D0881066

Iraq Since 1958

Iraq Since 1958

From Revolution to Dictatorship

Marion Farouk-Sluglett
and
Peter Sluglett

KPI
London and New York

IRAQ SINCE 1958
From revolution To Dictatorship

First published in 1987 by KPI Limited
11 New Fetter Lane, London EC4P 4EE

Distributed by
Routledge & Kegan Paul
Associated Book Publishers (UK) Ltd.
11 New Fetter Lane, London EC4P 4EE

Methuen Inc., Routledge & Kegan Paul
29 West 35th Street
New York, NY 10001, USA

Produced by Worts-Power Associates

Set in Times
by Margaret Spooner Typesetting
and printed in Great Britain
by Short Run Press Ltd.
Exeter, Devon

ISBN 0 7103 0238 X

In memory of
Omar Farouk Mahmoud al-Awqati,
1932–1963

Contents

Foreword

Since the Second World War the Arab states of the Middle East and North Africa have undergone a series of socio-political and economic upheavals that, whatever the political complexion of particular governments, have been broadly similar in content. These include the overthrow of the old landowning and politically dominant classes (or the expulsion of the European settlers, in the case of North Africa) and their replacement by social strata drawn largely from the ranks of the lower middle classes and the petty bourgeoisie; the dismantling of the political systems installed by the British or French and their replacement by one party systems that are often forms of military dictatorship; a growing concentration of economic activity in the hands of the state, or more accurately in the hands of the ruling party or the clique which dominates it, and the commitment of the state itself to 'development', however this concept may be defined by particular regimes. In broad outline, allowing for some local variations, particularly in the Arabian peninsula where the old social classes often managed to absorb and incorporate some of the social groups formerly excluded from power, most of these phenomena can be found in all the states between Morocco and Iraq.

In addition, a number of other significant and inter-related tendencies have emerged, particularly over the last two decades. First, there has been a very great acceleration in rural to urban migration, with the result that, on the one hand, agricultural production and productivity has declined in almost all Arab countries; and on the other, that the influx of new migrants has produced acute crises in housing, employment, transport and other services in most of the major cities of the region. Migration has also led to profound social and cultural dislocations for the newcomers, who have had to accommodate themselves to the new ways of life, attitudes and values of the city. In the poorer Arab countries, notably in Egypt, Morocco, Sudan and Tunisia, there have been spontaneous outbursts of popular anger in the urban areas, often triggered off by government decisions to remove subsidies on essential foodstuffs. It is also among the poor and uprooted migrants from the countryside that fundamentalist Islamic revivalism has found much of its support.

Secondly, there have been major changes in the balance of power in the Arab world since the oil price rise in the 1970s, which enabled Sa'udi Arabia and the Gulf states to become major forces in the region. An important by-product of the new oil wealth has been another sort of migration, of hundreds of thousands of individuals moving backwards and forwards between the poorer and the richer states. This has resulted in a certain degree of social and economic integration of the area as a whole, and more specifically in the dependence of large parts of the region on remittances from Libya, Iraq or the Arabian peninsula. The recent decline in world oil prices has therefore not only affected the economies of the oil-producing Arab states themselves but has also seriously influenced those of countries such as Egypt, Syria and North Yemen.

Thirdly, the phenomenal increase in investment in the richer states, particularly in infrastructure, and the rapid rise in the purchasing power of the population, have greatly accelerated the incorporation of the region as a whole into the Western world economy. In consequence, the West has begun to look more and more towards the Middle East as an essential market for western foodstuffs, consumer durables and capital goods. At the same time the Middle East has become increasingly affected by the economic crisis in the West, as is evident from the collapse of the Kuwaiti stock exchange in 1982 and the havoc caused by falling oil prices in the mid-1980s.

Fourthly, a degree of uniformity has begun to pervade the political outlook of Arab governments, which are now almost all inherently pro-Western. This leaves little scope for influence on the part of the Soviet Union except in the sphere of trade, particularly arms sales. This development can be attributed partly to the defeat or marginalisation of the Arab left in the 1950s and 1960s, and the subsequent emergence of dictatorships and authoritarian regimes in most states, and to the gradual depoliticisation of large sections of the population and their increasing involvement in the race for consumer goods.

Fifthly, a tendency can be observed towards more autonomous and inward-looking policies on the part of all Arab regimes. Events in one Arab state no longer necessarily assume the character of matters of fundamental concern to the other Arab states, unless their own vital interests are also thought to be affected. Although there is still an awareness that all Arabs share in a common linguistic and cultural heritage, and that most of them are Muslims, narrowly national rather than 'Arab' priorities have largely taken over the political arena. This seems to indicate that the nation states of the Arab world are gradually turning into distinct national political entities (like, for example, the states of South America), and growing further apart rather than closer together. Whether this phenomenon is to be deplored or applauded is less important than that it should be acknowledged as taking place, or more accurately as having taken place. It is only in this light that some sense can be made of the feebleness of the 'Arab' response to the Israeli invasion of Lebanon in 1982, or of the highly ambiguous attitudes of the Arab states towards Palestine and the Palestinians.

Finally, mention should be made of some important developments that have taken place in the Arab Middle East in 1986. The rapid decline in oil prices has created a new situation on an international and regional level whose future implications are not clear. At the moment, although the oil-producing countries, particularly Sa'udi Arabia, continue to maintain their dominance on a regional level, they have lost some of their economic and political muscle in the world arena. This has permitted the emergence of an increasing disregard on the part of the United States for the susceptibilities of the Arab states, and hence some deterioration in the relations between the United States and its conservative allies in the Arabian Peninsula. One manifestation of this has been the adoption of more outspoken and blatant support for the state of Israel on the part of the American administration. Equally, the United States' attack on Libya in

April 1986 was a clear humiliation for the Arab states as a whole; however little love existed between Qadhdhafi and the rulers of the Arabian Peninsula, the way in which the operation was carried out indicated that the West would not hesitate to embarrass its Arab allies if it was in its interests to do so.

It is most unlikely that such events will result in any radical changes in the basic attitudes of the Arab regimes towards the West or the United States. However, the feeling that the West is not a reliable ally for the Arabs has begun to permeate even those social groups in the Arab countries who have always been pro-Western in their political outlook. One consequence of this has been that sections of the population that have not previously shown any very strong attachment to Islam are now beginning to see the Islamic movement as a viable vehicle through which the Arabs may be able to defend their integrity and their standing within the world.

In writing this book on Iraq over the past four years, we have been made constantly aware of these very fundamental political and socio-economic changes, however imperfectly we comprehend their nature. It is too early to arrive at more than a tentative understanding of the transformations that lie beneath the surface. Not enough is known about the characteristics of the new social classes that have emerged or are in the process of emerging; too little is known about the decision-making process within the ruling elites in each state, their relationship to other social groups, and the nature and workings of the linkages between members of the ruling elite and private capital, both foreign and domestic.

In this connection, much of the stimulating writing of the 1960s and 1970s that attempted to provide an analytical framework for the study of the Third World in general and the Middle East in particular, including the work of Samir Amin and Anwar Abdelmalik, has not stood the test of time because it was not based on sufficient empirical research. However, an important reason for the lack of empirical research is the absence of adequate or reliable data, as students of the area are all too acutely aware. This problem is further compounded by the obstructions and restrictions that most Middle Eastern governments place in the way of both indigenous and foreign scholars wishing to undertake research into contemporary developments in their countries.

In the case of Iraq, the combination of the poor state of existing socio-economic data and the impossibility of collecting material ourselves has led us to write a political history rather than to attempt a socio-economic analysis of contemporary Iraqi society. It seemed important to write such a book, because with the exception of Hanna Batatu's *The Old Social Classes and the Revolutionary Movements of Iraq: a Study of Iraq's Old Landed and Commercial Classes, and of its Communists, Ba'thists and Free Officers*, published in 1978, a landmark in the historiography of the contemporary Middle East, most existing work on Iraq is either sadly superficial, excessively reliant on *ex cathedra* pronouncements by members of the present regime, or both. Furthermore, until fairly recently, the image of Iraq in both eastern and western writing was of a radical, socialist, pro-Soviet state, an image which, as we shall show, was always false. This book is an *unofficial* history; if it does not present the present regime in a particularly favourable light, that is because the evidence does not point towards a different conclusion. If we appear to emerge 'on the side' of those who have suffered so grievously at the hands of the Ba'th and its predecessors, this is an accurate reflection of our own sympathies.

Nevertheless, we have tried to present as objective a picture as possible and to give the most accurate account that the material permits, which may explain the neutral and somewhat detached style of much of the writing. It was often difficult for us to oppress our revulsion and horror in the face of some of the barbaric activities of a regime that has chosen — and this cannot be explained in terms of 'national character' — to oppress its people in such a cruel and vicious fashion. It is clear from conversations with Iraqis and non-Iraqi observers that the majority of the population fears and despises the present dictatorship; the totalitarian nature of Saddam Husain's rule, and the harsh penalties meted out to any manifestations of opposition to it have left the people of Iraq in a state of sullen and resigned acquiescence, in sharp contrast to the spirited defiance of those who fought so courageously for national liberation and social justice only a few decades ago. In addition the country is being devastated by a senseless war that has claimed more than 200,000 lives on the Iraqi side alone, started primarily in order to carve out a leadership role for Saddam Husain within the region as a whole. This desperate situation underlines the vital need for the establishment of democracy in Iraq, however broadly this may be defined. The tragedy is that it is difficult to see how this might be achieved under present conditions. The first requirements would be a change of regime and its replacement by one that might give the people of Iraq some breathing space and permit a degree of freedom of political expression.

Even for the modest objective of writing a political history, it has been difficult to find dependable and original source material. We have therefore relied principally on international press coverage, the BBC's daily *Summary of World Broadcasts*, unpublished theses, official and party political publications, and the two yearbook series *Middle East Record* and *Middle East Contemporary Survey*. We have also had stimulating discussions on Iraqi politics with Iraqi and other friends.

We have followed a strictly chronological presentation of political events, summarising the main economic developments in each period in passing but leaving a more detailed analysis of the economy to a separate chapter. A more integrated approach would have required more detailed and specific economic information than is available. Although written over the last four years, the book inevitably reflects some of the fruit of twenty years' of work on nineteenth and twentieth century Iraq; and also, for one of us, of the experience of nearly a decade spent in Iraq spanning the period before and after the 1958 revolution. The book is entirely a joint effort; all of it has been written by both of us together, and no part can be attributed to either of us alone.

We are deeply grateful to many friends for their help in the preparation of this book. In particular, we would like to thank Albert Hourani, who has read through the whole book in draft, for his penetrating criticisms, and, as always, for his generosity, kindness and encouragement. John Erpenbeck, Fred Halliday and Roger Owen have read through the manuscript and made a number of acute and stimulating suggestions, most of which have been incorporated into the text. None of them, of course, is in any way responsible for any of the shortcomings that remain. To Faisal Darraj, 'Abdulla Hanna, 'Abd al-Majeed al-Heeti and 'Isam al-Khafaji we owe many hours of convivial and stimulating discussion. We would also like to acknowledge our very great debt to Hanna Batatu and express our admiration for his scholarly, lucid and courageous writings on Iraq.

Katharine Monro read through the final proofs and helped us to eliminate a number of errors and inconsistencies. Malcolm Ferguson of the Oriental Section of Durham University Library has been exceptionally patient and helpful in tracking down obscure requests on Inter-Library Loan; our thanks to him and the other members of the Library staff. We are also grateful to the staff of the Press Library at Chatham House, and to the Staff Travel Fund of Durham University for the grant that enabled us to work there. Finally, we should like to express our affectionate gratitude to Joseph and Marjorie Sluglett, and to Marwan and Shaalan, who have shown remarkable forbearance and affection in putting up with our preoccupation with this book for so long.

MARION FAROUK-SLUGLETT
PETER SLUGLETT
June 1986

Chapter One
Iraq Before the Revolution of 1958

Early Modern Iraq: from Ottoman Frontier Province to British Military Occupation, c. 1550–1914

By the time that British Indian troops landed at Fao in the last weeks of 1914, the area that now forms modern Iraq had been at least nominally part of the Ottoman Empire for almost four centuries. The authority of the 'Abbasid caliphate, under which Baghdad had been the commercial, political, intellectual and spiritual capital of the Islamic world, had begun to decline as early as the tenth century; after many vicissitudes, the caliphate itself disappeared as an institution after Baghdad was sacked by the Mongols in 1258. In the next two centuries the area was ruled first by the Mongol Ilkhans and then by the formidable Timur, who died in 1405. The next century and a half saw a succession of different rulers of Turkic origin, the two Turcoman confederacies, the Kara Koyunlu and the Ak Koyunlu, the Safavids, and finally the Ottomans, who took Mosul and Kurdistan from the Safavids in 1516, and added Basra and Baghdad to their territories in 1555.

Although the Ottomans conquered Iraq in the sixteenth century the subsequent incorporation of the area into their empire was gradual and sporadic. The extent and intensity of Ottoman control varied considerably over the centuries, in such a way that the process was unlikely to have been a matter of obvious and

permanent significance to the contemporary inhabitants of the
area. Thus, to cite the example of Baghdad, the city was taken over
from the Ottomans by local forces at the beginning of the
seventeenth century, and subsequently captured once again in
1623 by the Safavids, who remained there until another Ottoman
conquest in 1639. By 1704 direct Ottoman control had lapsed once
more, this time in favour of a Mamluk 'dynasty' that ruled
Baghdad and most of the rest of 'Iraq' until 1831, when an
Ottoman army managed to defeat the Mamluks, and the process
of reintegrating, or perhaps more accurately integrating, the Iraqi
provinces into the Empire began. In general, therefore, Iraq, like
many other parts of the Empire, enjoyed relative administrative,
economic and fiscal autonomy for much of the period between the
original conquest and the mid-nineteenth century[1].

One result of this relative independence was that effective
administrative control was generally exercised either directly by,
or at least through the mediation of, provincial notables, tribal
chieftains or military adventurers. Although such individuals
would almost always attempt to obtain confirmation of their right
to rule from the Ottoman authorities in Istanbul, their base was
regional and local, so that few of those who lived in the three
vilayets of Basra, Baghdad and Mosul would have had a sense of
being part of a wider political entity. The distance from Istanbul,
combined with poor communications and the nature of much of
the terrain, ensured that at least until the mid-nineteenth century,
the authority of the central government rarely extended far outside
the towns where the main garrisons were quartered. In consequence the Arab tribes in the desert and riverain areas and the
Kurdish mountain-dwellers generally managed to resist the
penetration of the forces of central government with a fair degree
of success until the institution of the British mandate in 1920. A
further important factor militating against later efforts at state
formation was that there was no particular sense in which the
three provinces formed a geopolitical or economic unit, unlike, for
example, Egypt or Syria. Thus at least until the opening of the Suez
Canal in 1869, Basra looked towards the Gulf and India; Baghdad
was an important staging point on the land route between Syria
and Iran, and Mosul tended to have closer economic links with
Anatolia and Aleppo than with Baghdad.

However, by the middle of the nineteenth century both these
circumstances had begun to change. At that time Istanbul was

gradually taking a closer interest even in the more inaccessible parts of the Empire, and although the application of the new Ottoman laws and administrative arrangements known collectively as the Tanzimat was slow and hesitant, the main reforms did eventually penetrate to the three Iraqi *vilayets* and began to draw them into what was becoming an increasingly homogeneous imperial system[2]. These attempts by the central state to increase its control over the provinces coincided with a period of growing European commercial activity in the Ottoman Empire as a whole, the rise of British commercial activity in Iraq in particular[3], and the gradual transition of the area from a subsistence to an exporting economy.

Efforts to re-establish Ottoman control began in earnest under the administrations of two governors of Baghdad, Mehmed Reşid (1852–57) and Namik (1861–68), and were continued under their more famous successor Midhat Pasha (1869–72). All three sought to improve irrigation, to extend the control of the state over the tribes, and also to raise more revenue, attempting to achieve the two latter objectives by appointing local shaikhs to 'official positions' in the administration of their own tribal areas. This policy was to be carried out more single-mindedly and in a sense more effectively by the Ottomans' successors, although the object of the exercise under the British and later the Iraqi administrations was not so much to raise revenue as to pacify and control the countryside at minimal cost to the central government.

Economy and Society, c. 1850–1914

The opening of the Suez Canal and the gradual introduction of steam navigation on the Tigris and Euphrates rivers enabled Iraq to become an exporter of grain, mostly to the Gulf and India. The volume and value of cereal exports increased from an average of £140,000 a year in 1867–71 to an average of nearly £8 million a year in 1912–13, a twenty-fold increase in some forty years[4]. This rise in exports was accompanied by a 'substantial expansion of the cultivated area' from perhaps as little as 100,000 to as much as a million acres[5] over the same period. In such circumstances, boundaries, leases and conditions of tenure became issues of considerable importance as well as sources of friction under the largely free-for-all situation that prevailed.

During his tenure of office as *wali* of Baghdad, Midhat Pasha attempted to introduce the provisions of the Ottoman Land Code of 1858 into Iraq, and thereby to extend the powers of the state as tax collector[6], although these efforts were largely unsuccessful. The main purpose of the Code, in Iraq as elsewhere in the Ottoman Empire, was to retrieve the right to tax that the state had lost *de facto* in earlier times as a result of having to resort to various forms of tax-farming[7], but this could only have been achieved in situations where clearly defined individual property rights actually existed. In Iraq, where socio-economic and political factors had generally inhibited the development of private property in land[8], the Code conflicted directly with tribal custom, where land was held by the tribe as a whole and land-holding 'depended not on formal grants by the government but on the continued ability of the tribesmen to defend what they held against other tribesmen[9]'. The immediate result of the introduction of the Code was that title deeds (*tapu sanads*) confirming what were in practice inalienable possessory and usufructuary rights were issued on the most perfunctory evidence to city merchants, former tax farmers and tribal shaikhs and others astute enough to 'understand the advantages conferred by the possession of slips of paper'[10], who were thereby transformed overnight into large landowners.

This *de facto* alienation through *tapu* had the effect of relieving the *tapu* holder of any particularly pressing reason to pay taxes, given the general absence of any effective machinery to force him to do so, and the Ottomans soon found themselves faced with a serious threat to the very powers that they had sought to consolidate and establish. As a result, no further *tapu* grants were made after 1881[11], and the Ottomans made numerous attempts over the next thirty years to repossess the lands that they had almost inadvertently granted away. Thus on the eve of the British Occupation in 1914 only a relatively small proportion of state land had been registered in *tapu*, and the state and the would-be property owners were locked in a clear-cut conflict of interests[12].

Another consequence of this was that aspiring landowners, many of whom were tribal shaikhs, could not, under these circumstances, assert their authority excessively over their tribes-men, since to have done so would have been to risk putting themselves between the hammer and the anvil; 'in those days', one southern Iraqi tribesman recalled, . . . it was dangerous for the shaykh to have large numbers of tribesmen angry with him[13]'. In the same way the acquisition of *tapu* title by the Sa'duns, a major shaikhly family in the middle Euphrates, 'contributed to a further erosion of the deference Muntafik tribesmen had customarily accorded to the al-Sa'dun who were increasingly viewed as merely absentee landlords and were resented accordingly[14]'.

In general, in the conflict between tribal leaders, the Ottoman state and the tribesmen themselves over the possession of land, the Ottoman policy of 'divide and rule', together with the effects of the penetration of the market economy, would, if continued, have led almost inevitably to the gradual decomposition of the tribal confederations and a concomitant decline in the authority of the traditional tribal leaders[15]. As the subsistence economy became increasingly undermined with the growing involvement of Iraqi agricultural products with the world market, many shaikhs began to view their tribesmen more as a source of profit than as efficient fighters, while still being forced to depend on a loyal following to assist them against the encroachments of other tribes and of the Ottoman state.

These changing circumstances were accompanied by a gradual alteration in the occupational structure of the population. Such evidence as is available shows a rise in the numbers of sedentary cultivators after about 1867, and a concomitant fall in the number of nomads: expressed in percentages, the nomads fell from 35% to 17% of the rural population between 1867 and 1905, and to 7% in 1930, while the percentage of cultivators rose from 41% to 59% between 1867 and 1905 and to 68% in 1930[16]. Naturally, these figures must be used with caution because of the difficulty of distinguishing accurately between the various categories, but an overall tendency towards sedentarisation is unmistakable[17]. Thus the shaikhs' position was becoming somewhat ambiguous and insecure, and remained so until the British Occupation changed the situation once and for all by freeing them from their dependence upon their tribesmen and firmly uniting their interests with those of the state.

The Last Years of Ottoman Rule

Although the impact and significance of the institutions of the

Tanzimat should not be overestimated[18], it is clear that the general atmosphere of reform did have an important effect on the social and intellectual life of the Iraqi provinces. In particular, the government's foundation of several modern schools in the main cities towards the end of the nineteenth century meant that increasing numbers of young Iraqis were able to proceed to the civil and military establishments in Istanbul, where they could meet their contemporaries from similar backgrounds from other parts of the Ottoman Empire, many of whom were imbued with the ideas of constitutionalism and liberalism that were being widely discussed at the time.

During the period between 1839 and 1876 the notion of Ottomanism, *Osmanlilik*, according to which all citizens of the Empire, irrespective of whether they were Muslim or Christian, Arab, Greek, or Turk, were to be regarded as equal before the law, had been promoted fairly consistently by the Tanzimat reformers[19], and in 1876 a constitution and a form of pàrliamentary government had been introduced. However, during the long reign of 'Abd al-Hamid II, (1876–1909) these generally liberal tendencies were put into abeyance and replaced by a return to a more autocratic and despotic style. At the same time, the notion that the Arabs formed a distinct ethno-linguistic entity and, ultimately, that they were entitled to some form of autonomy within the Empire, was beginning to exert an important influence on Arab intellectuals, and the more repressive aspects of 'Abd al-Hamid's rule gradually gave increasing currency and respectability to this idea in the Arab provinces[20].

In the 1880s, the main opposition to the 'new despotism' came from the loose coalition known generically as the Young Turks, which consisted of a number of protest groups scattered throughout the Empire and in exile in Europe[21]. The Committee of Union and Progress, founded in 1887, which consisted largely of army officers, became the most important of these groups, with branches in Paris, Geneva, Cairo and London[22]. However, when the Committee succeeded in seizing power in 1908 (and eventually in forcing the abdication of 'Abd al-Hamid in 1909) it gradually became clear that its main aim was to foster and promote the position of the *Turkish* element in the Empire, and that there was to be no place in the new order for ideas of provincial autonomy and decentralisation. At this point many Arab intellectuals and political activists began to come round to the view that the cultural and political aspirations of 'the Arabs' would be better served by the separation of the Arab provinces from the rest of the Ottoman Empire, and, some felt, by the creation of an Arab state under an Arab king. A few of these individuals were also aware that the achievement of these aims would not be entirely unwelcome to the European powers, particularly Britain[23].

As a result, a number of Arab secret societies were founded in various parts of the Empire. One of these, *al-'Ahd*, founded by 'Aziz 'Ali al-Misri in 1914, was dominated by a number of Iraqi officers, many of whom were to become leading politicians under the mandate and monarchy, including Nuri al-Sa'id, Ja'far al-'Askari, Yasin al-Hashimi, Jamil Midfa'i, Naji Shawkat, Maulud Mukhlis and 'Ali Jawdat[24]. Hence by the time of the First World War the idea that the Arabs should break away from the Ottoman Empire (though generally not the more specific notion of forming a separate 'Iraqi state') had begun to gain ground among political activists in Iraq, and some of these Iraqi officers were to play a major role in the British-sponsored Sharifian army, which began the Arab Revolt in the Hijaz in 1916.

The Origins and Development of British Interests in Iraq and the Gulf Area

Britain's interests in Iraq, which have been mentioned briefly, originated as an extension of her concern to protect the route to India, and to prevent attacks on her shipping from pirates based on the Gulf coasts. In the early part of the nineteenth century, Britain entered into treaty relations with most of the rulers of the Gulf shaikhdoms, and the ensuing peace enabled British merchants to trade freely with both shores of the Gulf and with Iraq, whose exports, mostly of grain and dates, rose steadily in the period between 1870 and 1914. At the same time imports of British goods, mostly textiles through Basra, rose from £51,000 in 1868–70 to £1,128,000 in 1879–99 and to £3,066,000 in 1907–09; on the eve of the First World War Britain's share of the trade of Iraq and the Gulf area as a whole amounted to £9,600,000, about three-quarters of the total[25].

At the same time, another and more compelling factor was beginning to attract European governments and commercial interests to the area. Oil had been discovered in commercial quantities at Masjid-i Sulaiman in South Iran in 1908: a year later the Anglo-Persian Oil Company was formed, and in 1914 the refinery at Abadan exported a quarter of a million tons of oil. The enterprise soon attracted British government interest, especially with the combination of Admiral Fisher (known, apparently, as 'the oil maniac' since as early as 1886[26]) as First Sea Lord, and Churchill as First Lord of the Admiralty in 1911. Convinced that oil was the naval fuel of the future, Churchill and Fisher were anxious to find a source nearer at hand than the Gulf of Mexico, from which the bulk of world oil supplies then came, and as a result the British government decided to acquire a 51% holding in Anglo-Persian. This was effected by Act of Parliament a few days before the outbreak of war in August 1914.

At the same time, a number of rival international groups were making bids for oil concessions in the Ottoman Empire, particularly in the Baghdad and Mosul *vilayets*. In 1903, the Baghdad Railway Convention, signed between the imperial authorities and the Ottoman Railway Company of Anatolia (a German undertaking controlled by the Deutsche Bank) to build the Berlin to Baghdad railway, included mineral rights over the land 20 kilometres each side of the track. In 1911, African and Eastern Concessions, a consortium (in which British interests predominated) consisting of Royal Dutch Shell, C.S. Gulbenkian, the (British) National Bank of Turkey, and the Deutsche Bank was formed, which changed its name to the Turkish Petroleum Company in 1912. In 1913 the TPC was merged with the Anglo-Persian Oil Company, with the shares distributed between the TPC's British, German, Dutch and Gulbenkian interests. Thus when the British government took over Anglo-Persian in August 1914, it thereby obtained a similar interest in the TPC[27]. Clearly, the acquisition of these assets further strengthened British commercial and strategic connections with the area, so that in the autumn of 1914, when it became increasingly likely that the Ottoman Empire would enter the war on the side of the Central Powers, Britain began to make preparations to defend her interests at the head of the Gulf.

British Occupation and Mandate, 1914–1932

On 3 November 1914, the Ottoman Empire formally concluded an alliance with Germany, and declared war on Britain and France two days later[28]. On 6 November, an advance party of Indian Expeditionary Force 'D' landed at Fao, thus beginning the Mesopotamia campaign, 'which was eventually to wrest from the Ottoman Empire the whole of Turkish Arabia, as the . . . wilayets . . . of Basra, Baghdad and Mosul were then known in British official circles, and to lay the foundations of the Kingdom of 'Iraq[29]'. The small size of the force, and the limited objectives that it was assigned, indicate that it was not originally part of British policy to 'take over' Mesopotamia, but the lack of any substantial Turkish opposition, which enabled the Force to take Basra on November 22 and to advance as far as Qurna, some 100 miles up the Shatt al-'Arab, by December 9, seems to have produced a sense of euphoria that was to have serious and costly consequences[30].

Urged on by the men on the spot and by the Secretariat of the Government of India at Simla, the India Office in London gave its reluctant sanction to a more fully-fledged military campaign, which culminated in an ill-prepared attempt to march on Baghdad in the autumn of 1915. The Ottomans rallied; British forces were beaten back to Kut al-'Amara, where they were forced to surrender after a siege of five months. Eventually, the Government of India was relieved of its charge over the operation, which was transferred to the War Office; major reinforcements were despatched, and British troops finally captured Baghdad in March 1917. Early in 1918, Kirkuk, some 200 miles north of Baghdad, was taken, and three days after the Armistice of Mudros, Mosul town and most of the Mosul *vilayet* fell into British hands[31].

In the meantime, the British had consolidated their control over the area under military occupation by setting up a form of civil administration. Since most of the administrators had received their training in the Indian Political Service, they began to apply the principles that they had learnt there to Lower and Central Iraq, and since they were not given any firm instructions to the contrary until after the capture of Baghdad, it was not surprising that the administration of the area began to resemble that of an Indian province, in which the indigenous population were ruled directly by British officials with the help of such 'reliable' local leaders as could be persuaded to participate. However, particularly after the entry of the United States into the war on the Allied side in April 1917, it became uncomfortably clear first, that direct rule over

conquered territories was no longer going to be acceptable as part
of any post-war settlement[32]; and secondly, that few of the officials
on the spot understood, or wished to accept, the implications of
this new state of affairs. The result was a series of misunder-
standings about the nature of Britain's future role in Iraq and a
sense of bewildered outrage on the part of the administrators at
such expressions of liberal intent as President Wilson's Fourteen
Points[33] (put forward in a speech in January 1918 but not
published in Iraq until October 1918) and the Anglo-French
Declaration of 1918, that promised 'the establishment of indigenous Governments and Administrations in Syria and
Mesopotamia'[34].

The eighteen months between October 1918 and April 1920 were
to be crucial for the future of Iraq. During that period, many
former members of *al-'Ahd* were running the Arab kingdom of
Syria, under Faisal ibn Husain, with whom they had served in the
Arab Revolt in the Hijaz, while Iraq was still being ruled by British
officials. Thus it appeared that the British judged the Arabs
competent to run their own affairs on one side of the Fertile
Crescent but not on the other, a situation that was particularly
paradoxical since so many members of the Syrian administration
were Iraqis. In British Mesopotamia, on the other hand, in the
words of one official, 'any idea of an Arab state is simply blood-
stained fooling at present'[35].

In April 1920, the mandates were shared out between Britain
and France; France was awarded Syria and Lebanon and Britain
Iraq, Palestine and Transjordan. In July 1920 a French army under
General Gouraud defeated Faisal's army at Khan Maisalun on
the road between Beirut and Damascus; perhaps anticipating this
result, many of Faisal's Iraqi supporters in Syria had already
begun to turn their attention to Iraq itself, where opposition to
British rule eventually culminated in a widespread rising known
subsequently as the Revolution of 1920, which engulfed the
southern and central parts of the country for most of the summer
and autumn of that year.

The Revolution of 1920 is significant as the first manifestation
of a form of Iraqi national identity, but perhaps more so as
showing that the 'Indian' policies pursued by Britain over the
previous years could not be continued indefinitely. As well as
being embarrassingly costly for the British government in terms of
losses of 'blood and treasure' so long after the end of the war, it had

taken place at a time when Britain's policies in the Middle East as a whole were being subjected to considerable criticism in certain circles on the grounds of heavy-handedness and expense[36]. Hence, partly as a result of these wider financial and political constraints, it was felt necessary to introduce cheaper administrative policies into Britain's newly-acquired Middle Eastern territories. To this end a special sub-department of the Colonial Office was set up and a conference organised in Cairo in March 1921, where Churchill, now Colonial Secretary, laid down the new guidelines[37].

For Iraq, it was decided that direct rule by British officials should be abandoned in favour of indirect rule through an ostensibly Iraqi government and civil service, backed up by a small but powerful corps of British 'advisers', whose advice had to be taken. Britain was to control Iraq's foreign relations and to have what amounted to a right of veto in military and financial matters. The new national government was to be headed by an Arab ruler, and, for a variety of reasons, (principally that, as an outsider, he would be particularly dependent upon Britain), Faisal ibn Husain was regarded as the obvious candidate for the post[38]. In addition to the British civilian officials who were to advise and train their Iraqi charges, the defence and internal security of Iraq, and the protection of Britain's imperial interests in the country, were to be in the hands of British forces (or British-sponsored forces such as the Iraqi Levies, recruited from the Assyrian Christian community) and an Iraqi army, which Britain would also equip and train. In practice, the line between 'defence' and 'internal security' was somewhat blurred, and during the twelve years of the mandate the protection of the regime from threats both from within and from without was in the hands of the RAF, whose general effectiveness in these fields soon made itself felt[39].

The most immediate question facing the British authorities in Iraq itself in the spring of 1921 was how best to stage manage the matter of Faisal's 'election'. Of course, his adoption by Britain had effectively scotched the chances of any other candidate, but it seemed important both that public opinion in Iraq should be broadly in favour of him, and that he should at least not be seen to be widely opposed. Fortunately, the only other serious candidate, Saiyid Talib of Basra, effectively queered his own pitch in mid-April by making veiled threats of a tribal uprising if the 'elections' to the throne were not carried out fairly (in the course of a dinner party he had given for the French and Persian consuls and the correspondent of the *Daily Telegraph*), and was arrested and deported the next day[40].

In August 1921 Faisal was duly installed as king, and a national government formed. For appearances' sake, it was decided that relations between Britain and Iraq should be regulated by a treaty, an instrument that embodied the terms of the mandate without actually using the word. It took over a year for the Treaty to be accepted by the new Iraqi cabinet, and a further two years for it to be ratified by the Constituent Assembly; neither body was particularly anti-British, but the pretence that the Treaty was an agreement freely entered into between equals was too transparent for many to swallow[41]. During this period, and until his death in 1933, King Faisal did not prove quite as pliant as his British masters had expected him to be; he and his circle were constantly involved in a delicate balancing act, having to satisfy the exigencies of British policy while at the same time trying to retain some degree of credibility with what may loosely be termed Iraqi national aspirations.

Batatu has shown the variety of ways in which the British were able to maintain Faisal and his governments in power and at the same time to limit their freedom of manoeuvre[42]. From the beginning of the period of military occupation, it had been a cardinal principle of British policy to bolster the powers of tribal shaikhs and landlords by creating a system of jurisdiction specifically for the tribes that was to remain in force until the Revolution of July 1958 and by appointing 'suitable' tribal leaders as 'government shaikhs'. The *Tribal Criminal and Civil Disputes Regulation*, drawn up in 1916, was formally incorporated into the Iraqi constitution in 1925, and throughout the occupation, mandate and monarchy periods, political and tax-levying powers were given to individuals selected for their likely loyalty to the authorities. In the first few years of the monarchy the new government attempted to take some of these privileges away, but was soon forced into the realisation that it was only by the creation of some sort of alliance between itself and the local tribal leaders that it could maintain itself in power. By the middle 1920s an informal arrangement had grown up between the government and the larger landowners whereby, in return for their support, the landowners would be left to their own devices as far as the administration, taxation and policing of their local area was concerned[43].

Although the British were able to override Iraqi opposition to the Treaty, there were undoubtedly some awkward moments, especially as the question of the future status of the Mosul *vilayet* had not yet been finally decided. Britain was anxious to keep Mosul within Iraq in order to secure control over the oilfields, which were included in the TPC concession area, while Iraq itself needed Mosul for both economic and political reasons; the *vilayets* of Baghdad and Basra would scarcely have formed a viable state on their own, and, without Mosul, Iraq would have been a Shi'i-dominated state. The British and Iraqi governments were generally united in their pursuit of this goal, and the main opposition — apart from the claims of the Turkish government itself — came from the Kurdish population of the area itself, some of whom, while preferring no government at all to Anglo-Iraqi government, had decided to opt for a continuation of Turkish rule as a lesser evil.

By the middle of 1924 a certain impasse had been reached in Anglo-Iraqi relations, partly because Britain had not been able to secure Mosul definitely for Iraq at the Lausanne Conference. Furthermore, a lively 'Quit Mesopotamia' campaign had been raging between 1922 and 1924 in the British press, whose proprietors were apprehensive of the dangers posed by the revival of Turkish military strength and apparently unaware of the considerable potential of Mosul oil[44]. The lack of absolute certainty about Britain's intentions, (which coincided with the first Labour government's brief period in office in 1924), combined with the fact that the Treaty was highly unpopular with most of those Iraqis who understood its implications, encouraged many of the deputies elected to the new Constituent Assembly in March 1924 to make no secret of their reluctance to ratify it. After several months of stalemate, the High Commissioner threatened to suspend the constitution in June in order to bully the deputies into forming a quorum to produce the desired result[45].

In fact the League's arbitration commission *did* decide, in July 1925, that Mosul was to be awarded to Iraq, on the condition that the mandatory regime should continue for twenty-five years or until Iraq became a member of the League. A few months earlier, in March 1925, the Iraqi government had signed a concession with the TPC, on terms most unfavourable to itself, for the exploitation of Mosul oil, which meant that, provided the League's arbitrators found in Iraq's favour — which they were almost certain to do —

Britain would secure ultimate control over Iraqi oil. In an important sense, the award was the turning point of the mandate; in the course of 1925 the Iraqi government became aware, perhaps more sharply than before, of the urgency of maintaining its relationship with Britain and gave up any very serious attempts at defiance. Iraq needed the Mosul *vilayet* for its survival: only British aid, both diplomatic and military, could secure the area, keep the Turks out and, as we shall discuss later, restrain the Kurds. Thus the remaining seven years of the mandate form a period of general cooperation with Britain, in contrast to the sharp conflicts of the earlier years. This was reflected in the gradual loosening of the formal ties between the two governments; it seems likely that Britain, now so sure of her standing in Iraq, could afford some relaxation in control[46].

By September 1929, Britain had agreed to recommend Iraq for League membership in 1932. Britain insisted on maintaining the RAF in Iraq to ensure the security of imperial communications (and also, indirectly, to ensure that no Iraqi government could step too far out of line) and on an assurance that all foreign officials should be British. The question of conscription for the Iraqi Army, a cause of contention between the two governments for some years, was allowed to lapse quietly, and was eventually imposed in 1934. In 1930, a new Anglo-Iraqi Treaty was drawn up, designed to come into force when Iraq entered the League in 1932. There were a few hiccups between 1930 and 1932 when it became very clear that the Iraq government was not prepared to make any binding commitments actually to implement the various administrative and educational measures that it had promised to introduce into the Kurdish areas, but, as it was generally British policy to support League entry in 1932, the considerable weight of evidence showing that the Iraqi government was not in fact fulfilling its obligations to the Kurds was effectively hushed up; after Iraq became independent, Britain would, at least in theory, have no power to insist.

In the circumstances it was hardly surprising that the country's passage from mandated territory to independent state, which took place on 3 October 1932, occasioned little excitement among the people of Iraq, since, however disguised British power and influence might be, it was widely believed by many Iraqis that they were not the true masters of their country. The victory that had been won was strictly limited; moreover, it had been won by a small clique, imposed on the country from outside, which had few claims to the acceptance, approbation or trust of the rest of the population. The end of the mandate had significance for the small group of Sunni officials and ex-Sharifian officers gathered around King Faisal, in giving them a freer hand to exercise control within the country, but the British authorities retained supreme power, and the vast majority of the population continued to be excluded from any meaningful participation in government[47].

'Independent' Iraq

The next twenty-six years of what was now officially the independent state represent, to a very great extent, a continuation of the mandate, in the sense that overall control of the country still rested with Britain, and that the 'permitted political arena' continued to be occupied by the same groups of people who had become prominent in the 1920s and their close friends and associates. The most obvious difference between the politics of the 1920s and those of the 1930s, particularly after the premature death of King Faisal in 1933 and the succession to the throne of his flamboyant son Ghazi (1933–39), was the emergence of the armed forces, or more correctly of factions within the armed forces, as a new locus of political power, although in many ways this development was more a change of style than of substance[48].

The army had established its nationalist and patriotic credentials in the hearts of many members of the urban population in the summer of 1933 by its campaign against the Assyrians, who were considered as an important adjunct of the British presence[49]. In October 1936, taking advantage of the unpopularity of the government of Yasin al-Hashimi, and encouraged by King Ghazi's own desire to be rid of al-Hashimi's restraining influence, the army, under its acting Commander in Chief Bakr Sidqi, seized power after staging a military coup. One of the first acts of Sidqi's Prime Minister, Hikmat Sulaiman, after forming his cabinet, was to send a message to the British Ambassador assuring him that the new government wished to maintain the cordial relations with Britain that had been enjoyed by its predecessors[50]

In spite of this, the composition of Sulaiman's government gave some grounds for hope that a new political initiative might be possible. Three members of the cabinet, Kamil Chadirchi, Ja'far

Abu' l-Timman and Yusuf 'Izz al-Din, were associated with a reformist political association, *Jama'at al-Ahali*[51], and two other ministers, Salih Jabr and Hikmat Sulaiman himself, were known to have liberal views. However, it gradually became clear that Bakr Sidqi was either unwilling or unable to allow free elections or a free press, and was also prepared to intimidate his opponents; these soon included the Ahali ministers, who judged the situation sufficiently dangerous to flee to Cyprus after submitting their resignations in June 1937. Two months later Sidqi himself was assassinated, and Jamil Midfa'i, the nominee of a group of pan-Arabist officers, was asked to form a new government.

For the next four years, until the spring of 1941, governments were made and dismissed according to the wishes of the officers. The situation was complicated by the death of King Ghazi in April 1939, and the nomination of his pro-British cousin, 'Abd al-Ilah, as regent for Ghazi's four-year-old son Faisal, and further exacerbated by the outbreak of the Second World War. By this time, the military and the civilian politicians had become divided broadly into those who were, and those who were not, prepared to support Britain and her allies against Germany and Italy, a division that became more clearly apparent as the war continued. Britain's most prominent supporters were the Regent and Nuri al-Sa'id, and its most prominent opponents Rashid 'Ali al-Gailani and his circle, who enjoyed the support of a powerful faction of officers known as the Golden Square[52]. Again in rather broad terms, many of the officers were attracted towards various shades of pan-Arab nationalism, a body of ideas that enjoyed considerable vogue in certain circles in Iraq, but more particularly in other Arab countries, during the inter-war years.

Political Currents, c. 1920–1946

As has been mentioned, a number of Arab secret societies had been founded in the period before the First World War, with the general objective of freeing the Arab world from Ottoman domination and of setting up some form of Arab state, perhaps with the assistance or even under the aegis, of the European powers. In the aftermath of the peace settlement in 1918–1920, which did not produce the independent state that many Arabs had wished for or fought for, a new form of Arabism or Arab nationalism began to emerge, which, in its essentials, was subscribed to by almost all actors on the political stage in the Arab world in the inter-war and immediately post Second World War period. This consisted of a popular rediscovery of the common Arab 'heritage', and a recognition of the existence of an 'Arab nation', of which Iraq (or Syria, or Palestine), formed an integral part.

In the particular case of Iraq, this was accompanied by the propagation of the theme that twentieth century Iraqis were the direct descendants of the Mesopotamians and Babylonians, in an effort to promote feelings of loyalty to and pride in the new country. As both of these two streams — Arab nationalism and Iraqi patriotism — were widely expressed in the schoolbooks of the time a new feeling of national/patriotic cosnciousness or awareness filtered down to wide sections of the population, and gradually developed into a common ideological denominator around which all political actors had to orientate themselves. When 'genuine' political parties emerged, they could only attract widespread support if they succeeded in merging their political programmes with the wider concepts and aspirations of either Arab or Iraqi independence, according to the political situation at the time.

Here a certain caution is necessary, since the carriers of aspirations to Arab nationalism and the content of the aspirations themselves underwent important qualitative changes with the passage of time. In the case of the Sharifian officers who threw in their lot with Faisal and the Iraqi state after 1920, their original patriotic and nationalist attitudes are not in doubt. Furthermore they could argue, even at the beginning of the 1920s, that however faintly Iraq might resemble an independent Arab state, it was at least 'more Arab' in its administration and certainly more of a coherent entity, than the three provinces had been under Ottoman rule. By the end of the 1920s, however, it was clear that such figures as Nuri al-Sa'id and Ja'far al-'Askari had become content to accommodate themselves to the British, with the result that any Arab nationalist credentials they might once have had gradually ceased to count in their favour among the Iraqi population. The mainstream of Arab or Iraqi national awareness passed to different groups, which developed roots among wide strata of the population by merging the desire for Arab or Iraqi independence and reassertion with other immediately relevant political and social aspirations. Unfortunately for our understanding of these events, the politicians who served the monarchy have sometimes been described as 'Arab nationalists' long after the label ceased to have any meaning as a description either of their actions or of their perception of their role.

It is difficult to document the way in which the new national consciousness was diffused among the Iraqi population, since the publications of the various political parties only reflect some aspects of it. However, it is important to be aware that this general theme lay behind almost all party political activities during the period under discussion. The major indicators of the new awareness were the huge turn-outs and the militancy expressed in anti-British or anti-government demonstrations and activities, particularly in 1941 and after 1945. In addition, largely under the influence of communism and the Communist Party, much of the political thinking of the time became infused with ideas of socialism and communism, which permeated the vocabulary and much of the thinking of the political organisations. As we shall see, the appeal of the Communist Party was largely due to its success in merging the struggle for social change with the fight for national independence and against imperialism[53].

By the end of the 1920s, political life had become more and more to resemble an elaborate game of musical chairs, and such political parties as were permitted to function were normally short term alliances between groups of fortuitously like-minded individuals. The ideological and moral bankruptcy of the political system was glaringly evident, particularly to those who were excluded from full participation in it, and other 'extra-parliamentary' political tendencies and groupings had begun to emerge. In the period before the Second World War, that is, before the emergence of the Iraqi Communist Party as a major, if not *the* major, force in the organised opposition to the regime, two main trends can be discerned, a combination of social reformism and Iraqi nationalism on the one hand, and pan-Arabism on the other.

The social reformist/Iraqist tendency was most prominently represented by *Jama'at al-Ahali*, which had been founded by a group of Iraqi students at the American University of Beirut in the late 1920s. Its founder members were Muhammad Hadid, 'Abd al-Fattah Ibrahim, 'Abd al-Qadir Isma'il and Husain Jamil, all of whom were to have substantial influence in Iraqi politics in various capacities both in the opposition to the monarchy and after the Revolution of 1958. As young men, they were all active in student politics and participated in demonstrations against the mandate[54]. Their newspaper, *al-Ahali*, first appeared in January 1932 and soon became popular as a forum for progressive opinion. The ideology of *Jama'at al-Ahali* was drawn largely from British Fabianism, amounting to a belief in the necessity for a combination of political and economic independence with democratic social reformism, which, it was thought, could be achieved through the ballot box.

These beliefs were shared by many educated members of the middle classes, but any attempts on the part of members of *al-Ahali* and their supporters actually to achieve national independence and social reform could be and always were checked by those whose vested interests in the *status quo* were strong enough to prevent them ever being able to put their ideals into effect. A combination of the inherent weakness of the position of the bourgeoisie within the economy and the immense and ever-increasing polarisation between rich and poor that characterised the whole of the period between the foundation of the state and the Revolution of 1958 meant that bourgeois democratic ideology never gained more than the most precarious foothold in Iraqi society. Thus although many individual members of *Jama'at al-Ahali*, most notably, in addition to the founders themselves, Kamil Chadirchi and 'Aziz Sharif, later became highly respected political figures, the tradition that most of them represented in the 1930s, which was continued by the National Democratic Party after 1946, had few roots in the social formation of Iraq and was thus never able to command widespread support.

The second and more evidently influential political tendency of the period before the Second World War was pan-Arabism, an ideology generally associated with the educationalist Sati' al-Husri, whose ideas filtered through to a whole generation, particularly through his contribution to the school textbooks of the period[55]. In broad terms al-Husri developed a new form of Arab nationalism, which held that although the Arab countries had been liberated from Ottoman rule, the post-war situation in the Arab world simply amounted to the substitution of one form of control for another, and that the Arab world was essentially a single geopolitical entity, which had been divided artificially and arbitrarily by the Western powers after the First World War. The regeneration of Arab society could only be achieved through the re-unification of the 'Arab nation', of which Iraq was an integral part.

In fact the highly heterogeneous nature of the new state of Iraq, with its preponderantly Shi'i population and its important Kurdish minority, meant that these ideas did not enjoy such widespread popularity in the inter-war period as they did, for example, in mandatory Syria, where the notion of Arabism had originated, and where the sense of division and separation was compounded both by the separation of Palestine from the rest of geographical Syria and by the internal divisions within Syria itself imposed under the French mandatory regime. However, because Iraq was at least nominally independent, it had its own army, whose senior officers had all served in either the Ottoman or Sharifian armies (or both, in some cases), and were Sunnis almost to a man[56]. The Iraqi officer corps was thus particularly receptive to such ideas, and rejected what they considered to be the excessively 'regionalist' or 'Iraqist' ideology of *Jama'at al-Ahali*. However, apart from enjoying a certain vogue among members of the Muthanna' Club[57], who came from backgrounds broadly similar to the Arab nationalist officers and who were often connected with them by ties of family or friendship, these ideas were not widely shared *outside* the ranks of the military before the mid-1930s; at least before the rebellion of 1936, the Palestine cause, always a useful barometer of pan-Arab feeling, had not been espoused to any noticeable extent by any Iraqi government or political organisation[58].

Nevertheless, as we have indicated, a small group of military officers imbued with this ideology did in fact dominate Iraqi political life between 1937 and May 1941, a period in which opposition to Britain began to take new forms. In the first place, the officers showed that although they were not immediately concerned to attempt to make any dramatic changes in Iraq's relations with Britain, *they* were now the principal locus of political power within the country and could and did make or break the seven cabinets that came into office in these four years[59]. Secondly, by 1939 events in Palestine had begun to have greater impact in political circles in Iraq, particularly after the Round Table conference in London in January–March and the arrival in Baghdad of the mufti of Jerusalem, Hajj Amin al-Husaini, in October. Finally, the outbreak of a war in which a victory for Britain did not seem a foregone conclusion appeared to open up a new range of possibilities to those who had already been seduced by the new forms of nationalism in Nazi Germany and Fascist Italy, two countries that were perceived as having emerged as strong, militarised and united nation states after a long period of disunity and could be pointed out as exemplars for the future development of the Arab world.

In March 1940, Nuri al-Sa'id, Britain's most faithful Iraqi servant, resigned as Prime Minister (an office he had held since April 1939) and agreed to enter a cabinet headed by the most prominent civilian pan-Arab nationalist, Rashid 'Ali al-Gailani. Nuri had failed to persuade his colleagues either to declare war on Germany or break off diplomatic relations with Italy during his own premiership[60]; their stand contravened the provisions of Article 4 of the Anglo-Iraqi Treaty of 1930[61], but was generally popular in Iraq, especially after the arrival of the mufti and his party in October 1939. The confrontation between the Iraqi government and Britain began to develop in earnest when Italy declared war on Britain and the Allies in June 1940, since Iraq still refused to break off relations with Italy, whose legation in Baghdad had become the main link between the mufti (whose influence with Rashid 'Ali was increasing as Britain's strategic situation worsened) and the Germans.

Matters came to a head in the course of the next year, since Rashid 'Ali, who by now had most of the armed forces behind him, refused to bow to British pressure to resign if he was not prepared to honour the clauses of the Anglo-Iraqi treaty giving landing and transit rights to British troops. This was clearly a highly sensitive issue, since it seemed to constitute direct interference in Iraqi domestic affairs. Rashid 'Ali managed to hold out until January 1941, when he was replaced by Taha al-Hashimi, who lasted until April; by that time pressures from the officers enabled Rashid 'Ali to return to head a new cabinet, and the Regent and Nuri decided to flee the country with British assistance. At this stage Rashid 'Ali and his associate Yunis al-Sab'awi were probably counting on, or at least expecting, some form of assistance from Germany.

In spite of the obvious dangers signalled by the landings of British troops at Basra in mid-April, there was no doubt that Rashid 'Ali's government enjoyed very widespread popular support[62] because of its determinedly anti-British stand. Nevertheless, given the balance of forces involved[63], the defeat of Iraq at the end of the 'thirty days war' in May 1941 was more or less a foregone conclusion, but the episode showed how little support in Iraq there was for British control, or for Britain's Iraqi partners. Both Nuri and the Regent, who had never enjoyed anything like the popularity of his uncle or his cousin, compromised themselves irretrievably by their almost slavish support for British interests in April 1941[64]. A recent account correctly maintains that 'The year 1941 represents a watershed in the history of the British era in Iraq, and its significance is essential in understanding the nationalist rejection of the treaty of alliance with the British in 1948, and the end of the Hashemite dynasty ten years later'[65].

The remaining seventeen years of the monarchy were character-ised by a high degree of unrest and uncertainty, partly because of sudden shifts in the direction of policy brought about by changes in the international situation, and partly because of the new strength and sense of purpose of the opposition. Thus, although the Regent returned to Baghdad in June 1941, immediately after the defeat of Iraqi forces, and Nuri took over once more as Prime Minister between October 1941 and June 1944, which might have been thought to presage a more repressive political atmosphere, the German attack on the Soviet Union in June 1941 and the Soviet Union's subsequent joining forces with the Allies introduced a brief period of greater political freedom, which benefitted the political organisations of the left, including the social democratic forces associated with *Jama'at al-Ahali*, and the Iraqi Communist Party.

The Communist Party, founded in 1934, became a significant factor in Iraqi politics by the early 1940s[66]. The first show of strength on the part of organised labour had been initiated by the Artisans Association (*Jami'yyat al-Ashab al-San'a*) formed by Muhammad Salih al-Qazzaz in 1929. The Association organised a general strike against the Municipal Fees Law in 1931 and a boycott of the British-owned Baghdad Electric Light and Power Company in 1933–34; both actions were supported by the 'nationalist' politicians of the day, including Rashid 'Ali, Ja'far Abu'l-Timman and Yasin al-Hashimi[67]. However, after the electricity boycott, which lasted a whole month, labour unions were banned, their leaders imprisoned and the labour movement forced underground for the next ten years.

Hopes that Hikmat Sulaiman's government, which contained three members of *Jama'at al-Ahali*, might prove more receptive to demands for democratic reforms and trade union rights were soon dashed when it became clear that the government had neither the ability nor the will to embark on such measures. In addition, Ja'far Abu'l-Timman and Hikmat Sulaiman took the same pains to emphasise, in the course of press interviews, that although they were anxious for social reform, they had no sympathy with communism[68]. After a brief period in 1936-37 when the Communists (who were hardly a force to be reckoned with at this stage) came out openly in support of the government, Bakr Sidqi, presumably in an attempt to distance himself from them, launched an attack on communism in March 1937, declaring that his government would crack down on any manifestations of it. A few days later there were major strikes at Basra port, the National Cigarette Company and at the Iraq Petroleum Company, all organised either by al-Qazzaz or by members of the Communist Party. The strikes were suppressed, and the leaders and a number of prominent Communists sent into internal exile[69]. The Party largely disappeared from public view until the events of April/ May 1941 when, as we have seen, it decided to give its support to Rashid 'Ali's movement.

The Kurds under the Mandate and Monarchy

So far, only passing reference has been made to the Kurds, who constitute some 20% of the population of Iraq, partly because although the integration of the Kurdish area within Iraq has long been a cardinal principle of Iraqi politics, the background to the 'Kurdish question' is in many ways *sui generis*, and thus most conveniently discussed as a separate issue. Until the end of the First World War, the Kurds were at least nominally subject to the jurisdiction either of the Shah of Iran or of the Ottoman sultan, although the boundary between Iran and the Ottoman Empire was not finally charted until 1913.

In the course of the nineteenth century, as we have seen, the Ottomans attempted to assert their authority even over the more remote parts of their Empire. In the Kurdish areas, their efforts in this direction caused major risings in 1837-52 and 1880-81, but even as late as the outbreak of the First World War their authority was still not universally accepted in what is now eastern Turkey and northern Iraq. Like the Arabs during the same period, although to a very much lesser extent, the Kurds were affected by the currents of nationalism in Europe and Asia in the second part of the century, and began to found political associations demanding either some form of decentralised administration or, more rarely, complete independence from Ottoman control. In an essentially tribal society, such activities could only be effective if they were supported by powerful tribal leaders, who could produce the weapons and the men necessary to bring about the political changes desired by the 'intellectuals'.

During the First World War, the Turks and the Russians were on opposite sides, confronting each other within and across the Kurdish areas in eastern Turkey and western Iran. After Russia withdrew from the war in December 1917 there was a power vacuum in eastern Turkey until well into 1919, and in western Iran until Reza Khan's seizure of power in 1921. The absence of any recognized outside authority permitted widespread disorder and also facilitated the massacre and expulsion of most of the Assyrian and some of the Armenian population, who, as Christians, had generally supported the Russians[70]. Further south, as we have seen, Mosul town was occupied some days after the Armistice of Mudros (30 October 1918), and British occupation was soon afterwards extended over the whole of the Mosul *vilayet*. Kurdish nationalists in exile outside Turkey, and local tribal leaders in ex-Ottoman Kurdistan, saw the defeat of the Ottomans and the occupation of Mosul as a golden opportunity for pressing their claims, further encouraged by the promises of autonomy that seemed to be held out in President Woodrow Wilson's Fourteen Points.

At this time, it will be remembered, the two ex-Ottoman provinces of Baghdad and Basra were under direct British administration. Because of the circumstances of the occupation of northern Iraq, and the inaccessibility of much of the terrain, the Mosul *vilayet* could not be run in the same way, and it became British policy to encourage the appointment of 'suitable' local figures to administer the area with British political advisors. The most prominent of these notables was Shaikh Mahmud Barzinji, who was installed as governor of Sulaimaniya in November 1918. A variety of factors combined to ensure that this arrangement was not to be the prelude to the creation of an independent or quasi-independent Kurdish state.

In the first place, the British gradually became committed to the' establishment of an Arab government in Iraq under British auspices, and to the inclusion of the oil-bearing province of Mosul within the boundaries of the new state. Secondly, the defeat of the Ottomans in the war was followed by the rise of a national resistance movement in Anatolia in 1919; this turned out to be the prelude to a war of independence that ended with Atatürk and his forces victorious, compelling the British and Greek armies to withdraw by October 1922. In these circumstances, the Kurds both north and south of the present Turco-Iraqi frontier naturally hesitated to throw in their lot with Britain, since it was no longer clear whether Britain would remain in the area at all. Finally, and very significantly for the future, the concept of a 'Kurdish state' or even of 'autonomy for the Kurds within Iraq' required a degree of consensus in the recognition, on the part of the Kurds themselves, of suitable representatives. At this stage, the desire for Kurdish autonomy did not, because of traditional clan and tribal rivalries, produce any coherent movement towards Kurdish unity; Shaikh Mahmud had to be removed by the British in May 1919, because his support base was so inadequate that he could not control areas less than twenty miles from Sulaimaniya[71].

Throughout 1919 and 1920 there were constant risings in northern Iraq. Some were inspired by the Turks in an attempt to drive Britain out of the Mosul *vilayet*, but most were the expression of traditional Kurdish hostility to the imposition of any form of outside authority. In the summer of 1920, a few months after the distribution of the mandates at San Remo, the Istanbul government accepted the Treaty of Sèvres, against the wishes of Atatürk and his supporters in Ankara. This provided for the dismemberment of most of what was left of Turkey and its partition between Italy and Greece, with independent states in Armenia and Kurdistan. Although Atatürk's seizure of power meant that the Treaty was never ratified, it marked an important turning point in the evolution of the Kurdish movement, since it was the first formal declaration of intent to set up a separate Kurdish political entity.

By the early 1920s the political geography of the Kurdish areas had begun to assume the general shape that it has today, with the Kurds divided between the states of Iran, Iraq, Syria and Turkey. Turkish policies towards the Kurds in the 1920s and 1930s were extremely repressive, and the risings led by Shaikh Sa'id in 1925, the Khoybun revolt in 1929–30, and the Dersim rebellion in 1937 were all put down with great ferocity. In Iran, the early 1920s were

filled with uncertainty, as the continuing anarchy in the country
encouraged some Kurdish leaders there to think in terms of a
separate state or at least an autonomous province, though these
ambitions were finally dashed after their defeat by a revitalised
Iranian army in July 1922.

In Iraq, the situation of the Kurds was more complex. The
British authorities promised the Kurds a form of autonomy within
the Arab kingdom of Iraq in 1922, but by this time Shaikh Mahmud,
who had been reinstated, *faute de mieux*, in Sulaimaniya,
had decided to reject any form of Iraqi suzerainty. By the spring
his movement had gained sufficient momentum for the British to
judge it necessary to send troops to occupy the area, setting in
motion a series of military operations culminating in the bombing
of Sulaimaniya in December 1924. By this time the League of
Nations had decided to send a commission to make a recommendation on whether the Mosul *vilayet* should be part of Iraq or
part of Turkey, which, as has been described, found in favour of
Iraq. Early in 1926, the Iraqi Prime Minister declared that civil
servants in the Kurdish area should be Kurds, that Kurdish *and*
Arabic should be the official languages of the area, and that
Kurdish children should be educated in Kurdish[72]. Although
these provisions were never more than half-heartedly carried out,
it is fair to say that in Iraq, in stark contrast to the very much more
repressive situation in Iran or Turkey, (where, especially in Turkey,
Kurds have been persecuted *qua* Kurds), the Kurds' separate
ethnic identity has generally been recognised to a greater or lesser
extent, or at least not denied, by all Iraqi governments since then,
and token Kurds served as ministers in most of the governments
under the monarchy.

At the end of the mandate, the Kurds became alarmed that there
were no clauses in the Anglo-Iraqi Treaty of 1930 specifically
guaranteeing minority rights, and a number of Kurdish deputies
protested to the Prime Minister in 1929 that little had been done to
implement the promises made in 1926. Shaikh Mahmud, techni-
cally exiled from Iraq between 1926 and 1930, indicated that he was
prepared to go on the offensive once more after serious rioting had
broken out in Sulaimaniya in September 1930 in protest against
the terms of the Treaty. This time, he was decisively defeated and
exiled to southern Iraq, but, almost simultaneously, a new and generally more effective nucleus of opposition was developing in the
district of Baradost. Mulla Mustafa Barzani, the younger brother

of the Barzani religious and tribal leader Shaikh Ahmad, emerged in the early 1930s as the principal figure in Iraqi Kurdish politics, a position that he was to hold until his death in exile in 1979[73]. After organising a series of revolts against the Iraqi government in the Barzan area, the Barzani brothers were eventually forced to surrender and made to live under a form of house arrest in Sulaimaniya in 1936. In the course of his stay in Sulaimaniya (he escaped in 1943) Barzani came into contact with Kurdish political writers and thinkers, some of whom joined together to form the clandestine *Hewa* (Hope) Party in 1939[74]. *Hewa* was a fairly loose grouping that included both left and right wing factions; that is, those who held that revolution and socialism were essential preconditions for the attainment of Kurdish national rights, and those who considered that the key to obtaining these rights lay in Britain's hands, a view implying that some sort of alliance or association with Britain was necessary. Since such differences were to form the basis of important splits within the Kurdish national movement later on, it is as well to indicate their existence at this stage. As was to be expected of a traditional tribal leader, Barzani himself was inclined to favour some sort of association with Britain.

In addition to *Hewa*, the Iraqi Communist Party had become active in Kurdistan almost since the time of its foundation in 1934. The earliest Communist newspaper, *Kifah al-Sha'b*, carried slogans in favour of Kurdish rights, and Communist organisations were set up in Arbil and other Kurdish towns in 1941 and 1942. In addition, *Azadi*, the first Kurdish political paper, was edited by members of the Communist Party, and the ICP was the first national (i.e. not exclusively Kurdish) political party to develop a coherent policy on the Kurdish question, which amounted to an autonomy plan based on self-determination. During and after the Second World War the Party continued to have a wide following in the Kurdish area[75].

After the British re-occupation of Iraq in 1941 the authorities seem to have concentrated their attention on the southern parts of the country, with the result that much of the north was left more or less to its own devices[76]. In July 1943, Barzani escaped from Sulaimaniya and returned to Barzan, where he raised a revolt in the autumn, and subsequently made overtures to the British authorities in an attempt to induce Britain to support Kurdish autonomy. In the course of a remarkable correspondence with

Cornwallis, the British ambassador, Barzani expressed his willingness to obey him 'whatever your orders may be'[77]. Cornwallis encouraged Nuri al-Sa'id to make contact with Barzani to work out a settlement, but this infuriated the Regent and many of Nuri's colleagues, who saw, or purported to see, that any concessions in the direction of Kurdish autonomy were simply a prelude to separatism, and thus a derogation of the sovereignty of the Iraqi state, which, it should be remembered, had only assumed its final form in 1926, some seventeen years earlier, and the *pourparlers* were abandoned. For about a year (June 1944–April 1945) a tacit truce prevailed, but by the summer of 1945 the government had regained sufficient confidence to launch a campaign to restore its authority in the north. Fourteen thousand troops were assembled, and this force, assisted by the defection of Barzani's father-in-law, Mahmud Agha Zibari, succeeded in expelling Barzani from Iraq into Iran in October 1945.

After this, the Kurdish struggle moved outside Iraq, and became concentrated around Mahabad, a small town in Iranian Kurdistan just south of Lake Urmia. The full story of the Kurdish Republic of Mahabad cannot be related here[78], but in essence, after the collapse of the authority of the Iranian government in most parts of the country in the wake of the Anglo-Soviet invasion in 1941, Mahabad gradually developed into the headquarters of the movement for Kurdish autonomy. This was given added impetus in October 1944 when the leading citizen and judge of Mahabad, Qadhi Muhammad, decided to join it. At the same time another autonomist/separatist movement was forming in the adjoining province of Azerbaijan, where the population was ethnically Turkish and thus, like the Kurds, also of non-Iranian origin. The Azeri movement was encouraged by Soviet officials from across the border, and by the Iranian Communist (Tudeh) Party. The Soviets were regarded as natural partners by both the Kurds and the Azeris, since they were encouraging the autonomists in both areas and were of course also instrumental in keeping the Iranian government out of the area. In the autumn of 1945, Qadhi Muhammad and his associates founded the Kurdish Democratic Party (KDP), at almost exactly the same time as Mulla Mustafa Barzani and his followers were preparing to enter Iran from Iraq.

For Qadhi Muhammad and the KDP, Barzani's arrival meant the addition of some 3000 fighting men to the Kurdish cause, and the Iranian Kurds accordingly decided to proclaim an autonomous Republic of Mahabad, inaugurated by Qadhi Muhammad on 22 January 1946. However, the main factor enabling the Republic to function was the presence of Soviet troops (though in neighbouring Azerbaijan rather than in Mahabad itself), and with the beginning of the Cold War, Britain and the United States were calling for the withdrawal of all foreign forces from Iran. Although the prospects for the Soviet Union looked bright for the first part of 1946, with three members of the Tudeh in the Iranian cabinet, more conservative elements had rallied by October, and the government fell[79]. Its successor decided to make the restoration of government authority in the north-west a major priority, and Qadhi Muhammad and his colleagues were forced to surrender to the Iranian army on 16 December. Barzani, meanwhile, had decided to abandon the cause of Mahabad, and made an unsuccessful attempt to come to terms with the Iranian government through the good offices of the British Embassy in Tehran. In March 1947, the Iranian Army launched a major offensive against Barzani and his men, chasing them back across the frontier into Iraq; on 31 March, Qadhi Muhammad and two of his closest associates were hanged in public in the main square of Mahabad. By mid-May Barzani had decided that it would not be safe for him to stay in Iraq either. Some 600 men accompanied him on a daring journey to the Soviet Union across Turkey and Iran, crossing the Aras river between 15 and 18 June. They stayed in the Soviet Union until 1958.

With the fall of Mahabad and the departure of Barzani, Kurdish politics went into something of a limbo until the overthrow of the Iraqi monarchy. The most important development between 1947 and 1958 was undoubtedly the foundation and rise to maturity of the *Iraqi* KDP. At first, an Iraqi branch of the KDP had been formed in Mahabad by Barzani and Hamza 'Abdullah, and 'Abdullah was sent back to Iraq to organise the Party there. However, as events turned out, 'Abdullah's mission ended in the creation of a separate Iraqi KDP (with Barzani as president and himself as secretary) in August 1946. At the time, the Iranian (i.e. Mahabad) KDP in Iraqi Kurdistan was led by Ibrahim Ahmad, who denounced the Barzani/'Abdullah initiative as a potentially dangerous derogation of the authority of Qadhi Muhammad and the Mahabad Republic, which still seemed the most viable vehicle for Kurdish national aspirations. These details may seem trivial, but the effect of the foundation of separate parties was to formalise what has subsequently developed into a permanent political division between Iraqi and Iranian Kurdistan.

After the fall of Mahabad at the end of 1946, Ahmad's Mahabad-linked organisation ceased to have much relevance, and, with some reluctance, he joined the Iraqi KDP, attempting to push it towards the left, a task facilitated by Barzani's absence in the Soviet Union. By 1951, having ousted Hamza 'Abdullah, he had become secretary-general of the Party, called in Kurdish *Parti Dimuqrati Kurdistan*, generally known in Iraq as 'Hizb al-Parti', as the Kurdish word is a transliteration of the English. Because of its political orientation under Ahmad, the KDP worked mainly among students and intellectuals, and had little support in the Kurdish countryside, which remained dominated by tribal leaders and landlords. Although not formally a member of either of the opposition national fronts of the 1950s, the KDP generally supported their aims, and, as we shall see, gave its enthusiastic support to the Revolution of 1958.

Economy and Society Before the Revolution of 1958: Land Tenure and Rural Social Structure

From the beginning of the British Occupation, the authorities were concerned to secure, if not the loyalty, at least the neutrality of the local population, who were still nominally Ottoman subjects. In order to ensure that the tribes did not cooperate with the Ottomans, and also to secure regular food supplies for themselves, the British decided soon after landing in Iraq to bolster the authority of those tribal shaikhs and landlords whose domains lay along the lines of the army's advance, and to give them the security of tenure over the lands that they had been unable to claim as their own under the Ottomans[80]. In consequence, vast areas became the personal possession of selected tribal leaders and were subsequently registered in *tapu*. Thus the decline of shaikhly power and the gradual decomposition of the tribal structures that had begun in the last years of Ottoman rule were dramatically arrested, especially as the administration also began to appoint suitable shaikhs as the 'official' leaders of their tribes. 'Many of them were small men of no account until we made them powerful and rich', one Political Officer wrote as the Revolution of 1920 was beginning, and the same general tendency is confirmed in his

Chief's memoirs ten years later: 'The shaikhs were in most cases directly dependent on the civil administration for the positions they held; realising that their positions entailed corresponding obligations, they cooperated actively with the political officers . . .'[81]. The policy of bolstering the powers of the shaikhs continued throughout the mandate and monarchy periods, and large land-ownership became the social base of the regime. In some cases, particularly in the provinces of Kut and 'Amara, where some of the largest private estates in the Middle East came to be located, mostly created by a stroke of the pen between 1915 and 1925, government administrative penetration was light and revenue tiny, reflecting the partiality of the pre-revolutionary governments towards the landowners.

Since the settlement policies pursued by the various govern-ments promised substantial income from land with very little capital outlay, many individuals, both tribal shaikhs, and, increasingly, townsmen, hastened to acquire land. In 1913, the cropped area amounted to only 937,000 acres; by 1943 it had increased nearly fivefold, to 4,242,000 acres[82]. This increase was made possible largely through the widespread use of mechanical irrigation pumps to raise water from the canals and rivers to the fields[83]. The rise in the number of pumps was facilitated by a law in 1926 that gave complete tax exemption on the produce accruing from pump-irrigated land for the first four seasons. Needless to say, the installation of pumps in areas where ownership was only imperfectly defined led imperceptibly to the acquisition of what was in fact state or *miri* land by the pump owner, a process that was also made easier by the passage of timely legislation. In 1932, two laws, the *Taswiya* (land settlement) Law and the *Lazma* (pre-scriptive rights) Law, granted prescriptive rights of ownership to those who could claim continuous cultivation for fifteen years.

This process resulted in the formation of enormous private estates out of land that had previously been held in some form of common tribal ownership. By 1952, over half a million acres of former state land in the province of Kut were owned by two families, the brothers 'Abdullah and Balasim al-Yasin of the Muhiyya tribe, and the family of Muhammad al-Amir of the Rabi'a, the father-in-law of the Regent 'Abd al-Ilah. In the province as a whole, forty-nine families owned 775,000 acres in *lazma* in addition to the 370,000 they had already obtained in *tapu*[84]. In the province of 'Amara, seven landowners had individual holdings of between 60,000 and 250,000 acres in 1944, and nine others owned between 30,000 and 60,000 acres. In 1951 eight shaikhly families held 53% and eighteen other individuals 19% of all land-holdings in the province[85].

Although the concentration of property was particularly high in these two provinces, the picture for the rest of the country was not very different. In the vicinity of Baghdad a number of influential government officials, politicians and merchants also became large landowners[86]. In the country as a whole, eight landowners held a total of 855,000 acres, or about 107,000 acres each; by 1958, 2,480 individuals, about 1% of all landowners, owned over 55% of all land in private hands in 1958. At the other end of the scale, about 600,000 rural heads of households (out of a total rural population of 3.8 million in 1957) were completely landless and 64% of landowners held 3.6% of all cultivated land[87].

Irrigation was generally undertaken privately and for private gain; during the mandate period, relatively small amounts, about 5.5% of annual government expenditure, were devoted to irrigation[88]. Since there was an almost unlimited supply of land, the extension of cultivation did not need to be accompanied by the intensification of production. The principle animating both pump owners and landowners was the production of *more* rather than *better* crops, since the former involved very little capital outlay, and the only investment required was the purchase and installation of the pumps. Furthermore, as many shaikhs were of nomadic origin they were not likely to be familiar with sophisticated agricultural techniques and were, in any case, more concerned with immediate returns rather than investment. In consequence, as methods of cultivation were generally extremely wasteful, the soil deteriorated steadily, especially in pump irrigated areas, because of the lack of elutriation and drainage. Productivity declined from an average of 375 kg per acre in 1920 to 238 kg per acre in 1953–58[89]; many landowners abandoned land that they had effectively ruined and simply shifted cultivation elsewhere by digging new canals to divert irrigation water.

The profits from agriculture found their way almost intact into the pockets of the landlords, who generally moved to the cities to enjoy their new wealth. Most landlords consumed rather than invested[90], and played an essentially parasitic role in the economy while bearing down heavily on the peasantry. It is important to stress that these tendencies were the direct result of British policies during the mandate, and that, in addition, the policies had been elaborated at the time in order to produce this overall result. Given the fluid and vague system of land tenure that prevailed, the British were faced with having to decide whether to allocate land to the producers and cultivators themselves, or to the tribal shaikhs and their families[91]. From the very beginning, the latter group was favoured, in spite of a series of memoranda from concerned officials questioning the wisdom of this course[92]. Thus the land and fiscal policies pursued under the British Occupation and mandate, and continued under the monarchy, both created and consolidated the essentially non-productive stranglehold of the shaikhs and landlords over the system of agricultural production.

The fallahin were naturally the most affected by the landlords' enhanced socio-economic role. The fallah and his immediate superior, the *sarkal*, suffered a concomitant decline in status, income and independence of action. Sharecropping was the commonest form of agricultural production, where the fallah was paid in kind, taking a share that varied from region to region, generally between 30 and 50% of the crop, depending on whether he supplied seeds and draught animals, or owned his own tools. The fallah's share would be further reduced by the numerous customary tribal dues, so that it is difficult to estimate his actual income with any precision. Most commonly, a fallah could not supply any of the components required for cultivation and had to borrow money to buy his seed from the shaikh, the sarkal, or the local money lender, at exorbitant rates of interest, thus initiating an unending cycle of poverty, wretchedness, and indebtedness. As recently as 1953, a British medical expert described the Iraqi fallah as a 'living pathological specimen' and estimated average life expectancy at between thirty-five and thirty-nine years[93]. In the nature of things the majority of the fallahin became more and more deeply indebted, and also had no incentive to produce more, since the greater part of any increase in production would go straight to the landowner.

Hence migration from the land began at the end of the 1920s and continued throughout (and of course beyond) the rest of the period of the monarchy, particularly from the southern provinces to Baghdad. Partly in response to this, the government enacted the *Law Governing the Rights and Duties of Cultivators*, which defined the legal responsibilities of landowners, sarkals and fallahin[94].

Under the provisions of the Law, the fallah could be held responsible for almost any disaster that might befall the crop, and was liable to summary eviction for a variety of reasons. Similarly, if he was in debt, he was not allowed to leave the land until his debts were paid off, which, for the reasons that have been outlined, was almost impossible. The only way to break out of the circle was to run away from the farm.

Hence, with the passage of time, a combination of the prevailing relations of production in the countryside and the attendant social and economic conditions reflected in the peasant's poverty — debt, almost total subjection to the will of the shaikh or landlord, un- and underemployment — encouraged increasing numbers of fallahin to move away from the land to seek work in the cities, especially after the relatively rapid economic expansion that accompanied the beginnings of the oil boom in the 1950s. A study carried out in 1957 showed that in spite of natural increases, migration was causing the population of the southern provinces to decline, while the population of Greater Baghdad rose from 515,459 to 793,183 between 1947 and 1957. In 1956 it was estimated that there were 16,400 *sarifas* (shacks made from palm branches, the Iraqi equivalent of the North African *bidonville*) in the vicinity of Baghdad, housing about 92,000 people[95].

Most migrants came from those areas in which the concentration of land-holding was highest and peasant oppression most acute[96]. They naturally had no industrial skills, and began to flood the labour market, especially as labourers in the construction industry, porters in the markets, *farrashin* in government offices, or servants and gardeners. One important effect was to reduce the bargaining power of workers, which resulted in low wages[97], friction, and higher unemployment. The city could not, ultimately, absorb this mass of landless fallahin, and the majority were forced to stay behind, eking out an existence on the land.

More importantly, while large landownership came to furnish the social base for the monarchy, and for the continuation of British influence, the socio-economic structures that emerged in the rural areas had the effect of arresting and distorting the historical processes of change within this sector of the economy. This state of affairs contributed to the lopsided and uneven development of the Iraqi economy as a whole; more precisely, capitalist penetration under these particular conditions resulted in the perpetuation of pre-capitalist relations of production in the countryside. Thus a system directed increasingly towards production for an urban capitalist market managed to exclude most of the rural producers from all but the most marginal participation in the money economy.

Economy and Society Before the Revolution of 1958: Urban Life and the Urban Economy

Iraq became integrated into the international economic system as an exporter, first of grain, and then, in the 1930s, of oil. The latter accounted for 49.3% of national income in 1953, but Iraq had been dependent on oil to balance the country's budget since as early as 1934[98]. However, the government had little control over either production or prices, which were both determined by the Iraq Petroleum Company. Furthermore, the Iraqi dinar was linked to sterling, which meant that the economy was always affected by changes in the value of the pound. Internally, the pattern of economic activity remained typical of a colonised or semi-colonial Third World country. The vast majority of the population continued to be employed in agriculture, although because of the value of oil exports, agricultural production only accounted for a relatively small proportion of national income, some 29% by 1951. Industry was still very underdeveloped, contributing only about 8% in that year and 10% ten years later[99]. State intervention was minimal; 'agriculture, almost the whole of mining and quarrying, construction, almost the whole of wholesale and retail trade, and ownership of dwellings, was wholly within the private sector'[100].

The concentration of wealth, and by extension of political power, in the hands of a very few landowners, was paralleled in the pattern of commercial and industrial holdings in the cities, although the picture here is more complex, and varies over time. In the larger towns, the middle class (in which we include all those strata that were taking advantage of the expansion of the domestic market) had been accumulating industrial, commercial and real estate capital since the early days of the mandate. Industry, as has been mentioned, functioned on a relatively small scale and owed much of the impetus for its development to the special conditions created by the Second World War. By 1957, fixed investment in industrial capital (ID 27.25 million) exceeded that of commercial capital (ID 20.80 million), but here an important characteristic of the middle classes at this time should be mentioned:

> Often a bourgeois at one and the same time owns
> irrigation pumps and agricultural land and some urban
> real estate, undertakes transactions in one or more
> branches of commerce and owns industrial stocks and
> shares if he is not the main founder of an industrial
> establishment'.[101]

There was a substantial rise in the growth of a few large private
fortunes, particularly marked after the oil boom of the early 1950s.
The speed at which this new capital was acquired is well illustrated
by a list of the seventeen Baghdadi families worth ID 1,000,000 or
more in 1958. Only one of these had ranked as first class in the
Baghdad Chamber of Commerce in 1938–39, which then meant
having a 'financial consideration' of between ID 22,500 and ID
75,000; all the others had made their fortunes over the previous
twenty years, together owning some 30–35 million dinars worth of
assets, the equivalent of 55–65% of all private corporate commercial and industrial capital. In commerce and business, some
90,000 individuals were engaged in domestic and foreign trade in
1957–58, and about 9,000 made their living from real estate
transactions[102].

At the other end of the scale, the 'working class', including those
employed in transport and services, was estimated at just under
half a million, between one fifth and one sixth of the urban
population. About 100,000 workers were employed in industrial
production and a further 15,000 in the oil industry. Most of the
'industrial enterprises' in existence were no more than workshops;
45% were one-man businesses and 93% employed less than five
people, although 44% of all industrial workers were employed in
294 large firms. A large proportion of the labour force were
illiterate rural migrants; here the contrast with Syria, with its long
tradition of skilled urban labour, is striking[103]. Hence the working
class was essentially still in the making in the 1940s and 1950s, a
dynamic process only slowed down by the overall economic
weakness of the industrial bourgeoisie.

The lower middle classes, or petty bourgeoisie, a wide and
growing group including professionals, army officers, and civil
servants, greatly outnumbered both the bourgeoisie and the
working class. Their numbers were continually increasing as a

result of the expansion of education and the armed forces, the main avenues of upward social mobility for those with no fortunes or property of their own. Many of these officers, doctors, teachers, businessmen and civil servants had themselves come from poor families, and thus often brought to their new positions a certain degree of concern for social justice and equality, born from their own experience. However, although this factor was important, it should not be unduly stressed, since they normally concentrated on securing their own progress up the social ladder, and preserved, or acquired, a disdain for manual labour.

Since this stratum was relatively well-educated, it was also one of the most important carriers of nationalist and anti-imperialist ideas, and formed the core of the political parties whose emergence has been discussed earlier. Many, probably most, people in this stratum were against the monarchy and the existing political structure, which was perceived as serving British rather than Iraqi interests; it was rather less clear, and there was certainly no consensus, about what they were *for.* There were wide disparities in their political thinking and social consciousness but their common opposition to the status quo gave them a certain degree of solidarity, and their desire for national independence was shared by members of most other social classes and strata. Of course, these social divisions were far more fluid than this brief description may suggest, but in general the incorporation of the economy into the world market had affected all strata of society, particularly in the cities.

In spite of this, the uneven nature of the process, combined with the backwardness of the rural economy, meant that the position of the national bourgeoisie was extremely precarious, both economically and, as has been emphasised earlier, politically. No bourgeois political party could muster anything like mass support, or promote its ideology as that of the nation as a whole, with the result that quite different and generally more radical forces tended to dominate the 'extra-parliamentary' political scene under the mandate and monarchy. The notion of economic development became closely linked with the demand for social justice, equality and 'socialism', which left little scope for the emergence of traditional bourgeois political values. Hence, despite the heterogeneity of the social structure, and the absence of a single dominant class, there was a general consensus of opinion in the last decade of the monarchy that the country's most urgent needs

were national independence and economic evelopment, both of
which were being blocked or denied by the *ancien régime*. At the
same time, in Iraq, as in many other underdeveloped countries,
the *state* had become widely regarded as the most 'natural' vehicle
to carry out the necessary transformation.

The Last Years of the Monarchy, 1946–1958

As well as inaugurating a certain degree of cautious democratisation in Iraq, and even, for a short while, bringing about a lull in the
persecution of the Communist Party, the circumstances of the
Second World War had important effects upon the Iraqi economy
that gradually came to make themselves felt in political terms. The
presence of the Allied armies of occupation meant a sudden influx
of a large body of newcomers with substantial purchasing power,
while the absence of normal supplies of manufactured goods from
abroad gave local firms and industrialists an obvious incentive to
expand or initiate production, and thus facilitated capital
accumulation on a larger scale than had previously been
possible.

Nevertheless, the doubling of the population of Baghdad
between 1922 and 1947 and the concomitant growth in the size of
the labour force, combined with the new political circumstances
that have already been described, created conditions that favoured
the development of a labour movement. Furthermore, a number
of political parties were licensed in 1946, notably the National
Democratic Party, the heir of the non-Marxist wing of *Jama'at al-
Ahali*, and the Istiqlal (Independence) Party, which favoured a
somewhat less extreme form of the pan-Arabism associated with
the Muthanna' Club, which had been broken up after the events of
1941.

The events of the immediately post-war years were to be of
paramount importance in consolidating opposition to Britain and
the monarchy. Under the ministries of Hamid al-Pachachi and
Tawfiq al-Suwaidi between 1944 and 1946 (Nuri had fallen
temporarily out of favour as the Regent had become tired of being
dictated to and was attempting to assert his independence)[104], a
total of sixteen labour unions, twelve of which were controlled by
the Communists, were licensed. The largest unions were formed in
the country's most important industrial undertakings, Basra Port,

and the Iraqi Railways, which were both under British management. Major strikes for higher wages took place on the railways in 1945 and at the port in 1947, and again in the late 1940s.

In the other major British-directed concern, the Iraq Petroleum Company, based in Kirkuk, permission to form a union was refused, and the workers went on strike for higher wages in July 1946. After nine days of strike, the workers were gathering to hear a report from the strike committee when the meeting was suddenly charged by armed police, and ten people were killed[105]. This tragic incident was a foretaste of the terrible violence of 1948, the year of the great national rising known as *al-Wathba*, the leap. The immediate cause of this mass disavowal of the current status quo and the whole governmental system was the so-called Portsmouth Agreement, the outcome of negotiations between Britain and Iraq in 1947–48 which, if implemented, would have had the effect of prolonging the Anglo-Iraqi Treaty of 1948 for a further twenty years, or, in Batatu's words of 'extending the treaty under the guise of revising it'[106].

Although a number of British officials and some British ministers had come to realise that 'with the old gang in power this country cannot hope to progress very far'[107], there were evidently limitations on the extent to which pressure on 'the old gang' to mend its ways would ever be brought to bear, since vital imperial communications, in terms of bases and other military facilities, as well as access to Iraqi oil, were to be maintained in any recasting of Anglo–Iraqi relations. The anxieties expressed by some British officials in 1946 and 1947 were temporarily allayed when Iraq's first Shi'i Prime Minister, Salih Jabr, took office after the elections of March 1947; in particular, it was believed that Jabr would be interested in implementing some of the social reforms that were judged necessary to prevent popular discontent reaching dangerous proportions, since Nuri, while acknowledging that reforms were desirable, did not seem sufficiently convinced of the volatility of the situation.

In office, Jabr proved as illiberal and repressive as Nuri. Fahd, the Communist Party leader, and two members of the Party's Central Committee, who had been arrested early in 1947, were given death sentences in June, although these were commuted on appeal. The leaders of the more moderate leftist parties, Kamil Chadirchi and 'Abd al-Fattah Ibrahim, were brought to trial in September 1947 and the parties banned. In these circumstances, which also coincided with enormous rises in the cost of living, and increasing public hostility towards British policy in the region and in Palestine in particular[108], any renegotiation of the Treaty that fell short of a major revision in Iraq's favour was likely to prove unacceptable to most politically conscious Iraqis.

The main discussions took place in Baghdad between May and December, and the Iraqi delegation left for Britain at the beginning of January; the new Treaty was initialled at Portsmouth on 15 January. Even before the delegation had arrived in England there were large student demonstrations in Baghdad, initiated, apparently, by the Istiqlal Party[109], but when the terms of the treaty were announced on 16 January the tide of popular discontent became a flood, in which 'the Communists emerged unmistakably as the fundamental force . . .'. On 20 January a mass march of railway workers and poor *sarifa* dwellers was fired on by the police, and a number of people were killed. The next day the Regent was forced to announce that he would not ratify the Treaty, and on 26 January Jabr and his colleagues returned from London. On 27 January there were huge demonstrations, which soon developed into clashes between the police and demonstrators, who retaliated by throwing stones and erecting barricades of burning cars. On that day alone some 300 to 400 people lost their lives through police and military action[110]. The opposition political parties put out a united call for the 'immediate abolition of the Treaty, the dissolution of parliament, a new, free election, and a prompt supply of bread'[111]. On the evening of the same day Jabr presented his resignation to the Regent.

Although another ten years were to pass before the overthrow of the *ancien régime*, the hatred that was revealed in these terrible scenes in Baghdad was a portent of the wrath to come. Jabr's ministry was replaced by a caretaker cabinet under another Shi'i, Muhammad al-Sadr (January to June 1948), who had been active in the Revolution of 1920. al-Sadr's main task was to organise new elections in the summer, which were again rigged in favour of the 'old gang'. During the spring and summer, violent opposition spread outwards from Baghdad to other parts of the country[112]. In what became the most legendary of all the uprisings of that period, the IPC's pumping station K3 near Haditha was brought to a standstill in April and May 1948 by a strike of the 3000 workers and clerical staff, organised by the Communist Party. The strike committee put forward wage claims of between 25 and 40%, which were not conceded, and the pumping station came to a halt. After two and a half weeks, the government and IPC cut off supplies of food and water to the strikers; after three weeks, they decided to march on Baghdad, some 250 kilometres away. On their way they were fed and sheltered by the inhabitants of the small towns and villages on the road, and even lent trucks by the people of Ramadi. When they came to Fallujah, some 70 kilometres from Baghdad, the police intervened and arrested them. This act of defiance, known in Iraqi history as the 'great march', *al-Masira al-Kubra*, was a major expression of popular determination to stand against the political order, even in the face of overwhelming odds. Almost all manifestations of opposition by organised labour during the 1940s and 1950s tended to combine claims for higher wages and better living conditions with the struggle for national independence, and it was often against British-owned and British-controlled concerns that the strikes and demonstrations were concentrated. This made the labour movement both more articulate and more effective than either its numbers, its cohesion, or its apparent lack of economic muscle might suggest.

The elections in 1948 coincided with the beginning of the war in Palestine, which aroused further strong anti-British (and hence anti-regime) feelings in Iraq, to the extent that martial law was introduced in the autumn. Nuri took over the premiership once again in January 1949, after having overseen the Iraqi Army's withdrawal from its forward position in Palestine the previous November. Nuri's crude answer to all opposition, which was to crack down upon it with an iron fist, was given savage expression on the mornings of 14 and 15 February 1949 when Fahd, the First Secretary of the Communist Party, and two members of the Politbureau, Husain Muhammad al-Shabibi and Zaki Basim, who had all been in prison since their arrest at the beginning of 1947, were hanged in public in Baghdad, ostensibly for having continued to organise the Party while in prison; 'their bodies were left hanging for several hours so that the common people going to work would receive the warning'[113]. The Party took some time to recover from this blow; a large number of senior cadres had either been arrested with Fahd in 1947, or between then and 1949, with the result that many of the most experienced members of the Party spent much of the last decade of the monarchy in prison[114]. On the other hand, Fahd and his two colleagues became martyrs and popular heroes, and their own supreme sacrifice, as well as the draconian punishments meted out to other Communists for their political activities, ensured that the Party gained widespread popular support.

The last ten years of the monarchy saw some twenty cabinets in and out of office, and represented the peak of Nuri's personal power; if he or his close associates were not actually running things, it was only a matter of months before they had to be called back in again. At this stage, another important factor began to emerge; as Table 1.1 indicates, oil revenues were beginning to grow rapidly, and although the British were well aware of the unpopularity of the Iraqi government, and of the corruption and venality of many of its members, there was a certain optimism, at least at the beginning of the 1950s, that both British interests and the regime's survival might be ensured by the possibilities now being opened by 'development', in which Nuri was beginning to take a lively and genuine interest.

Table 1.1 *Oil Production and Revenues, 1946–1958*

Year	Million Tons	Revenue (ID Million)
1946	4.6	2.3
1948	3.4	2.0
1950	6.5	5.3
1951	8.6	13.3
1953	28.0	49.9
1955	33.0	84.4
1958	35.8	79.9

Source: Y. Sayigh, *The Economies of the Arab World: Development since 1945*, p. 37.

Unfortunately for the regime and its backers, the activities of the Development Board, established in 1950, were quite insufficient to hold back the flood tide of discontent. The Board concentrated mainly on flood and irrigation control, communications and construction, the kind of large scale projects that, however sensible, could not produce immediate and visible results, but would take several years to materialise. It was also widely believed that whatever the ultimate benefits of industrial, agricultural or irrigation projects, the most obvious spin-offs were the rich pickings which went to those fortunate enough to be awarded the contracts[115].

Events in the world outside Iraq inspired some of the major incidents of the 1950s, particularly the nationalisation of Iranian oil in 1951, which gave rise to the ventilation of similar demands in Iraq, the negotiations leading to the Baghdad Pact in 1955, and perhaps above all Nasser's rise to power in 1952 and his successful defiance of Britain, France and Israel in 1956. The Partisans of Peace, a Communist front organisation whose members came mainly from the professional and middle classes, began to be active in the early 1950s, and the Communist Party itself began to revive under the leadership of Baha' al-Din Nuri, who, together with a number of Party associates, led and organised the huge demonstrations in Baghdad in November 1952 known as *al-Intifada*, the tremor[116], originally sparked off by student discontent. In response, martial law was declared and General Nur al-Din Mahmud was appointed to head the government (23 November 1952 to 29 January 1953). Eighteen people were killed as a result of military action; political parties were banned, and some 300 political leaders were arrested, including Siddiq Shanshal and Fa'iq al-Samarra'i of the Istiqlal, Kamil Chadirchi of the National Democrats, and 'Ali Mahmud of the Partisans of Peace[117].

In 1953, Faisal II, then aged eighteen, came of age, but the Regent, unwilling to lose the control he had exercised since 1939, did not step into the background and continued to act as if nothing had changed. In Nuri's absence in Europe, 'Abd al-Ilah planned to hold a relatively free parliamentary election in June 1954, which he hoped might produce a chamber of deputies where his arch rival's influence would be diminished. In May, the three main political parties, the National Democrats, the Istiqlal and the Communists (represented by their 'auxiliary forces')[118], had agreed to join together in a National Front, a unique and potentially influential political alliance, which actually won eleven out of the 135 seats in the elections in June. However, as the Anglo-Iraqi Treaty of 1930 was about to expire, 'Abd al-Ilah thought it prudent to bring Nuri back for the negotiations; he returned in August, prorogued parliament and on forming the twelfth of his fourteen cabinets began to rule by decree.

The intensity of the repression that followed was unparalleled in the previous history of the monarchy; all opposition parties and newspapers were banned, and a totally servile parliament assembled. However, although Nuri's diplomatic activities in 1954 and 1955, which resulted in the conclusion of the Baghdad Pact in February 1955, were every bit as unacceptable, if not more so, than those which he and Salih Jabr had perpetrated in 1947 and 1948, and the social and economic problems that had existed in the earlier period had not been seriously alleviated, the response was less well organised and coordinated in the mid-1950s than it had been in 1948. In Egypt, Nasser's reaction to a new western-sponsored defence agreement for the Middle East was predictably hostile. His vigorous denunciation of the Pact, and his triumphant emergence as an international figure at the Bandung Conference in 1955, served greatly to enhance his status, strenghtening his claim to be the leading representative of a new kind of pan-Arabism, which soon became very popular in Iraq and in other parts of the Arab world[119]. Furthermore, Nasser's passionate speeches over Cairo Radio were reaching an eager and appreciative audience in Iraq.

In this atmosphere, the Suez crisis put the Iraqi regime in a particularly difficult position. There were huge demonstrations in Baghdad and other cities, most notably in Hayy and Najaf; even the government itself (Nuri was Prime Minister between August 1954 and June 1957) was obliged to make a face-saving statement of protest to Britain, but clamped down violently on demonstrations and imposed martial law once more. Increasingly, as in Egypt at the beginning of the 1950s, it was clearly only a matter of time before the regime fell, and Suez made its isolation almost complete. By the end of 1956, the Iraqi regime was out of step with the governments of almost all the other Arab states, and the humiliation caused by this isolation was compounded by almost universal dissatisfaction with the slow rate of material progress and the absence of civil liberties.

Perhaps most ominously for the regime, and in spite of considerable improvements in its status, pay and conditions, discontent was spreading in the army, where Nasser's pan-Arab doctrines were finding a ready and appreciative audience. The Iraqi Army had expanded greatly from its small beginnings in 1920, and the rapid growth of the officer corps provided an important means of advancement for members of social groups without fortune or family. Although the most senior officers in the late 1950s were still closely associated with the regime through ties of family, friendship or material interest, the younger generation came from more disparate social backgrounds and their views reflected the various political trends circulating in the country as a whole, including Communism, Nasserism, and other forms of pan-Arab nationalism.

Although the year before the July Revolution was fairly uneventful in comparison with the turbulence of the early 1950s and the violent response to Suez in 1956, the disfavour in which the regime was held made a profound impression on observers at the time[120]. A second national opposition front was formed in February 1957, which included the National Democratic Party, the Istiqlal and the Communists, this time under their own colours, and the Ba'th Party, the Iraqi branch of a pan-Arab organisation founded in Syria, which had some 300 members in Iraq in 1955[121]. However, given the extremely volatile circumstances that have been described, and given the powerlessness of the opposition politicians in the face of the government's monopoly of the means of coercion, the actual overthrow of the regime could only be carried out by force. Thus it was to be a group known as the Free Officers, a secret organisation within the military, which brought about the coup which became the Revolution of 14 July 1958.

Chapter Two

1958–1963

The Revolution of 14 July 1958 was almost universally welcomed by the people of Iraq. For the poor, particularly the *sarifa* dwellers and the masses of unemployed, as well as for most other social groups, it was a time of great hope and optimism for the future. At last, many believed, a government had come to power that would not only free the country from the tutelage of Britain and her clients, but would pursue policies directed towards the fulfilment of their own interests. Indeed, such views were largely shared by many of the Free Officers, who also believed that if they could only liberate their country everything else would somehow fall naturally into place.

Preparations for the Coup: Qasim and the Free Officers Before July 1958

The original organisational structure of the Free Officers cannot be traced with any precision before 1956, although a number of discontented officers had been meeting secretly since 1952[1]. The movement, if it can be so described at this stage, attracted increasing numbers of adherents after the accession of Iraq to the Baghdad Pact in 1955, and even more so after the tripartite invasion of Egypt in 1956. In December 1956 a Supreme Committee of the Free Officers was formed, consisting of Muhi al-

Din 'Abd al-Hamid, Naji Talib, 'Abd al-Wahhab Amin, Muhsin Husain al-Habib, Tahir Yahya, Rajab 'Abd al-Majid, 'Abd al-Karim Farhan, Wasfi Tahir, Salih 'Ali Ghalib and Muhammad Saba', all of whom were army or air force officers of the rank of major and above. At this stage the Supreme Committee did not include the two men who were eventually to emerge as the prime movers of the group, 'Abd al-Karim Qasim and 'Abd al-Salam 'Arif, both of whom were stationed in Jordan. However, Qasim and 'Arif were members of another group of Free Officers, who included 'Arif's brother 'Abd al-Rahman, Fu'ad 'Arif (not a relation), Nadhim al-Tabaq chali, 'Abd al-'Aziz al-'Uqaili and Khalil Sa'id. Altogether the Free Officers numbered about 200, 'less than five per cent of the entire membership of the officer corps'[2], although the virtual absence of opposition to the movement from within the armed forces at the time of the Revolution itself indicates a higher level of support than this small percentage implies. Nevertheless, it was a clandestine movement, operating under a fairly repressive regime, and those involved lived in constant fear of discovery. In the summer of 1956, for example, a number of those whom the authorities suspected of being involved in a secret society were either transferred to less sensitive posts at home or appointed military attachés at Iraqi embassies abroad. As a result, contacts between Qasim's group and the Supreme Committee were suspended until the spring of 1957, when the two groups merged.

A major problem facing the conspirators in the months immediately before the July Revolution was that, for security reasons, few army units were issued with live ammunition. The successful accumulation of sufficient quantities of ammunition was apparently the work of Naji Talib, who was Director of Military Training and could thus requisition supplies 'for use on manoeuvres'[3]. The actual timing of the coup seems to have been decided by 'Arif and Qasim on their own, without any real coordination with opposition political leaders, although Kamil Chadirchi of the National Democratic Party, Kamil 'Umar Nadhmi of the Central Committee of the Communist Party and Fu'ad al-Rikabi of the Ba'th Party were given the date some days in advance[4]. The final date was chosen to coincide with the overland transfer to Jordan of the 20th Infantry Brigade, two of whose three battalions were commanded by Free Officers, presumably to be on hand in the event of any escalation of the fighting in the Lebanon.

Originally planned for 3 July, the move was postponed until the night of 13–14 July.

The Coup and the Revolution of 14 July 1958

The execution of the coup has been described in detail elsewhere and need not detain us here[5]. Briefly, while Qasim stayed at al-Mansur camp some distance outside the city with the 19th Infantry Brigade, 'Arif, who was one of the three battalion commanders of the 20th Brigade that was leaving camp at Jalawla for Jordan late in the evening of 13 July, managed to take control of the whole Brigade and directed it to march on Baghdad. Part of the Brigade moved to occupy strategic points in and around Baghdad, while other sections surrounded Nuri al-Sa'id's house and the Royal Palace. Nuri managed to escape capture until the following day, but the King, the Crown Prince and several female members of the royal family were shot in the palace courtyard. Early in the morning of 14 July the citizens of Iraq awoke to the strains of martial music on the radio, especially the nationalist song 'Allahu Akbar'. At 6.30 a.m. 'Arif read out the first proclamation of the new regime, to the effect that the army had liberated 'the beloved homeland from the corrupt crew that imperialism installed', and appealed to the nation for support. Qasim and 'Arif appeared on television soon afterwards and declared that a popular government under a republic would be inaugurated and called for the maintenance of 'order and unity . . . in the interest of the homeland'[6]. Martial law was declared a few hours later. Huge crowds poured into the streets of Baghdad chanting enthusiastic slogans of support for the 'Revolution' and its leaders, celebrating the downfall of the *ancien régime*, especially the death of 'Abd al-Ilah. In this highly volatile situation, where the intensity of popular feeling against the monarchy and the British seemed almost uncontrollable, it is remarkable that the number of casualties was not higher.

In the afternoon, the first cabinet was announced, containing a mixture of officers, prominent political personalities and 'representatives' of a number of political parties. It was generally moderate and nationalist in its complexion; neither the Communist Party nor the Kurdish Democratic Party was invited to participate. The Free Officers occupied the most important posts: Qasim, 'Arif and Naji Talib took the portfolios of Prime Minister (and Defence), Interior, and Social Affairs; two leading members of the National Democratic Party, Muhammad Hadid and Hudaiyib al-Hajj Humud, were Ministers of Finance and Agriculture; the Ba'th secretary-general, Fu'ad al-Rikabi, became Minister of Development; and the secretary-general of the Istiqlal Party, Siddiq Shanshal, Minister of Guidance. The remaining portfolios of Foreign Affairs, Justice, Economy, Education, Health and Communications, and Works were filled by Dr 'Abd al-Jabbar Jumard, Mustafa 'Ali, Dr Ibrahim Kubba (who had vague Marxist sympathies), Dr Jabir 'Umar (an Arab nationalist), Dr Muhammad Salih Mahmud, and Baba 'Ali, the son of Shaikh Mahmud of Sulaimaniya. At the same time, 'reliable' Free Officers were appointed as commanders of the army, air force and national security.

The first acts of the new government were to abolish the main institutions of the *ancien régime* (such as the monarchy and the two parliamentary chambers), and to arrest those most prominently associated with it. It also carried out purges of the higher ranks of the armed forces, the civil service and the police, replacing those whose loyalty to the Revolution might be suspect. However, the vast majority of those employed in these institutions did not lose their posts, thus ensuring that many of the attitudes and much of the ethos of the *ancien régime* continued to survive. In terms of foreign policy, the federation between Iraq and Jordan, which had been cobbled together in February 1958, the *ancien régime*'s somewhat half-hearted response to the United Arab Republic of Egypt and Syria, was quickly dissolved; Iraq no longer attended the meetings of the Baghdad Pact (although formal withdrawal did not take place until March 1959, when the British technical mission also left the Iraqi air force base at Lake Habbaniyya), and relations were immediately established with China, the Soviet Union and other socialist countries, a series of acts that indicated the new government's desire to pursue foreign policies independent of Britain and the West. The government remained noncommittal about its intentions towards the oil companies, probably well aware of the potential dangers of a major confrontation at this early stage.

The Political Climate in the Immediate Aftermath of the Revolution

Such actions, which were taken almost immediately, were particularly welcomed, and were accompanied by enormous demonstrations of popular approval and expressions of confidence in the new regime. Qasim's public appearances were greeted with rapturous enthusiasm, and contemporary photographs and eyewitness accounts of the enormous crowds that filled the streets in the first few weeks after the Revolution are striking testimony to the support that it enjoyed. Beneath the surface, however, tensions and differences were at work, which were soon to erupt into open conflict. Among the small circle of the new rulers themselves, these conflicts were often of a personal nature, but they were understood, translated or adopted by members of the public as expressions of divergent or conflicting political viewpoints.

In the first place, although the Free Officers shared and were able to reflect some of the more widely-felt political aspirations as far as domestic and especially foreign policy was concerned, most of them, and the majority of their civilian cabinet colleagues, were essentially reformist, even conservative, in their political thinking. They were therefore considerably more cautious and very much less 'revolutionary' than many of their supporters in the streets, who were acclaiming the success of their movement with such enthusiasm. Secondly, although Qasim and 'Arif had emerged as those principally responsible for the coup that brought about the Revolution, neither was widely known at the time, and as differences between them emerged almost within the first few days, there was considerable confusion about their respective roles. They soon became identified in the public mind as exemplifying 'left wing' (Iraqi nationalist and communist) and 'right wing' (Arab nationalist) attitudes, and political alliances gradually crystallised around these two poles.

On a broader level the sudden lifting of political constraints had led to widespread feelings of optimism, a sense of almost unlimited possibilities for the future of the country, and an upsurge in popular demand for the immediate enactment of radical social reforms. In these euphoric days and weeks it was widely believed (and even expressed by some of those in power, particularly 'Abd al-Salam 'Arif) that major social evils and injustices could easily be swept away at the stroke of a pen. Many of these notions were both naive, as illustrated by those who took food from shops without payment in the belief that the Revolution had made money obsolete[7], and far 'in advance' of the thinking of most of the government. Those in power lacked both experience and a shared ideology, with the result that fundamental issues of principle, such as who was in command, and what form of governmental and political system should be adopted, remained unresolved. The parallel with Egypt in the first few months after July 1952 is striking[8].

The clearest expression of the disunity at the top was the growing rift between Qasim and 'Arif, which was a struggle for supreme power as well as a clash of personality and ideals. Ostensibly, the main grounds for the eventual showdown between the two were connected with what became the burning issue of whether or not Iraq should join with Egypt and Syria in the United Arab Republic, which had been constituted in February 1958. For most politically conscious Iraqis, the success of the Egyptian Revolution of 1952 had been a source of inspiration and example, and the figure of Nasser had attracted devotion, even adulation, although this had not been expressed in the formation of a Nasserist political party. It is difficult to pinpoint this group accurately before the Iraqi Revolution, since the appeal of Nasser while Nuri was still in power was almost irresistible to almost all shades of political opinion, and in fact remained so until the split between Qasim and 'Arif began to reach ominous proportions in the autumn of 1958.

The Emergence of 'Abd al-Karim Qasim

It is difficult to overestimate the suspense and uncertainty that pervaded the political atmosphere in the summer and autumn of 1958. In the first place, after nearly two decades of 'neutrality', members of the armed forces had once more emerged as active, and indeed decisive, participants in politics. Of course, their intervention in 1958 was of a very different order from the series of coups carried out between 1936 and 1941[9], in that the latter were essentially struggles for power between different factions of officers and politicians, while the July Revolution was specifically intended to overthrow the *ancien régime*; nevertheless, many of the Free Officers had already begun their military careers by the late

1930s, and Qasim himself was related to Muhammad Jawad, who had been Commander of the Iraqi Air Force under Bakr Sidqi.

In common with the population at large, the Free Officers and those members of the armed forces who supported them were a highly heterogeneous and disparate group, united only by their desire to overthrow the *ancien régime.* Thus there were considerable differences of opinion among them over the policies that the new government should pursue. In addition, because many senior military officers had been retired or dismissed in the aftermath of the coup, and as the main perpetrators had been middle-ranking or even junior officers, it was not immediately clear who was actually in charge. As the organisational structure of the Iraqi Army was still 'apolitical', that is, based on hierarchy and rank, and was profoundly influenced by military values such as the 'honour of the officer' and 'respect for the uniform', the fact that most of the Free Officers were of approximately the same age and rank, and that none of them had emerged as undisputed leader by the time the coup actually took place, meant that there was no pressing reason for any of them to defer to any particular individual or individuals among their colleagues, although Qasim and 'Arif emerged relatively quickly as the main contenders for power. Furthermore, none of the officers had yet been able to build up a consistent body of supporters within the armed forces based on either regional, tribal or party loyalties, so that the power struggle in these early months became concentrated crucially around obtaining mass popular acclaim.

In this highly-charged atmosphere, where the state apparatus was still extremely weak, popular approval was essential for the very survival of the government and its leaders. However, as we have seen, representative legal political parties had not been permitted before the Revolution, and even those that had been allowed to function from time to time, such as the Istiqlal or the National Democratic Party, were never able to test or widen their influence in properly-held elections, with the result that effective opposition to the monarchy had been forced underground. Since the Ba'th and the nationalists/Nasserists were relative newcomers to the political scene, such opposition had been organised almost exclusively by the Communist Party, which also controlled most of the mass organisations and the trade unions. After the Revolution, the Communists were able to come out into the open for the first time, and in particular to direct the emotions of the crowds in the streets of Baghdad, on whom the new government so vitally depended.

In such circumstances, the position in which Qasim found himself was highly anomalous, since his own political views were reformist rather than revolutionary, and were far closer to those of Muhammad Hadid and the National Democratic Party — patriotism (*wataniya*), the encouragement and protection of domestic industry and agriculture, and the creation of a welfare state — than to the Communists. However, the reformist wing of the national bourgeoisie, whom Muhammad Hadid and his party represented, had not been able to establish their economic or ideological hegemony in the country as a whole, and had also been prevented from building up an effective political organisation or party machine because of the repressive and corrupt conditions that prevailed during the latter years of the monarchy.

Furthermore, the sudden rise in oil revenues in the early 1950s had occasioned a burst of conspicuous consumption that further widened the gap between the very rich and the rest of society, and underlined the pressing need for major social reforms that the monarchy was evidently unwilling to undertake. In the absence of an effective bourgeois social democratic party that might have concerned itself with such issues, the ICP was increasingly regarded as the only organisation able to voice the aspirations of wide strata of society, especially as it stressed the need for democratic reforms as well as revolutionary change. The Party's policy was to press for improvements and radical reforms *within* the existing social order; while socialism was always represented as the ideal society that, given the right economic and social conditions, would one day be built in Iraq, this was not considered as a practical possibility in the immediate future. Thus the Party concentrated on such issues as improvements in living and working conditions, a more equitable distribution of wealth, and better health, educational and welfare services for all. Similar aspirations for a more equitable society were also held by the pan-Arab nationalists and Ba'thists; but, for historical and demo-graphic reasons, pan-Arab ideology had exerted little influence outside a number of suburbs in Baghdad, most parts of the city of Mosul, and the small towns of 'Ana, Falluja, Haditha, Rawa and Takrit, where, presumably because of their physical proximity to Syria, the ideals of *'uruba* had always been strong, and where communism had generally not taken root[10].

Thus, in the immediate aftermath of the Revolution, the Communist Party and its sympathisers were undoubtedly the largest political force in Iraq, and Qasim, who had neither kin nor regional networks at his disposal — unlike 'Abd al-Salam 'Arif at the time, or Saddam Husain a few years later — let alone a political party, found himself almost entirely dependent on mass support in a situation where the 'masses' were more sympathetic to the aims and ideals of the Communist Party than to any other ideology or party. *Faute de mieux*, Qasim had little choice but to make an accommodation with the Communists, for whom, as a reformer rather than a revolutionary, his enthusiasm was distinctly lukewarm.

'Unity Now' versus 'Federation'

At the end of July 1958, Michel 'Aflaq, the secretary-general and co-founder of the Ba'th Party, arrived in Baghdad from Damascus to try to press the new government to join the UAR, of which he himself had been a prime mover. This prospect naturally found favour with the Ba'th and the nationalists (*qawmiyyun*); that is, individuals attracted by Nasser's achievements but who had no formal political organisation in Iraq. As unity with Egypt and Syria, *wahda*, is generally taken as having constituted the principal point of disagreement between the Ba'thists and nationalists on the one hand and Qasim and the ICP on the other, it is useful to try to clear up some common misconceptions that have become part of the received wisdom of many accounts of this period[11].

In the first place, although the long-term ideological contradictions are obvious, there had been little practical hostility between the Middle Eastern communist parties and Arab nationalist organisations in the pre-independence period, and at various times even a degree of cooperation between them, since both were united in their opposition to the British and French colonial presence. In addition, particularly under the leadership of Fahd, the communist movement in Iraq had developed in an atmosphere imbued with notions of both Iraqi-Arab and pan-Arab nationalism (although the fact that a very high proportion of Iraqis were Shi'is or Kurds meant that the former or 'patriotic' sentiment tended to predominate), and the policies pursued by the ICP had successfully merged notions of 'class struggle' with those of national independence. The Iraqi Communist Party had both grown out of and formed an integral part of the struggle for national independence and had gained wide support very largely because the leadership had understood that the achievement of independence was an essential prerequisite for social liberation. Against the background of the immense impact of the rise of Nasser, and in particular of the effect of the nationalisation of the Suez Canal in 1956, the ICP's party conference that year adopted the slogan of 'Towards a National Arab Policy', declaring that the Arabs are one nation and acknowledging that they have a 'fervent desire for unity', although it 'tied the fulfilment of the pan-Arab idea to the "disappearance of imperialism from the Arab world and the carrying out of democratic reforms" '[12].

By July 1958 the increasing popularity of Nasser and the new situation created by the formation of the United Arab Republic had greatly widened the appeal of pan-Arabism, particularly among the Sunni Arab urban population, at a time when the Communist Party was widely regarded as a, if not the, leading political force within Iraq. With the gradual entrenchment of the Qasim regime and the widespread propaganda to the effect that Qasim was simply a tool of the Communists, the nationalist/ Nasserists and the Ba'th gradually developed into the main focus of opposition to the Communists, in which, as we shall see, they were assisted materially and morally by Nasser and his supporters in Syria.

From this it may be inferred that the ICP's unenthusiastic reaction to the suggestion of immediate *wahda* with Syria and Egypt in 1958 was less a matter of principle than a reaction to their Syrian and Egyptian comrades' unhappy experience of the practical workings of the UAR. In Syria, the Ba'th leaders Michel 'Aflaq and Jamal al-'Atasi, who were nominally in alliance with the Syrian Communists, had produced an internal party document in 1956 that had emphasised the fundamental incompatibility between communist internationalism and their own way of thought, and expressed alarm at the effect that rising Soviet popularity was having on support for the communists in Syria[13]. This coincided with a period in which the Syrian Ba'th itself was disintegrating into a number of warring factions, and the leadership seems to have seized on the expedient of a constitutional union with Egypt as a sort of *deus ex machina*. Although the terms of the Union required the Ba'th to dissolve, the Party command assumed (wrongly, as things turned out) that their positions would be strengthened by the distribution of office to senior Party members in Syria, while the Union had the further advantage for the Ba'th that the Egyptian anti-communist laws would be introduced, forcing the Syrian Communist Party to dissolve itself as well[14].

In such circumstances it is hardly surprising that 'Aflaq and his colleagues should have hastened to Baghdad to try to persuade the Iraqis to join them in the Union, and equally unsurprising that the Communists were entirely averse to the proposal, under, let it be stressed, such conditions. Furthermore, as the clamour for Union was loudly supported by 'Abd al-Salam 'Arif, who was known to be profoundly anti-communist, the Iraqi Communists had few illusions about the effects such a step would have on their own position. Accordingly, the ICP organised a huge demonstration in Baghdad on 7 August, under the slogan 'Federal Union and Soviet Friendship'. This opposition to Union was also congenial to Qasim for two reasons: first, along with many non-Communist Iraqis, he was much more of an Iraqi patriot (*watani*) than a pan-Arab nationalist (*qawmi*); and secondly, he had no particular desire to play second fiddle to Nasser[15].

For most of the political leaders who called for immediate Union (though not, of course, for many of the rank and file), pan-Arabism and *wahda* were largely tactical notions, and 'Union' was far more a stick with which to beat the Communists — whom they could accuse of being traitors to the Arab nation — than a genuine political aim or option, as is evident from the total absence of any progress in this direction in the periods in which either the nationalists or the Ba'th have actually held power. Thus *wahda* was the symbol rather than the substance of the rift between the Communists and their opponents, and the fact that Qasim's personal predilections happened to coincide with the Communists' more nuanced opposition to the practicalities of the UAR was almost fortuitous.

More fundamentally, even if the Qasim regime decided to maintain the existing social and political system — and the options remained open throughout 1958 and most of 1959 — there was still a wide variety of possible trajectories. For example, how far should land reform, or the nationalisation of oil and of industry, actually go? These were important issues that divided the population, and that particularly worried the religious conservatives and other influential sections of society that were becoming increasingly fearful of what they imagined[16] to be the pressures being exerted from the left. Thus an alliance emerged between those forces who feared that their interests or their way of life were being threatened by Qasim and those who believed, or professed to believe, that the Communists were simply awaiting a suitable opportunity to take over and thus exclude them from power. Thus *wahda* developed into a rallying cry for opposition to the left, since for many, the prospect of Union with Egypt and Syria (itself fairly vague and distant) was a far lesser evil than the radical social and economic changes that they feared the ICP might press Qasim to introduce. Thus many of the vested interests that had not been destroyed in July 1958 gradually came to seek, and find, common cause with the Ba'thists and pan-Arab nationalists, joining them in their opposition to Qasim and the Communists.

The Split between Qasim and 'Arif, August to November 1958

A few days after the revolution, 'Arif, who was Deputy Prime Minister and Minister of Interior, paid a visit to Damascus, where he met and appeared in public with Nasser and the Syrian president Shukri al-Quwwatli. This was the first of a series of meetings between Iraqis, Syrians and Egyptians, which were concerned with the planning of joint ventures and mutual cooperation in a number of fields, including defence, economic and financial matters, communications and education. At this stage, the merger of Egypt and Syria into the United Arab Republic was less than six months old, and it seems most probable that these early exchanges were principally designed to receive Iraq into the revolutionary fold from which British tutelage had hitherto excluded her.

Although Arab unity was a key concern of the nationalists and the Ba'th — whose adherents in Iraq were very few in number at this stage — it is highly unlikely that the precise articulation of this notion into a concrete plan for the enlargement of the UAR to include Iraq had predated the July Revolution. There are no suggestions that such a plan had had any currency among the Free Officers; the creation of the UAR itself had been accidental, the brainchild of the Syrian Ba'th rather than of Nasser. Hence the translation of these vague aspirations for unity into a concrete scheme for the enlargement of the UAR probably dates from 'Aflaq's visit to Baghdad at the end of July, and was eagerly seized upon by 'Abd al-Salam 'Arif, to whom the idea was particularly attractive.

It is clear that 'Arif's enthusiasm for the UAR at that time and his devotion to the person of Nasser were genuine, but it was equally clear that Qasim regarded his second-in-command's repeated public assertions of his beliefs as at best ill-advised, and at worst as simply disloyal. For his part Qasim did not consider that Iraq's salvation would be achieved by her joining the UAR and regarded 'Arif's convictions to that effect as threatening his own position as well as being downright imprudent. For 'Arif, although any unity scheme would mean deferring to Nasser as the senior partner, the prospect seems to have been infinitely more attractive than deferring to Qasim and remaining outside the political framework that he fervently wanted Iraq to join. Here it must be remembered that less than a month had elapsed since the Revolution and nothing, including of course Qasim's leadership, was yet firmly established; furthermore, 'Arif's own ambitions were constantly encouraged by suggestions from a variety of sources that he was the rising star of the Iraqi Revolution, and that he might soon be in a position to kick Qasim upstairs in the way that Nasser had done to Naguib[17].

This growing division brought Qasim to the realisation that he would have to counter 'Arif by a vigorous espousal of the anti-unity cause, which, for reasons which will now be clear, brought him even closer to the Communists. Thus he encouraged the huge demonstration in favour of 'federation' with the UAR organised by the ICP on 7 August 1958, and attempted, although without success, to bring 'Arif into line. 'Arif continued to proclaim his support for *wahda* and *'uruba* in the course of several provincial speaking tours in an attempt to whip up nationalist support for his own leadership in August and early September, but only succeeded in securing his dismissal as Deputy Commander-in-Chief of the armed forces on 10 September. From then on things went from bad to worse; 'Arif refused to accept that he had lost this round and continued to voice his views. He was eventually relieved of his political functions on 30 September, and appointed ambassador in Bonn on 12 October. At first he indignantly refused to take up the post, but was eventually persuaded to accept it after an incident in which he threatened Qasim with a revolver in the Ministry of Defence. He returned secretly to Baghdad in November, was immediately arrested, tried *in camera*, and sentenced to death, but reprieved in February 1959.

'Arif's fall was important for a number of reasons. In the first place the commutation of his death sentence was an expression of Qasim's belief that his former deputy was easily led rather than fundamentally wicked, and of course 'Arif's survival meant that he was there to rally opposition elements around himself in Qasim's later years. More immediately, his disappearance from the political scene served to weaken the position of the nationalists in government and marked the beginning of a clampdown against them and the Ba'thists. As well as relieving 'Arif from his posts as Deputy Prime Minister and Minister of Interior on 30 September, Qasim also dismissed a number of other prominent Arab nationalists, including Dr Jabir 'Umar, the Minister of Education, and demoted the secretary general of the Ba'th Party, Fu'ad al-Rikabi, from his post as Minister of Development to Minister of State. Brigadier Ahmad Muhammad Yahya, a political moderate and a close friend of Qasim's, was brought in as Minister of Interior, and the other ministries were given to Muhammad Hadid and Hudaiyib al-Hajj Humud in addition to the portfolios they already held. The fact that Qasim's 'victory' over 'Arif seemed to be so closely connected with the issue of Arab unity meant that it affected most other prominent Arab nationalists in Iraq, and increased the sense of polarisation between the various political groups. This accounts in considerable measure for the fanaticism and vehemence with which the struggle between them was to be waged in the years to come. Finally, after 'Arif's removal Qasim had no serious rival, and could become 'sole leader', as he was known after October 1958[18].

The Rashid 'Ali 'Coup'

Huge demonstrations in support of Qasim followed 'Arif's arrest, with bloody clashes between Qasim's supporters, now usually identified as 'Communists', and the nationalists and their supporters in various parts of the country. The next months saw a hardening of the positions of what now developed into two distinct sides, the Communists and their sympathisers and the nationalists and theirs, although the latter group also included individuals who were motivated more by feelings of solidarity against the Communists rather than by any fervent desire for Arab unity. This 'opposition' embraced a multiplicity of political and socio-economic groups, ranging from members of the *ancien régime* who feared what Qasim and his associates might have in store for them, to members of the Muslim Brethren and other religious groups including the Shi'i *'ulama'* as well as Nasserists and Ba'thists. However, the see-sawing ambiguity of Qasim's actual relations with the Communists should not be forgotten; it was not until the end of January 1959 that the Communists were permitted to publish their own newspaper, *Ittihad al-Sha'b*, although some other newspapers had adopted a generally pro-Communist line over the previous months. More significantly, Qasim could still not be persuaded to appoint any ICP representative to a sensitive executive or ministerial position.

For a time, after the decline of 'Arif's star had become obvious to many of his potential supporters even if not to 'Arif himself, it seemed possible that the mantle of the nationalist leadership might fall upon the veteran politician Rashid 'Ali al-Gailani, who had returned to Baghdad in September at the age of sixty-six after seventeen years of exile in Germany, Sa'udi Arabia, Egypt and Syria. Although Qasim had been anxious to invite this legendary figure back to Baghdad, the substance of the quarrel with 'Arif and the fact that Rashid 'Ali was an avowed pan-Arabist meant that his presence became something of an embarrassment. In the circumstances Qasim did not, as Rashid 'Ali almost certainly expected, offer him a post in government, much to his evident chagrin[19].

Whether out of pique at what he interpreted as Qasim's snub, or out of genuine conviction of the error of Qasim's ways, Rashid 'Ali set about planning the sort of coup that he had organised to bring down governments in the 1930s, an utterly unrealistic scheme to overthrow Qasim by raising a rebellion among the Middle Euphrates tribes. This plot, planned for early December, quickly ended in failure, as the conspirators were amateurish in the extreme and bragged of their intentions to members of the secret police. More ominous, perhaps, than the plot itself, was the fact that several senior Free Officers, including Tahir Yahya, Rif'at al-Hajj Sirri, Nadhim al-Tabaqchali, 'Abd al-Wahhab al-Shawwaf and 'Abd al-'Aziz al-'Uqaili, were known to be at least privy to

Rashid 'Ali's plans, if not actually involved in them in some way. These officers were to form the nucleus of a far more serious revolt in Mosul in March 1959, in which, as in Rashid 'Ali's attempted coup, the UAR was to be heavily involved. Perhaps the most significant feature of the earlier incident, coming as it did so soon after the Revolution, was the feeling of uncertainty and tension that it created, contributing to the general sense of insecurity and impermanence surrounding the Qasim government.

The Communist 'Threat'

On 21 July 1958 a special court was set up to try the 'enemies of the people', meaning, at this stage, various politicians and officials of the *ancien régime*. The 'People's Court', under the presidency of a distant cousin of Qasim, Colonel Fadhil 'Abbas Mahdawi, soon developed into a national spectacle; its proceedings were televised, and it served as a barometer of the political climate, with extempore speeches and declarations by the witnesses, the public gallery, and by the president and his colleagues. In remarkable contrast to the savagery of the 'judicial proceedings' that took place under Qasim's successors, the court, and Qasim himself, who acted as final arbiter, showed — at least before the Mosul revolt in 1959 — a fair degree of leniency towards those who came before it, since most of the sentences handed out were either commuted or reduced on appeal. Four particularly infamous figures from the past were eventually executed: Sa'id Qazzaz, a former Minister of Interior; Bahjat al-'Atiya, the former head of the CID, who had been instrumental in organising the persecutions of Communists and leftists in the late 1940s and early 1950s; 'Abd al-Jabbar 'Ayyub, formerly director of the prison for political offenders in Baghdad; and 'Abd al-Jabbar Fahmi, a former *mutasarrif* (governor) of Baghdad.

At the same time, a popular militia, the People's Resistance (*al-Muqawama al-Sha'biya*), was organised by the government. Immediately after the Revolution the Communists had set up their own informal resistance groups to defend the new regime[20] and had urged Qasim to set up an official militia without delay. Qasim seems to have understood the dangers inherent in such a force acting on its own initiative, and issued a decree six days later forbidding any non-governmental agency to recruit or organise bodies of armed men. However, although this decree was intended to check Communist influence within the militia, the ICP's organisational ability and experience ensured that it soon gained control over it, and every action of the militia or its members was subsequently identified with the Party itself. By mid-August, the commander of the People's Resistance had some 11,000 volunteers at his disposal. The Resistance was informally linked to Qasim's personal intelligence service, headed by Taha al-Shaikh Ahmad[21] and separate from the Directorate-General of Security (*al-amn al-'amm*), which was never fully purged. As such it served as an important support base for the regime, albeit at ground rather than at command level.

Unlike the militias of later years, the People's Resistance was never allowed to develop into a force that could compete with the armed forces themselves, and as Batatu points out, a close check was kept on its weapons, which members had to turn in to police stations — still manned, of course, by policemen appointed under the monarchy — after each duty session[22]. Thus the militia was largely a paper tiger, although taken seriously both by the Communists themselves and by their opponents. However as the flamboyant and provocative behaviour of many members of the Resistance served to inflate its actual importance, and as the organisation and all its actions were widely identified with the ICP, there was a general impression that a major communist advance through the state institutions was taking place.

What was actually happening in the latter part of 1958 and the beginning of 1959 was that the ICP and its front organisations were gaining in strength and popularity, and to the extent that the Party was able to command the streets of Baghdad it was a power to be reckoned with. The appeal of the Party was such that it was forced to announce in January 1959 that it could not accept any new members, since it lacked the administrative capacity to deal with them[23]. This spectacular rise in its fortunes, and the gradual takeover by Communists of the executive committees of the Students' Union, the Youth Federation, the Women's League, and the Lawyers', Engineers' and Teachers' Unions, as well as the great popularity of the Partisans of Peace, a Communist front organisation founded in 1950, created a profound sense of alarm in the minds of those who had no sympathies for communism and who feared the emergence of a genuinely left-wing government.

Born in opposition and secrecy in 1934, the ICP was ill-qualified

to adapt itself to this unexpected new situation. It had no experience of 'open' or non-clandestine political activity, and had
not yet gained, and was not to gain — and then by the most terrible
of ironies — official permission to operate legally until 1973.
Although the Party interpreted the events of July 1958 as a
bourgeois democratic rather than a socialist revolution (both at
the time and in subsequent analyses), and called for free elections
and a democratic constitutional government[24], its opponents,
who, it must be remembered, were as ill-prepared by their own
political experience within the Iraqi context as the Communists,
simply did not believe them. Furthermore the fact that the
Communists controlled the Baghdad 'street' and seemed to have
the ear of Qasim was so much more relevant to the realities of
everyday experience that their calls for democracy went largely
unheeded. Hence those who feared or opposed the Communists
for whatever reason — and some Communists were behaving as if
they were actually in power — began to make preparations to
combat what they saw as the two most likely consequences of the
enormous and visible rise in support for the ICP; either an election
in which the Party would win a substantial share of the vote, or a
sudden seizure of power, by whatever means, on the part of the
Communists.

At this stage, the ICP confined its demands to the creation of
bourgeois democratic institutions and a functioning parliamentary
system; it was not until the spring of 1959, after the events of Mosul,
that it pressed for direct representation in government. Significantly, the ICP now attempted — unsuccessfully — to revive the
pre-revolutionary Front of National Unity in November 1958; at
that stage the three main participating bodies, the ICP, the Ba'th
and the NDP, had still not been legalised, and the ICP tried to
organise a united approach to the government on the matter. The
Mosul revolt, which polarised the opposing political forces more
sharply than ever before, ended any possible future viability for
the Front.

As far as the nationalists were concerned, the struggle to win the
hearts and minds of Iraqis to the ideals of *wahda* was decisively
lost in 1958 and 1959. Since the ICP had captured substantial sections of 'progressive opinion' not only in Baghdad but in most
of southern Iraq and in many parts of Kurdistan, the nationalists
and their associates decided to promote their cause partly by
relying on anti-communist or religious elements[25], but more

crucially on members of the armed forces who were unhappy with Qasim's rule and still had ambitions for themselves. The nationalists and Ba'thists formed themselves into loosely co-ordinated underground groups and hit squads, and began to attack the Communists and their supporters in a systematic fashion, often with the connivance of members of the police, who had themselves been brought up to hunt out Communists and leftists under the monarchy[26]. They also started smear campaigns about alleged Communist misdemeanours and began to create a potent image of 'the Communist enemy'.

One important result of these activities was that the Baghdad 'street' gradually passed out of control of the Communists and became a battle ground between the two sides. By 1961, the secretary-general of the ICP reported that 286 Party members and sympathisers had been murdered by nationalist hit squads, and that thousands of families had been forced to leave their homes in nationalist strongholds as a result of threats and other kinds of intimidation. In a conversation with the secretary of the Mosul branch of the NDP in 1966, Batatu was told that some 400 people, only a very small number of whom were actually ICP members, had been murdered in Mosul for similar reasons during the Qasim period[27].

The peak of Communist influence lasted approximately one year; the bloody events at Kirkuk on the first anniversary of the Revolution (14 July 1959) marked the beginning of the end of this phase. Communist support was probably most widespread early in 1959; we have already mentioned that ICP members had been elected to the majority of seats on the governing bodies of many of the leading professional associations. On 25 January trade unions were legalised, although peasants' unions, for which there was considerable clamour, were not permitted until the short-lived high tide of ICP power immediately after the Mosul revolt. In spite of this the only Communists ever to have positions of real power were Jalal al-Awqati, the commander of the air force; Wasfi Tahir, Qasim's principal *aide de camp*; Salim Fakhri, the director-general of broadcasting; a dozen or so brigade or battalion commanders of the rank of brigadier, colonel or lieutenant-colonel; and Taha al-Shaikh Ahmad, whose loyalties were never entirely clear[28]. Apart from this handful of senior appointments, and the elevation of a single Communist and two leftists to minor cabinet posts between July 1959 and May 1961, Qasim never allowed ICP members or sympathisers to hold positions of power in the government, civil service or armed forces. Nevertheless, the extent of support for the ICP in the country, and Qasim's evident lack of enthusiasm for the UAR, meant that it was widely believed, or at least widely alleged, that the Communists were about to take over in Iraq, or indeed that they were already in power.

This view was particularly vigorously voiced by Nasser himself, partly because of his displeasure at Qasim's refusal to acknowledge his superiority, and partly because of constant and generally accurate criticisms of the actual functioning of the UAR on the part of Khalid Baqdash, the secretary-general of the Syrian Communist Party, criticisms of the kind of Egyptian over-assertiveness that eventually caused the breakup of the UAR in 1961[29]. Thus at the end of 1958 Nasser began to attack all Arab Communist Parties, particularly those of Syria and Iraq, and a vituperative war of words against Qasim and his associates became staple fare on Sawt al-'Arab radio. At the same time the UAR authorities began to make contacts with disaffected individuals among the Free Officers, particularly those who had been in some way involved in or aware of Rashid 'Ali's plot, many of whom were serving with the Iraqi Army in Mosul.

Mosul, March 1959

Whether because of its historical trading links with Syria[30], or because of a combination of cultural and religious conservatism and the control of almost all the surrounding countryside by a small group of urban based landowners, Mosul had the reputation of being one of the most profoundly conservative cities in Iraq. In the course of a description of the town some fifty years earlier, the British vice consul noted: 'Probably there is no place which has been so little affected by the events in other parts of the [Ottoman] Empire'[31], and some of this insularity seems to have lingered on. Political consciousness was largely intertwined with religious traditionalism, which meant that 'atheist' ideas of any sort (whether Communist or Ba'thist) were unable to take root, and as a result the 'dominant ideology' was a form of vague Sunni pan-Arabism. The main exceptions to this were certain predominantly Christian or Kurdish quarters of the city, which had traditionally sympathised with the left.

Thus the large numbers of disaffected Free Officers stationed around Mosul who were offended either at what they regarded as Qasim's sell-out to the Communists and infidels, or his failure to set up an effective Revolutionary Council on which the Free Officers themselves would be more prominently represented, found a sympathetic audience for their grievances. The anti-Qasim forces in Mosul and Qasim's opponents in the Mosul garrison included Nasserists, nationalists (*qawmiyyun*), Ba'thists and Muslim Brethren, as well as large landowners such as Ajil al-Yawar of the Shammar and members of the Farhan, Kashmula, Khudair and Shallal families, whose interests seemed directly threatened by the fall of the monarchy. All these individuals had gravitated more closely together after the announcement of 'Arif's sentence on 7 February 1959, which was followed by the resignation of Muhammad Mahdi Kubba from the Sovereignty Council, and of Dr al-Jumard, Naji Talib, Baba 'Ali Shakh Mahmud, Fu'ad al-Rikabi, Dr Muhammad Salih Mahmud and Siddiq Shanshal from the Cabinet[32].

Precisely how the disaffected Free Officers originally planned their revolt is not clear. Khadduri suggests that Rif'at al-Hajj Sirri, the head of military intelligence in Baghdad, encouraged Tabaqchali, the commander of the Kirkuk garrison, to raise a revolt there which he, Sirri, would then join with his supporters[33], and that 'Abd al-Wahhab Shawwaf, the Commander of the Mosul Garrison, was only brought in later. The decision to focus all activity on Mosul was presumably directly related to the announcement in the ICP's paper *Ittihad al-Sha'b* on 23 February that the Partisans of Peace would be holding a nationwide rally in Mosul on 6 March, although Batatu suggests another and in fact more accurate sequence, that the rally was held to underline the strength and support of the left in the country as a whole in the face of mounting rumours of a revolt in the Mosul garrison[34].

In any case, in spite of two visits to Baghdad by Shawwaf to warn Qasim of the possible consequences of permitting the rally to take place, it duly went ahead. The rally itself passed off without violence; special trains were organised to ferry the participants from further south, and after an impressive march through the streets of Mosul, most of the visitors left the city by the evening of the same day, 6 March. Violent confrontations only began the next day, when fighting broke out between local nationalists and Communists, and early in the morning of 8 March some sixty ICP members and sympathisers were arrested and imprisoned. At 7.00 a.m. the same morning Colonel Shawwaf announced his rebellion over the radio; although claiming to be acting independently he mentioned Tabaqchali and other Free Officers by name as being sympathetic.

The next four days were chaotic, horrifying and confused. The assistance apparently promised by the UAR did not materialise, although enthusiastic sabre-rattling could be heard on the radio from Damascus, where Nasser was celebrating the first anniversary of the Union[35]. Fighting broke out between rival army units, who were joined by other groups from the suburbs and surroundings of the city. As emerges from Batatu's detailed description (based on both eyewitness accounts and police records[36]), much of the subsequent fighting had more to do with long standing ethnic and inter-tribal rivalries between Arabs and Kurds and between different Arab tribal factions, and with the hatred of peasants for their landlords, than with strictly party political matters. Shawwaf himself was killed in the course of the fighting, as was the loyalist commander of the Engineering Regiment, 'Abdullah al-Shawi. However, after the news had leaked out of the murder — in prison — of the much-loved Peace Partisan leader, lawyer and poet Kamil Qazanchi, who had spectacularly defended Fahd at his trial in 1947, and who had led the huge demonstrations against the Portsmouth Agreement in Baghdad in January 1948, the Communists and their supporters began to wage a campaign of indiscriminate revenge against suspected 'nationalists'. These terrible days of fighting, during which at least 200 people were killed, hardened and widened the bitter divisions between the two sides in the country as a whole. Order was eventually restored and the leaders of the revolt were arrested and taken to Baghdad to await trial in the People's Court.

The significance of Mosul was twofold. In the first place the confidence of the ICP leadership increased still further after the foiling of the revolt, and the Party and its supporters staged huge demonstrations demanding that the People's Resistance militia should be armed and pressing for Communist representation in government[37]. Secondly, the Qasim government began to initiate purges and dismissals of those whose 'loyalty to the Revolution' was suspect, in other words, prominent nationalists and Ba'thists in the ministries and in the armed forces.

At this point ICP support was growing rapidly in both the army and the air force, and the ICP-backed People's Resistance expanded from 11,000 members in August 1958 to about 25,000 in May 1959. The Party itself now had between 20,000 and 25,000 members and its associated organisations such as the Women's League, the Youth Federation, the trade unions and the Peasants' Union, were going from strength to strength. How deeply committed this vast influx of new members and sympathisers actually was is hard to estimate; nevertheless, 'in 1963, when the boot was on the other foot, the Ba'th was never able at any time to bring together one-third of the crowds that the Communists attracted in 1959 . . . When all is said, it must be recognised that the Communists also possessed genuine mass support'[38].

Under these circumstances the ICP began to press harder for due recognition of its vital role in safeguarding and supporting the regime and began to demand that their strength should be adequately reflected in the government. This was expressed most dramatically in the largest demonstration of the period on May Day 1959, when the Party managed to bring hundreds of thousands of people into the streets of Baghdad calling for Communist representation in government[39]. Qasim viewed this as a fundamental challenge to his own authority and rapidly began to regard the Communists as a threat rather than an asset. For the time being he took refuge in issuing a blanket ban on party politics, implying that the time was not yet ripe for the restoration of constitutional democracy.

Qasim's refusal to accept the Communists' demands either for Party representation in government or for some form of parliamentary democracy prompted many Party members to ask whether it should not seize power by force as long as it was still in a position to do so. However, after heated arguments within the Politbureau it was agreed that while the Party might well succeed in *taking* power, its original analysis of the essentially bourgeois character of the revolution was correct. The constellation of national and international forces was not favourable, and the Party's opponents would be able to combine successfully against it; a civil war would follow in which the left would be defeated. Thus the Party decided to moderate, or at least not to press, its demands and generally began to pursue an accommodating line towards Qasim[40]. The decision not to attempt to seize power when the opportunity was most favourable was to cause a serious rift in the Party in later years. The effect of the adoption of this line at the time was to cause it to lose much of the impetus that had carried it forwards over the previous year, forcing it to give up much of its revolutionary spirit.

Kirkuk, July 1959

For some months — as early as the end of 1958 — Qasim had been proclaiming that he was 'above' political parties and factions — 'nahna fawq al-muyul', as he expressed it on a number of occasions. In other circumstances, such a declaration might have been an acceptable statement of neutrality, but after a year in which 'Arif, Rashid 'Ali, and some of Qasim's own closest associates had tried to overthrow his government, and at a time when the ICP and its supporters were providing virtually all his mass support, its real implication was that he had no intention of giving in to any of the Communists' major demands. At the end of June 1959 he greatly restricted the role and operation of the People's Resistance forces in order to weaken their military potential, and a few days later half a dozen of the better known ICP army officers were retired. In the face of these obvious blows, the Party remained firm but fundamentally accommodating, presumably in the expectation that time and circumstances would eventually force Qasim to give due acknowledgement of his dependence on its support.

In this sense the appointments announced on 13–14 July 1959 may have had the effect of showing the hardliners of the Party that the 'accommodationists' had in fact judged the situation correctly[41]. A prominent member of the ICP, Dr Naziha al-Dulaimi, was appointed Minister of Municipalities, and two individuals close to the Party, Dr Faisal al-Samir and 'Awni Yusuf, were appointed to the Ministries of Guidance and Public Works and Housing. At the same time, in order to appear to be acceding to demands for a return to some form of democratic government, Qasim announced that political parties would be legalised on or by 6 January 1960.

These appointments did not, of course, change the fundamental structure of power within the state, which was in real terms being slanted increasingly against the Communists through the purges and dismissals in the armed forces that have already been mentioned. Nevertheless the fact that Communists and pro-

Communists were now actually in the cabinet was sensational enough in itself, and the nominations were widely regarded by both its enemies and its supporters as a victory for the left. Those who were predisposed to be fearful and apprehensive at what they saw as the growing power of the left, and of the Communists in particular, now saw their worst misgivings about the Qasim regime being fulfilled. The complexity and volatility of the situation was further exacerbated by the tragic events of Kirkuk a few days later.

Even more than the Mosul battles, much of the fighting at Kirkuk was only incidentally concerned with party politics; it was far more profoundly rooted in the deep-seated antagonism between the original Turcoman population of the city and the more recent Kurdish incomers. The ICP had considerable support among the Kurds, while the Turcomans, who were generally both better-off and more conservative politically, were united by ethnic solidarity rather than party affiliation. Since the end of 1958, a number of sensitive appointments in the city had been given to Kurds, with the result that the Turcomans, who had always dominated the socio-economic and political life of the town, now felt themselves increasingly at a disadvantage. It is unclear who started the fighting — apparently over the route of the procession to celebrate the first anniversary of the Revolution — but the result was that between thirty-one and seventy-nine people were killed, most of them Turcomans[42].

The massacre at Kirkuk, for this was certainly how it was regarded at the time[43], although in no way 'planned' by the ICP, was eagerly seized upon by its opponents and particularly by Qasim himself, since it gave him the opportunity he needed to distance himself from the Communists and to try to end his identification with them. Baghdad television laid the blame for the massacre squarely at the Communists' door, broadcasting horrific pictures purporting to show 'what the Communists are really like', and a wave of arrests of ICP members in Baghdad and other parts of the country began that continued throughout July and August. Further restrictions were put on the activities of the Popular Resistance, and control of the Peasant Unions was taken away from the Communist-controlled General Federation of Peasant Unions and given to provincial governors. However, the most crucial losses sustained by the Communists were undoubtedly in the armed forces, where, throughout the remainder of the Qasim period, officers suspected of being Communists or Communist sympathisers were either arrested, dismissed or appointed as recruiting officers in the provinces with no soldiers or weapons at their disposal. At the same time, the Party itself published a profoundly self-critical report, analysing its shortcomings over the previous year; although in many ways admirable for its frankness, the timing of the document's release was not opportune and seems to have caused considerable confusion in the minds of many Party members and sympathisers[44].

The Attempt on Qasim's Life, October 1959

The failure of the Mosul revolt had led the nationalists and the Ba'th to the conclusion that the only way to reverse the political situation was to assassinate Qasim and then to assume power themselves, a strategy that reflected a more realistic appreciation of the political situation than that of the Communists, to the extent that the 'normal' method of obtaining political power in the Middle East was through the coup rather than through the ballot box. Fu'ad al-Rikabi and his associates[45] had come to this conclusion by the middle of 1959, but at that point feared that an untimely assassination would simply hand over power to the Communists, and the plot was postponed. In the meantime the Ba'th began to widen their contacts and to establish ties with officers sympathetic to themselves and their 'project'. Major Salih Mahdi 'Ammash, a Ba'thist who had recently been released from detention and reinstated in the army by Qasim in an attempt to pacify the opposition, became their liaison officer.

Although it took some time to become obvious, the decline of Communist influence both at street level and within the state system after the autumn of 1959 was very rapid. This decline was partly related to the indecisiveness being displayed by the leadership, which had the effect of giving the Party an image of 'weakness' in the minds of many of its potential supporters and sympathisers. More importantly, Qasim had evidently decided to try to regain the confidence of the more moderate forces, and thus began to make important concessions towards them, while simultaneously clamping down on the Communists and their associated organisations, as we have shown. Thus nineteen nationalist officers who had been dismissed after the Mosul revolt were reinstated into the army at the beginning of August, and Qasim also made conciliatory overtures to a number of prominent nationalists, including Jabir 'Umar, 'Abd al-Rahman al-Bazzaz, Shaikh Mahmud al-Shawwaf, 'Adnan al-Rawi and Naji Talib.

Thus the political situation had changed profoundly in the aftermath of Kirkuk. The nationalists and the anti-Qasim camp were gaining rapidly in confidence and also attracted a measure of public sympathy for their cause during the trial of the leaders of the Mosul revolt in the People's Court, which was shown on television. Tabaqchali made a moving speech on behalf of himself and his fellow defendants, and many of the accused alleged that the statements that they had made before the trial had been extracted from them by force or under torture[46]. The Court proceedings became a microcosm of the political conflicts being fought out on a broader scale in the country as a whole, and almost everyone was glued to the television in anticipation of what Mahdawi and his colleagues would do next. While Qasim had previously shied away from judicial executions, and had in fact pardoned almost all of those previously sentenced to death by the Court, he felt he had to show his hand over the Mosul revolt. On 20 September Tabaqchali and Rif'at al-Hajj Sirri were executed, together with eleven other fellow conspirators and the four members of the *ancien régime* already mentioned[47].

These executions, coming so soon after the events of Mosul and Kirkuk, had the effect of polarising public opinion beyond the point of no return. The Ba'thists now felt that the time was ripe for their assassination plan, and on 7 October an attempt on Qasim's life was made as he was driving down Rashid Street. Although his driver was killed, Qasim himself escaped, with extensive though not serious injuries. The assassins, who included the twenty-three year-old Saddam Husain, managed to get away into the narrow alleyways off the main thoroughfare, and most of the plotters, including the Ba'th secretary-general Fu'ad al-Rikabi, managed to escape to Syria[48]. Seventy-eight other people implicated in the incident were subsequently brought before Mahdawi, including 'Ayyad Sa'id Thabit and his sister Yusra, who made defiant and emotional speeches, using the Court as a forum for their political views. Although six of the accused were sentenced to death, the sentences were never carried out.

The Breaking of the Radical Left

Qasim's narrow escape from the attempt on his life served to restore his aura as 'Sole Leader'. He himself came round to the belief that divine providence had stayed the hand of the assassins, and the massive and spontaneous demonstrations of crowds calling his name must also have encouraged his sense of having been 'chosen'. Furthermore, the mass support he was still able to rally as the incarnation of the July Revolution made him underestimate the real vulnerability of his position and perhaps also to overestimate his ability to act as an arbitrator between the opposing political forces. To this end he continued to pursue a conciliatory policy towards the nationalists and to reinstate many of them into the armed forces and the civil service, while simultaneously cutting the ICP down to size. Unfortunately it was already too late for him to win over the sympathies of the nationalists; too much blood had been spilled, and the political polarisation had gone too far, with the result that his attempts to conciliate the moderate forces by clamping down on the Communists merely served to undermine his only secure source of support.

In addition, any illusions that the Communists may have cherished of a degree of benevolent neutrality on Qasim's part were soon to be rudely shattered. In apparent fulfilment of the pledge he had made the previous July, Qasim announced on 1 January 1960 that political parties would be legalised, and the ICP immediately applied for registration. At the same time a similar request, on behalf of an organisation calling itself the Iraqi Communist Party, was made by Da'ud al-Sayigh, who had been associated with the League of Iraqi Communists in the 1940s and early 1950s[49]. This fictitious Communist Party, which had no organisation or members, was Qasim's answer to the real ICP, and was, incredibly, actually registered instead of the ICP, along with the Kurdish Democratic Party and the National Democratic Party[50]. Hence the ICP 'hardliners' had been right about Qasim after all; the 'accommodationists' would not, in the end, be able to get their way with him. From now until the terrible days of February 1963, the Party was to fight a continuous rearguard action in a vain attempt to regain what it had lost, or at least to maintain some of its positions. In spite of the enormity of Qasim's rebuff on the registration issue, the ICP now found itself hoist on the petard of its own moderation; having decided not to attempt to seize power in 1959, it now had no other option but to continue supporting Qasim while attempting to convince him of the folly of his ways, since any weakening of his position would simply play into the hands of their opponents.

It is difficult to say what the Communists' line should have been, or what the practical alternatives actually were. In Iraq, as in most other Middle Eastern countries, in which political power was and is generally obtained and maintained by means of the military and the police, it is not usually possible for political parties to gain power through democratic political processes or elections (and in this sense things have gone from bad to worse in Iraq since 1958); rather, they have to be *asked*, or *permitted*, to participate by the powers that be. Thus the ICP found itself in the dilemma that it was to face again in the 1970s, of attempting to operate and organise a political party along lines that could only work properly in a functioning democratic system. In the absence of such a system, in which a party could test its own popularity in elections, it either had to go underground, or work within the existing system and try to obtain power by force, or accommodate itself to the political realities.

In situations where a measure of democratic practice still prevailed the Party was able to assert itself in the face of mounting pressure and intimidation from its opponents. Thus Communists were able to retain majority control of the executive committees of a number of professional associations, including the Students', Economists' and Teachers' Unions, and even the General Federation of Trades Unions, until the spring of 1960[51]. In the months that followed, however, the Party gradually lost its substantial influence over the press. *Ittihad al-Sha'b* was banned sporadically between April and October in various parts of southern Iraq, and disappeared altogether after its editor, 'Abd al-Qadir Isma'il, was imprisoned in October. Other papers that generally supported the Party (*The Iraqi Review, Sawt al-Ahrar, al-Hadara* and *al-Thabat*) were all suspended by the end of the year. This was accompanied by efforts to dislodge Communists from any important offices they held in trade unions, often, in Qasim's typically roundabout manner, by the creation of duplicate committees packed with non-Communists.

Thus in Basra Port the ICP leadership was arrested, and several activists imprisoned; in the Iraqi Railways the workers were threatened with redundancy if they voted for the Communist list and when they did so the elections were simply rigged in order to secure a more acceptable committee[52]. The offices of the ICP's mass organisations were raided and their files seized, and by May 1961 the Youth Federation, the Partisans of Peace and the Women's League had all been closed down. Dr Dulaimi and 'Awni Yusuf were dismissed from the cabinet in November 1960, and Dr al-Samir in May 1961. At the same time, the nationalists, often aided by their 'Islamic' allies[53], intensified their reign of terror against individual leftists in the nationalist areas, notably Kirkuk, Mosul, the Euphrates towns north of Falluja and in the Baghdad suburb of 'Adhamiya[54].

Social and Economic Policies, 1958–1963

In spite of the setbacks to progress in the field of civil and political liberties over these years, Qasim continued to be identified by wide sections of the population as a man of principle who had their interests and those of the nation at heart. His reputation as the personification of the Revolution was further enhanced by the broad appeal of many of the economic and social policies that he promoted. Thus the government devoted considerable resources to increasing the numbers of places available at all levels in the educational system, to improving health care, and enacting progressive labour legislation. A far-reaching land reform was inaugurated in October 1958, which, in spite of many inadequacies in design and subsequent execution, did in fact succeed in breaking the political power of the large landowners. The law imposed ceilings on individual holdings (618 acres in irrigated areas, 1236 acres in rainfall areas), and promised that the sequestrated land would be redistributed to landless fallahin in plots of about 20–40 acres each. In addition, cooperatives were to be set up and new contracts, more beneficial to the peasants, were introduced to regulate relations between landlords and their tenants and sharecroppers[55].

Another particularly popular measure with which Qasim was always associated was the construction of Madinat al-Thawra, a large, low-cost housing complex, designed for the *sarifa* dwellers on the outskirts of Baghdad. For the better-off, notably for officers and professional people working for the government as civil servants, teachers, engineers, and so forth, housing associations were founded that provided low interest loans to enable members either to buy plots of land and build their own houses on them or to purchase government-built houses at very favourable rates[56]. These houses became the private property of the owners once the payments had been completed. In addition Qasim appeared genuinely concerned to improve the lot of the poor, and this, combined with his anti-imperialist credentials, ensured that he never entirely lost a bedrock of populist support. Furthermore, the Iraqi patriotic component of Qasim's nationalism, together with his evident lack of religious fanaticism (which may have derived from his half-Sunni/half-Shi'i parentage[57]) had the merit of embracing all sections of the population, with the result that Shi'is, Christians and Jews, and members of the various ethnic minority groups within the country could feel at ease with his rule.

Like most other revolutionary governments in the area at the time, the post-revolutionary regime was publicly committed to 'development'. In this context 'development' meant 'state sponsored economic development and industrialisation', and the state itself was regarded as the proper vehicle to set the appropriate economic and social changes in motion to achieve these ends. This view of the state's function was shared by social democrats, Arab nationalists, Communists, and Ba'thists alike, all of whom supported the principle of centralised economic planning and state investment in the economy, and in fact some steps in this direction had already been taken with the establishment of the Development Board in 1950. Immediately after the Revolution a plethora of new committees and departments was set up to cover all aspects of economic planning. Although the lack of experience of the administrators and the general incapacity of a highly personalised bureaucratic system to delegate responsibility and to decentralise its activities led to the creation of major administrative bottlenecks, the general principle of development through industrialisation was accepted as a major priority and was enshrined as such in both the 'Provisional Economic Plan' (1959/60–1962/63) and the 'Detailed Economic Plan' (1961/62–1965/66). Hence a variety of public works and infrastructural projects were inaugurated with great ceremony, and capital investment in the public sector almost doubled between 1957 and 1960, admittedly from a very small base[58].

Since Qasim's own economic and financial advisors, notably

Muhammad Hadid and Husain Jamil, were essentially middle-of-
the roaders, and since Qasim himself was by inclination more
interested in improving the living standards of the poor than in
reducing those of the rich[59], it may be anticipated that the
preservation of private property — even the maximum holdings
permitted under the land reform were fairly generous — was to be
an important feature of the regime's economic philosophy. The
government encouraged private investment in industry through
special loans and fiscal exemptions, and even repealed its own
early legislation on death duties and inheritance taxes. Here
Qasim's attacks on the oil companies, and in particular the
celebrated Law 80 of 1961 reclaiming the unexploited areas of the
Iraq Petroleum Company's concession, must be seen in terms of
'repossession of the national patrimony' rather than as an
ominous portent of 'socialism'.

Naturally, demands that 'something should be done' about the
oil industry had been vigorously expressed at the time of the
Revolution. Most Iraqis felt that the *ancien régime* had allowed the
oil companies to cheat the country out of the profits that should
have been channelled into national economic development.
Qasim himself, conscious of the immense power of the companies,
and perhaps mindful of Muhammad Musaddiq's experience in
Iran a few years earlier, hastened to assure the companies
immediately after the Revolution that existing agreements, which
dated from 1952, would be honoured[60]. Oil output rose steadily
between 1958 and 1963, from 731.3 mn b/d to 1161.9 mn b/d, an
increase of 60%, although revenues rose less rapidly than had been
anticipated ($ 224 mn in 1958 and $ 353 mn in 1963), because of
reductions in posted prices in February 1959 and August 1960[61].
Negotiations over the price of oil, Iraqi equity participation in
IPC, and the return to Iraqi control of the unexplored portions of
the concession area, took place between the government and the
Company between August 1960 and October 1961. The Company's
failure to meet the government's demands led to the passing of
Law 80, under which the government repossessed 99.5% of the
unexploited concession area. The Company immediately retaliated
by slowing down the rate of production, and the state's revenues
certainly grew less rapidly than they would otherwise have done,
but in spite of this the 'political popularity of Law 80 with the Iraqi
people was never in doubt in spite of the cost to the country of [the]
confrontation with the IPC'[62].

The Kurdish Question, 1958-1963

Under the mandate and monarchy, Kurdish aspirations had never been permitted any proper development or expression, and the Kurds had been forced into submission in the 1920s and 1930s by the Royal Air Force, backed up by the Iraqi Army. After the collapse of the Republic of Mahabad in 1946, the military wing of the Kurdish resistance under the command of Mulla Mustafa Barzani went into exile in the Soviet Union, while the organisation that later became the Kurdish Democratic Party, the political party of the 'urbanised' Kurds, was banned under the monarchy and its leader Ibrahim Ahmad placed under house arrest. However, the Kurdish leaders had some contact with the Free Officers through the intermediary of the Kurdish brigadier Fu'ad 'Arif.

When the Free Officers took over in July 1958 the KDP, in common with the other political organisations, was not directly involved, but welcomed the Revolution in the belief that the new regime would be generally sympathetic to their cause. The new constitution stated that 'Arabs and Kurds are partners in the Iraqi homeland and their national rights are recognised within the Iraqi state'[63]. In October, Ibrahim Ahmad was sent to Prague with passports for Barzani and three of his closest associates and a week later Barzani returned from twelve years of exile to a rapturous welcome from his supporters and what appeared to be expressions of genuine cordiality on the part of 'Abd al-Karim Qasim. A new era in Arab-Kurdish relations seemed to have begun.

For their part the Free Officers had no special interest in or commitment to finding a solution to the Kurdish question, but their general attitude seemed friendly, if not in any way actively sympathetic. Thus the three-man sovereignty council, which was to exercise the ceremonial functions of a president, contained a Sunni Arab, a Shi'i Arab and a Kurd from a well-known religious and landowning family, Khalid Naqshbandi, a former Army officer who had been governor of Arbil before the Revolution. Although this body enjoyed virtually no power, Naqshbandi's appointment to it was clearly a gesture of goodwill.

In the struggles that followed between Qasim and his supporters and opponents, the Kurds' natural suspicions of schemes for Arab unity — in which their own position was most unlikely to be improved[64] — led them to range themselves against those who were calling for unity with the UAR, and for this and other historical reasons the KDP was fairly closely associated with the ICP in the early months. However, the Kurds themselves were by no means of one mind or one voice, and splits soon emerged, notably between Barzani, the leader of the Kurdish 'tribals', who had an army of Kurdish irregulars to back his leadership, and Ibrahim Ahmad, who represented the more sophisticated and more directly 'political' aspirations of the urbanised Kurds. Furthermore, in spite of a general unity of aims, tensions soon broke out between the KDP and the ICP, especially as the KDP claimed to be a Marxist–Leninist party, which led to a good deal of confusion over their respective roles.

In April 1959 the KDP was given permission to publish *Xébat*, a daily paper in Kurdish. In the same month some 850 Kurds returned from exile in the Soviet Union, arriving at Basra on board a Soviet ship. However, by this time relations with Qasim were already under a certain amount of strain, as the Kurds had taken his vague assertions of benevolence towards them at more than their face value, and were beginning to formulate demands that Qasim was no longer in a position to grant. For most of the Free Officers — many of whom had been involved in fighting in the Kurdish area under the monarchy — any suggestion of a devolution of power, let alone autonomy, for the Kurds was anathema, and even if Qasim himself had been strongly committed to such a policy he would have found it extremely difficult to rally his supporters, especially those in the military, to his side.

In these circumstances relations rapidly deteriorated. Qasim either would not or could not make any concessions towards Kurdish autonomy, and both Mulla Mustafa and Ibrahim Ahmad would lose credibility if they failed to register a protest at the slow rate of progress in some tangible way. On the other hand, many of the more sophisticated members of the KDP (which had been registered officially for the first time in February 1960) shared the ICP's general view that Qasim should be supported because of his general commitment to anti-imperialism and his refusal to join the UAR. In the winter of 1960–61 Mulla Mustafa paid a visit to the Soviet Union, presumably intending to ask the Soviet leadership to put pressure on Qasim, but he returned empty-handed and left Baghdad for Barzan soon afterwards. In March 1961 Ibrahim

Ahmad was arraigned on a trumped-up charge of complicity in the murder of Sadiq Miran, a Kurdish associate of Qasim's, although he was eventually acquitted for lack of evidence. By the summer of 1961, fighting had broken out between the Barzani tribes and their traditional enemies the Herki and the Surchi, who were tacitly supported by the government. In September the Barzani forces occupied Zakho; government forces retaliated by bombing Barzan village, causing considerable loss of life. This was to be the start of a prolonged campaign that continued intermittently until 1975, and which the government side had little chance of 'winning' since the Kurdish guerillas were completely at home in the mountains and had overwhelming support from their own people. However, just as the government was unlikely to defeat the Kurds in any meaningful sense, it was also impossible for the Kurds to extract a satisfactory settlement. Thus by the winter of 1961, some — though by no means all — of the Kurdish leaders began to think that it would be sensible to make contact with Qasim's potential successors.

At this point, since neither the NDP nor the ICP and their sympathisers were prepared to go into an anti-Qasim alliance, the only obvious partners for the Kurds were, paradoxically, the Ba'thists and the nationalists, in spite of their apparent lack of enthusiasm for any concrete acknowledgement of the validity of Kurdish national aspirations and their avowed commitment to Arab unity, which seemed an unlikely vehicle for the realisation of Kurdish national or autonomist aspirations. The KDP made contact with Tahir Yahya as early as the spring of 1962, and as a result of these talks Ibrahim Ahmad gave assurances that if Yahya and his associates succeeded in overthrowing Qasim, he and Barzani would announce a ceasefire[65]. There were also a number of inconclusive meetings between KDP representatives and 'Ali Salih al-Sa'di, the Ba'th secretary-general, early in 1963. Whatever actually passed during these meetings, the conspirators knew that they could at least rely on the Kurds not intervening to support Qasim in the event of their staging a coup.

The Kurdish war was yet another example of Qasim's apparent incapacity to remain on good terms with those who should have been, and were certainly originally prepared to be, his natural allies. The left did not desert him, but it is a measure of the Kurds' desperation and frustration, or, as some would say, of the opportunism of some of their leaders, that they were prepared, in however vague and general terms, to throw in their lot with Qasim's opponents, whose commitment to the Kurdish cause can only have been superficial in the extreme.

Qasim's Last Years, 1961–1963

By the end of 1960, all hope of the establishment of democratic institutions had gone. The NDP had become divided over whether or not to continue supporting Qasim, and had broken up into a number of factions by October 1961; the Istiqlal Party had long ceased to play any effective political role, although some of its members gravitated towards the Ba'th Party. The Communist Party and its organisations, Qasim's principal support base, had been so savaged by him and were by now so hamstrung by their own lack of direction that they could only react to events rather than initiate them, and the field was now open for any group with sufficient tenacity and organising ability to seize the crucial power centres and stage a coup against the regime. Conventional political life had virtually ceased and the 'thirty months of stagnation'[66] that followed were filled with a terrible sense of foreboding, a sense of waiting for what many knew would be the fatal blow to fall.

Perhaps the most charitable view of Qasim during this period is that he simply underestimated the sticking power and desire for revenge that animated the Ba'th and the nationalists, and the extent of the polarisation of political forces that had taken place. Furthermore, after the failure of the attempt on his life, the split in the Ba'th that followed al-Rikabi's defection to Nasser in June 1961, and the collapse of UAR in the same year, no obviously dangerous enemies remained in sight. Qasim's over-confidence was expressed in a series of erratic and reckless acts that gave rise to serious doubts about his sanity. His extraordinarily quixotic attempt to annex Kuwait in the summer of 1961 is an example of the atmosphere of almost total unreality that pervaded these last years. Apart from souring relations with Kuwait itself, Qasim managed to unite almost all members of the Arab League against Iraq, and damaged his reputation both at home and abroad by the palpable hollowness of his claims and the absurdity of the manner in which he pursued them[67].

In spite of his bombast, and his irrational and capricious

behaviour, Qasim lacked the viciousness and vindictiveness of those who came after him, and even they, who were anxious to paint him as the devil incarnate, were unable to make any charges of corruption or dishonesty stick. His inflated view of his own abilities and his exaggerated sense of mission do not seem to have included salting away fortunes in Swiss banks. Again, apart from his confirmation of the death sentences on the Mosul plotters, he showed considerable magnanimity towards those who had sought at various times to overthrow him. In October and November 1961 he released all those who had been sentenced by Mahdawi, including 'Arif and Rashid 'Ali, and the rest of those who had been condemned either to death or to periods of imprisonment for their involvement in plots against the regime. Qasim's failings, serious as they were, can scarcely be discussed in the same terms as the venality, savagery and wanton brutality characteristic of many of the regimes which followed his own.

In the general atmosphere of paralysis and inertia of these years it was not difficult for a determined band of conspirators to capitalise on the population's growing disillusionment with the regime and plan its downfall. Although the failure of the attempt on Qasim's life in 1959 had considerably damaged the Ba'th Party organisation, it did not prove difficult to rebuild, and by April 1960 'Ali Salih al-Sa'di, who had escaped to Syria after the assassination attempt, had returned to Iraq on the orders of the Ba'th National Command[68] in Damascus to reorganise the Party with a view to overthrowing Qasim. By May 1962, when he had become regional secretary-general, he had built up an effective network with links to a number of groups opposed to the regime, including former members of the Istiqlal Party, members of the professional associations, and, most crucially, with a number of key military officers.

Ba'th membership at this stage was tiny; al-Sa'di himself estimated that there were 850 'full members' and 15,000 'sympathisers' in 1963, and even these numbers are probably an exaggeration[69]. The February 1963 coup was to be a textbook example of its kind: detailed planning; close coordination with sympathetic officers, who were to seize key military and communications installations; the killing of the head of state and his entourage; and the nomination of a 'military figurehead' as the new president. The actual perpetrators of the coup were a group of Ba'thist and nationalist officers, of whom the most prominent were the Ba'thists Ahmad Hasan al-Bakr, Salih Mahdi 'Ammash, 'Abd al-Sattar 'Abd al-Latif, Hardan al-Takriti and Mundhir al-Wandawi, and the nationalists Makki al-Hashimi, Tahir Yahya and Rashid Muslih. As two-thirds of the army was in Kurdistan, the conspirators had only to seize Abu Ghuraib and Rashid camps and Habbaniya air base — in each of which there were sympathetic unit commanders — and then take over the radio station before marching on the Ministry of Defence where Qasim had his headquarters. After two false starts the coup was eventually launched on 8 February, a Friday in Ramadan.

It came as no surprise. The Communists had warned Qasim that it was imminent, but his only response had been to arrest 'Ammash and al-Sa'di on 4 February. When the conspirators began to broadcast over the radio early in the morning of 8 February — with the martial music and the strains of 'Allahu Akbar' that had accompanied the Revolution of 14 July — there were immediate demonstrations in support of Qasim all over Baghdad, and people poured into the streets in a desperate effort to defend his regime. The crowds that gathered outside the Ministry of Defence begged Qasim to give them weapons, but, presumably counting upon some deep-seated belief in his own capacity to find a way out of the situation, he refused. The most bitter resistance took place in the poorer parts of the city. In Karkh, Karrada and 'Aqd al-Kird, and especially in the area around the Shi'i shrine in Kadhimain, where fighting continued until the next day, crowds fought the tanks with sticks and pistols. Most of those who had gathered outside the Ministry of Defence were killed in the course of the day, either mown down by the tanks of the Fourth Tank Regiment or shot by members of the Ba'th National Guard. Although it took another twenty-four hours for the besiegers to penetrate into the Ministry itself and proceed to the summary 'trial' and execution of Qasim and his colleagues, the eventual outcome was not in doubt.

Chapter Three

1963-1968

The months between February and November 1963 saw some of the most terrible scenes of violence hitherto experienced in the post-war Middle East. Acts of wanton savagery and brutality were perpetrated by the Ba'th and their associates on a scale that no assertions of 'revenge for Mosul and Kirkuk' could possibly justify. Having captured the main strategic points, and having executed Qasim, the Ba'th set about the physical elimination of their rivals. This was largely achieved through the agency of their irregular paramilitary force, the National Guard, whose number rose from about 5,000 to about 34,000 between February and August[1]; its duties were described in a proclamation issued by the Revolutionary Command Council on the day of the coup:

> In view of the desperate attempts of the agent-Communists, the partners in crime of the enemy of God ['adu al-Karim] Qasim, to sow confusion in the ranks of the people and their disregard of official orders and instructions, the commanders of the military units, the police and the National Guard are authorised to annihilate anyone who disturbs the peace. The loyal sons of the people are called upon to cooperate with the authorities by informing against these criminals and exterminating them.[2]

Although the Communist Party leadership had been aware for some time that a coup was being prepared, it had not made any detailed contingency plans. More particularly, as it must have been equally aware that such a coup would be directed primarily against the Party and its members, its failure to take any systematic measures either to get them out of Iraq or to organise a proper underground network was almost inexplicable. Rank and file Party members and sympathisers were rounded up in their homes, or shot in the streets in the first few days if they went out to join the crowds in brave but futile attempts to 'defend the revolution', which Party leaflets were actually calling upon them to do. Salam 'Adil, the first secretary of the Party, and many members of the Central Committee were arrested and subsequently murdered. It is impossible to establish exactly how many people were killed, but many thousands were arrested, and sports grounds were turned into makeshift prisons to hold the flood of detainees. People were killed in the streets, tortured to death in prison, or executed after mock 'trials'. Many of those who escaped with their lives were condemned to long periods in prison under atrocious conditions. The killings, arrests and torture continued throughout the Ba'thists' period in power, and their direct responsibility for these crimes is not in doubt. As almost every family in Baghdad was affected — and both men and women were equally maltreated — the Ba'thists' activities aroused a degree of intense loathing for them that has persisted to this day among many Iraqis of that generation.

Although individual leftists had been murdered intermittently over the previous years, the scale on which the killings and arrests took place in the spring and summer of 1963 indicates a closely coordinated campaign, and it is almost certain that those who carried out the raid on suspects' homes were working from lists supplied to them. Precisely how these lists had been compiled is a matter of conjecture, but it is certain that some of the Ba'th leaders were in touch with American intelligence networks[3], and it is also undeniable that a variety of different groups in Iraq and elsewhere in the Middle East had a strong vested interest in breaking what was probably the strongest and most popular Communist Party in the region.

Although its most prominent and notorious members were Ba'thists, the group that overthrew Qasim was a loose 'coalition' of Ba'thists and nationalists, whose members rapidly fell out with each other over the details of the distribution of power. The conspirators attempted to demonstrate their nationalist credentials by immediately proclaiming 'unity' with Egypt, but this turned out to be no more than a rhetorical gesture, and the announcement had no practical consequences. Although the UAR had collapsed in September 1961, and the recreation of a similar structure was not a practical possibility, the fact that none of the regimes between 1963 and 1968 ever took any serious steps even in the direction of greater inter-Arab cooperation must cast doubt on the seriousness of their original intentions.

In the first few months of the new regime, neither the President, 'Abd al-Salam 'Arif, nor the rest of the government, held undisputed power. The streets were controlled by the National Guard, whose commander, the notorious Mundhir al-Wandawi, took his orders directly from the Ba'th secretary-general 'Ali Salih al-Sa'di, who was also Deputy Prime Minister until his dismissal in November and held the important post of Minister of Interior until May. Thus the nationalist members of the 'coalition' and the 'non-Sa'dist' Ba'thists, most of whom were career officers, quickly gravitated towards one another in an attempt to establish their own centre of power as against that of al-Sa'di, not so much out of repugnance at his activities but because of his virtual monopoly of power. Moreover, the fact that al-Sa'di was widely regarded as little more than a petty gang leader meant that his continuation in office would not improve the regime's profoundly unsavoury image.

The Origins of Ba'thism

The Ba'th Party was founded in Damascus in 1944 by three French-educated Syrian intellectuals, Michel 'Aflaq, a Greek Orthodox Christian, Salah al-Din Bitar, a Sunni Muslim, and Zaki al-Arsuzi, an Alawite[4]. Briefly, the Ba'th was founded at a time when Syria was still under French mandate, and developed partly as a national liberation movement in opposition to the French and partly in response to what its founders regarded as the political and ideological inadequacies of the older generation of Syrian nationalists, who came to power for a short period after Syrian independence in 1946. The expansion of the Ba'th into a mass political organisation dates from the end of the Second World War and more particularly from the defeat of the Arab armies in Palestine, for which 'the older generation' of Arab politicians was widely regarded as being responsible.

By 1953, 'Aflaq and Bitar (al-Arsuzi had dropped out of the leadership by then) had joined forces with Akram Hawrani's Arab Socialist Party, and were in exile in Lebanon plotting against the dictatorship of Adib Shishakli[5]. Partly because the political structure of post-war Syria was somewhat more democratic than that of contemporary Iraq, and partly because Arab nationalism had always enjoyed considerable popularity in Syria, sixteen Ba'thists were elected to parliament in 1954. By this time the Ba'th was gaining adherents in other countries, and there were branches in both Iraq and Jordan in the early 1950s.

Perhaps the most distinctive feature of Ba'thism at this stage was its pan-Arab ideology, and its belief that the individual Arab states were all part of a single Arab nation, as expressed in the slogan 'One Arab nation with an eternal mission'. This was symbolised in the organisational structure of the Party, so that the supreme body, the 'National Command', was composed of members from different 'regions' (that is, conventionally, countries) of the Arab world. According to 'Aflaq, Arab society could only be revitalised through Arab unity; the Ba'th Party was to be the standard bearer and vanguard of the new Arab nation, and while Ba'thism was essentially a secular idea, Islam was the prime 'moment' of Arabism in which Christians as well as Muslims could and should take pride[6]. In common with other nationalist ideologies, Ba'thism is vague, romantic and mystical, and makes constant reference to an idealised vision of the past. Some idea of 'Aflaq's style is conveyed in this quotation from the 1950s, picked at random from an anthology published by the Iraqi government in 1977:

> Our attachment to the Spirit of the nation and its heritage will increase our drive, strengthen our forward march and ensure our orientation; thus we shall not be irresolute for we shall then be confident that everything will be consistent with the spirit of our nation. When our point of departure is strong which is the saturation in the spirit of our nation and the clear understanding of ourselves and our reality, truly sensing our needs, we shall not be susceptible to the assumption of artificial ideas or imitating others.[7]

A more specific vision of the future was embodied in the Party's constitution, although this is full of internal contradictions. For example, Article 26 says:

> The Party of the Arab Ba'th is a socialist party. It believes that the economic wealth of the fatherland belongs to the nation.

While Article 34 reads:

> Property and inheritance are two natural rights. They are protected within the limits of the national interest.

The Party is anti-imperialist; it believes in land reform, free social, educational and medical services. As a whole the notion of socialism is extremely vague, and socialism as such is only mentioned specifically in one other Article:

> The Party of the Arab Ba'th is a socialist party. It believes that socialism is a necessity which emanates from the depth of Arab nationalism itself. Socialism constitutes in fact the ideal social order which will allow the Arab people to realise its possibilities and to allow its genius to flourish, and which will ensure for the nation constant progress in its material and moral output. It makes possible a trustful brotherhood amongst its members.[8]

As in the Nasserist version of Arab nationalism, the Ba'thist vision of socialism is essentially non-Marxist, and in fact anti-Marxist, in the sense that it stresses the primacy of national/ethnic identity and rejects the notion of antagonistic social classes; once the Arabs are liberated and united, class conflict will somehow melt away (*tadhwib*). This belief was generally accompanied by a similar conviction that development and modernisation would come about as a result of national liberation and unity, and that the Arabs would then be able to recapture their former glory. However, there is no indication in early Ba'thist thinking of how power should be achieved or how it is to be wielded later[9].

As we have mentioned, the Syrian Ba'th, which had managed to capture certain crucial political positions in 1956, agreed to dissolve itself as the price to be paid for entering the United Arab

Republic in 1958. This caused a major crisis when, as happened very quickly, the Union began to turn sour and became little more than a mechanism for the exploitation of Syria by Egypt. Different factions arose within the Syrian Ba'th, many of which were deeply critical of 'Aflaq and Bitar for having accepted both the unity scheme and the dissolution of the Party. In March 1963, one of these factions seized power; there was a further intra-Ba'th coup in 1966 and another in 1970, which brought the regime of Hafiz al-Asad into power[10]. 'Aflaq enjoyed chequered fortunes in these years; when the Iraqi Ba'th came to power briefly in 1963 he acted as an intermediary in the negotiations with their Nasserist partners. In 1966 the new Ba'thist regime in Syria decided to disown the 'old guard' of 'Aflaq and Bitar, and this was to cause an irrevocable split between the Syrian and Iraqi wings of the Party; 'Aflaq went to Baghdad, where he is still based at the time of writing.

The Ba'th in Iraq

Ba'thist ideas were first brought to Iraq by a few Syrian teachers late in 1949, and by 1951 Fu'ad al-Rikabi, a Shi'i engineer from Nasiriya, had taken control of an organisation of about fifty people. By 1955, according to police records, there were 289 of them. Most of the early Ba'thists were Shi'is and friends or relatives of al-Rikabi himself, primarily because recruitment had as much to do with family and social networks as with ideology. In 1957 al-Rikabi took the Ba'th into the opposition National Front, a grouping that consisted of itself, the Communists, the National Democratic Party and the Istiqlal Party, and welcomed and supported the Revolution of 1958 along with the other parties. In the period of sudden political freedom that followed, the Ba'th claimed to have attracted '300 active members, 1200 organised helpers (*ansar*), 2000 organised supporters and 10,000 unorganised supporters', according to al-Rikabi[11].

As we have seen, the main polarisation of political forces after the Revolution, which had emerged clearly by the spring of 1959, was between Qasim and the Communists and their supporters on the one hand, and the nationalists, Ba'thists and their supporters on the other. Arab unity, *wahda*, became the symbol, if not the substance, of the difference between them. In November 1959 a

group of Ba'thists attempted to assassinate Qasim; the failure of
the operation led to a temporary breakdown in the organisation of
the Party, which was further weakened by a number of arrests and
by al-Rikabi's founding a rival body in 1961. Meanwhile 'Ali Salih
al-Sa'di, with the blessing of Michel 'Aflaq, had begun to
reorganise the Party in Iraq, although several other Ba'thist
groupings also existed, either alongside the main body of the Party
or as factions revolving around individuals. Hence, at the time of
the Ba'th/nationalist takeover in February 1963, the Ba'th was not
a homogeneous body, and was made up of a number of elements
that could not always be relied upon to act in unison, since
relations between 'the Party' and what purported to be its
constituent parts were of an informal and personal nature and
might or might not be expressed by the adoption of or the
adherence to an agreed political line.

The main difference between Ba'thism in Syria and in Iraq
before the split in the Party in 1966 was that the movement had
deep and well-defined roots in Syria, the traditional home of
Arabism. As we have already explained, this tradition was very
much weaker in Iraq, which meant that even in different
circumstances it is difficult to imagine that Ba'thism would ever
have attracted substantial numbers of supporters, as is evident
even from the (presumably) somewhat over-optimistic figures for
the late 1950s and early 1960s — when it had no power — given by
Party officials to Batatu.

Again, the Ba'th found it extremely hard to function effectively
in the relatively limited spheres where a form of electoral
'competition' was possible, such as in the elections to the executive
committees of labour and professional unions. Here the field was
usually dominated by the Communists, who had often founded
the organisations in the first place and had a long tradition of work
within them. Thus even after four years of persecution the
Communists were able to gain a majority in the elections to the
Federation of University Students in March 1967[12]. However, it
was not the Iraqi Ba'th's policy to seek to gain power by means of
elections or through the appeal of its programmes; on the
contrary, it relied on the use of force and the coup d'état, using its
loose organisational structure and its efficiently organised and
committed conspiratorial groups to make direct bids for power. In
fact, these groups consisted largely of gangs of thugs, the most
well-known of which were those associated with 'Ali Salih al-Sa'di

in Bab al-Shaikh, or with Saddam Husain and Sabah Mirza in Ju'ayfir and Karkh, whose links were regional and personal rather than ideological. Hence the general clampdown on the Party that followed the attempt to assassinate Qasim had little effect on its basic ability to take power, since this depended on organisational skills rather than on the more mundane and tedious process of building up mass support. Given the nature of the Party's activities in Iraq, and the irrelevance and vagueness of its 'ideology', it is clear that it did not come to power in 1963 with any specific programme beyond that of establishing itself at the expense of its principal opponents.

The Ba'th/Nationalist Alliance, February–November 1963

Political developments in the period between February and November 1963 were extremely confused, and consisted largely of different groups jockeying for power against a background of indiscriminate murder and terror carried out by al-Sa'di, Wandawi and the National Guard. However, by June, al-Sa'di had lost the Ministry of Interior, his faction had quarrelled with both Nasser and the Iraqi Nasserists, and fighting had broken out again in Kurdistan. He now faced increasing hostility both from other Ba'thists in the army and from his Ba'thist colleagues in Damascus, who were also becoming increasingly critical of some of his methods. In order to counter this, he suddenly announced that he and his group were 'Marxists' and 'leftists', attempting to assert, in a style which Ba'thists were often to adopt in the future, his own ideological purity over his opponents, who were now dubbed 'rightist' and 'reactionary'. al-Sa'di was a man of violence rather than an ideological activist and his 'socialism' was more a bid to gain support among particular factions within the National Command of the Party in Damascus than a change of political line. Thus Devlin's claim that 'Sadi and his supporters were eager to spread socialism in Iraq', or that their views 'harmonised with the extreme socialist views held by a group of party members in Syria' cannot be taken seriously[13]. At the Sixth National Congress in Damascus in October he ranged himself against 'Aflaq and Bitar, who were consequently voted out of office by al-Sa'di and his new friends. This development and al-Sa'di's apparent monopoly of power within Iraq itself seems to have encouraged his opponents within the Iraqi Ba'th to try to remove him and his clique from office; as his gangs had more or less succeeded in eliminating the influence of the Communists, they were becoming increasingly redundant.

Accordingly, Wandawi was dismissed from his post as commander of the National Guard on 1 November, but refused to budge. This proved the last straw; on 11 November, when al-Sa'di and his companions were holding an 'Extraordinary Regional Conference' to expel the 'rightists' (Ahmad Hasan al-Bakr, Hardan al-Takriti, Salih Mahdi 'Ammash, Tahir Yahya and their friends) from the Party, they were arrested by armed officers, hustled to Baghdad airport at gunpoint and put aboard a plane to Madrid. Two days later Wandawi, who was still at large, started bombing Rashid Camp from the air. Amin al-Hafiz and 'Aflaq hurried from Damascus to try to bring about a reconciliation, but it was too late. The National Guard took to the streets, where it was allowed to rampage for five days until it was crushed by units loyal to 'Arif. It was then summarily dismantled, and with al-Sa'di's faction now ousted, 'Arif, with the support of the armed forces, moved to exercise his own personal control.

The Regime of 'Abd al-Salam 'Arif, 1963-1966

By the time that 'Arif and his allies seized power in November 1963 the constellation of political forces in Iraq had greatly changed. Perhaps most significantly, all hope of the establishment of any form of democratic political life based on representative institutions had been crushed, and a system had emerged that had no other source of legitimacy except that conferred by military force and the possession of a monopoly of the means of coercion. 'Abd al-Salam 'Arif's regime can be divided into two parts, the first lasting from February to November 1963 and the second ending with his death in April 1966. In the first period rival Ba'thist and nationalist groups were jockeying for power, with the 'Sa'dist' Ba'th relying substantially on their paramilitary support forces, which doubled as the shock troops and the bodyguard of the regime but were essentially additional and external to the state apparatus. After November a more integrated force, the Republican Guard, was created, based largely on men from the 20th Infantry Brigade[14] — that is, from a unit within the armed forces — to be the elite corps of the regime. The Republican Guard developed into a special praetorian group within the army, and acted as the President's personal instrument, a system later developed to perfection by 'Arif's Ba'thist successors.

'Arif, who continued as President and Commander-in-Chief of the armed forces, now moved to ease out the remaining 'right wing' Ba'thists, notably the Vice-President, Ahmad Hasan al-Bakr, and the Minister of Defence, Hardan al-Takriti, whose support had been crucial in the crushing of al-Sa'di and Wandawi. Tahir Yahya, a recent and not particularly committed recruit to Ba'thism, was appointed Prime Minister, and by the spring of 1964 'Arif had engineered the resignations of al-Bakr and al-Takriti with the aid of his other associates, including the Ministers of Foreign Affairs and Guidance, Colonel Subhi 'Abd al-Hamid and Brigadier 'Abd al-Karim Farhan, the commander of the air force, 'Arif 'Abd al-Razzaq, and the directors of military planning, military intelligence and public security, all of whom were of course army officers. However, the core of 'Arif's personal support came from his own family and relatives, notably from his brother 'Abd al-Rahman and Colonel Sa'id Slaibi, who controlled key army units including the Republican Guard, which was largely formed from members of al-Jumaila, the tribe from which the 'Arifs originally came[15].

Although the new regime was relatively coherent to the extent that most of its members were nationalists or Nasserists of some kind, personal and ideological differences persisted, especially over the question of Iraq's relations with Egypt. While 'Arif himself had quietly abandoned his earlier enthusiasm for immediate union with Egypt, some senior members of the regime, notably 'Abd al-Karim Farhan and 'Arif 'Abd al-Razzaq, remained committed to the idea, and also considered Nasser's whole political and economic system as the model that Iraq should follow as closely as possible.

As far as 'Arif and his closest supporters were concerned, the conditions that had fired their original zeal for unity no longer existed. In the first place the UAR experiment had failed, and in addition Nasser had now entered into a more radically 'socialist' phase, introducing measures that aroused fears among the Iraqi middle classes that the application of 'Nasserism' might involve a similar fate for them. However, as 'Arif and the nationalists had opposed Qasim precisely on the grounds of his lukewarmness for

Arab Unity, they could scarcely be seen to be acting in vigorous opposition to those who were still committed to it. Hence in 1964 and 1965 a number of high-sounding 'unity projects' were launched with great ceremony: a preliminary accord on unity between Nasser and 'Arif in June 1964, the establishment of a 'unified political command' in December 1964, and the adoption of the eagle of the UAR as the national emblem of Iraq in 1965. Of course none of these projects had to be, or indeed could possibly be, taken seriously by the principals on either side, but they were useful ammunition for 'Arif as proof of his continuing enthusiasm for Arabism.

'Arif's principal concern in the first year of his presidency was to maintain himself in power. This he managed to achieve by building up a loyal elite corps in the army and by putting his friends and relatives in key positions. Naturally these pre-occupations meant that he could give little attention to the wider economic and social problems of Iraq, which had been growing in intensity over the previous years and which a 'revolutionary' government might reasonably be expected to be trying to alleviate. Furthermore, the continuing political instability had created a general crisis of business confidence and had encouraged those in a position to do so to liquidate their capital assets and transfer them abroad[16]. Thus there was an urgent need for the government to take some action that would both stop the flow of capital and satisfy the aspirations of some of its members and supporters for the state to play a more vigorous part in the economy.

To this end, some two months after issuing a provincial constitution that stressed the 'inviolability of private property', 'Arif announced, on the sixth anniversary of the Revolution (14 July 1964), the nationalisation of all banks and insurance companies, and thirty-two large industrial and commercial firms, which would now be run by an autonomous state economic organisation[17]. This measure had the effect of heightening rather than easing the economic crisis, without in any way dimming the enthusiasm of the Nasserists for these policies. Needlesss to say, the lack of qualified personnel, the way in which the policies were applied and the absence of real commitment to them on the part of many members of the government, contributed more to the general malaise than any major defects in the principle; given the general weakness of private capital and the fact that oil was the country's main source of wealth, it is difficult to see how any upturn in the economy could have been achieved other than by increased, skilfully applied, state intervention. The regime's economic policies soon became the subject of major disagreement between the various factions, particularly over the negotiations with the Iraq Petroleum Company, which took place between May 1964 and June 1965.

The Minister of Oil, 'Abd al-'Aziz al-Wattari, 'an intelligent non-political technocrat'[18] who had held office since the overthrow of Qasim, was primarily concerned to clear up the differences between the government and the Company in order to raise oil output and thus oil revenues. IPC and its associates had been thoroughly alarmed by the wider international implications of Law 80, and the effect that any capitulation to the Iraqis might have on their activities elsewhere. On the other hand, the principle asserted in the Law, of the nation's inherent right to control its own assets and resources, which had been vigorously and successfully upheld by Nasser in the nationalisation of the Suez Canal, had become firmly embedded in the public mind in Iraq and particularly among the Nasserist faction in the government.

The details of the negotiations have been described elsewhere; the main points of the agreement reached in July 1965 were that in return for the payment of £20 million, equity participation by the government and some of the IPC associates in a national oil company, and substantial increase in production levels, the government would restore IPC's right of access to all those unexplored parts of the concession area from which the provisions of Law 80 had excluded it[19]. Although this would have brought a rapid short term increase in revenues, it would also have resulted in the reinstatement of IPC in its controlling position over Iraqi oil, since Law 80 had in effect ensured that future oil development would be determined by the Iraqi government rather than by IPC. When news of the agreement leaked out, the six Nasserist ministers resigned in protest and it was never ratified.

Eight weeks later 'Arif replaced Tahir Yahya with the commander of the air force, 'Arif 'Abd al-Razzaq, a staunch Nasserist, as Prime Minister and Minister of Defence. A few days later, while the President and his Minister of Foreign Affairs, 'Abd al-Rahman al-Bazzaz, were attending a summit meeting in Casablanca, 'Arif 'Abd al-Razzaq attempted to seize power himself. The coup was discovered and successfully foiled by the President's close friend and relative Brigadier Slaibi, and 'Arif 'Abd al-Razzaq and his associates had to flee the country. This incident marked the end of any significant Nasserist influence within the regime, and al-Bazzaz, a 'moderate' nationalist, was appointed Prime Minister on 21 September, the first civilian to hold the office since July 1958.

The Government of 'Abd al-Rahman al-Bazzaz, September 1965 to August 1966

Like 'Abd al-Salam 'Arif himself, al-Bazzaz, who had been an academic and a diplomat, was a conservative Sunni nationalist for whom the attachment to Islamic principles in private and public was of considerable importance. The National Council of the Revolutionary Command, hitherto an exclusively military body created in February 1963 and consisting of the President and the chiefs of staff and other senior military officers both inside and outside the cabinet, dissolved itself and legislative power was transferred to the cabinet, giving the impression that real power was at last passing into civilian hands. However, a new military organisation, the National Defence Council, maintained the overall control of the military over the cabinet, and, together with the Republican Guard, constituted the essential mainstay of the regime[20]. Hence, given the nature of the 'Arif government, al-Bazzaz' much vaunted civilian cabinet[21] was almost inevitably largely dependent on 'Arif himself for its continuation in office.

A prominent if somewhat conservative politician, al-Bazzaz sought to introduce more market-oriented and less *dirigiste* economic policies, and generally to promote a more liberal political line. In an attempt to reassure private capital and to regain the confidence of the industrial and commercial community, he declared that he was going to pursue what he described as a 'prudent' or 'rational' form of socialism suited to current conditions in Iraq, that there would be no further nationalisations, and that stability and the rule of law would prevail. In addition, he also undertook to put an end to the arrest and imprisonment of the regime's political opponents, to permit free expression of political opinion and ultimately to re-establish a parliamentary system[22].

al-Bazzaz stayed in office for almost a year, between September 1965 and August 1966, but his effectiveness was greatly weakened by the sudden death of his patron and protector 'Abd al-Salam 'Arif in a helicopter accident in April 1966, and by the ensuing political uncertainty. Although al-Bazzaz managed to secure the smooth succession of 'Arif's brother 'Abd al-Rahman to the presidency, the power struggle between the Prime Minister and the officers, which had been latent from the time of his original appointment, became more and more acute in the course of the summer of 1966. As well as antagonising the officers by his independent stance, and later by his controversial efforts to achieve a settlement of the Kurdish question, al-Bazzaz' conservative approach to the economy also aroused misgivings outside a fairly limited circle of commercial and industrial entrepreneurs. The notion that the state should be in charge of the overall direction of the economy and thus act both as the main promoter of economic development and as the principal provider of all social and educational services had taken such firm root that al-Bazzaz' efforts to reverse this process were viewed with concern by many politically conscious Iraqis. Such measures as the relaxation of import controls and an increase in the compensation payable to landlords expropriated under the provisions of the Land Reform of 1958 seemed specifically designed to benefit the privileged classes of the *ancien régime*.

al-Bazzaz tried to ensure that some basic civil liberties were respected, and claimed to be anxious to pave the way for the eventual introduction of some kind of democratic structure. Political parties were still illegal, and the regime's only attempt to float its own party, an Iraqi version of the Egyptian Arab Socialist Union, in July 1964, had collapsed in the face of general public indifference. In the course of an interview in the summer of 1966, al-Bazzaz stated that he intended to embark upon 'the resumption of elections as the next step to be taken towards representative government'[23]. However, it also emerged that he was firmly opposed to any unconditional legalisation of political parties, since this would inevitably have involved recognising the Communists, an interesting reflection of the influence the ICP still wielded in spite of the persecution to which it had been subjected since February 1963. Since the Ba'th was widely detested because of its activities in 1963, and both the National Democratic Party and the Istiqlal Party had virtually ceased to exist, it is difficult to imagine what sort of elections al-Bazzaz could have had in mind.

The Presidency of 'Abd al-Rahman 'Arif, April 1966 to July 1968

The death of 'Abd al-Salam 'Arif and the succession of his much weaker brother made al-Bazzaz' position especially vulnerable[24]. 'Abd al-Rahman 'Arif had emerged as the most suitable candidate for the presidency largely because he was an officer and the former president's brother; moreover, the cabinet and the National Defence Council who elected him had themselves been appointed by 'Abd al-Salam. The factionalism and rivalry between the officers that 'Abd al-Salam had been able to contain or balance now gradually came to the surface; the officers especially resented having to put up with a strong-minded civilian Prime Minister, who had begun to ask awkward questions about military expenditure, and, as we shall see, was pursuing a constructive and conciliatory policy in Kurdistan. A second attempted coup by 'Arif 'Abd al-Razzaq gave the officers a major opportunity to demonstrate their indispensability as the mainstay of the regime, and five weeks later 'Abd al-Rahman 'Arif was forced to ask al-Bazzaz to resign.

The next two years, from al-Bazzaz' departure to the Ba'th coup of July 1968, saw a further succession of military governments. After al-Bazzaz, Naji Talib emerged as a suitably weak compromise candidate for the premiership, acceptable to all the military factions. Here Khadduri's valiant attempt to fit the various *groupuscules* into neat ideological boxes[25] should not obscure the fact that they were all vying with each other for political power, and generally grabbed at whatever ideological labels they felt would best suit their immediate purposes. Naji Talib's government consisted of seven officers and twelve civilians, most of whom were civil servants or technocrats with no obvious political affiliations. Needless to say, no more was heard about the democratisation of the political system, and negotiations with the Kurds came to an abrupt end.

At the end of 1966, the regime was faced with a crisis that was not of its own making, a dispute between IPC and the Syrian government over oil transit fees. As a result no oil was pumped across Syria from Iraq to the Mediterranean oil terminals, and Iraq's oil income, which formed 70% of government revenue, was immediately cut by two-thirds. In spite of broad hints from the Syrians that their attitude might change dramatically if Iraq decided to nationalise its oil, Naji Talib's government chose a line of *realpolitik*, judging, probably correctly, that the time was not ripe for such a step, given the glut of oil on the world market. Eventually a face-saving formula was found that satisfied both the Syrians and IPC, and after agreeing on the payment of compensation for Iraq's lost revenues, pumping was resumed in March 1967. The episode served yet again to highlight Iraq's dependence on the Company and its widely detested powers, at a time when calls for more radical action against 'imperialism and Zionism' were being loudly voiced in both Egypt and Syria[26].

The depths of inaction to which the Iraqi government had fallen, and above all the hollowness of its claims to have any serious commitment to 'Arab brotherhood' were nowhere more strikingly illustrated than in its failure to send more than a token force to the front to fight in the Arab–Israeli war of June 1967. By this time, 'Arif had taken over the premiership himself, since the inter-factional quarrels had become too acute for Naji Talib to handle. After the war, on 19 July, 'Arif once more entrusted the premiership to the more forceful Tahir Yahya, who immediately embarked upon a more vigorously anti-imperialist line, breaking off diplomatic relations with Britain and the United States and apparently launching a more determinedly independent oil policy. This was expressed in two Laws, Nos. 97 and 123 of 16 August and 1 October 1967, which paved the way for the government to play a more active part in the development of the country's oil resources. Briefly, the two Laws gave an enhanced role to the state oil company, INOC, which was given wider powers and the exclusive right to develop the North Rumaila oilfield, where the existence of oil had long been proven, but which IPC had been prevented from developing under the provisions of Law 80. INOC began negotiations for a service contract with the French consortium ERAP, which was signed on 24 November. At the same time the state company declared its intention to seek Soviet assistance for the development of North Rumaila and other fields, the most important of Iraq's early ventures in technological cooperation with a socialist country. Thus Yahya's government showed itself determined to continue the policy of excluding IPC that had begun under Law 80, and insisted on its clear intention of developing the country's oil resources on its own. The decision that INOC should definitely develop North Rumaila without IPC assistance was the subject of a dramatic declaration on 10 April

1968, which was greeted with immense satisfaction. As we shall see, the principle of extending government control over the country's oil resources was carried to its logical conclusion by the Ba'th government's nationalisation of IPC in 1972.

Social and Economic Policies, 1963-1968

The political confusion and discontinuity of the years between Qasim's overthrow and the assumption of power by the Ba'th in 1968 had their counterpart in the economic policies of the period. Some indication of the chaotic and uncoordinated planning of these years may be gauged from the fact that between 1964 and 1968 there were eight ministers of industry and transport, seven ministers of public works, six ministers of agrarian reform and six ministers of planning. The changes at the top were usually accompanied by transfers of civil servants within the ministries, so that almost all sense of continuity was lost[27].

In general terms the various governments remained broadly committed to state sponsored economic development, which they called Arab socialism, within an institutional framework largely based on the Egyptian model. The authors of the 1965-1969 Plan declared that they aimed to establish a dynamic industrial sector that would lessen the country's dependence on oil and also pave the way for Arab unity. The Plan only achieved 40% of its target, some indication of the distance between the ideal and the reality. However, the depth of the commitment to 'socialism' may be inferred from the preamble to the 1964 nationalisation decrees, which stated that:

> ... our Arab socialism does not mean state control of all economic activities. We have left a wide opening for the private sector and for individual initiative to work on activating the economic life of the country.[28]

Land reform continued slowly; by 1968 some 3.5 million acres had been sequestrated, although this represented only a little more than half the area to be taken over under the provision of the Law of 1958. Of the sequestrated area only 39%, 1.4 million acres, had actually been distributed by 1968; the rest was rented out by the Ministry of Agrarian Reform. The scarcity of trained and committed personnel caused acute dislocations in agriculture generally, and although living standards and working conditions in the countryside undoubtedly improved, food production began a decline from which it has never recovered[29].

The Kurdish Question under the 'Arifs

At the time of Qasim's overthrow there had been a lull in the fighting in Kurdistan, partly because of the winter and partly because of some hope on the part of the Kurds that Qasim's enemies, with whom they had been in informal contact[30], might if successful be inclined to grant concessions on Kurdish autonomy. These hopes, which must be regarded even without hindsight as having been wildly over-optimistic, were soon dashed. In the first place, the regime was primarily interested in establishing itself in power, and secondly its members were committed, at least in theory, to some form of Arab unity and in that context Kurdish autonomy was a contradiction in terms. Thus no early proclamation of the regime's intentions for the Kurds was forthcoming, although two token Kurds, Baba 'Ali Shaikh Mahmud and Brigadier Fu'ad 'Arif, were appointed to the cabinet.

In the middle of February Jalal Talabani and Salih al-Yusufi began negotiations on the Kurdish question with the new government, but little progress was made. Barzani, who was still in the north, declared on 28 February that he would not hesitate to start fighting again if the government did not declare its positive commitment to Kurdish autonomy. Not wishing to antagonise the Kurds, but not wishing to offer them anything concrete either, the government sent a delegation headed by Tahir Yahya to meet Barzani, who refused to be fobbed off with anything less than autonomy. A few months of energetic logic-chopping over the precise meaning of such terms as 'decentralisation' and 'self-administration' and the definition of the area to be included in 'Kurdistan' ended in June 1963, when fighting broke out once more.

On assuming personal control in November, 'Abd al-Salam 'Arif immediately declared his own desire to end the war, which, as always, looked unwinnable by conventional military means for reasons that have already been explained. In addition the various coups and purges had deprived the armed forces of many of their ablest commanders. 'Arif now approached Barzani secretly to explore a possible ceasefire, which was negotiated on 10 February 1964. By this time, however, the latent divisions within the Kurdish ranks between the 'tribals' and the 'politicals' had broken through to the surface, and Barzani was forced to take the challenge to his authority now being posed by the KDP more seriously. Hence, when 'Arif bypassed the KDP and began to negotiate directly with him, Barzani seized what appeared to be a golden opportunity to dispense with the KDP, whose leaders, notably Ibrahim Ahmad and Jalal Talabani, immediately denounced the ceasefire as a sell-out and refused to cooperate. Barzani and his group attempted to be conciliatory, but when no progress was forthcoming expelled their opponents across the border into Iran.

Of course, the 10 February agreement *was* a sell-out; it fell far short of granting Kurdish autonomy, and was in fact a tactical device to give both Barzani and 'Arif breathing space for their various purposes. It enabled Barzani to crush the KDP at least for the time being and 'Arif to reorganise and strengthen the army as the main bulwark of his regime. Sporadic fighting broke out again in the winter of 1964/1965 and by April 1965 the war had begun in earnest once more. For a short time Barzani and his Kurdish opponents patched up their differences and fought together against the common enemy. Although the government scored some strategic successes in the winter and spring of 1965/1966, there were few hopeful signs of a satisfactory outcome from the government's point of view by the time of 'Arif's death in April 1966. Its sole achievement had been to widen the breach between the Ahmad–Talabani group and Barzani to the point where units led by the former, paid for by the regime in Baghdad, were fighting alongside government troops against Barzani's forces[31].

On his appointment as Prime Minister in September 1965 al-Bazzaz had undertaken to try to restore peace 'to all parts of Iraq and to "safeguard the unity of its territory" '[32], although his Minister of Defence, General 'Abd al-'Aziz al-'Uqaili, was well-known for his hawkish attitude towards the Kurdish problem. By May 1966, Barzani and his followers, supported increasingly by money and weapons from Iran, had inflicted a crushing defeat on the Iraqi Army (under the command of General al-'Uqaili himself) and the pro-government Kurds at Mount Handrin on the road between Ruwanduz and the Iranian frontier. Serious doubts now began to be expressed in both military and civilian circles over the conduct of the war, and although not reported on the Iraqi media[33] it was widely unpopular in the country at large. The severity of the defeat, and the personal set-back this represented for al-'Uqaili, seems to have enabled al-Bazzaz to seize the initiative and to make contact with both Barzani and the KDP leaders.

On 15 June 1966 al-Bazzaz appeared on radio and television and declared himself ready to recognise 'Kurdish nationalism and the Kurds' national rights'. After twelve days of negotiations he announced the Declaration of 29 June, which recognised clearly and unequivocably the 'binational character of the Iraqi state'[34]. This was the most far-reaching attempt ever made at a solution, and the principles of the Declaration were to be echoed in the Ba'th's later attempt at a settlement, the Manifesto of 11 March 1970.

al-Bazzaz' farsightedness and sincerity in promulgating the Declaration were not in doubt; far less sure, however, was his capacity to put it into practice. Influential sections of the Army were hostile to any negotiated settlement at all, let alone a settlement on these lines; in part, 'Arif 'Abd al-Razzaq's foiled coup was an attempt to demonstrate this. As has been described, al-Bazzaz fell a few weeks later and the agreement fell with him. The officers' opposition proved an insuperable obstacle; even 'Abd al-Rahman 'Arif's visit to Barzani in October and his evident willingness to reopen negotiations could not carry the day against their will. Thus a stalemate ensued; 'Arif could not deliver a settlement to Barzani, whose position in Kurdistan now appeared impregnable, and the Army was in no position to force the issue. Naji Talib's government made a few feeble efforts to attack Barzani by arming supporters of Ahmad and Talabani to raid his positions in Kurdistan, but Barzani's overwhelming strength on the ground made this a futile exercise. The situation persisted throughout 1967 and 1968; Barzani gradually consolidated his position further with Iranian (and possibly Israeli) assistance, and the impasse continued until and well beyond the Ba'th takeover in July.

The Communists under the 'Arifs[35]

The relentless campaign carried out against the Communists by the Ba'th and their allies after February 1963 had severely weakened the Party. After the fall of the Ba'th in November the intensity of the persecution diminished somewhat, and Amir 'Abdullah, Baha' al-Din Nuri, and 'Abd al-Salam al-Nasiri managed to slip back into the country, reactivate some of the Party cells, and begin a limited handwritten circulation of *Tariq al-Sha'b*. Outside the country, the Communist Party in exile, based in Prague, co-ordinated the international publicity campaign against the regime.

For a number of reasons the ICP's original stance of unrelenting hostility underwent certain modifications in the summer of 1964. By this time the Ba'th were no longer in the government, the Kurdish war had come to a halt, both Egyptian–Soviet and Iraqi–Soviet relations had improved, and the national-isations of July 1964 seemed to indicate, at least to some members of the Central Committee, that things were generally moving in the right direction. These apparently positive developments led to the formulation in Prague of what became known as 'the August Line'[36], which amounted to an acceptance of the doctrine of the non-capitalist road as an interpretation of events in both Egypt and Iraq, which entailed, by extension, a recommendation that the Party should support the 'progressive Nasserist elements' within the 'Arif government.

For many of the rank and file, both inside and outside Iraq, this line evoked 'great indignation'[37]. To them, the 'Arif regime was indistinguishable from the Ba'th, and was equally responsible for the atrocities of 1963. As a result the Central Committee was forced round to a view that was more in line with the sentiments and aspirations of the ordinary membership and by April 1965 came to adopt a policy of advocating armed struggle to overthrow the dictatorship and to establish a 'provisional national coalition government' while appealing to the Nasserists to withdraw from the regime.

Although this more militant line was a more faithful reflection of the opinion of the grass roots of the Party, it was far from clear what form armed struggle could possibly take, and the prac-ticalities of this question became the cause of considerable disagreement. Eventually this manifested itself in a split in the Party between the Central Committee and what became known as the Central Command, which took place in September 1967. 'Aziz al-Hajj, who had returned to Iraq early in 1967 to organise the

Baghdad branch of the Party, was the leader of this breakaway group, which advocated guerilla action against the regime from bases in the marshes in southern central Iraq. The terrain does not in fact lend itself to this sort of activity, as the group was to be made tragically aware, but although the Central Committee managed to retain the loyalty of the majority of Communists, the Central Command continued to attract supporters even after their capture and defeat by the Ba'th in the spring of 1969.

Chapter Four

1968–1972

With the accidental death of 'Abd al-Salam 'Arif in April 1966, the regime that he had headed for the previous three years lost most of the symbolic capital it may ever have possessed, since this was so closely bound up with his own person and personality. As the senior Free Officer after Qasim, and the country's leading advocate of Arab socialism and Arab unity, 'Arif was probably the most prominent political figure to have survived the 1958 Revolution and its aftermath. He was able to command a significant degree of respect within the disparate factions of the government over which he presided, and also had a certain following among nationalist and conservative circles in the country as a whole. His political heirs showed their awareness of 'Abd al-Salam's importance by promoting his brother as his successor, an expedient whose effectiveness was considerably impeded by 'Abd al-Rahman's relative obscurity and lack of personal authority[1].

In an important sense, therefore, 'Abd al-Salam 'Arif's death created a vacuum that lasted until the Ba'th takeover in 1968. This was expressed in the lack of leadership and the absence of any discernible economic policy[2], the failure to participate effectively in the Arab-Israeli war of June 1967, the continuing conflict in the north, the vacillations and evasions shown towards IPC, and the growing loss of confidence in the government on the part of the mass of the population. In this extremely fluid situation any

organised political party or group with access to individuals in
sensitive positions in the armed forces stood a good chance of
being able to take over the government, and it is highly likely that
only the June war and the Nasserist euphoria that preceded it
prevented a coup taking place in the course of 1967[3]. The group
that did eventually succeed in taking power at this point was the
Ba'th Party, and before discussing the course of events before,
during, and after the two coups of 17 and 30 July 1968, it is useful to
make a number of observations about the structure, function and
nature of the Party as an entity in the 1960s.

The Background to the July 1968 Coups: the Ba'th Party and the Struggle for Power

Most accounts of the Iraqi Ba'th Party[4] suggest that it has a highly
structured organisation, comparable in many ways to a Communist party, with a central committee, a carefully elaborated
ideology and an agreed line which is either followed or formally
amended at party congresses. To the extent that the Ba'th does
necessarily have some sort of organisational structure the picture
given is not entirely false, but it is a mistake to attribute too much
importance either to structural or to ideological matters, since
personal and family ties have usually played a considerably more
important role than ideological purity. Thus, particularly before
the Party's seizure of power, personal relationships and common
sectarian or geographical origins have been decisive factors in
Party affiliation, which was often, though certainly not always,
more a declaration of group solidarity or of fealty to a particular
individual than a political or ideological statement. It was only
after 1968 that a more thorough-going administrative apparatus
was created, and even then the informal personal networks
continued to be decisive at the highest levels in the Party. But this
is to anticipate.

The extent of the importance of personal ties can readily be
appreciated from a brief survey of the fortunes of the Party since its
origins. Thus Fu'ad al-Rikabi, the Shi'i founder of the Iraqi Ba'th
in the early 1950s, presided over an organisation that was almost
entirely composed of his Shi'i relatives and classmates; 'Ali Salih
al-Sa'di's supporters were generally petty criminals like himself
from the Bab al-Shaikh area of Baghdad, and the Ahmad Hasan

al-Bakr/Saddam Husain group that came to power in 1968 had a following based in the first instance on Sunnis from Takrit. Similar examples exist outside Iraq; the core of the Syrian President Hafiz al-Asad's support comes from members of his own community, the Alawites, a compact minority from the mountains behind Latakia. In fact Ba'thism is sufficiently flexible to be adopted as an ideology by virtually any group in the Arab Middle East, as we have shown[5], (whether 'majority' or 'minority'), since it is couched in extremely wide and vague terms, and lacks both an analytical framework and clearly defined objectives. As a result, the mere reiteration of pious nostrums about, for example, 'Arab unity', was and occasionally still is thought sufficient to confirm the generally erroneous impression that Ba'thist parties or governments were or are actually working actively towards this end.

Thus, while some organisational structures probably did exist, these features should not be unduly emphasised, since the main focus of Party activity in Iraq in the period between November 1963 and July 1968 was in small, loosely interconnected conspiratorial groups of like-minded friends and kinsmen. At this stage Ba'th 'policy' was more the organisation of the steps necessary to seize power than the construction of a political party that would actually attract people to its ranks by virtue of its social and economic programmes. In such circumstances assertions of ideological purity like those expresssed by 'Ali Salih al-Sa'di in 1964–65 were simply *prises de position* on the part of competing groups or *post hoc* justifications for actions that had been taken on entirely pragmatic grounds[6].

By the beginning of 1964, the senior Ba'thist officers who had sided with 'Arif against their comrades at the end of 1963 had decided to distance themselves formally from al-Sa'di, although they were unable to secure his actual expulsion from the Party until 1965. These moves had begun at a time when 'Arif was gradually tightening his personal hold on the reins of government, and in fact al-Bakr, Hardan al-Takriti and Salih Mahdi 'Ammash were gently but firmly removed from positions of power by the spring of 1964. Both al-Bakr and Hardan came from Takrit, and they were almost certainly responsible for the appointment of al-Bakr's relative, Saddam Husain, then aged twenty-seven, as principal full-time organiser of the non-military wing of the party in 1964.

Although it is difficult to follow the Party's progress during this period of its clandestine existence, Saddam Husain's own version of these years states that he was arrested and imprisoned in October 1964 'in the wake of a large scale round-up'[7], and released, or rather 'sprung' in 1966. By September of that year he had become deputy secretary-general of the Party[8]. Other prominent Party members in these years were 'Abd al-Karim al-Shaikhli (from Baghdad, one of Saddam Husain's associates in the attempt to assassinate 'Abd al-Karim Qasim in 1959), Murtada al-Hadithi, originally from Takrit, 'Abdullah Sallum al-Samarra'i and 'Abd al-Khaliq al-Samarra'i, all of whom became members of the Regional Command (meaning, in Ba'th parlance, the national command for Iraq) in 1964; and Taha al-Jazrawi, now known as Taha Yasin Ramadan, from Takrit, Salah 'Umar al-'Ali, from Takrit, and 'Izzat Mustafa, from 'Ana, who were appointed to the same body in 1966 after the major internal upheavals that resulted in the formation of two separate Ba'th parties in Syria and Iraq[9].

Although the Ba'th's activities were officially proscribed between 1963 and 1968, and many Ba'thists were arrested for parts of the period, there was never any serious attempt under either of the 'Arifs to identify, still less to punish, the real perpetrators of the bloodbath of February–March 1963. Indeed, many of the senior officers and officials who bore much of the responsibility for these atrocities reappeared in July 1968, and never made any public expression of regret for the brutalities committed in the course of the campaign against Qasim and the left. Thus in May 1966 'Ali Salih al-Sa'di and Hardan al-Takriti were referred for trial, but only on vague charges of misappropriation of funds after Qasim's death; in any event the cases never actually came to court[10].

In fact such 'repression' of the Ba'th as actually took place was directed largely against the al-Sa'di group; naturally enough, since the others had been instrumental in assisting 'Arif to bring about al-Sa'di's downfall. Thus senior Ba'thists, especially al-Bakr, were almost invariably invited to the meetings convened at various times by 'Abd al-Rahman 'Arif between 1966 and 1968 in his efforts to form governments of national unity[11]. In addition, 'ex-Ba'thists', such as 'Abd al-Sattar 'Abd al-Latif, who had served as Minister of Communications between February and November 1963, and his better-known comrade in arms Tahir Yahya, both became cabinet ministers between 1964 and 1968, Yahya serving as Prime Minister under both 'Arif brothers. Thus, given the essentially conservative nature of the 'Arifs and their governments, and the fact that they did not differ substantially from the Ba'th on matters of principle, it was relatively easy for al-Bakr and his colleagues to sit out the interregnum between 1964 and 1968 waiting for circumstances to change in their favour.

As we have already suggested, the situation became particularly volatile after 'Abd al-Salam 'Arif's death in April 1966. In May 1967, for example, Naji Talib's resignation produced a crisis that was only resolved by 'Arif taking over the premiership himself; al-Bakr was widely tipped at the time as a possible successor[12]. On this occasion the Ba'th leadership seems to have judged, probably rightly, that the time was not ripe and that it would be unwise to risk rocking the boat at this crucial juncture in Arab affairs.

In the spring of 1968, 'Arif himself approached a number of Ba'thists and nationalists in order to sound out their opinions, and if possible to associate them more closely with the government, then headed by Tahir Yahya. Two days before the meeting, most of those who had been invited met at al-Bakr's house to discuss tactics. The thirteen men involved, all former officers, included three ex-Prime Ministers (al-Bakr, Naji Talib and 'Arif 'Abd al-Razzaq), and five other ex-Ministers (Hardan al-Takriti, 'Abd al-Sattar 'Abd al-Latif, Rashid Muslih, 'Abd al-Ghani al-Rawi and 'Abd al-'Aziz al-'Uqaili). The discussions with 'Arif broke down, largely because of Tahir Yahya's fears for his own authority, but a few weeks later, most of the thirteen, with some abstentions but with the addition of Salih Mahdi 'Ammash, (who brought the number of Ba'thists involved up to five), submitted a note to 'Arif calling for the formation of a government of national unity[13]. This may have represented an attempt on the group's part to take power, or perhaps to be admitted to power, without a military coup.

This initiative also came to nothing, but it is interesting for a number of reasons, especially in the context of the events of the following July. First, it showed that the Ba'th were evidently still prepared to collaborate with the nationalists if this would enable them to enter a government. Secondly, the government itself, or at least 'Arif himself, clearly regarded the group as *ministrables* rather than as 'opposition'. Finally, it illustrates how essentially accessible and amenable to the Ba'th those in power still were, in spite of having pushed them out in 1963-64.

The Coups of July 1968

In July 1968, al-Bakr's patience was finally rewarded. Infighting within the regime, and in particular within the armed forces, had reached its peak, to the extent that Tahir Yahya threatened to resign on 12 July, and did in fact do so three days later[14]. The Ba'th, possibly in common with other 'opposition' *groupuscules*[15], had made contact with three of the four key individuals upon whom the security of the 'Arif regime ultimately rested: Colonel 'Abd al-Razzaq al-Nayif, Director of Military Intelligence; Colonel Ibrahim 'Abd al-Rahman al-Da'ud, the commander of the Republican Guard, which acted as the regime's 'anti-army', and Colonel Sa'dun Ghaidan, the commander of the 10th Armoured Brigade, which was the Republican Guard's tank regiment. In an interview with Batatu in 1970, 'Arif declared that al-Nayif had been bought by foreign oil interests, and that both al-Nayif and al-Da'ud feared the vengeance of the Nasserists because of their prominent role in suppressing the pro-Nasserist revolt of 'Arif 'Abd al-Razzaq in 1966.

It is not clear whether the Ba'thist officers or al-Nayif and al-Da'ud made the first contacts with each other, but it is evident that mutual interest drew them together. From the point of view of al-Nayif and al-Da'ud, their previous track record with the Nasserists must have made the Ba'th seem more immediately congenial partners, and there is also some suggestion that they were becoming increasingly concerned at Tahir Yahya's attempts to carve out a stronger and more independent position for himself within the 'Arif regime by a series of military transfers, whose general effect seemed likely to undermine their own power base[16]. On the Ba'th side, the arrangements that al-Bakr and his friends arrived at with al-Nayif and al-Da'ud were naturally entered into in circumstances of the greatest secrecy, so much so in fact that even after the coup had taken place, the extent of Ba'th involvement and participation in it as a party rather than as a group of like-minded individuals was not clear either to the public at large or to the party rank and file. Indeed, it is legitimate to ask in what way the Ba'th as a *political party* was involved at all in the events of 17 July 1968.

The timing of the coup seems to have been partially connected with the political crisis occasioned by Tahir Yahya's resignation, but a further important factor was that this hiatus also happened to coincide with the absence in Britain of the fourth key figure, Brigadier Slaibi, who had hitherto provided the continuity and acted as the ultimate anchor of the regimes of both the 'Arif brothers[17]. Early in the morning of 17 July, Sa'dun Ghaidan brought al-Bakr, Hardan al-Takriti, 'Ammash and a number of other Ba'thist officers into the headquarters of the 10th Armoured Brigade; al-Da'ud took over the radio station, (which was controlled by the Republican Guard that he commanded), and al-Nayif took charge of the Ministry of Defence. As the conspirators had foreseen, the regime, deprived of its essential foundations, offered no resistance.

Since they had no scores to settle with 'Arif, and as he was not considered to constitute any real threat, the actual transfer of power took place in an entirely gentlemanly fashion, and 'Arif was allowed to go into honourable exile. Eric Rouleau described how Hardan al-Takriti insisted on taking 'Arif to his own home, made him coffee and urged him to lie down before his flight; 'after a few hours' rest', 'Arif is quoted as saying, 'I bade farewell to all the officers and wished them every success'[18]. These homely details serve to underline the essential community of outlook between the victors and the vanquished; at this stage the coup seemed to represent the defeat of one faction by another.

At this stage the '17 July Revolution' seemed to exhibit all the elements of a classic military coup, where key members of the armed forces take power simply by seizing a few vital installations or by gaining control of key military units. However, it soon became apparent that the successful execution of these manoeuvres was only the prelude to much more far-reaching developments, which culminated in the emergence of the al-Bakr/Saddam Husain wing of the Ba'th as 'the government' thirteen days later. Meanwhile, al-Bakr was proclaimed President on 18 July, with al-Nayif and al-Da'ud respectively Prime Minister and Minister of Defence; 'Ammash, the most senior of the eight Ba'thists in the cabinet, became Minister of Interior. The rest of the cabinet included six supporters of al-Nayif and al-Da'ud, including the Minister of Foreign Affairs, Nasir al-Hani; the leader of the Muslim Brethren, 'Abd al-Karim Zaidan; four Kurds, one of whom, Muhsin Dizahi, represented Mulla Mustafa Barzani, and three 'conservative specialists' holding the ministries of Finance, Planning, and Oil[19].

Although this cabinet may have seemed reasonably representa-

tive in its own terms, the most decisive forces within the new
regime were the two power circles centring around the al-Nayif/al-
Da'ud faction on the one hand and the Ba'thist officers on the
other. On 18 July, the formation of a seven-man Revolutionary
Command Council (RCC) was announced, consisting entirely of
officers (see Table 4.1).

Table 4.1 *The Revolutionary Command Council (RCC)*

Name	Civilian Function	Military Function
Ahmad Hasan al-Bakr (B, †, *)	President of the Republic	President of the RCC and C-in-C Armed Forces
Salih Mahdi 'Ammash (B)	Minister of Interior	—
Hardan al-Takriti (B, *)	—	Chief of Staff; Commander of Air Force
'Abd al-Razzaq al-Nayif	Prime Minister	Formerly Director of Military Intelligence
Ibrahim 'Abd al-Rahman al-Da'ud	Minister of Defence	Deputy C-in-C, Armed Forces; formerly Commander of Republican Guard
Hammad Shihab al-Takriti (I, †, *)	—	Commander of Baghdad Garrison
Sa'dun Ghaidan (I)	—	Commander of Republican Guard; formerly Commander of 10th Armoured Brigade (Republican Guard Tank Regiment)

B = Ba'thist
† = cousins
* = from Takrit
I = Independent; no known party affiliation in July 1968

Through their access to the military, the RCC and the President
exercised — and continue to exercise, as will be discussed below —

supreme executive and legislative authority. The Ba'th faction was eventually able to seize control by successful approaches to the commander of the Baghdad garrison, Hammad Shihab al-Takriti, (a cousin of Ahmad Hasan al-Bakr, but not, so far as can be ascertained, a Ba'thist before 1968) and Sa'dun Ghaidan, who had been promoted after 17 July from the command of the Republican Guard's Tank Regiment to the command of the Guard itself. According to Batatu, Ghaidan had 'briefly flirted' with the Ba'th Party in 1963[20]; although evidently once a close associate of al-Nayif and al-Da'ud, he seems to have considered that they had not given him, and were unlikely to give him, adequate reward for his part in the events of 17 July.

The new regime's somewhat anodyne and often contradictory pronouncements after 17 July (apart from routine denunciations of Zionism and assertions that Palestine would be liberated 'immediately') gave little clue of its likely policy orientation, and attempts to delve more deeply beneath the surface were ably fielded at a press conference by the Foreign Minister, Nasir al-Hani[21]. Thus the absence in the early communiqués of what had become the almost obligatory forelock-tugging towards Nasser was followed by the despatch of fulsome congratulations to the Egyptian president on the anniversary of the Egyptian Revolution on 23 July; similarly, the regime's declaration of its intention to pursue 'an oil policy independent of the international oil monopolies' was followed a few days later by an announcement that the ERAP agreement[22], widely regarded as a sell-out to French interests, would be respected[23]. The whole of this brief period was marked by rumours and prophesies of imminent collapse, which were to be amply justified by events. Behind the scenes, al-Bakr was busily consolidating his position, in particular by appointing over 100 Ba'thist officers to positions in the Republican Guard and other key units.

The Ba'th takeover on 30 July was considerably facilitated by the departure on 29 July of al-Da'ud, the Minister of Defence, for a tour of inspection of the Iraqi troops stationed in Jordan, which left the Chief of Staff, Hardan al-Takriti, one of al-Bakr's most trusted associates, in charge of the armed forces. Khadduri, who provides a detailed account of these events (given to him, presumably, by Saddam Husain), says that the Prime Minister, al-Nayif, was arrested by a 'group of officers led by Saddam Husayn' after having had lunch with al-Bakr at the Presidential Palace[24].

Having won over Sa'dun Ghaidan and Hammad Shihab al-Takriti to their side, the Ba'th were easily able to isolate al-Nayif and al-Da'ud, who were powerless without their military units. al-Da'ud was told to remain in Jordan and not to attempt to return to Iraq, and al-Nayif was exiled to Spain; al-Da'ud held various ambassadorial posts until he was retired in 1970, while al-Nayif went to London, where he was eventually assassinated by the Ba'th in 1978, having survived an earlier attempt on his life in 1973.

The Government of 30 July 1968

The coyness displayed by al-Bakr and his associates about the nature and extent of Ba'thist participation in the events of 17 July was immediately discarded after their successful consolidation of power thirteen days later. Although the membership of the RCC was not announced for some time, its composition remained as before, except of course for the exclusion of al-Nayif and al-Da'ud. Rather quaintly, Shihab and Ghaidan, neither of whom, as has been mentioned, had any previous connection with the Ba'th Party, were soon 'declared to be Ba'thists' in a party circular[25], and in this sense the composition of the RCC was now solidly Ba'thist. The day after seizing power (31 July) al-Bakr announced that the 17 July Revolution was a 'natural extension of the 14 July (sc. 1958) Revolution, and a profound re-assertion of the pro-Union progressive leanings for which the 8 February 1963 Revolution was carried out'[26], and it is of course (if rather incongruously) 17 July rather than 30 July that the Ba'th has chosen to celebrate as the anniversary of its return to power.

Like all other post-coup governments in Iraq, al-Bakr and his colleagues had no very clear idea about politics or administration on a day to day basis. The new twenty-six man cabinet included ten members of al-Nayif's ministry, but consisted only of Ba'thists (14), independent nationalists (9) and Kurds (3). Real power lay with the RCC, and especially with al-Bakr himself, who was the only member of the government to have personal and political links with important figures both in the armed forces and in the Ba'th Party. Furthermore, at fifty-four, al-Bakr was at least ten years older than any of his colleagues on the RCC, as well as being the only Free Officer and the only one to have held senior military rank before 1963.

As far as the population as a whole was concerned, memories of the Ba'th reign of terror in 1963 were all too fresh, and the anxieties that were widely harboured were to be amply justified in the months and years to come. In the course of the first two years of their rule, al-Bakr and his associates devoted themselves to imposing Ba'thist rule on the country, and to trying to ensure that all opposition was either absorbed or stamped out. In particular, the regime endeavoured to secure its base in the armed forces and the security apparatus, by removing, transferring or retiring any officers whose loyalty was thought suspect, and replacing them with trusted, if often inexperienced, Ba'thists[27].

At the beginning, it was some time before the regime's pronouncements gave any discernible indication of a consistent political line. al-Nayif and al-Da'ud were castigated for being 'anti-socialist' and for favouring the abolition of INOC, the state oil company. A firm commitment to maintain the 'joint Iraqi-Egyptian political line' on 12 August was followed fifteen days later by the closure of the Iraqi offices of the Arab Socialist Union, and the dissolution of the preparatory committee engaged in overseeing the arrangements for the eventual union between Iraq and Egypt[28].

Again, in the first few months, the Ba'th made gestures of conciliation both to the KDP and to the Communists, but not on terms that either was likely to accept. Overtures to Barzani soon failed because of the regime's evident partiality for Jalal Talabani, and the former's two supporters in the cabinet resigned in protest on 26 August over the continuing presence in the cabinet of Talabani's representative, Taha Muhi al-Din Ma'ruf. The Ba'th's failure to make any immediate headway with the KDP was paralleled by its experience with the Communists, who were astonished to find themselves offered three ministerial portfolios at the beginning of August. This was all the more remarkable, as Eric Rouleau comments, since al-Bakr, who was now 'extending the hand of friendship to them, was the same man who, in 1963, had presided over a government responsible for the death of tens of thousands of sympathisers or militants of the extreme left and the arrest of more than a hundred thousand others'[29]. The Communists refused to participate unless full civil liberties were restored, political parties legalised and democratic elections held, demands to which the Ba'th was either unable or unwilling to respond.

In September, the new regime issued its first provisional constitution, which declared Islam to be the religion of the state, 'socialism' as the foundation of the economy, and the RCC (and, by extension, its chairman) as the supreme legislative and executive authority[30], to which the cabinet and the (projected) national assembly were to be subordinate. The third of these provisions, stressing the supremacy of the RCC, is evidently the one that has been most assiduously respected since 1968. The RCC is accountable to no one, except to the Ba'th Party; even this degree of accountability is no more than formal. As far as the two other institutions are concerned, the cabinet has never exercised more than technocratic authority, and the national assembly, which eventually came into being in 1980, has deliberative rather than legislative powers[31]. Hence, with an absolute monopoly of all judicial, legislative and executive authority, the RCC, at least while al-Bakr was still at the helm, is best described as a form of collegiate dictatorship.

A few days after the promulgation of the provisional constitution, the regime began what was to become its all too familiar practice of combining a campaign of terror with blandishments of various kinds and assurances of its ultimate good faith. At this stage it hit out quite indiscriminately at both 'right' and 'left', and Communists, Nasserists, pro-Syrian Ba'thists, former ministers and ex-officials, and 'spies' were rounded up. Some were so maltreated in prison that they died there or soon after their release, while others were executed, often in public, for their alleged participation in plots against the regime, or for crimes they were supposed to have committed in the past. By the end of the year, several hundred officers had been arrested, together with some forty businessmen, generally Iraqi representatives of Western firms, and a host of ministers and former civil servants, including 'Abd al-Rahman al-Bazzaz, Adib al-Jadir and Khair al-Din Hasib. In November, Nasir al-Hani, who had served briefly as Foreign Minister under al-Nayyif and had been 'openly critical' of the Ba'th, was found murdered[32].

Hence the atmosphere of indiscriminate terror familiar to Iraqis from the Ba'th's previous campaign in 1963 soon returned, with raids on private houses in the middle of the night and gangs of armed thugs roaming the streets. The Ba'thist militia, the National Guard, became a familiar sight at demonstrations and strikes, arresting and even killing those taking part in them[33]. In general, the period between the autumn of 1968 and the middle of 1969 is one of extreme chaos and confusion, in which the only thread that can be followed is the Ba'th leadership's clear determination to stay in power this time at all costs, to smash all actual or potential opposition, to entrench itself in key positions, and to extend and develop the machinery of the Party as an instrument of control. In broader terms, the policies actually pursued by al-Bakr and his circle in these early months do not indicate any startling departures from those of the 'Arif brothers. Thus there were no further nationalisations and no immediate changes in oil policy; relations with other Arab states remained as indifferent as in the middle 1960s; economic policy was still uncertain, and the restoration of democracy and civil liberties as far away as ever.

The absence of any clear political line should come as no surprise, given the organisational structure of the Ba'th Party of 1968, and the fact that the coup of 30 July had been carried out by a group of officers, each of whom felt equally entitled to play a, or *the*, key role in government, and each of whom also knew that unless he succeeded in securing an unassailable power base, he would always be vulnerable to the ambitions of his other colleagues. As we have seen, Sa'dun Ghaidan and Hammad Shihab had played essentially subordinate and ancillary roles in the two coups, and were thus not serious contenders for supreme power. At this point the real struggle was between al-Bakr (backed by Saddam Husain), 'Ammash, and Hardan al-Takriti, all of whom had some kind of following in the armed forces, which, if properly activated, could easily constitute a threat to the others. It was thus not long before disputes between the three came to the surface.

Providentially for al-Bakr, the main focus of disagreement seems to have been an argument between his two rivals over the lines of demarcation between their respective ministries, Interior ('Ammash) and Defence (Hardan al-Takriti). Both men were trying to build up separate security bodies to strengthen their own power bases, which led to mutual accusations that each was trespassing on the proper sphere of the other's ministry. In the meantime, al-Bakr, who had greater experience and a far shrewder grasp of the overall situation, was quietly making sure of his own position, but by very different means. He too was building up his own security apparatus, headed by his younger relative Saddam Husain, but his chosen instrument was the newly developed Ba'th Party apparatus, also controlled by Saddam Husain, who, as we have seen, had been in charge since the Party's split with the Syrian Ba'th in 1966.

Early in 1969, (following the Party conference that had begun in November but whose deliberations had been postponed to make way for negotiations with the Kurds), a new Regional Command was announced, whose members were al-Bakr, 'Ammash, Saddam Husain, 'Abdullah Sallum al-Samarra'i, 'Abd al-Khaliq al-Samarra'i, 'Abd al-Karim al-Shaikhli, Shafiq Kamali, Murtada al-Hadithi, Taha Jazrawi (= Taha Yasin Ramadan), Salah 'Umar al-'Ali, 'Izzat Mustafa, 'Abd al-Wahhab Karim and 'Izzat al-Duri, all but one of whom ('Abd al-Wahhab Karim, who died in a car accident in September 1969) were to become additional members of the RCC in November 1969. Apart from al-Bakr and 'Ammash, none of the group were from military backgrounds; all came from the 'Sunni triangle' bounded by Baghdad, Mosul, Takrit, on the Tigris, and the small mid-Euphrates towns of 'Ana, Rawa, Haditha and Falluja, an area that had always been more exposed or at least more susceptible than the rest of the country to the ideological waves of Arab nationalism emanating from Syria, and had been either junior civil servants, school teachers, or (the majority) full-time party workers, before their elevation[34].

At the same time as having manoeuvred themselves into a position where they could take greater control of the RCC, al-Bakr and Saddam Husain were also assiduously 'Ba'thising' the armed forces. In addition to the arrests of officers in the autumn of 1968 that have already been mentioned, the Chief of Staff, Faisal al-Ansari, and eight divisional commanders, were dismissed at the end of December and replaced by Ba'thists or trusted sympathisers. al-Ansari was succeeded by Hammad al-Shihab of the RCC, whose own post as commander of the Baghdad garrison was taken over by his colleague Sa'dun Ghaidan. On a broader level, more than 3000 new commissions were announced by the end of 1970, enabling al-Bakr and Husain to install what amounted to political commissars at all levels, individuals who were part of a chain of command that effectively bypassed the formal military hierarchy and led ultimately to Saddam Husain[35]. Here it may be appropriate to mention that while the Iraqi Ba'th regime of the 1970s and 1980s is normally described as 'civilian', and while the civilians have always outnumbered the military on the RCC since 1969, these civilians have also always been buttressed by an officer corps that has become increasingly Ba'thised with the passage of time, thus making the distinction somewhat less clearcut than the 'civilian' label might otherwise imply.

The close ties between al-Bakr and Saddam Husain, together with Husain's shrewdness and utter ruthlessness, presumably account for the latter's rise from relative obscurity in 1966 to the second most important position in the state apparatus only three years later. Husain controlled the National Security Bureau of the RCC (*maktaba al-amn al-qawmi*), the President's personal security apparatus, which dealt particularly with the collection of information on political and religious opposition movements within the country. He also had overall control of the 'official' security service (*al-amn al-'amm*), which was run on a day-to-day basis by Nadhim Kazzar[36], and was in charge of the Ba'th militia, the National Guard. Hence al-Bakr was able to concentrate on trying to maintain or to gain the support of the armed forces (and also on isolating 'Ammash and Hardan al-Takriti), while Saddam Husain, at the apex of the various security services and also at the head of the Party organisation, was able both to check all potential threats to the regime and to ensure that Ba'thists, and especially Ba'thists loyal to him, were placed in key posts in the security apparatus and in the civil service generally. At this stage, and, as far as can be ascertained, until shortly before al-Bakr's departure from politics in July 1979, the partnership seems to have been a complementary one, in which the two men together managed to achieve a degree of domination that neither could have achieved on his own.

While this process of consolidation was taking place, the regime put on a series of show trials, presumably in an attempt to discourage further manifestations of opposition. In December 1968, a special Revolutionary Court, in which, apparently, no defence lawyers were allowed, and whose judges were not legally qualified[37], was established to try the 'enemies of the people', and seems to have sat continuously throughout 1969. Fifty-three people were executed, many in public, in the course of 1969, for alleged offences against the state; some of the accused were forced to confess their 'crimes' on television[38].

At one of the first trials, which was televised in January 1969, fourteen people, of whom nine were Jews, were found guilty of 'spying for Israel', and hanged in public[39]. This was merely the beginning: in May, another group was sentenced for its alleged links with the CIA; in a series of trials in June, the late 'Abd al-

Salam 'Arif was named as a former CIA agent, the former Interior Minister Rashid Muslih made a similar confession on his own behalf, and Zaki 'Abd al-Wahhab, the former manager of the Coca Cola company, admitted having been a British agent since 1956[40].

This spate of accusations and executions was further evidence of the regime's consciousness of its vulnerability and also perhaps of its general inability to attract support. On a regional level, these fears were further heightened by the evident hostility to the regime displayed by Iraq's neighbour Iran (and indeed, although to a lesser extent, by most Arab states). Iran chose to take much of the Ba'th's 'anti-imperialist' rhetoric seriously, increasing its aid to Mulla Mustafa Barzani as well as conducting a vigorous propaganda campaign against Baghdad, and a state of extreme tension between the two countries persisted, constituting a permanent source of insecurity for the Iraqi regime. Thus in 1969, the Iranians declared that they would henceforth make free use of the waters of the Shatt al-'Arab without respecting Iraq's rights under the Treaty of Saadabad, and also massed troops on various disputed sectors of the southern part of the frontier between the two countries. In January 1970, Iraqi security uncovered a plot to overthrow the regime, apparently masterminded by Tehran, which appears to have been the most serious threat to the Ba'th since its seizure of power[41]. Another special court, consisting of Taha al-Jazrawi of the RCC, Nadhim Kazzar, the director general of security, and his deputy 'Ali Rida, sentenced forty-two people to death between 21 and 24 January for their part in the affair. The executions were carried out immediately.

A few months earlier, the regime had meted out equally draconian punishments to those involved in far more quixotic attacks upon it. These had been undertaken by a group calling itself the 'Central Command' (*al-qiyada al-markaziya*) of the Communist Party (ICP-CC), led by 'Aziz al-Hajj, which had broken off from the main body of the ICP in September 1967. The group attracted widespread support from those Communists who believed very strongly that the Party should not under any circumstances even consider entering into any sort of alliance with 'Arif (or, later, with the Ba'th), because of the ruthless anti-communism he had displayed in 1963. Influenced by Che Guevara and Maoism, they preferred to adopt a policy of armed struggle. Briefly, al-Hajj and his companions had begun a campaign of sabotage against the regime in January 1969; most of those involved were soon caught, and many of them were subsequently tortured to death. al-Hajj himself, a major figure on the left in the 1950s and 1960s, who had been imprisoned for his political beliefs between 1948 and 1958, broke down under interrogation and subsequently appeared on television, castigating both his own organisation and the 'official' ICP for their past and present opposition to the Ba'th Party, and praising the Ba'th as the only truly progressive force in the country[42]. A Fa'ili Kurd himself, he also urged the Kurds to disassociate themselves from Barzani, in line with current Ba'th policies. Later in 1969 a long letter signed by al-Hajj and seventy of his colleagues was read out on Baghdad radio, in fulsome support of the regime's decision to recognise the German Democratic Republic.

Although the recapitulation of these grim details may give the impression of an indiscriminate campaign of terror against all opposition from whatever quarter, a close examination of events reveals a more consistent pattern. In the trials and in its propaganda pronouncements generally, the regime made every effort to demonstrate its opposition to Britain, the United States, the Shah, Israel, and 'imperialism, Zionism and reaction' in general. At the same time, through such foreign policy departures as the recognition of the German Democratic Republic in July 1969 and the development of closer links with the Soviet Union and other socialist countries, it was attempting to prove that it was now able to match or outbid the Communist Party in its claim to constitute the 'real' left.

The First Steps on the Road to Oil Nationalisation: Negotiations with the Soviet Union, March–July 1969

To put the developments that have just been described into a wider context, it is important to remember that in the years after the humiliation of 1967 many Arabs had come to identify the United States with Israel, and had also become convinced that the military and economic strength of Israel depended almost entirely upon American support. Thus any regime that wished to give itself a revolutionary image had to present itself as opposed to the West in general and the United States in particular. Furthermore, in these years Nasser and Egypt still provided the 'natural' leadership

of the Arab world, and Nasser enjoyed very cordial relations with
the Soviet Union. Again, all the 'revolutionary' governments in the
Arab world had been buying arms from the Soviet Union since the
middle 1950s, and all of them still had fairly extensive trade
relations with the socialist countries, although many Arabs had
been somewhat disappointed at what they considered to have
been the Soviet Union's failure to intervene effectively on the Arab
side in 1967. Finally, at this stage, before the oil boom of the 1970s,
Sa'udi Arabia and the Gulf States had comparatively little
economic muscle, and their rulers were widely regarded and
almost ritually lampooned as 'agents of imperialism' because of
their avowedly pro-Western stance.

Given this general atmosphere in the Middle East, the Iraqi
government's approaches to the Soviet Union at the beginning of
1969 could be seen not only as the continuation of a process begun
under Qasim and the 'Arifs, but as a step that would also serve to
enhance its image as a 'progressive' regime. Specifically, the
regime was concerned to reactivate the 'Letter of Intent' signed by
its predecessors in December 1967, which 'envisaged Soviet
assistance in the development of the Iraqi oil industry'[43], and
Soviet cooperation in other fields. Early in 1968, Tahir Yahya's
government had signed an agreement with the French consortium
ERAP, under which the latter undertook to develop a 4000 square
mile area on behalf of the national oil company, INOC, in return
for a preferential option on a third of annual production for
several years[44]. The agreement was the object of considerable
criticism, both at the time and later, since although it marked a
step away from IPC, it was still regarded as being unnecessarily
generous to the French company[45]. Since the signature of the
ERAP agreement the oil question had remained largely in
abeyance, and the new regime was too busy consolidating its own
power base to pay proper attention to it for several months.
However, negotiations with the Soviet Union were resumed in
earnest in March 1969, and on 21 June a major agreement was
signed in Moscow, providing for Soviet technical aid for the
Halfa'iya and other oilfields, for which the Iraqis were to pay the
equivalent of $70 million in dinars. A further more wide-ranging
agreement concluded a few weeks later announced Soviet
assistance for the development of the key North Rumaila oilfield,
and the construction of a 70 mile pipeline linking North Rumaila
with the port of Fao on the Shatt al-'Arab, to be financed by a

rouble loan, which the Iraqis would repay in crude oil[46].
These two agreements marked the beginning of the end of a
period that had started in 1924, when the Iraqi government had in
effect been forced to grant the Turkish Petroleum Company a
concession for the exploitation of Iraqi oil[47]. Every government
since the Revolution of 1958 had attempted to restrict the scope of
IPC's operations, and the Company had responded by a series of
punitive measures, either by not increasing (or even cutting back)
production or delaying royalty payments[48]. The most far-reaching
measure taken by any Iraqi government before the conclusion of
these agreements with the Soviet Union had been Qasim's Law 80
of 1961, a first and essential step in the reassertion of the state's
sovereignty over the oilfields within its borders. This had been
followed by the creation of the national oil company, INOC, in
1964, which was to develop the country's oil resources without
recourse to the multinationals. However, no major steps in this
direction could be taken while Iraq was still fundamentally
dependent on IPC, a dependence which had been underlined in
the course of the Company's dispute with Syria in 1966-67[49], as
Table 4.2 illustrates.

Table 4.2 *Government Oil Revenues 1965-68*

Year	Government Oil Revenue	Government Revenue	Oil as % of Revenue	Government Expenditure	Surplus Deficit
1965	ID 133.9	ID 179.0	74.8	ID 187.5	−ID 8.4
1966	ID 140.7	ID 158.6	88.7	ID 192.4	−ID 33.8
1967	ID 128.9	ID 210.4	61.3	ID 205.5	+ID 4.9
1968	ID 170.0	ID 220.4	77.1	ID 241.9	−ID 21.5

At the time of the negotiations that had culminated in the
promulgation of Law 80 in December 1961, it was known that
North Rumaila oilfield in southern Iraq contained very substantial
proven reserves of oil. However, the government could not allow
IPC to initiate production as this would enable it to consolidate its
monopoly position even further. Conversely, it was not possible
for Iraq to develop an independent oil policy *without* starting
production in North Rumaila, but this could only take place

within a framework that satisfied three main criteria: first, that Iraq's sovereignty would not be infringed; second, that IPC was not involved; and finally and most imponderably, that the sales and distribution of the oil actually produced should be undertaken without having recourse to the networks controlled by IPC and the oil majors.

The agreements with the Soviet Union in June 1969 satisfied the first two criteria, and the state of the world market in the late 1960s, combined with greater confidence on the part of the oil-producing countries in general, seems to have favoured the auguries for the satisfactory resolution of the third. Needless to say, the widely repeated *canard* that Iraq was simply substituting dependence on the Soviet Union for dependence on IPC was misconceived as well as inaccurate; Soviet assistance had been planned on a reducing scale, involving the construction of a set of key infrastructures, and did not involve an open-ended period of *sales*. In a variety of ways, therefore, the agreement satisfied long-established and widely held aspirations in Iraq, and was undoubtedly a feather in the regime's cap and further proof of its progressive intentions at a time when it was desperately trying to expand the basis of its support.

Relations with the ICP and KDP, 1969–1970

In the prevailing atmosphere of distrust between the Ba'th and the two other main political organisations, the Communist Party and the Kurdish Democratic Party, it was of vital importance for the regime to try to neutralise the potential opposition that both groups could muster, whether together or on their own. In spite of the severe depletion of its cadres during and after 1963, and the confusion caused by the breakaway of 'Aziz al-Hajj's Central Command group in 1967, the ICP had shown much of its traditional resilience, and still commanded a measure of support far beyond the circle of its official membership. As far as the Kurds were concerned, the Ba'th regime was 'ideologically' closer to the Ahmad/Talabani group, but was faced with the reality of Barzani's greater appeal in, and de facto control of, the Kurdish areas. In such circumstances the Ba'th seems to have realised fairly quickly that there was little to be gained in practical terms from attempting to set up Ahmad and Talabani as the 'real' Kurdish leadership.

After its early approaches to the Communists had been rebuffed, largely because of the Communists' unwillingness to participate in government before civil liberties were guaranteed or the ICP itself legalised, the regime continued its carrot and stick policy, continuing to negotiate with the Party leadership while simultaneously harassing rank and file members. An official Party declaration in November 1968 protested against Ba'thist interference in trade union elections, and accused the Ba'th militia of a series of attacks on Communists, including firing on strikers at a vegetable oil factory near Baghdad on 5 November, causing at least two deaths, the disruption of a protest demonstration on the anniversary of the Balfour Declaration, and a more serious incident on 7 November, when a demonstration commemorating the October Revolution was fired on by the National Guard, causing at least three deaths among the demonstrators[50].

Throughout 1969 and 1970 the ICP reiterated its demands for a coalition government with the Ba'th and what it described as other 'progressive national parties', but on conditions similar to their original demands, namely assurances of free speech, freedom to organise and the release of political prisoners[51]. At the same time the ICP was closely monitoring the government's policies, and was evidently impressed by the Soviet oil contracts in June and July 1969 and the award of a major concession for sulphur extraction to a Polish company a few weeks earlier[52]. Little progress towards agreement was made at this stage, but it is clear that the Ba'thists were anxious to come to some sort of arrangement with the Communists, who had more influence among certain sections of the population and in certain areas of the country than the Ba'th themselves. However, as before, formal concessions were accompanied by seemingly random acts of violence at 'street' level.

It was of the utmost importance for the Ba'th to be able either to weaken or in some way to absorb the Kurdish and Communist movements, which were still the two most important political forces within the country, without giving them any concessions in terms of actual power sharing, in order to expand its own power base. It was therefore necessary to keep the Communists at bay by means of relatively insignificant gestures, and at the same time to make it clear to them and to the world at large that it was the Ba'th who were in power and were going to stay there. Thus while the Communists were given permission to publish their monthly review, *al-Thaqafa al-Jadida* in March 1969, there were several

attacks on individuals, including the assassinations of Sattar
Khudayr al-Haidar and 'Abd al-Amir al-Sayyid in June and
September 1969[53].

Like the ICP, the various factions of the Kurdish movement
were suspicious of the Ba'th, although neither the KDP nor the
Kurds in general had suffered particularly in February 1963. In
fact, as we have described, the KDP had agreed to collaborate with
the Ba'th just before Qasim's overthrow, at least to the extent of
making an informal agreement to suspend hostilities in Kurdistan
to improve the plotters' chance of success[54]. Of course, neither the
Ba'th nor the nationalists had any interest in granting Kurdish
autonomy, and the KDP leadership soon fell out with them, with
the result that intermittent fighting both between the different
Kurdish factions and between Barzani and the various governments had been taking place since June 1963. Barzani's major
victory at Handrin in May 1966 had forced a temporary change in
government policy, culminating in the June Declaration on
Kurdish rights drawn up by the Prime Minister, 'Abd al-Rahman
al-Bazzaz. Because of opposition from the armed forces, the
Declaration had proved impossible to implement, and a period of
stalemate ensued, punctuated by sporadic fighting, which had
lasted over eighteen months by the time the Ba'th took over.

It seems likely that the Ba'th had made overtures both to Barzani
and his rivals in the period before July 1968. Although precise
details of these contacts are elusive[55], the fact that the cabinet of
the 30 July coup included representatives of *both* main Kurdish
factions (a notable coup for Ahmad and Talabani) suggests that
some minimal preparations must have been made. Although
Barzani withdrew his own men some three weeks later in protest at
Taha Muhi al-Din Ma'ruf's presence, he did not break off relations
with the regime entirely. At this stage neither the Ba'th nor Barzani
wanted any kind of showdown, Barzani presumably because he
feared that the Ba'th might be tempted to 'adopt' his enemies more
wholeheartedly, and the Ba'thists because they were not yet in a
position to resume the war in Kurdistan.

Indeed, the regime's first steps seemed promising. It was almost
immediately announced that the June 1966 Declaration should be
enforced and an amnesty was proclaimed for all those who had
taken part in the fighting. However, the regime continued to
favour the Ahmad/Talabani group, partly because it found them
more congenial and partly because it hoped to make some

progress in detaching Barzani's traditional supporters through the concessions that they were making. These tactics eventually goaded Barzani into action, both against his Kurdish rivals and against the regime itself, and in mid-December 1968 his forces attacked a train between Kirkuk and Arbil, killing twenty soldiers and civilians[56]. A period of serious fighting ensued, the first outbreak on this scale since the spring of 1966.

This potentially dangerous turn of events coincided with the 7th Regional Congress of the Ba'th Party, in the course of which, as we have seen, al-Bakr, Saddam Husain and their associates emerged as the majority group on the Revolutionary Command Council. Two considerations seem to have been uppermost in shaping the resolutions on the Kurdish question that emerged from the Congress. First, the regime was still profoundly insecure, and rested on an extremely narrow support base. Secondly, five months after the coup, the armed forces were by no means purged of those who might, under certain circumstances, wish to take power themselves, and the army and air force were the respective support bases of Salih Mahdi 'Ammash and Hardan al-Takriti, whose personal ambitions were very evident. For such reasons it would not do for the regime to let the conflict in Kurdistan be contained, still less in any sense decided, by the military. Accordingly, the Congress resolutions on the Kurdish question were mild and conciliatory, and stressed the need for a peaceful settlement based on the June 1966 Declaration. However, this more cautious approach on the part of the Ba'th, and its cordial relations with Ahmad and Talabani, seems to have put new heart into Barzani and his followers, who interpreted caution as a sign of weakness and proceeded to step up their operations once more as soon as the snows began to melt and the campaigning season started.

Early in March 1969 an audacious attack by Barzani's forces on the IPC installations at Kirkuk — using long range artillery almost certainly supplied by Iran — succeeded in causing some $5 million worth of damage and reducing oil pumping capacity by 70% for about ten days[57]. This marked a particularly serious escalation of the conflict, as the location of the plant made it almost impossible to defend against similar attacks in the future. The situation was further exacerbated by the Kurds' Iranian allies unilaterally abandoning the Saadabad Treaty in April 1969, claiming navigation rights in the Shatt al-'Arab on the grounds that it was an international waterway[58]. Although the Iranians had been using the Shatt al-'Arab without any particular regard for Iraqi sensibilities for the previous three or four years, the combination of an apparently harder line on Tehran's part with greatly increased financial and military assistance to the Kurds seemed to pose a major threat to the stability of the regime in Baghdad.

Again, the advocates of conciliation on the government side seem to have won the day; in a speech in Arbil in May, Sa'dun Ghaidan held out the promise of Kurdish autonomy, and on 28 June the government announced the creation of the new all-Kurdish province of Dohuk, which had been promised in the June 1966 Declaration[59]. The effects of such earnests of good intention were somewhat dampened by the government's counter-offensive in August; according to Kurdish sources (as usual, the campaign was not reported in the Iraqi media) the army massacred the inhabitants of two villages, Dakan and Sora, and a number of bombing raids were carried out on civilian targets[60].

Later in the autumn the regime appears to have reverted once more to a conciliatory policy; on 9 October several important linguistic and cultural concessions were announced[61], possibly the first fruits of the negotiations with Barzani that had been going on in secret since September through the intermediary of 'Aziz Sharif, a respected elder statesman of the Iraqi left[62]. By this time the Ba'th seems to have understood once and for all that however politically sophisticated the Ahmad/Talabani group might seem, its support on the ground in Kurdistan was relatively limited, and that the only way of arriving at a long term resolution of the Kurdish problem was to conclude a viable agreement with Barzani himself.

For obvious reasons the Ba'th's attitude towards the Kurds had been entirely governed by pragmatic considerations. In the first place, it was desirable and sensible that an acceptable solution should be achieved, and every effort was expended to this end, principally, as subsequent relations between the Kurds and the regime were to show, to give the latter the necessary breathing space to consolidate its own still shaky authority. Secondly, the Ba'th had learnt from its predecessors that, given the cordial relations between Iran and Barzani, the Kurds were, for all practical purposes, invincible in terms of the kind of offensive the Iraqi armed forces could mount against them. Finally, the continuation of this costly and apparently endless war in the North would undoubtedly strengthen the hand of the non-Ba'thist officers in the armed forces, who still constituted a potential source of opposition to the regime.

By January 1970 a businesslike dialogue was under way, conducted partly in Baghdad and partly at Barzani's headquarters in the North, led by Mahmud 'Uthman, Barzani's *chef du cabinet*, and Saddam Husain for the government, although the latter appears to have left the detailed negotiations to other members of the RCC[63]. The fragile stability of the Ba'th regime was dramatically underlined in the middle of the negotiations with the announcement of the discovery of the army plot at the end of January[64]. The swiftness and scale of the punishments suggested that the regime did have something tangible to be apprehensive of, over and above simply taking advantage of the situation to rid itself of a tiresome nucleus of opposition in the army, and it is also possible that the plotters may have been spurred on by indications that the negotiations with the Kurds were moving towards a conclusion that would greatly enhance the standing and stability of the government[65].

The negotiations ended with the publication by the government of the Manifesto of 11 March 1970. If actually implemented, this document would have gone as far as, if not further than, the Declaration of June 1966 towards a solution of the Kurdish question[66]. In essence, it recognised the 'legitimacy of the Kurdish nationality', and promised Kurdish linguistic rights, Kurdish participation in government, and Kurdish administrators for the Kurdish area. It also envisaged the implementation of the agrarian reform laws in the North, and perhaps most controversially, as future events were to show, stated that 'necessary steps will be taken to unify the governorates and administrative units populated by a Kurdish majority as shown by *the official census to be carried out*'[67] (our italics). If undertaken, such a census would almost certainly have shown a Kurdish majority in the area around Kirkuk, where the principal oilfields are located, and in other areas that were not included in what was eventually designated the 'autonomous area' in March 1974. The government's failure to implement this part of the Manifesto, and its deliberate efforts to change the ethnic composition of the Kirkuk area over the following years, which began almost immediately[68], boded ominously for the future of the Manifesto, although the fact that a watertight definition of the precise area under discussion had not been arrived at in advance made such controversy almost inevitable.

In fact, as future events were to show, the main function of the Manifesto was to enable the Ba'th to gain time and to establish itself sufficiently to be able to recast its Kurdish policy more to its own advantage at some future point, a purpose that it succeeded in serving at least for the next two years[69]. Barzani duly broke off relations with Iran, and gave his full, if somewhat reluctant, support to the Ba'th regime. A high level body, consisting of Kurdish and Ba'thist representatives, was charged with the task of working out the detailed application of the Manifesto over a four-year period. Thus, at least on the surface, the framework of a durable settlement appeared to have been laid, and the Party was able both to congratulate itself and to gain the approval of others (particularly the Communists) for its 'success' in having begun to 'solve' the Kurdish problem. With these negotiations with the Kurds under way, and the development of North Rumaila proceeding apace, the Ba'th leadership could now devote itself more single-mindedly to the task of consolidating its hold on the state apparatus.

The Ba'th and Black September

The Ba'th's trenchant and uncompromising stance on foreign policy matters was particularly evident from its apparent in-transigence on the Palestine question. After July 1968 it soon aligned itself with those Arab states and those factions of the PLO that rejected Resolution 242 and all other attempts to find a peaceful solution. Hence it was bound to oppose the Rogers plan, put forward by the United States at the end of 1969, and accepted by Israel, Egypt, Jordan and the Soviet Union by July 1970[70]. A virulent slanging match between Egypt and Iraq soon followed, with Iraq committing itself to 'the goal of liberating the whole of Palestine [by means of] armed struggle', and refusing to take part in the second Arab summit in Tripoli. Two days later, Nasser put a pertinent question to President al-Bakr in a letter read out on Cairo radio:

I do not conceal from Your Excellency that I sometimes

ask myself why your forces at the front [i.e. in Jordan]
have not at any time received orders to engage the enemy,
or why not a single one of your aircraft has raided enemy
positions.[71]

At this stage there were about 17,000 Iraqi troops stationed in
Jordan, with some 100 tanks.

At the very end of August 1970, Egypt, Jordan and Syria
withdrew from the Eastern Command, which left the Salah al-Din
forces, as the Iraqi contingent was called, as the only sizeable unit
of regular troops in the country other than the Jordanian army.
Earlier in 1970 there had been a number of more or less serious
clashes involving members of the various Palestinian guerilla
organisations and the Jordanian army. The root cause of the
clashes was King Husain's unwillingness to allow the guerillas to
operate freely in and from Jordan, and more generally the
challenge they appeared to pose to his own authority; it will be
remembered that it was not until 1974 that the PLO was recognised
by the Arab states as having the sole right to negotiate on behalf of
the Palestinians, a role that King Husain had assiduously sought
for himself since the 1960s.

At the beginning of September, Husain's forces began an all out
attack on the Palestinian guerillas; by the time the fighting ended,
some 300 Palestinians had been killed and some 10,000 wounded,
mostly civilians, with some 2000 casualties on the Jordanian
side[72]. On 1 September, Iraq declared that the shelling of the
guerillas by the Jordanian army had put Iraq firmly on the
guerillas' side, and Hardan al-Takriti, the Minister of Defence,
pledged Iraq's support to the Palestinians in ringing tones the next
day. On 9 September, Baghdad Radio announced:

> Revolutionary Iraq, which declared to the world that its
> forces were at the disposal of the Resistance forces,
> reaffirms to the masses that it will not remain idle in the
> face of current events in Jordan.[73]

In fact, Iraqi troops played no part whatsoever in the fighting, thus
substantially facilitating the victory of the Jordanian Army.
Although one of the guerillas actually denied the persistent
rumour that the Iraqis had gone so far as to permit Jordanian
troops to pass through Iraqi lines, his assertion that 'the

revolutionary regime in Iraq had given the Resistance great assistance in the form of arms, ammunition and supplies during the recent events in Jordan' was telling[74]. Similarly vigorous but essentially empty sabre-rattling was to be a prominent feature of Iraq's 'contributions' to the Palestine question throughout the 1970s and 1980s, which were almost always of a diversionary and disruptive nature.

Further Power Struggles: The Emergence of Saddam Husain

The war of words over Palestine waged on Baghdad radio in the autumn of 1970 accompanied, and to some extent concealed, the bitter struggle for supremacy within the higher echelons of the Ba'th that had been continuing intermittently since July 1968. This struggle centred primarily around the person of Saddam Husain, in the sense that the capacity of any other individual to remain in a position of power was almost entirely dependent on the degree of his acceptability to the Deputy Chairman of the RCC. Equally, those who disagreed with Saddam Husain, or who posed a threat, actual or potential, to his position, were either summarily dismissed, or, if they had a major power base of their own, gradually eased out[75].

In view of these highly personalised politics, it is of course absurd to analyse the struggles that accompanied the rise of Saddam Husain in *ideological* terms[76]; as well as investing an essentially sordid and violent series of events with a certain dignity, this characterisation obscures rather than clarifies the real nature of what was taking place, as if a historian of inter-war Chicago was to attempt to explain the interaction between Capone and his rivals in terms of competing political theories. Furthermore, since all internal Party decisions are secret, and as the RCC has never published a record or minutes of its proceedings, the details of actual decision-making are naturally a matter for conjecture[77]. Hence the account which follows, describing the events that culminated in the emergence of Saddam Husain, can only be based on an analysis of the *results* of the various steps taken by the leadership, since it is not possible to reconstruct the processes that produced these results.

At the end of 1969, and indeed for some time afterwards, there

were substantial pockets of opposition to al-Bakr and Saddam
Husain within both the armed forces and the party leadership[78].
One civilian member of the RCC, 'Abdullah Sallum al-Samarra'i,
the Minister of Culture and Information, was demoted to Minister
of State in December 1969, then dismissed from the RCC and put
out to grass as Iraq's ambassador in India in 1970. In November
1969, it was announced that the deputy premiership had been
abolished, a move directed against the two holders of the post,
Salih Mahdi 'Ammash and Hardan al-Takriti; as a result, neither
could chair cabinet meetings in Ahmad Hasan al-Bakr's absence.
Their powers were further reduced in April 1970, when both were
relieved of their ministries (and replaced by Sa'dun Ghaidan at
Interior and Hammad al-Shihab al-Takriti at Defence), and
appointed 'Deputy President'. A series of high level military
transfers and promotions accompanied this reshuffle.

All in all, it proved rather harder to get rid of 'Ammash and
Hardan al-Takriti than Saddam Husain had perhaps envisaged,
but eventually the events in Jordan in September 1970 provided
Husain and al-Bakr with the excuse they needed to remove
Hardan al-Takriti and purge his leading supporters from the
armed forces[79]. The non-intervention of the Iraqi Army on the side
of the Palestine Resistance could be laid fairly and squarely at the
door of Hardan al-Takriti as Deputy Commander-in-Chief of the
Armed Forces, and it was also widely put about that Saddam
Husain had favoured intervention but that Hardan had insisted
on thwarting his wishes[80]. Hardan was exiled to Algeria in October
1970, and later took refuge in Kuwait, where he was assassinated in
1971[81]. 'Ammash was not finally ousted until September 1971,
when he was appointed to the Iraqi Embassy in Moscow at the
same time as another of Saddam Husain's rivals, 'Abd al-Karim
al-Shaikhli, was also dismissed from the RCC and appointed
Iraq's representative at the United Nations. The various changes
between November 1969 and September 1971 are summarised in
Table 4.3.

However, although Saddam Husain had evidently managed to
establish himself as the strong man of the regime well before
September 1971 when 'Ammash and Shaikhli were dropped,
neither the degree to which he had succeeded in doing so nor the
means that he had employed to this end were entirely obvious to
the majority of Iraqis, including most members of the Ba'th Party.
This was because al-Bakr, Husain and their immediate circle

Table 4.3 *RCC Reshuffle, November 1969 to September 1971*

RCC November 1969	RCC September 1971
Ahmad Hasan al-Bakr	Still serving
Saddam Husain	Still serving
Hardan al-Takriti	Removed October 1970*
Salih Mahdi 'Ammash	Removed September 1971
Sa'dun Ghaidan	Still serving
Hammad Shihab	Still serving†
'Abd al-Karim al-Shaikhli	Removed September 1971
Salah 'Umar al-'Ali	Removed July 1970
'Abdullah Sallum al-Samarra'i	Removed (?) March 1970
'Abd al-Khaliq al-Samarra'i	Still serving‡
Shafiq Kamali	Removed (?) 1970
Taha al-Jazrawi (= Taha Yasin Ramadan)	Still serving
'Izzat Mustafa	Still serving
'Izzat al-Duri	Still serving
Murtada al-Hadithi	Still serving

* Assassinated in Kuwait, March 1971
† Killed by Nadhim Kazzar, July 1973
‡ Removed after Kazzar plot, July 1973[82]

always contrived to present their rule as that of the Ba'th Party as a whole, and to foster the image of the RCC (and the Regional Command, since all members of the RCC except Sa'dun Ghaidan were now also members of the Regional Command) as a collegiate body in which collective decisions were arrived at in a democratic fashion. This image of the 'Party in government' was further reinforced both by the systematic penetration by Party members of all governmental and military institutions and all mass organisations, and also in the media by the constant use of the Party's ideological cachet to legitimate the various pronouncements issued by the regime. Thus it was always 'the Party' or 'the Revolution' that was hailed as having brought the regime to power, and in whose name the totality of its actions were carried out. Of course, the leadership took great pains to build upon and improve the existing Party apparatus, with the result that by 1976, when the regime had been in power for eight years, the Party could claim some 10,000 'activists' (*'udu*) and half a million 'sympathisers' (*mu'ayyid*)[83]. While the Ba'th was still trying to secure itself in power in the years after July 1968, fairly strict vetting procedures were imposed upon aspiring members, but such restrictions had virtually ceased to be applied by the end of 1973.

Although many of those who flocked into the Party in the middle 1970s were undoubtedly motivated by opportunistic considerations, the Ba'th was also able to win more genuine converts to its ranks by drawing upon a long established canon of populist–nationalist ideology, particularly suitable for mass mobilisation and mass organisation, which had been developed by Michel 'Aflaq since the middle 1950s. In the nature of things, the Party had increasingly little difficulty in attracting members the longer it held on to power, and particularly when it became clear that personal, political, economic and social advancement were to become intimately dependent on an individual's connections with or within the Party. In addition, of course, the regime's growing insistence on extracting positive affirmations of loyalty from civil servants and others (rather than tacit acquiescence in its authority), and its well-known ruthlessness towards its opponents, also assisted Party recruitment. Even more importantly, the Ba'th made strenuous efforts either to include or to gain popular support from much wider sections of the Iraqi population than the 'Arif brothers had done, and here 'the Party', with its populist/nationalist doctrines, was to play an important role.

Social and Economic Policies, 1968–1972

The agreement with Barzani in March 1970 came some nine months after the successful conclusion of negotiations with the Soviet Union for the future development of the North Rumaila oilfield, and the Ba'th seems to have acquired new confidence from these signs of its apparent ability to solve some of the country's more pressing political and economic problems, particularly as their solution had so evidently eluded its predecessors. It is impossible to assess the actual effects of the regime's economic policies in these early years, but it is important to mention some of the main items of social and economic legislation that were introduced, and which helped to further its image as a 'progressive' and 'leftist' government.

The agrarian reform legislation since 1958 had succeeded in breaking the social and political power of the semi-feudal landlords, thus facilitating the more rapid penetration of market relations into the countryside, but it had not destroyed the dominance of private ownership of land and agricultural machinery. The speed with which the reforms were enacted and the widespread inexperience of those who were in charge of applying them meant that the pace and extent of the reforms had begun to falter well before Qasim's fall in February 1963. Although sequestration had been carried out fairly quickly[84], distribution was rather slow, and this had had the effect of leaving large areas either uncultivated or available for rent[85]. Living conditions in the countryside in the decade since the Revolution of 1958 had remained extremely backward, and it was obviously necessary that the regime should be seen to be concerning itself with the situation of the rural poor if its radical postures were to be taken at all seriously. Apart from the enormous practical difficulties that those who framed the Law had apparently not foreseen, such as the failure to substitute appropriate managerial and credit institutions for the administrative and credit facilities hitherto provided by the landlords, the 1958 Law (and the amendment of 1964) also required the payment of compensation to the former landlords by the beneficiaries, a provision that was very unpopular at the local level.

At the beginning of 1969, it was announced that these compensation payments would be cancelled, and in May 1970 a 'much more sophisticated'[86] agrarian reform was promulgated, with the size of plot per beneficiary now being more carefully related to factors such as location, access to water and soil fertility. New cooperatives and extension services were created over the next few years, and the average annual percentage of development expenditure devoted to agriculture rose from 16.75% over the period 1965/1968 to 34.25% over the period 1969/1972[87]. Nevertheless, while the pattern of tenure was evidently changing in the peasants' favour in comparison with the situation before 1968, and their standard of living was certainly improving, property relations in the countryside were still slanted in favour of the big and middle landowners. In 1972, the last year for which data on the size and distribution of holdings appears in the official statistics, less than 3% of all landlords still owned at least 30% of all agricultural land[88] (see Table 4.4).

Table 4.4 *Size and Distribution of Land Holdings, 1972*

Size of Holding	Percentage of Total Area	Percentage of Landlords
0–25 acres	32.2	79.6
25–75 acres	36.5	17.7
Over 75 acres	31.3	2.7

On the other hand, there were signs of progress in the rural areas, particularly with the wider provision of health and educational services, although the introduction of these facilities was accompanied by increasing state control over the countryside and the wider propagation of Ba'thist doctrines there.

In addition to this major agrarian reorganisation, the regime also enacted a series of measures between 1969 and 1971 regulating such matters as conditions of work, labour unions, pensions and social security. The new laws set minimum wages and maximum working hours, prohibited child labour and protected workers against arbitrary dismissal[89]. A comprehensive national insurance scheme was introduced in 1971 on the basis of pension and social security contributions from employees, employers and the government. In October 1970 a new Labour Law regulated the organisation of cooperatives and trade unions; 'all accounts and records of cooperatives and unions were made subject to government supervision, and . . . members who violate[d] the laws . . . would be subject to penalties'[90].

Unfortunately, there has been no 'unofficial' research on the Iraqi labour force since 1958, with the result that there is no empirical evidence of the effect of these and other measures on workers and employees[91]. However, while the new laws apparently provided workers 'with a security which they have never enjoyed before'[92], their long term effect has been to incorporate the labour force into the political system and to create exclusively 'Party unions', which have come entirely under the control of the Ba'th, and have thus lost the independence[93] for which they had struggled in the course of the 1940s and 1950s[94]. Nevertheless, the effect of the ensemble of these and other decrees on 'left-leaning' Iraqis at the time should not be under-estimated. The Ba'th appeared to have turned over a new leaf and now seemed anxious

to satisfy many of the demands that had traditionally been put
forward by the Communists and the left.

The Uneasy Road to Reconciliation: The Ba'th, the Communists and the Kurds, 1970–1972

The Ba'th's relations with the Communists in the period before the
nationalisation of the Iraq Petroleum Company in June 1972 were
at least partly conditioned by the state of its relations with Barzani
and the KDP. This was particularly evident after the negotiations
culminating in the Manifesto of March 1970, which ushered in a
brief period of Ba'th/Kurdish amity and gave the Ba'th sufficient
confidence to resume its verbal and physical attack on the
Communists. On 23 March, the body of Muhammad Ahmad al-
Khadri, a prominent Baghdad Communist, was found in the
street, and there were reports in the spring and summer from
Communist sources outside Iraq of numerous arrests and assassinations of ICP members[95]. Judging from the regime's own
pronouncements at the time, the Ba'thists knew that the Communist's conditions were unacceptable. In June, speaking to a
mass rally in Kirkuk, where he shared the platform with Idris and
Mas'ud Barzani, Taha Jazrawi complained: 'We extended our
hand to the ICP and other national forces . . . but our calls [were]
either rejected or . . . met with frustrating conditions'[96].

The Ba'th's exasperation at the Communists' continuing unwillingness to participate in a National Progressive Front was
expressed in some detail in the media a few weeks later. The tone
of these statements is a further indication of the regime's evident
distaste for the Communists on the one hand, and on the other of
its recognition that, given the nature of the social and economic
programmes it was attempting to implement, and its growing
reliance on the Soviet Union and the socialist countries in the
continuing battle with IPC, it was increasingly in need of their
positive support. Thus the Communists were criticised for their
support of Qasim, and also, rather paradoxically, because they
'never took power and never staged a revolution'. They were also
roundly criticised for:

> Their unjustifiable campaign of lies and distortions [sc.
> against the Ba'th] They [carry out this campaign] despite

the fact that this authority acted in an admirably democratic manner when it released all [sic] political prisoners, including the Communists and reinstated them in their jobs ... [This] means that the Communist leaders have failed to make their political attitudes and behaviour consistent with their ideological concepts and principles. Consequently they are incapable of leadership. This means that the Communists have no right to lead the National Front because they lack the ability to lead.[97]

The implication is, of course, that only the Ba'th is entitled to lead because it had 'set off the revolution single-handed', and that in the event of a national front being formed it must be understood that the participating bodies must accept Ba'thist hegemony. Thus what was proposed was not a form of genuine power-sharing but an alliance in which the Ba'th was to be the senior and dominant partner. The Communists' evident unwillingness to accept such conditions at the time was castigated as 'irresponsible negativeness' by President al-Bakr in the course of a press conference on 20 July 1970[98].

Although the National Front that actually materialised in 1973 was an arrangement that did not differ very materially from the one just described, it is fair to point out that by that time the Ba'th were giving what appeared to be earnests of their good intentions in a manner and to an extent that the Communists found difficult to continue to ignore. It is also important to recall that the Communist parties of the Third World were very much influenced at this time by theories of the 'non-capitalist road' to socialism and the 'objectively progressive' role of the national bourgeoisie, which were much in vogue in the Soviet Union and the socialist countries in the early 1970s and indeed for some time afterwards[99]. Thus at its Second National Congress in September 1970, the ICP praised the Ba'th regime's positive achievements in the social and economic fields and its avowedly anti-Zionist and anti-imperialist foreign policy, while criticising the continuing absence of democratic liberties and the suppression of the 'struggle of the masses for freedom'[100].

In the months that followed, the Communists were faced with the cruel paradox of increasing attacks and harassments from the Ba'th at the same time as increasing evidence of the regime's efforts to cement its relations with the socialist countries. Thus in

January 1971, commenting on the increase in trade with Eastern Europe, a member of the RCC stated 'The socialist countries are our friends, and we buy from our friends'[101]. On the other hand, the Communists announced a few weeks later that they would not take part in trade union elections because of extensive intimidation and malpractice on the part of the Ba'th authorities. Again, in the course of the year, a number of Communists were arrested and later either found dead — in such cases, as in Argentina or Guatemala, the regime would deny knowledge or responsibility — or tortured to death in prison. Among the more prominent victims at this time were Qasim Jawad, 'Aziz Hamid, Thabit Habib al-'Ani and Shaikh 'Ali al-Barzanchi[102]. By November 1971, however, the regime began to change its tactics, professing to be more seriously interested in forging a durable alliance with the ICP, although Communists were still being arrested, tortured and imprisoned[103].

Part of the reason for what was to become an increasingly evident change of direction was the deterioration of relations between the Ba'th and the Kurds, although the appearance of continuing Ba'th/Kurdish cordiality was maintained long after this ceased to be any reflection of reality. For the first few months after the announcement of the Manifesto of March 1970, everything seemed to be proceeding according to plan: Barzani's guerillas, the Peshmerga, were redeployed, demobilised, or otherwise brought into line[104]; regular meetings of the Ba'th/Kurdish joint supervisory committee and other friendly high-level encounters were reported[105]; schoolbooks were being printed in Kurdish[106]; Muhammad Sulaiman, a Sudanese member of the Ba'th National Command, attended the KDP's 8th Congress at Nawperdan in July, and fraternal greetings were duly exchanged between the two parties on appropriate occasions. The high watermark of this period was the inclusion of a number of clauses in the new (provisional) constitution of July 1970, stating explicitly for the first time that 'The People of Iraq is formed of two principal nationalities, the Arab nationality and the Kurdish nationality. This constitution shall recognise the national rights of the Kurdish people and the legitimate rights of all minorities within the unity of Iraq'. In addition, Kurdish was made the official language in the Kurdish region, and 'The area whose majority of population is Kurdish shall enjoy autonomy in accordance with what is defined by the law'[107].

It did not take long for cracks to appear in the facade; naturally enough, since, essentially, the regime was buying time and not seriously concerned to implement Kurdish autonomy. For his part, Barzani clearly intended that Kirkuk should be the capital of the 'autonomous area' rather than the regime's choice, Arbil. If a census had been taken, it would have shown that the area round Kirkuk, where the main oilfields were located, had a substantial and most probably a majority Kurdish population, but, precisely for that reason, none was ever taken, in spite of constant complaints from the Kurdish side that the regime was dragging its feet on the issue[108]. Another early rebuff for the KDP was the Ba'th's refusal to accept its nominee for the vice-presidency, Habib Karim, in September 1970[109], and the lengths to which Barzani's enemies (whether fellow Kurds or members of the regime) were prepared to go to thwart him were revealed after a botched attempt to assassinate his son Idris early in December 1970[110].

This uneasy atmosphere continued throughout 1971, with the appearance of correct and friendly relations being maintained even after the spectacular failure of an attempt to assassinate Barzani himself in September, which, even if allegedly master-minded by the notorious Nadhim Kazzar, was carried out at a time when Kazzar enjoyed the full backing and protection of Saddam Husain. In May 1971, Saddam Husain took over the chairmanship of the Ba'th/Kurdish committee, presumably in an attempt to speed matters along, and perhaps also in view of the evidently impending crisis in Iraq's relations with Iran, in which it would be clearly to Baghdad's advantage to have Barzani more firmly on its side. However, Barzani himself had never been entirely convinced by the Ba'th's protestations of good faith, and, as we shall see, Iran's increasing belligerency and its evident intention to act as the United States' stalking horse in the Gulf after Britain's withdrawal at the end of 1971[111] seems eventually to have persuaded him that a closer alliance with Tehran would offer him greater security than the vague and generally inadequate assurances he had been able to extract from Baghdad.

However, at the end of 1971 the final rupture still lay some way ahead, and the Ba'th's National Action Charter, announced in mid-November, seemed to represent another attempt to gather support for the regime from as many quarters as possible. The Charter reiterated the main points of the March Manifesto on Kurdish autonomy; spoke about reorganising the national economy, freeing it from foreign dependence and developing relations with 'friendly and socialist countries'; declared that the state was responsible for guiding economic activity and that the target of the revolution would be 'the liberation of oil wealth from foreign domination and exploitation'; and stressed the regime's intention to seek 'the realisation of the broadest coalition among all the national, patriotic and progressive elements in a democratic, popular and unitary system'[112].

There were good reasons for this appeal. By the autumn of 1971, the regime found itself threatened simultaneously from a number of different quarters. In the first place, there was the long-standing dispute with Iran over the Shatt al-'Arab and other parts of the frontier, which had taken on a new and potentially ominous dimension with Britain's departure from the Gulf, the simultaneous creation of the United Arab Emirates and the well-publicised increase in American military supplies to Iran[113]. Iraq's relations with most Arab countries were scarcely more cordial; the Sa'udis and most of the new rulers of the Gulf were both suspicious and fearful of what the Ba'th might do; the Syrians regarded the regime as heretical in Ba'thist terms (and apart from a brief and rather half-hearted attempt at reconciliation in 1978–79 have generally maintained this attitude); the Jordanians were not a major force in the Middle East in the early 1970s, and in any case regarded Iraq's radical posturings over Palestine with understandable, if in fact unwarranted, alarm; and relations with Egypt, already sour under Nasser, had deteriorated further under his successor. Further afield, although trade continued to be fairly buoyant, Iraq's formal relations with the West were in some disarray. Relations with the United States had been broken off in 1967; two British diplomats were asked to leave the country as *personae non gratae* in July 1971, and diplomatic relations with Britain (and Iran) were broken off on 30 November 1971 following Iran's occupation of three small islands in the Gulf, the Tunbs and Abu Musa. The boom in Iraqi/West German and Iraqi/Japanese relations was still to come, which meant that Iraq's only firm West European 'friend' was France. Apart from this connection, whose importance in 1971–72 can hardly be over-estimated, the ensemble of Iraq's diplomatic, political and economic future was predicated almost exclusively on its relations with the Soviet Union and the other Comecon countries.

The Background to the Nationalisation of the Iraq Petroleum Company

One important reason for Iraq's political isolation from the West at this point was its uneasy relations with IPC, which had deteriorated further since the signature of the agreement with the Soviet Union to develop the North Rumaila oilfield in 1969. In the 1960s, IPC was the 'chief financier of the ... government'[114], providing an average of 80.4% of total government revenue between 1959 and 1970. The only way that the government could increase these revenues was by initiating the production of more oil, but, apart from North Rumaila, oil production was entirely controlled by IPC. Although the international price of oil rose substantially after the Tehran Agreement in 1971, Iraq remained a relatively poor country, with income per capita less than $120 in that year, about a third of the amount it was to reach only six years later[115].

Hence for Iraq to develop, or even to keep pace with the rate of its own population growth, a substantial increase in oil revenues was essential, and it was very evident that IPC was either unable or unwilling to respond to the pressures for greater production from the Iraqi side. Exactly how apprehensive the Company was at the obvious signs of progress emanating from North Rumaila is difficult to gauge, but its negotiators did not seem particularly flexible in 1971 and 1972. In fact, the sudden fall in shipments from the Mediterranean terminals in the autumn of 1971[116] showed the Iraqis how vulnerable they still were in spite of the Tehran price rise, and this is likely to have been an important factor in encouraging the Ba'th to try to forge closer political alliances at home.

At this stage, in the autumn of 1971, IPC (and its associates the Basra Petroleum Company, BPC, and the Mosul Petroleum Company, MPC) were producing all the oil in Iraq. Although it had been formed in 1964, INOC, the national oil company, had no physical plant until 1968, and had not yet started production in any of the parts of the concession area that the government had repossessed under the terms of Law 80 of 1961. In a major speech in November 1971, a few days after the proclamation of the National Action Charter, President al-Bakr hinted to IPC that the regime had no intention of letting the present unsatisfactory situation continue, and, as we have seen, the Charter itself had suggested that the regime was thinking of taking a stronger line with the Company. Moreover, events in the Gulf in November and December 1971 and Libya's nationalisation of BP (which held a 23.75% share in IPC) in December also encouraged the regime to take more positive steps, evidently fortified by the knowledge that North Rumaila would begin production in the spring of 1972; at that point 'markets [would be] about the only card IPC [would have] to play'[117].

A few days after the publication of the National Action Charter, a Communist Party spokesman, the economist Safa' al-Hafidh, declared that the document contained 'certain very positive elements'[118], and it is clear that the Communists regarded it as a *prise de position* to which they could make a constructive response. The rationale behind the Communists' subsequent alliance with the Ba'th will be discussed in more detail below[119], but it can be appreciated that, along with the Ba'th's domestic and international enemies, the Communists (from a different perspective but for essentially similar reasons) regarded the regime's policy of friendship with the Soviet Union, its expressed determination to arrive at an appropriate settlement of the Kurdish problem, and its apparent desire to end the IPC monopoly as mounting and ultimately convincing evidence of commitment to a left-leaning political line. For the regime's enemies, this served to confirm its negative character, while the Communists found themselves under increasing pressure to give their support to policies for which, at least in broad outline, they themselves had been agitating for years.

At the end of December 1971 it was announced that negotiations would soon take place with IPC in an effort to resolve the differences between the Company and the government. On 13 January, Baghdad Radio assured listeners that 'Iraq's full rights [will] be wrested from the oil companies . . . and there [will] be no bargaining of concessions affecting the people's interests'. The talks made no immediate progress, and were adjourned after a week; Saddam Husain immediately flew to Moscow with a high level delegation, calling for a 'solid strategic alliance with the Soviet Union'[120]. At the same time, Mukarram Talabani, a member of the central committee of the Iraqi Communist Party, confirmed in Beirut that serious discussions were under way between the Ba'th and the Communists on the basis of the terms of the National Action Charter.

While conceding that there were still disagreements 'on a number of issues', Talabani affirmed the ICP's wholehearted support for the Ba'th's apparently serious intention to solve the Kurdish problem and its anti-imperialist stand[121]. By April, the ICP had come out more unequivocally in support of the Ba'th, asserting that recent developments 'marked a turning point in the people's struggle' and declaring its willingness to participate in a National Progressive Front[122]. In March, negotiations with IPC were resumed, and the principle that the Iraq government would be permitted 20% equity participation in the Company (in line with OPEC resolutions) was agreed; on 7 April, Alexei Kosygin, the Soviet Prime Minister, personally inaugurated production at North Rumaila, and two days later he and al-Bakr signed a fifteen-year Iraqi–Soviet Friendship Treaty, providing for cooperation in political, economic, technical, cultural and other fields. It was obviously impossible for the Communist Party to distance itself from such a dazzling achievement.

These were certainly heady days. A week after the opening ceremony, the first shipment of North Rumaila oil left Fao for the Soviet Union; a series of sales deals for the new oil had been concluded with governmental agencies or private firms in Brazil, Italy, the USSR and the GDR in the course of February and March. The rapprochement with the Communists was given concrete form by the appointment of 'Amir 'Abdullah and Mukarram Talabani to the cabinet on 15 May; three days later, the government delivered an ultimatum to IPC, to the effect that it must either restore previous production levels and sort out its outstanding differences with the government, or face national-isation. The Company refused, and was duly nationalised on 1 June; Syria followed suit a few hours later[123]. No action by any Iraqi government since the 1958 Revolution was greeted with such universal enthusiasm, and the Ba'th was able to live off the moral capital it generated for many years.

IPC immediately threatened (and actually initiated) legal proceedings against purchasers of 'its' oil, and it was by no means clear, in spite of all the efforts that had been made to arrange sales with other countries, whether sufficient money would in fact be forthcoming from these sources to fund the country's ambitious development projects, or even to pay its armed forces and civil service. Iraq was not greatly beloved in OPEC, whose members feared that she might resort in desperation to flooding the world market with cheap oil[124]. However, Saddam Husain and his colleagues had obtained the maximum amount of assurance both from the socialist countries and their own political rivals before taking any irrevocable steps; even so, they could not have known that a settlement with IPC would be arrived at within eight months, still less that long term marketing problems would be solved once and for all in the aftermath of the fourth Arab/Israeli War in October 1973.

Chapter Five
1972–1975

The situation of the Ba'th during the period between the nationalisation of IPC in June 1972 and the Algiers Agreement in March 1975 continued to be both precarious and vulnerable. In order to establish its position securely the Ba'th had to overcome two interconnected obstacles. In the first place, it had to obtain the support, or at least the acquiescence, of those political forces and organisations that had traditionally been radical and/or supported the Communist Party, and thereby to gain support on a scale that had eluded it so far. Secondly, it was clear that the Ba'th would have to bring the Kurds securely under control if it wanted to establish its rule in all parts of the country, and more generally to create the stable conditions that were an essential prerequisite for the consolidation of its power.

Since coming to power the Ba'th had succeeded in achieving both these objectives to a certain extent, validating its left-wing credentials by a series of apparently progressive policies, and keeping the Communists at bay partly by stealing their clothes in this way and partly through a combination of repression and conciliation. As far as the Kurds were concerned, the Ba'th leadership had attempted to buy time for itself by the March Manifesto of 1970, which not only freed its hands for the time being but also contributed to the 'progressive' image that it was trying to project as part of its drive for populist support. All this had been necessary before going ahead with the nationalisation of IPC, an act that, as well as being widely acclaimed in itself, helped to overcome much of the Ba'th's unpopularity.

A further consequence of the nationalisation was that the state now had absolute control over the country's oil resources, which greatly increased its power. However, when Mulla Mustafa turned out to be unimpressed by the nationalisation, continued to press for the implementation of the Manifesto and resumed the fighting in Kurdistan, the Ba'th began to pursue a clearer policy of cooperation with the Communist Party, inviting the ICP to join them in a National Front. Although the formalisation of the Front did not take place before the fall of Kazzar in 1973, it seems certain that the inclusion of the Communists as the major 'partner' of the Ba'th at that precise point was related as much to the new threat being posed by the Kurds as it was to the need felt by Saddam Husain and his allies to strengthen their position within the party leadership by incorporating the Communists in circumstances under which such a step could not pose any threat to their own rule.

Another factor complicating the situation was that the apparently radical and 'anti-imperialist' stance taken by the Ba'th inevitably aroused expectations of a wider degree of political participation than the leadership was, in the long run, prepared to permit. Furthermore, while appealing to the progressive constituency within the country by constant references to 'building socialism', and even initiating wide-ranging discussions on how this might be achieved, the Ba'th was alienating itself from its 'natural allies' among the middle classes and other social groups not in favour of such policies. On the other hand, as events were to show, this alienation was never total, and the Ba'th's capacity to tap this key reservoir of support enabled it to modify many of the developments that it had promoted in the first place.

This period of Ba'th rule until March 1975 is both confusing and contradictory, in which things are rarely what they seem. In the context of the various middle strata, it is clear that although the Ba'th's apparent enthusiasm for 'socialism' and its alliances with the Soviet Union and the Iraqi Communist Party must have caused considerable misgivings, some of these policies brought them quite tangible benefits. Greater state control over a rapidly expanding and developing economy necessarily implied greater state expenditure, and thus almost unlimited opportunities for those in a position to undertake the wide range of tenders offered in such fields as the construction of roads, schools and hospitals, and equipping what was virtually an entire industrial sector. Furthermore, protectionist policies, import controls[1] and the generous provision of cheap credit enabled industrialists and businessmen alike to make substantial profits without having to risk either their own capital or foreign competition[2]. In these circumstances, the alliance between the Communists and the Ba'th was almost bound to be short-lived, although this seems not to have been obvious to the West, the Soviet Union, the Communists, or even many of the Ba'th themselves at the time.

For the time being, however, the regime's apparently decisive turn towards the left, symbolised by the oil nationalisation, the Soviet Friendship Treaty, and the formation of the National Patriotic Front, aroused a wave of hostility both in the West and in the more conservative states in the Gulf. One of the consequences of this was that Iran became more closely involved in the affairs of Iraqi Kurdistan in an attempt to weaken the regime in Baghdad, supplying Barzani with extensive quantities of money and sophisticated weapons. As a result, the Ba'th was able to portray itself as the victim of campaigns and conspiracies masterminded by 'Western imperialism' and carried out by the West's local 'agents', and as the champion of progress in the face of attacks from the 'reactionary' Shah of Iran. In such circumstances, the Iraqi Communists felt that they could do no less than give the regime their support. However, given the Ba'th's fundamentally anti-Communist outlook, and Saddam Husain's personal inclination to maintain as absolute control as possible over the state apparatus in the regime's hands, it became clear that once the regime had managed to find the most effective way of dealing with the Kurds — which turned out to be by making its peace with Iran — it no longer had any pressing need for the Communists, nor, for that matter, of the Soviet Union, and almost immediately began to cast about for more congenial partners.

For and Against the National Patriotic Front

Although the first Communist ministers had been appointed to the Cabinet in May 1972[3], it was not until July 1973 that the Communist Party took the collective decision to participate in the National Patriotic Front. Despite the Ba'th's socialist rhetoric and its declared enthusiasm for the Soviet Union, a degree of profound distrust continued to characterise relations between the two parties, particularly on the part of the Communist rank and file, who had suffered so grievously at the hands of the Ba'th only a few years before. However, precisely because of the line the regime now appeared to be pursuing, the Communist leadership found it difficult to continue to withhold its support, or, ultimately, to reject the Ba'th's proposals for a closer alliance between the two parties. It was clear, however, that any such alliance would be one between unequals, as all centres of power and coercion within the state were, and would certainly continue to be, firmly in the hands of the Ba'th alone[4].

However, the legalisation of the Party that accompanied the constitution of the Front gave the Communists more freedom to disseminate party literature and to recruit new members. The Communist leaders also believed that they would be able to influence some of the Ba'th leaders, particularly Saddam Husain, who was now made out to be almost a second Castro, in view of his increasingly congenial initiatives in domestic and foreign affairs. It was also the case that the Soviet Union and the socialist countries made no secret of their approval of the principle of a Front, and strongly urged the ICP to abandon its reservations and join in[5].

In retrospect, the Communists' adhesion to the Front seems an almost suicidal act, and indeed it appeared so at the time to many Iraqis, both Communists and non-Communists. For others, however, the presence of two Communist ministers in the cabinet, the ability to publish a weekly paper and a monthly discussion journal (admittedly both subject to considerable self-censorship), greater freedom of manoeuvre, and the possibility of a return, after over a decade of persecution or at least enforced clandestinity, to some semblance of normal life, seemed to represent substantial achievements for the Party. Many regarded the opportunities that now seemed to be presented as the beginning of a period in which the Party would be able to rebuild and consolidate its cadres, and re-establish its links with the mass organisations (women, youth, students, trade unions, and so forth), with which it had been traditionally associated. For others, the Front held out the possibility of a return to Iraq, sometimes after years of exile abroad, with the added incentive of being able to engage in legal political activity.

The Party's decision to enter the Front in 1973 must also be considered against the background of its evaluation of the situation in the Middle East and Iraq in 1959[6], which had led the Party to the decision not to attempt to seize power when the opportunity had presented itself. As the line had never been revised, largely because this unique opportunity had passed, and as there were no possibilities for any form of democratic participation in government, the ICP had no alternative but to support the government of the day or go underground. The logical extension of the 1959 line some fourteen years later was that, at least for the time being, some form of power-sharing with an apparently progressive and left-leaning partner was the most the Party could expect. This approach also accorded with an important general principle of Soviet policy in the region, which was that the Soviet Union itself preferred to work with governments rather than with opposition parties wherever possible[7].

In spite of the arguments in favour of the formation of a Front, many Communists continued to have serious misgivings. Apart from their antipathy to many aspects of Ba'thist dogma and their conviction that anti-Communism was too integral a part of Ba'thism ever to be discarded, they felt that the nature and extent of the proposed Communist participation in government would have severely negative repercussions for the Party. Critics of the idea of a Front also felt that an alliance between the Communists and the Ba'th would simply have the effect of muzzling the regime's most vociferous and best organised opponents, and furthermore, that any association with the Ba'th would discredit the Party, particularly in the eyes of those who had suffered at the hands of the Ba'th, both in 1963 and since 1968. There was also a strong feeling that the Ba'th leadership was simply making use of the Communists, and that, sooner or later, it would turn against them once more.

Ba'th Party members were also divided in their attitudes to an alliance with the Communists. Those on the left of the Party, who were more seriously committed to constructing some form of socialism, welcomed it; many others, who had been more attracted by the nationalist side of Ba'thism, and who had been greatly influenced by a variety of anti-Communist sentiments and particularly by allegations of Communist responsibility for the 'massacres' in Mosul and Kirkuk in 1959[8], either acquiesced reluctantly or were vehemently hostile. In spite of these varying attitudes, the formation of the Front clearly served to consolidate the position of the regime within Iraq, and, as a corollary, to isolate it further from its 'moderate' neighbours.

The Consequences of the Nationalisation of IPC

Although the economic difficulties caused by the nationalisation of IPC turned out to be comparatively short-lived, the regime could scarcely have afforded to proceed on this assumption at the time. Thus the decision not to nationalise the Mosul Petroleum Company and the Basra Petroleum Company, both wholly-owned subsidiaries of IPC and thus playing exactly the same 'exploitative' and 'monopolist' role as the parent company, showed a fair degree of pragmatism. Between them, the two smaller companies accounted for about 25% of Iraqi oil production, which could still be disposed of through normal channels. The immediate task was to find alternative outlets for the remainder of the oil formerly produced by IPC, now renamed the Iraqi Company for Oil Operations (ICOO). Some arrangements had already been made with the Soviet Union and other (mainly socialist) countries before nationalisation, but these appear to have involved mostly barter or credit facilities[9] that provided goods or technical assistance, rather than income, in return for Iraqi oil. Hence, throughout the negotiations with IPC, in which, judging from the tenor of the discussions, 'each side knew that the outcome . . . would probably be . . . nationalisation . . . before very long', the Iraqis had been particularly careful to try to preserve good relations with France, the second largest purchaser of Iraqi oil[10].

Accordingly, almost immediately after the nationalisation of IPC, its French participant company, Compagnie Française des Pétroles, was offered 'special treatment'[11], and a few days later, at the end of a state visit to France by Saddam Husain, an agreement was concluded under which Iraq undertook to sell France 23.75% of the oil produced by ICOO operations. This effectively restored the supply situation to what it had been before nationalisation, since the amount corresponded exactly to CFP's former share in IPC. Over the next few months, mediators from CFP and OPEC organised meetings between the two sides, and compensation terms that have been described as generous to IPC[12] were arranged in February 1973. After the third Arab-Israeli War in October 1973, the Dutch and American shares in BPC were nationalised, followed by Gulbenkian's share a few weeks later; by December 1975 all the remaining foreign holdings had been taken over[13].

Of course, in comparison with the situation in Iran in 1951-53, when Muhammad Musaddiq's attempted takeover of the Anglo-Iranian Oil Company was countered by the Company simply cutting back production by 95%[14], the Iraqi regime had carried out its nationalisation at a time when OPEC had begun to develop some cutting edge as a sellers' cartel, and also at a time when oil purchasing governments were generally more concerned to ensure stable markets for their goods and the stability of supplies for their countries' greatly increased consumption than to secure 'justice' for the oil companies. By mid-June 1972, several governmental delegations and numerous freelance oil salesmen had already arrived in Baghdad to make offers for Iraqi crude[15], and by the end of August major deals had been concluded with energy ministries and other state oil organisations in Japan, India, Greece and Brazil[16]. An important feature of these arrangements was that even at a time when political and economic relations with the socialist countries seemed at their closest, the regime was always careful to maintain solid commercial links with the West.

As far as the domestic economy was concerned, some austerity measures had been enforced before nationalisation, and more were introduced in the summer and autumn of 1972. Travel and foreign exchange operations were strictly controlled, and imports for 1972 (ID 235 mn) were slightly down on 1971 (ID 248 mn). However, by April 1973 most of these austerity measures had been lifted; Saddam Husain's warning at a Peasant Union rally in June 1972 that Iraq would have to live for two years as a non-oil producing country proved unduly pessimistic[17]. Politically, the regime took every opportunity to make use of the nationalisation to bolster its support among the population by creating a feeling of victorious euphoria throughout Iraq.

The nationalisation of IPC brought the country behind the Ba'th as no other policy had done or could have done, and the regime made the fullest possible use of the new mood, by encouraging the belief that the victory over the Company was not won by the Ba'th Party alone but by the Iraqi people under the Party's leadership, a line that was also part and parcel of the Ba'th's own image as the standard bearer of the Arab nation. In a

speech on 1 March 1973 outlining the main features of the final
settlement that had been concluded with IPC the previous day, al-
Bakr declared:

> Compatriots, congratulations to you on your victory.
> Congratulations to you on this honourable result of
> your battle, which you have waged confidently and
> determinedly. ... You have truly proved what we said
> on 1st June [1972] — that the battle we are waging
> against the oil companies is a model of the great battles
> which are rightly called the battles of history, because it
> heralds the beginning of a new stage that puts to the test
> the steadfastness and capability of our masses and their
> national and progressive forces.[18]

Six months later, Iraq broke ranks with the other Arab oil
producers by refusing to reduce output and sales after the October
War, although sales to Holland, Portugal and the United States
were officially suspended for a time[19]. Claiming to be working for
the 'real' interests of the Arabs, the Iraqi regime criticised the
embargo and cutback policy as misconceived, and declared its
readiness to 'supply oil to all those countries which respect the
legitimate ambitions of the Arab nation, regardless of their
political aspirations[20], and urged other Arab states to follow its
example of nationalising the assets of oil companies associated
with unfriendly powers. In fact, as Stork points out, this apparently
uncharacteristically soft line both reflected and fulfilled the
regime's pressing need for a rapid increase in production to enable
it to proceed with and expand its ambitious development
programmes.

The Formation of the National Patriotic Front

The appointment of the two Communist ministers to the cabinet
at the end of May 1972 had been preceded by lengthy negotiations
between the Ba'th and the Communists that had begun at least as
early as the proclamation of the National Action Charter in
November 1971. By the beginning of 1972, 'only' fifty Communists
were still in prison[21] and many of those who had formerly been
civil servants had apparently been reinstated in their posts. The

security service now turned its attention to rooting out nationalist opponents of the regime; in November 1971, Fu'ad al-Rikabi, who had been the first Secretary-General of the Ba'th Party between 1952 and 1959 and had subsequently forsaken the Ba'th for the Nasserists, was killed in prison, allegedly by a fellow inmate, but, according to the Arab press[22] by the security service. In January and February 1972 Ba'th assassination squads were active in London and Cairo; in London, 'Abd al-Razzaq al-Nayif, the former Prime Minister, was wounded in an attack, while in Cairo attempts were made on the lives of three prominent Iraqi Nasserists. The organiser of the Cairo hit squad, Arkan al-Takriti, told the Egyptian authorities that he and his associates were working directly under the orders of the head of Iraqi security, Nadhim Kazzar[23].

However, this ostensible change of direction was of comparatively recent origin, as Communists were still being murdered and attacked by the Ba'th in the summer of 1971[24], and although the Communist Party continued to voice its support for the 'positive' aspects of the regime's policies[25] its situation was still extremely precarious. A visible improvement in relations followed the dismissals of 'Ammash and Shaikhli in September 1971, which further strengthened Saddam Husain's position[26], and gave the impression that he was the principal pro-Communist within the RCC. A few weeks later, the National Action Charter was proclaimed, and although it did not mention the Communist Party by name, the document stressed the desirability of an alliance between the Ba'th and the 'national and patriotic progressive forces in Iraq', claiming that the Ba'th 'right from the very first days of the July 17 Revolution [had] embarked upon preparing the appropriate conditions for the emergence of a genuine and powerful unity among all national and patriotic progressive forces'[27].

There were of course to be major constraints upon the activities of any future 'partners' of the Ba'th in such an alliance: al-Bakr stressed a few days later that 'the responsibility for leading the Army and directing it politically falls on the RCC alone . . . no Party other than the Ba'th Party will be able to carry out any forms of political or organisational activity within the armed forces'[28]. As the statement also implies, there would be no place for members of the KDP or ICP on the RCC, which, at least in theory, was the supreme decision-making body. Even so, the Communists decided that the Charter could serve as a basis for 'national cooperation'[29].

The Kurds and the National Front

A major factor determining relations between the Ba'th and the Communists was the state of the regime's relations with the Kurds, or more specifically with the Mulla Mustafa, which, in spite of the optimism expressed in the National Action Charter, had been deteriorating steadily for many months. Barzani and his circle seem to have come round to the view that the regime was no longer showing any serious interest in implementing the March Manifesto, and that it was trying to buy time in order to undermine the Kurdish movement. As early as May 1971 Barzani was again complaining that the regime was attempting to create demographic 'facts' by moving Arabs, particularly Christians, to Kirkuk[30]; *al-Taakhi*, the Kurdish newspaper, was forced to suspend publication several times in 1971, and early in October an elaborate attempt to assassinate Barzani came to light after the would-be assassins had succeeded in killing themselves rather than their target when the explosives concealed beneath their clothing were accidentally detonated. After Nadhim Kazzar's attempted coup had been foiled in June 1973 such incidents could be attributed to his personal malevolence — his hostility towards both Communists and Kurds was proverbial — but at this stage (October 1971) Kazzar's loyalty to Saddam Husain, and hence the latter's implication in this and other assassination attempts, can scarcely be doubted.

A further cause of conflict between the regime and Barzani was the deportation of between forty and fifty thousand 'Iranians' across the border to Iran in late 1971 and early 1972, apparently as a reprisal for Iran's seizure of the Tunbs and Abu Musa. Those involved in the deportations were of Iranian origin only in the sense that they or their forbears had originally come from Iran and settled in Iraq. Many now had only the most distant connection with Iran, but nevertheless found themselves in refugee camps on the other side of the frontier[31]. The deportation of so-called Iranians was to prove a favourite device of the Ba'th in the future, but in 1971–72 many of those expelled were Fa'ilis, Shi'i Kurds from the area extending roughly between Khaniqin and 'Amara. In the circumstances Barzani interpreted the move as an attempt to reduce the number of Kurds in Iraq.

Barzani's growing disenchantment with the Ba'th was also fuelled by the intense suspicions of the regime's good faith that he had entertained from the very beginning[32], and by the spring of 1972 he had resumed the contacts with Iran that he had broken off after the signature of the March Manifesto. At the same time, Iraq's pro-Soviet stance, its apparently uncompromising foreign policy pronouncements and the threat it appeared to be posing towards the 'stability' of the Gulf area[33], had combined to arouse intense concern on the part of the United States and Iran. Hence, although the interests of the Kurds were otherwise by no means identical with those of Iran, both Barzani and the Shah had a common interest in trying to weaken the Iraqi regime. Unfortunately for the Kurds, Barzani does not seem to have been sufficiently alert to the fact that the Shah's desire to undermine the Iraqi regime did not imply unconditional support for an autonomous Iraqi Kurdistan under his leadership.

The early 1970s marked a major policy departure on Barzani's part. Previously, he had always maintained cordial links with his former hosts in the Soviet Union, but now, apparently influenced by emissaries from the CIA, he seems to have decided to exchange Soviet for American support. It is probable that this change of heart was prompted by the assumption that the United States had more complete control over the Shah's actions than was ever in fact the case, and having obtained what he considered to be cast-iron assurances from the CIA and Dr Kissinger, he evidently felt that he had sufficient guarantees against any future defection on the Shah's part[34].

Nevertheless, contacts and indeed negotiations between the Ba'th and the Kurds continued, although the prospects of a settlement did not seem bright. Serious incidents broke out in the summer between government and Kurdish forces in Sulaimaniya and in Sinjar, where several thousand Yazidis were later (in February and March 1973) forced to leave their homes in another of the internal population 'redistribution' exercises engineered by the Ba'th[35]. By the autumn, the Ba'th's efforts to present a picture of Ba'th/Kurdish amity were clearly under considerable strain; a series of articles attacking the Kurdish leadership appeared in the Ba'thist daily *al-Thawra* in October and November; the Kurds were advised to sever their links with Iran and put an end to their campaign of sabotaging railway lines and oil installations[36]. At the end of the year the Iraqi Air Force was bombing villages in the north, and a new 'Kurdish war' seemed imminent[37], although a major conflict did not in fact break out until the spring of 1974. In

such circumstances there was little immediate prospect of
meaningful Kurdish participation in a National Front, and as a
result, despite the evident misgivings and reluctance of some
leading Ba'thists, the regime became increasingly reliant on
Communist support.

Thus a considerable degree of interdependence existed beween
the Ba'th's relations with the Kurds and its relations with the
Communists, in that a rapprochement with the Kurds (such as
had occurred in the immediate aftermath of the March Manifesto)
would have lessened the urgency for an alliance with the
Communists. It is probably also correct to say that the antipathy
felt by many Ba'thists towards the Kurds was less deep-seated than
their hostility to the Communists, in the sense that while the Kurds
may have been an infernal nuisance to the Ba'th the two were not
competing in the same political or ideological arena. In consequence, it is possible that if Barzani had shown more
willingness to compromise with the Ba'th, and if the Ba'th
leadership itself could have arrived at a more satisfactory working
relationship with him, those elements within the Ba'th leadership
who were most deeply opposed to an alliance with the Communists
might well have swung al-Bakr and Saddam Husain away from
this course. In the event, Barzani and the KDP could not in fact be
fashioned into suitable coalition partners, and a Ba'th/Communist
alliance did materialise. However, this could not come into
existence until al-Bakr and Saddam Husain had won yet another
power struggle within the Ba'th leadership, and had ousted the
last major opponent of the prospective alliance.

The Defiance and Defeat of Nadhim Kazzar, June–July 1973

Even when judged by the fairly undemanding standards set by
most of his colleagues and contemporaries in the Ba'th leadership,
Nadhim Kazzar's reputation as a sadistic torturer and murderer is
particularly unsavoury[38]. However, 'Despite his repulsive methods,
which aroused criticism within the Party, Kazzar's influence rose
high because he eliminated elements considered dangerous to the
party when the position of the Ba'th regime was uncertain'[39].
Kazzar had gradually become estranged from his former patron
Saddam Husain, who, presumably well aware of his particular

talents, had appointed him to head the security services in 1969[40].

This estrangement has sometimes been explained in ideological terms, to the effect that Kazzar could not stomach Saddam Husain's new-found enthusiasm for the Communists, but it is far more probable that Kazzar, who had been able to build up an increasingly independent position within the security system, anticipated that al-Bakr and Saddam Husain were unlikely to allow him to remain in almost unchallenged control of such an important power base, and would not hesitate to use force to oust him. The only way he could prevent this happening was by staging a pre-emptive coup against them[41].

Thus Kazzar devised a plan that had the attraction of enabling him to dispose of almost all his rivals more or less simultaneously. Taking advantage of one of al-Bakr's relatively rare visits abroad, and realising that protocol would demand that most of the Party leadership would be on hand at Baghdad Airport to greet the President on his return on 30 June, Kazzar invited the two key military members of the RCC, Lt-General Hammad Shihab, the Minister of Defence, and Lt-General Sa'dun Ghaidan, the Minister of Interior (who were in charge of the armed forces and the police) to a 'banquet'[42], or, according to Ghaidan, to visit his headquarters to inspect some newly installed surveillance equipment[43]. On their arrival, the two ministers were bundled down to the cellars, while a special detachment of Kazzar's own men was despatched to the airport to assassinate both the President and his reception committee on the former's return from Poland. Fortunately for most of the RCC, the aeroplane was delayed and the would-be assassins left the airport, presumably under the impression that the President had somehow got wind of the plot. Meanwhile, Kazzar, having watched al-Bakr's arrival on television and thus having seen for himself that the plot had misfired, left Baghdad by road, taking the two ministers with him as hostages, threatening (over the radio) to kill them if he was not given safe conduct out of the country. Unfortunately for 'Abd al-Khaliq al-Samarra'i, Kazzar apparently offered to meet al-Bakr at the former's house to 'discuss his differences with the regime'[44], thus implicating al-Samara'i in the plot. There is no other evidence linking Kazzar with al-Samara'i, who, unlike Kazzar, had good standing in the Ba'th Party and was an important rival of the al-Bakr/Saddam Husain group[45]. In the end Kazzar decided that his safest course of action was to try to reach Iran with his two hostages. When the party was sighted by Iraqi forces near the Iranian border Kazzar killed Shihab and seriously wounded Ghaidan before being captured himself.

The successful foiling of the plot was immediately announced on Baghdad radio, and a special court under the presidency of 'Izzat al-Duri was set up to 'try' the conspirators. On 7 July, it was announced that the court had found Kazzar and twenty-one others guilty, and that they had been executed immediately afterwards. A further fourteen were executed the next day, including Muhammad Fadhil, head of the Ba'th military bureau[46]; 'Abd al-Khaliq al-Samarra'i, apparently saved from the firing squad only by the personal intervention of Michel 'Aflaq, was given life imprisonment. On 10 July 1973 Shibli 'Aisami, assistant secretary-general of the Party, declared that 'the Ba'th Party will learn a good lesson from this criminal and treacherous incident', adding without obvious irony that the experience would prompt the Party to 'cling even more tenaciously to democracy, legality and morality'[47].

Kazzar's fall had a number of important consequences. In the first place it enabled the regime to lay the blame for many of its previous excesses at his door, although, as we have already indicated, Kazzar's close connections with Saddam Husain meant that the latter could not possibly have been unaware of the activities of his subordinate[48]. In addition, since the executions were followed almost immediately by the formal conclusion of the alliance between the Ba'th and the Communists that had been in the air for the previous fifteen months, it was widely believed that the 'leftist' element within the Ba'th leadership had succeeded in gaining the upper hand. The Communist Party certainly seems to have come to this conclusion; even before the 'trial' of the conspirators it indicated its willingness to join in 'a single united front', which it considered as 'the firm answer to the plots being hatched by the enemies of the country'[49].

Although the attempted coup was largely confined to Kazzar himself and his immediate supporters, the al-Bakr/Saddam Husain group immediately took a number of administrative and 'constitutional' measures to safeguard and consolidate its position. Thus al-Bakr himself took over the Defence portfolio, the intelligence services were reorganised under Sa'dun Shakir al-Takriti and Barzan al-Takriti, Saddam Husain's younger brother[50], and the Provisional Constitution was amended to 'redefine' the powers of the President. Under Article 57, he now became Commander-in-Chief of the armed forces as well as Head of State, and could exercise his powers 'either directly or through the Council of Ministers'. Article 58 conferred a further wide range of powers on the President: he was charged with the preservation of the 'independence of the country and [the] integrity of its lands', supervising the 'application of the Constitution, laws, resolutions, judicial decisions and development projects in all parts of... Iraq', appointing and dismissing ministers, judges, civil servants and officers, and directing and controlling the work of Ministries and other institutions[51].

The RCC, now reduced to seven members (Ahmad Hasan al-Bakr, Saddam Husain, Sa'dun Ghaidan, 'Izzat Mustafa, 'Izzat al- Duri, Murtada al-Hadithi, Taha Yasin Ramadan) after the assassination of al-Shihab and the imprisonment of 'Abd al-Khaliq al-Samarra'i, seems to have lost some of its former importance, and no new members were added until a major reshuffle in September 1977[52]. This greater concentration of power on the part of the regime was accompanied by the announcement that a National Assembly, whose members were to be 'selected' by the RCC, was shortly to be convened, although the project in fact remained a dead letter until 1980. However, the most visible consequence of the affair was the announcement within a few days of the fall of Kazzar of the formation of the National Patriotic Front[53]. The absence of any Kurdish participation indicated the next major item on the regime's agenda, the task of finding a permanent solution to the Kurdish problem, which was to be its principal preoccupation over the following twenty months.

The difficulties in which the regime was finding itself both internally and internationally had enabled Saddam Husain to present himself as an embattled leader, besieged by imperialism and reaction, even comparing his own situation with that of Allende in Chile[54]. In the same vein, partly in response to the mood within the country, and partly because it had become a prisoner of its own rhetoric, the Ba'th leadership began to make declarations giving the impression that the newly-created National Front was a step towards greater democratisation. Thus al-Bakr claimed in September 1973 that since the formation of the National Patriotic Front in July, 'governing authority' had actually been in the hands of the Front, and that its members 'bear responsibility for governing along with the Ba'th party', calling on the KDP to join in[55].

However inexplicable it may seem in retrospect, the ICP leadership seemed prepared to accept such statements at their face value and to ignore the fact that all real power still remained entirely in the hands of the Ba'th. It hoped to be able to use its influence to push the Ba'th in a generally 'leftward' direction, and also attempted to act as a mediator between the regime and the KDP. The Party tried to nudge the Ba'th into implementing the March Manifesto, using the regime's own overblown rhetoric: 'Our joint march on the path of alliance, democracy and national fraternity on the basis of the March Manifesto and the application of autonomous rule for the Kurdish people within the framework of the Iraqi Republic ... will turn our country into an invincible fortress. We share your confidence that our people's revolution will not stop'[56]. The Communists must also have been greatly encouraged by pronouncements such as al-Bakr's declaration in July 1973 that the Ba'th wanted 'a lasting and solid front, a front with a strategic outlook and with long-range strategic tasks [which would act as] a fine model for all progressive and national forces in the Arab homeland', and also by the Ba'th's attitude towards the Soviet Union. In the course of the same speech al-Bakr declared that the nationalisation of IPC would have been impossible without the assistance of the Soviet Union, and that the episode 'proved the validity of faith and confidence in the relations between our people and revolution and the forces of progress and socialism in the world, foremost of which is the friendly Soviet Union — forces which have stood on our side and rendered us real and fruitful support'[57].

The Ba'th, the Kurds and Iran, 1973–1974

Although the October War provided a brief respite in the hostilities between the regime and the Kurds, as well as leading to a temporary resumption of diplomatic relations with Iran, the situation in the Kurdish area became increasingly critical with the passage of time. In addition it was clear that there had been an important change in the nature of the conflict by the end of 1973, in that the 'Iranian' dimension had assumed greater significance than ever before. By October Barzani had a sophisticated anti-

aircraft system in position around his headquarters in Hajj
'Umran, and had rallied a number of Kurdish deserters from the
Iraqi Army as well as a host of Kurdish students and intellectuals
from both inside and outside Iraq to the Kurdish cause[58].
Ironically, however, this period of apparent triumph and strength
was in fact the beginning of Barzani's end. Due to the institu-
tionalisation of the movement, the emergence of an 'apparatus'
with its own security forces, the Parastin[59], which had substantial
financial resources at its disposal, and the gradual transformation
of the conflict from a guerilla war into a conventional war
supported by a powerful foreign state, Barzani had allowed
himself to be manoeuvred into a position of great vulnerability
and almost total dependence on the goodwill of the Shah of Iran
and the United States[60].

For its part, the Ba'th now started to make more overt
approaches to potentially less intransigent elements within the
Kurdish movement in an attempt to bypass Barzani. Thus in
September 1973 Saddam Husain declared that the KDP was not
identical with the 'Kurdish people' and that the Party had been
'infiltrated by counter-revolutionary forces'[61]. The adoption of this
line was greatly facilitated by Barzani's celebrated interview with
the *Washington Post* in June 1973, in which he had declared that
the Kirkuk oil fields were the inalienable property of the Kurdish
people, and offered the United States participation in 'Kurdish oil'
if it would only send its forces to assist him in his struggle against
the 'wolves' in Baghdad[62].

In addition to trying to convince the more 'reasonable' Kurds
that it was Barzani who was creating the obstacles preventing the
fulfilment of the March Manifesto, the regime's general line until
the outbreak of fighting in 1974 was to maintain that it was in
reality giving the Kurds as much as they could possibly expect, and
that any further concessions would be tantamount to separatism.
Barzani and the KDP were accused of being separatists at heart,
and merely pretending to be committed to the principles of
'autonomy'. Thus in a review of his discussions with various
Kurdish leaders over the previous four years in a speech in March
1974, Saddam Husain claimed to recall an occasion on which the
Ba'th negotiators had been obliged to point out to the Kurdish side
that 'we were debating a draft for autonomy and not for a new state
in Iraq'[63].

Discussions between the Ba'th and the KDP continued from

September 1973 until March 1974, but even the regime's official pronouncements show that the Ba'th was determined to impose its own version of 'autonomy' in the Kurdish areas, and that it was in no mood to give serious considerations to proposals put forward by the KDP. For example, on 17 October 1973, Saddam Husain declared: 'You know that our brothers in the KDP have already submitted a draft, but we have not discussed it. The fact is that in our opinion their draft is far removed from the concept of autonomy'[64]. At this stage, the differences between the two sides could not simply be reduced to semantics; the Kurds were not prepared to join the National Front without any solid guarantees of meaningful participation in government[65], and also consistently refused to accept the Ba'th's definition of the physical extent of the Kurdish area, which excluded the province of Kirkuk[66]. The Ba'th was behaving as if it was faithfully implementing all the provisions of the March Manifesto in the most generous manner, while at the same time managing to preserve the 'national unity' of Iraq. In the course of a speech on the fifth anniversary of the revolution of 17th July 1968 al-Bakr declared:

> The past three and a half years from the date of the manifesto until today have witnessed active and intensive efforts to implement the provisions of the proclamation. It can be said that the greater part of those provisions have actually been implemented as far as the SABP and the revolutionary regime are concerned. Very regrettably however, this same period has witnessed negative aspects, acute crises and mistakes which have harmed national unity and to a certain extent obstructed the progress of the peaceful and democratic solution of the Kurdish question.[67]

The Kurdish view of these developments as expressed by Mahmud 'Uthman shortly before the outbreak of hostilities in the late spring of 1974 was more down to earth:

> In the RCC we have nothing. In the army, we have nothing, no key positions. In the security and intelligence services we have nothing. In the Oil Ministry, we have nothing. In the Ministry of the Interior we have nothing. In the Ministry of Foreign Affairs we have nothing. In

fact, we hold no key positions. The Kurds have no part in decisions relating to domestic or foreign policies. Everything is done by the Ba'th Party. We have no participation in the regime. We only have participation on an *administrative* level (our emphasis).[68]

A substantially similar conclusion was reached by Vanly in his account of the actual steps taken by the Ba'th regime towards the implementation of the March Manifesto between 1970 and 1974, which has the merit of dealing with each clause of the Manifesto document in turn. Apart from the failure to hold a census and the forced movement of populations that have already been described, little progress had been made even on less obviously contentious issues such as the introduction of Kurdish as the language of instruction in schools; in addition, it was claimed, the five Kurdish ministers appointed in March 1970 had 'no decision-making power at all'. More generally, outside the context of the Manifesto, there was little evidence of any active commitment on the regime's part to reverse the severe economic, infrastructural and educational deprivation of the Kurdish area[69].

In such circumstances, relations between the ICP and the KDP had become extremely precarious by the end of 1973, particularly because the Parastin had begun to mount systematic attacks against Kurdish Communists[70]. In November, the Communist daily *Tariq al-Sha'b* complained that the KDP was waging an anti-Communist campaign in Kurdistan, about which the ICP could no longer remain silent, because it had recently taken on 'the proportions of an organised military action to exterminate the Kurdish Communists'. Numerous Communist delegations had been sent to Kurdistan during the summer, the paper added, 'in an attempt to try to achieve cooperation between the KDP, the Ba'th and the ICP, but the Kurdish Democratic Party failed to stop its campaign against the Communists, who were sponsoring the national cause of the toiling Kurdish people long before the KDP had been established'[71].

Open Warfare, 1974–1975

Well before the negotiations between the regime and the Kurds were finally abandoned in the spring of 1974, and hostilities broke out in earnest, relations between Iraq and Iran had begun to resume their familiar pattern of cross-border violations and military incidents. In mid-February 1974 the situation had become more than usually tense, with over a hundred casualties on the two sides and both parties requesting the despatch of United Nations observers to the frontier area[72]. As far as it is possible to judge, these particular incidents seem to have originated on the Iranian side, although reports later in the year and in 1975 show that Iraq was also taking the offensive[73].

The negotiations with the Kurds continued after a fashion until a few days before the official inauguration of the Autonomy Law in March, but the regime was evidently determined to press ahead, whether or not it managed to secure the active consent and cooperation of the KDP. The regime's unwillingness to accept any of the basic objections put forward from the Kurdish side was made out to be an example of admirable firmness and reliability, and a sign that, unlike previous Iraqi governments, it was determined to fulfill its commitments[74]. When the Law was announced on 11 March[75], Barzani was given a further fifteen days to join the National Patriotic Front; the KDP countered by demanding an extension of the autonomous area proposed by the regime, and a percentage of the country's oil revenues in proportion to the Kurdish population[76].

In the bitter fighting that followed, there is no doubt that Barzani attracted the support of the vast majority of the Kurdish movement, including those who had long entertained doubts both on the score of the 'feudal', 'reactionary', and 'tribal' style of his leadership and on the propriety of his contacts with outside powers and forces whose disinterestedness, as well as good faith, was highly questionable. The Ba'th were never able to attract a significant number of Kurds, or any particularly distinguished Kurdish personalities, to their own cause, with the possible exception of Barzani's eldest son, 'Ubaidullah, who broke with his father in April 1974. According to Kutschéra, generally the most reliable source for this period, even those Kurds on the left wing of the KDP who were vehemently opposed to the alliance with Iran and were the most eager for an alliance with the Ba'th 'admitted in the spring of 1974 that Saddam Husain and the other Ba'th leaders did not want an agreement'[77].

When the fighting began, Barzani could count on some 50–60,000 Peshmerga fighters and another 50,000 irregulars, while the

Iraqi forces comprised some 90,000 men, 1200 tanks and armoured cars and 200 aircraft[78]. Iraqi reservists were called up on 6 April; in spite of Saddam Husain's denial a few days later that military operations were taking place in the North — in accordance with previous practice, the regime imposed a complete news blackout on the war throughout its duration — it was evident that serious fighting had already broken out by the end of March, when an army brigade was temporarily besieged by Kurdish forces in Zakho[79]. Thousands of Kurdish volunteers from all over Iraq flocked to Barzani, while a mass of refugees made their way to the North; by the end of 1974, there were at least 110,000 Iraqi Kurdish refugees in makeshift camps in Iran, where they had fled to escape from the war zone[80].

The Iraqi armed forces certainly had superior fire power, and were also able to launch devastating bombing raids against civilian targets[81]. However, in spite of such attacks, which were accompanied by a fairly thorough-going economic blockade of the area, there was no sign of any wavering on the Kurdish side, and especially after taking delivery of 122 mm guns from Iran in the autumn the Kurds seemed dug in for an indefinite period. In one battle at the approach to the Hamilton Road in September, in which the Kurds controlled the heights overlooking the pass along which the government forces were trying to penetrate, the Kurds claimed to have killed some 500 of their opponents while sustaining only eight losses on their own side[82]. Almost all the Iraqi armed forces were now concentrated on the Kurdish front, and casualties were extremely high; by the end of the fighting in March 1975, 1640 men had been killed and 7903 wounded, according to official Iraqi figures[83].

By the beginning of 1975, the stalemate familiar from previous confrontations between the Kurds and the government in Baghdad had begun once more, although this time Baghdad appeared to be under greater pressure than ever before. In addition to the high human cost of the war, military expenditure escalated sharply, from ID 102 mn in 1972 to 236 mn in 1974 and 356 mn in 1975[84]. In January, Iranian assistance was stepped up further with the supply of Rapier missiles and 155 mm cannon to the Kurds[85] and the Iranians had apparently bombarded Iraqi Army positions from their own side of the frontier at the end of December[86]. At this point the conflict had developed in such a way that it was in danger of escalating into an all-out war between Iran and Iraq. Furthermore, there was no obvious end in sight, because according to a KDP analysis of these events — although Iran was prepared to step up its support for the Kurds as soon as the Iraqi Army went onto the offensive, Iranian military assistance was always either inadequate or slow in coming as soon as the Kurds themselves began to take the offensive[87]. The Shah had no intention of allowing the Kurds to become strong enough to defeat the Iraqi Army, since this would give great encouragement to the Iranian Kurds, among whom the war had already created considerable ferment[88].

However, Barzani and his supporters were by now totally dependent on Iranian assistance, a dependence that Barzani himself was desperately trying to modify by constant appeals and wild promises to the United States. If the Shah could be convinced to stop supporting the Kurds their resistance would collapse, as both Barzani and the Iraqi regime were well aware. However, in addition to the different interests of the three parties most directly concerned with the conflict, other powers both inside and outside the region were anxious to find some way of reaching an acceptable settlement or at least of containing the situation. The Soviet Union's attempts to mediate both between the Ba'th and the Kurds and between Iran and Iraq as early as 1973 had not succeeded[89], but after the Rabat summit in October 1974, King Husain of Jordan managed to arrange preliminary meetings between representatives of Iran and Iraq[90]. These contacts were followed up by meetings between the two sides at ministerial level in Istanbul in January, and separate discussions with Presidents Sadat and Boumedienne.

The outcome of these negotiations was the Algiers Agreement, concluded by Saddam Husain and the Shah at the beginning of March, which effectively terminated hostilities in Kurdistan and paved the way for a swift and permanent demarcation of the disputed frontier between Iraq and Iran. Within forty-eight hours of the signature of the Agreement, the Iranians removed their 155 mm field guns, and the Kurdish resistance collapsed; the Iranians even threatened to join the Iraqis in a combined attack on the Kurds if the latter refused to accept the terms of the Agreement[91].

Chapter Six

1975-1980

In both the long and the short term, the wider implications of the Algiers Agreement should not be underestimated, and go far beyond the interests of the parties most closely involved in the settlement. The Kurdish movement, though perhaps not completely crushed, was dealt such a fearsome blow that the nature and scope of the activities it was subsequently able to undertake were greatly altered. For the Ba'th, it meant the settlement of the Kurdish question on its own terms, as well as an enormous boost to the authority of the regime as a whole and of Saddam Husain in particular. In addition, the Agreement meant the 'final' resolution of a frontier dispute that had bedevilled relations between the two countries since the late 1930s.

The main features of the Agreement, which were incorporated in a treaty signed in June 1975[1], were a settlement of the boundary between the two states at the *thalweg* line in the Shatt al'Arab, and elsewhere on the basis of the Constantinople Protocol of 1913, and, effectively, the closure of the Iranian border in such a way as to prevent Kurdish forces from being supplied from, or to regroup in, Iran. Consequently, as the Turkish border had been closed since the beginning of the fighting in 1974, the Kurds now had to choose between carrying on the resistance in the mountains of Iraqi Kurdistan, surrendering to the Iraqi authorities, or entering Iran as refugees. Significantly, neither the Agreement nor the Treaty contained any reference to the three small islands in the

Gulf that Iran had occupied in November 1971, and in addition, the final demarcation of the frontier meant that Khuzistan, to which Iraq had often laid claim, was now firmly in Iran. Both these issues were allowed to drop quietly out of sight until their resurrection by the Iraqis in the spring of 1979. The Treaty also covered navigation rights in the Shatt and the movement of pilgrims between the two countries; further subsidiary agreements on commerce, tourism, agriculture, railways and fishing were signed in 1977[2]. In general, a very cordial atmosphere characterised relations between the two countries until the overthrow of the Shah at the beginning of 1979.

The Agreement was widely welcomed by Iraq's neighbours in the Gulf[3], and was a vital stage in the slow but definite process of Iraq's integration into the 'moderate' camp in the Arab world. Finally, and perhaps most significantly, the cessation of hostilities with both Iran and the Kurds meant that the Ba'th was no longer so dependent upon the Soviet Union and the Communists, and could begin to edge away from both. The steps it took in this direction gradually brought about a further improvement in Iraq's relations with most of the other Arab states except Syria. But this is to anticipate.

1973-1975: The Ba'th Dig In

Although the change of direction that followed the Algiers Agreement had already been anticipated by some observers[4], the actual process was very gradual and uneven, to the extent that what was actually taking place seems not to have been fully comprehended even by the Ba'th's allies in the National Front. In fact, the first steps had already been taken well before the Algiers Agreement, in the wake of the oil price increase after the Arab-Israeli War of October 1973, when oil revenues soared from $575 million in 1972 to $1,840 million in 1973 and to $5,700 million in 1974[5].

This sudden acquisition of very great wealth enabled the regime to finance a series of expensive and prestigious development projects, and to introduce major new programmes in such fields as education, housing, health and welfare. The very considerable progress made meant that throughout the 1970s and 1980s apologists for the regime made much of its achievements in these fields. However, since all oil states have pursued similar policies since the early 1970s it seems a little curious to attribute the pace and quality of developments in Iraq to the far-sightedness — or, even more bizarrely, to the generosity — of those in power. The Iraqi economy has prospered because of Iraq's huge oil reserves rather than because of the genius or the bounty of the country's rulers.

The enormous expenditure involved in these programmes had the effect of initiating Iraq's rapid integration into the world market and eventually of reducing its reliance on the Soviet Union to all but the military sphere. Trade with the United States, with whom Iraq had no diplomatic relations, and whose actions were vilified almost daily in the Iraqi media, grew steadily from $32 million in 1971 to $284 million in 1974; and trade with both Japan and West Germany expanded dramatically over the same period[6]. Again, since the regime, which had become coterminous with 'Saddam Husain and his circle', controlled the economy to an infinitely greater extent than any of its predecessors, it found itself in a position to dispense patronage and contracts on an almost unlimited scale. The main local beneficiaries were businessmen, speculators, contractors and entrepreneurs of all kinds, who came to constitute an extensive social base for the regime[7]. Furthermore, the social welfare programmes, the subsidies on essential foodstuffs, the increases in wages and salaries and the new employment opportunities provided by the general expansion in economic activity in a country that was neither over-populated nor (at least initially) required a major importation of foreign labour, all helped to bring about rapid and visible improvements in living standards for the population as a whole and undoubtedly encouraged a wide acceptance of the regime in many quarters in the early 1970s[8].

It is true that many of these apparently positive developments were followed by consequences that were both damaging and unforeseen. Thus agricultural production underwent a severe decline, aggravated by rural to urban drift and over-hasty and often inequitable land redistribution[9]. There were major and seemingly insuperable bottlenecks in industry, the civil service and elsewhere, which resulted from the general unwillingness, and fear, on the part of subordinates to take decisions without constant reference to higher authority[10]. However, in the middle 1970s much of this was still in the future.

On a more narrowly political level, the National Front's efficacy as a forum for political debate rather than as a rubber-stamp for the regime did not long survive the Kurdish settlement[11]. As we have seen, the Communist Party had thrown its weight fully behind the Ba'th[12], and, at least initially, refrained from serious criticism of its policies. Perhaps more crucially, the ICP's participation in the Front under the existing constellation of forces in Iraq created favourable conditions for the strengthening of Ba'th rule, and allowed the regime to build up its own organisations and institutions almost unopposed.

Soon after the formation of the National Front, the Ba'th Party began to use the Front's 'regulations' to extend its control over the mass organisations and trade unions, which had traditionally been dominated by the Communists. It was announced that the Front, as a 'collective' body, should put up common lists of candidates for office in all popular organisations, and that the separate Communist or Ba'thist associations should now be absorbed in unified national associations in which, on the model of the Front, the Ba'th would have a 'privileged role' (*dawr mutamayyiz*)[13]. Since the Ba'th controlled the state apparatus, had almost limitless funds at its disposal and was in any case determined to take these organisations over, the Communists were inevitably at a great disadvantage. In general terms, while making use of the Communists' experience in such matters as the formulation of a new Labour Law, the regime fought and constrained Communist influence wherever it could[14].

In addition, conditions in Iraq were changing dramatically in directions that greatly affected both the composition and the attitudes of the labour movement. The spin-off effect of the new oil revenues meant that employment opportunities increased everywhere and in particular that easy money could be made. This in turn set in motion a rapid and almost total transformation of the demographic structure of the country, which was accompanied by an equally comprehensive process of social differentiation. One consequence of this was that many of the ICP's traditional centres of support in the cities were now being swamped with migrants from a background with little tradition or experience of working class struggle[15]. Nevertheless, the Communist Party attempted to continue to work within the mass organisations and the trade unions in spite of increasing restrictions and difficulties. The Ba'th began to change the trade union regulations in such a way that it became impossible for a non-Ba'thist to become a member of the union leadership, and the unions and the other mass organisations were turned into bureaucratic institutions that had no initiative of their own and that were entirely subservient to the regime. In addition, many of the union officers were not representatives of the workforce but were full-time Ba'th Party officials and sometimes members of the security services[16]. Such policies were accompanied by continual pressure on the Communist Party to confine its activities to the Party alone and not to work within the mass organisations or the unions. In 1974 this pressure became so strong that the ICP dissolved the Party 'centres' that it had organised in order to preserve at least some of its influence within the unions, and tried to confine its work to the Party itself, only taking up working class questions and grievances in its own publications[17].

As far as the Kurds were concerned, a faction calling itself the KDP under the leadership of 'Aziz 'Aqrawi broke with Mulla Mustafa and the 'real' KDP when the fighting started in March 1974. Members of the Neo-KDP were among those appointed to the legislative assembly in Arbil in August 1974, and its representatives, along with a number of Kurdish 'independents' and members of various other pro-Ba'th Kurdish organisations, such as the Kurdish Revolutionary Party, were subsequently appointed to the National Front. The Kurdish paper, *al-Taakhi*, which had been edited by Dara Tawfiq, a Kurdish leftist who had long opposed Barzani on ideological grounds but could not bring himself to side with the Ba'th against him, was handed over to the Neo-KDP in March 1974. As we shall show, the regime was never able to attract a great deal of positive support in the Kurdish areas[18], largely because the 'self-government' promised in 1974 turned out to be the sham that most Kurds had anticipated, and also because atrocities like the burning of villages, and the torture, mutilation and execution of 'dissidents' carried out by the regime during the fighting were continued in the course of an equally brutal 'pacification' campaign that followed the conclusion of the Algiers Agreement[19].

In January 1974 a new Ba'th Regional Command had been announced on the occasion of the 8th Party Congress. Thirteen members were appointed, including all seven existing members of the RCC except Sa'dun Ghaidan and Murtada al-Hadithi. The eight newcomers were Na'im Haddad (a Shi'i from Nasiriya),

Tayih 'Abd al-Karim (a Sunni from 'Ana), Muhammad Mahjub (a
Sunni from Dur), 'Adnan Hamdani (a Shi'i), Ghanim 'Abd al-Jalil
(a Sunni from Takrit), Tahir al-'Ani (a Sunni from 'Ana), 'Abd al-
Fattah Muhammad Yasin (a Sunni from Takrit), and Hasan al-
'Amiri (a Shi'i).

The significance of the 1974 Congress lay in the leftist line of
much of the Report[20], which seemed to indicate that the alliance
with the Communists was having some effect upon Ba'thist
policies. Furthermore, as the next Party Congress did not take
place until 1982, after the outbreak of the war with Iran, the Report
of the 8th Congress continued to be quoted as embodying Party
policy over the intervening years. By 1982, however, 'politics' had
become so bound up with the cult of personality surrounding
Saddam Husain that it becomes difficult even to identify any
specifically Ba'th 'ideology', let alone to attempt any coherent
analysis of it[21].

Iraq's Relations with its Neighbours, 1973–1975

In the course of the early 1970s the Iraqi Ba'th acquired the
maverick reputation in Middle Eastern politics that it took many
years to shake off. Part of the explanation for this lay in its
apparently determined adoption of a particularly hard line on the
Arab–Israeli conflict, its close relations with the Soviet Union and
the socialist countries between 1969 and 1973 and its militant
declarations on Arab socialism and Arab unity. Although, as we
shall see, there was in fact a wide gulf between rhetoric and reality,
the regime's apparent extremism had succeeded in convincing
Iraq's more moderate neighbours, and indeed much of the rest of
the world, that it was intent on pursuing genuinely revolutionary
policies, and as a result the Iraqi regime found itself either feared
or loathed by most of the states in the region.

Given the basic premises on which the Ba'th was forced to
operate in the first few years after its seizure of power, it is probably
true to say that this line was both 'necessary' and 'inevitable'. The
regime had inherited a relatively radical line from its predecessors,
who had themselves been influenced by the strong leftist tradition
in Iraqi politics, both before and after the Revolution of 1958. In
addition, it had to justify its own existence in the face of the
ideological *non sequitur* posed by the existence of another Ba'thist

regime in Syria, with which it was in profound conflict. The mere existence of two branches of a movement that might reasonably be expected to have a least a measure of *internal* coherence gave rise to a number of awkward questions, which were particularly difficult for the Iraqi Ba'th to duck in view of Syria's inevitably closer involvement in the Arab-Israeli conflict. In this situation, the Iraqi Ba'th was more or less forced to try to outbid the Syrians in its efforts to appear more truly Arab and more truly nationalist — or perhaps 'more truly Ba'thist' — than they. In addition, with Egypt's gradual withdrawal from the main stream of Arab politics under Sadat, the 'Struggle for Syria'[22] that had been conducted by Egypt and Iraq at various times in the 1950s and the early 1960s receded into the background in the 1970s and was replaced by a bitter rhetorical battle for ideological legitimacy between the two rival Ba'th factions in Damascus and Baghdad.

The October War and the oil price rises that followed occasioned a series of major and apparently lasting changes in the political geography of the Middle East. Many of these changes took some time to work themselves out, particularly, perhaps, Egypt's gradual disengagement after the Sinai Accord in 1975, which was the most obvious, though perhaps not the earliest, indication that Sadat was prepared to come to terms with Israel[23]. Another important consequence of the War was that it became clear that although the Soviet Union had given its full support to the Arab countries, it was not, ultimately, prepared to come to their aid in a way that might threaten the continued existence of Israel and thus risk a direct confrontation with the United States. For this and other reasons, the Soviet Union's relations with most of the Arab states gradually deteriorated throughout the 1970s[24].

Of comparable if not of greater significance was the fact that the oil price rise enabled the states of the Arabian peninsula, whose previous influence in the region had been comparatively modest, to play a more vigorous part in its affairs, to such an extent that Sa'udi Arabia gradually developed into the richest, and certainly one of the most influential, of the states in the Middle East. The failure, or the petering out, of the oil embargo by March 1974 showed that the Gulf states and Sa'udi Arabia were evidently not prepared to use that particular weapon to force an 'equitable' settlement of the Arab-Israeli conflict, but, since they now had quantities of wealth at their disposal that far exceeded their most lavish domestic requirements, they were able to buy support from their less well-endowed neighbours, or to finance one or other of the organisations attached to the PLO. Here too an important development had taken place; partly because of King Husain's decision that his country should not take a major part in the War[25], and partly as a consequence of Kissinger's diplomacy, which meant that the Americans were unable to force the Israelis into making concessions that might enhance the King's credibility, Husain was no longer in a position to put himself forward as a spokesman for the Palestinians. Hence, at the Rabat summit almost exactly a year after the ceasefire, the PLO was finally recognised as the sole representative of the Palestinians, and, thus, incidentally, as another 'legitimate' vehicle for inter-Arab intrigue.

In the context of these momentous changes, the 'revolutionary' states in the Arab world, which had determined the political atmosphere of the area in the 1950s and 1960s, were either, like Egypt and Sudan, bought up by Sa'udi Arabia and the United States or, like Syria, under tremendous pressure from the same quarters. However, Syria was able to make use of its political and geographical position in the area to maintain a certain degree of economic and political independence[26], while Iraq could use its own oil wealth and economic resources for the same purpose.

Hence, in addition to the fact that both Syria and Iraq were ruled by the same Party, Syria might have been expected to be Iraq's closest and most 'natural' ally in the area. However, as the two countries remained constantly at loggerheads, the reverse was in fact the case. Some indication of the degree of Iraq's isolation from its Arab neighbours in the early 1970s emerged in the course of the October War, when Saddam Husain complained that the Iraqis had 'heard the news of the ceasefire over the radio in the same way as they had heard about the beginning of the war'[27]. The régime marked its disapproval of Arab policies in general by refusing to participate in the subsequent 'oil embargo', and also by not sending representatives to the Summit in Algiers in November 1973.

Domestic Politics 1975–1979

Two particularly significant developments characterise the years between the Algiers Agreement and Saddam Husain's eventual emergence as President in July 1979. As we have already noted, the

Iraqi regime gradually loosened its ties with the socialist countries, moving into the general orbit of the West on a global level and towards the moderate Arab states on the regional level. Of course, there were a number of constraints and obstacles to be surmounted, and the process was uneven as well as being made less straightforward than it might have been by actions on the part of the United States or some of Iraq's near Arab neighbours — such as Sadat's visit to Jerusalem in November 1977 — with which it could not afford to be directly associated. Nevertheless, the general tendency is clearly visible.

The other principal overall characteristic of Iraqi politics during this period was the growing — and apparently irreversible — concentration and accumulation of power in the hands of Saddam Husain and a few particularly trusted subordinates. By the time Saddam Husain took over from al-Bakr in July 1979, even the 'Takriti' cliché had become outmoded, as many of the original Takritis had shown too much ambition, or had not been prepared to give sufficient blind obedience, to be tolerated at the real centre of power. In September 1977 all members of the Party's Regional Command became members of the Revolutionary Command Council[28], which meant that the Party and the state (*al-dawla*) were now virtually indistinguishable. Thus the Party was no longer — if, indeed, it ever had been — a body in which policy discussions and debate took place, and became simply a further means of asserting the authority of the state, or, more accurately, that of Saddam Husain.

As we have seen, almost all the austerity measures introduced to guard against any possible adverse consequences of the oil nationalisation had been repealed by the summer of 1973, and the oil price rise after the October War meant that the country was unlikely ever to be beset by any conventional economic difficulties. Within five years (1973-1978) the state's income from oil rose almost tenfold; by 1976, the contribution of crude oil to total revenues had risen to 87%. Thus the state now emerged more emphatically than ever as the principal focus, and principal agent, of economic activity and capital accumulation[29]. Much of the new wealth was handed out directly. In February 1974 substantial tax cuts and wage rises were announced; in addition, essential foodstuffs were subsidised and minimum wages raised each year[30]. The 1977 investment plan provided for the expenditure of $2357 million, and was directed towards education, social services, housing, health, water and sewage projects in particular[31], and a wide-ranging campaign to eradicate illiteracy was launched in May 1978[32]. Huge sums were also spent on major industrial and public works projects, perhaps most notably the construction of an oil terminal at Fao to serve the North Rumaila oilfield, undertaken by the American conglomerate Brown and Root, the Kirkuk/Dörtyol oil pipeline, completed by Mannesmann in January 1977, the Tharthar canal, constructed by the Soviet Union and opened in October 1976[33], and a wide variety of other projects undertaken mainly by Japanese, French, American and British concerns. As we shall see, the pace of this very wide-ranging development programme only began to slacken when the adverse effects of the war with Iran began to be felt more keenly in 1982–83.

The regime's move away from the Soviet Union was partly connected with its desire to implement its development programme in the shortest possible time, but it also reflected a conscious policy decision on the part of the Ba'th leadership. Clearly, many of the major infrastructural and industrial projects required a degree of sophisticated technology and expertise that, if not exclusively confined to the West and Japan, was generally not as highly developed in the socialist countries. 'What we want', said Jawad Hashim, a leading economist and Minister of Planning in March 1975, 'is the best technology and the fastest possible fulfilment of order and contracts ... That is more important than price'[34]. This enthusiasm for Western technology had been apparent as early as July 1973[35], but the theme was elaborated somewhat wryly in the course of an interview given by an under secretary in the Economy Ministry to the *International Herald Tribune* in April 1975.

> We cannot sacrifice technology for ideology ... Of course, we have to keep our friends happy and throw some business their way. Thus we buy your Boeing aircraft and let you build our oil refineries. But a less important project, like a brick factory, will go to Bulgaria, even though we know we can get a better one from France.

Thus, although the socialist countries continued to do a fair amount of business with Iraq — the contract for the Basra/Baghdad pipeline, one of the major undertakings of the middle 1970s, was awarded to a Soviet firm[36] — complaints about 'socialist trading methods' and delivery dates became increasingly frequent[37]. However, while the Ba'th was gradually distancing itself from the Soviet Union, its continuing professions of anti-imperialism meant that the change of direction was not immediately discernible. In fact, although never regaining the closeness and cordiality of the halcyon days of 1972–73, Iraqi–Soviet relations have always remained at least superficially cordial and generally 'correct', with no reverses for the Soviet Union on the scale of the humiliations inflicted by Sadat or Numairi; on the other hand, in more pragmatic terms, trade with the socialist countries as a proportion of Iraq's total foreign exchanges reached a peak of 13% in 1974, went down to 7% in the first half of 1975, and thereafter declined steadily to 2.6% in 1981[38].

Perhaps the clearest sign of the regime's desire to change direction was its attempt to diversify its sources of military *matériel*, which it effected by substantial purchases of arms from various Western countries in the second half of the 1970s. Until the Algiers Agreement this kind of diversification had been impossible, partly because it would have been difficult to train the armed forces to use entirely different weapons systems when they were in a state of almost permanent alert and, more importantly, no Western country would have considered supplying arms to Iraq on a large scale while it was still apparently a Soviet 'satellite'. According to Kutschéra, Saddam Husain assured the Shah and President Boumedienne in the course of the negotiations in Algiers in March 1975 that 'he had only turned to the Soviet Union because he had been forced to do so by the isolation of Iraq'[39]. The first major order of Western arms dates from September 1976, when France agreed to supply between 60 and 80 Mirage F 1s, followed by an order for 200 French AMX 30 tanks in 1977[40]. Further large orders were placed with Brazil (200 Cascavel armoured transport vehicles in July 1978) and Italy, the latter supplying a number of sophisticated naval vessels[41]; France, Italy and Brazil are also among the major consumers of Iraqi oil.

Nevertheless, for a variety of reasons, the Soviet Union inevitably remained Iraq's principal supplier of tanks, artillery and military aircraft, so that the disengagement could not be as total as the regime might have desired. In the first place the West was not prepared to carry out a complete replacement of Iraq's weapons systems unless it had greater control over Iraq. At the same time, although Ba'th 'ideology' was gradually being replaced by a personality cult around Saddam Husain, such a cult needed to be founded on the kind of populist and national–chauvinist sentiments in which he very probably believed himself, and a 'sell-out' to the United States and the West could not easily feature in this scenario. In addition, the fact that Iraq had significant oil revenues meant that, unlike Sadat or Numairi, Saddam Husain had considerable room for manoeuvre. Hence there was never any real need for a showdown with the Soviet Union, although this would not prevent the regime gradually moving over to Western weapons systems if the West would permit it to do so.

These important departures in commercial and foreign policy were paralleled by other significant developments at home. The combination of the new oil money and the 'settlement' of the Kurdish question gave an unprecedented boost to the Ba'th's confidence, and it now began to work even more systematically towards the development of a political system over which it had exclusive and total control. Thus power became concentrated increasingly in the various organs of the state and the Ba'th Party apparatus, and the regime also began to subject the various mass organisations to its own authority. Of course, this process could scarcely coexist even with the relatively limited political plurality provided for in the National Front, and in consequence the Ba'th's partners gradually found themselves faced with more overt demands to restrict their activities, especially within the mass organisations, and to endorse increasingly unpalatable policies. Since the regime's repressive policies in Kurdistan quickly lost the 'Neo-KDP' most of the support it had ever attracted from those opposed to Barzani on ideological grounds, the Communist Party remained the Ba'th's only serious competitor.

In the beginning, the ICP made use of the relative freedom of action permitted under the terms of the Front to expand and consolidate its support throughout the country. It is obviously difficult to assess how successful it was in this respect, but one indication of the Party's resilience was that its daily newspaper *Tariq al-Sha'b* sold over 6.7 million copies in 1975, a third of the sales of *al-Thawra*, the official government newspaper[42], and in the spring of 1976 its publications were evidently available in bookshops in Baghdad[43]. However, the widely expected turn against the Communists had already begun at the end of 1975, when a number of rank and file party members were arrested apparently at random, imprisoned for relatively short periods, often tortured, and then equally suddenly released.

The Communist Party began to complain about this state of affairs at the beginning of April 1976, and by June it was evident that its activities were becoming subject to greater restrictions[44]. The report of the Third Party Congress, held in Baghdad in May, contained the first unambiguous articulation of the Party's dissatisfaction with the Ba'th[45]. The Communists demanded that the National Front should be transformed into an apparatus that would be genuinely representative of all 'progressive forces and organisations', and that the terms of the original agreement between the two Parties should also be applied to the mass organisations, particularly the Federation of Trade Unions (*Ittihad Niqabat al-'Ummal*), and the Peasant Associations (*al-Jam'iyat al-Fallahiyya*). In addition, the Ba'th was asked to abandon its demands for the dissolution of the Democratic Youth Federation (*Ittihad al-Shabab al-Dimuqrati*), the General Federation of Students (*Ittihad al-Talaba al-'Amm*) and the Women's Association (*Rabitat al-Mar'a al-'Iraqiyya*), all of which had been historically under Communist Party leadership. The Communists had been made to freeze their activities in these associations and also to withdraw their representatives from the international organisations to which they were affiliated. In more general terms they demanded the introduction of democratic liberties in accordance with the original agreement, the establishment of the rule of law, and a return to constitutional principles. Although these criticisms and demands were still phrased in a conciliatory and constructive tone it is clear that, within the context of what was very nearly a dictatorship, they constituted an unacceptable 'attack' on the way in which the Ba'th was running the country.

From this time onwards there was a steady deterioration in relations between the two parties, accompanied by an increasingly vitriolic propaganda campaign against the Communists, culminating in witch hunts comparable to those launched by the Ba'th in 1963. Simultaneously, the regime began to extend and perfect its security apparatus, and to accelerate its policy of ensuring that all key positions in the civil service, the police and the armed forces were purged of non-Ba'thists. Hitherto, 'apolitical' individuals had still managed to retain relatively important posts, but after 1976 even the most 'harmless' non-Ba'thists were compulsorily retired, although usually allowed to set up in business on their own. Early in 1976 there were apparently four separate internal intelligence structures watching each other, and the regime's evident obsession with security and the omnipresence of the Ba'th Party and its agents was a matter of widespread comment[46].

This process gathered increasing momentum over the next few years. In addition to the Republican Guard, which acted as the regime's 'bodyguard', there were the Special Forces, with two brigades in 1976, and the People's Army, an adjunct of the Ba'th Party[47], created in 1976 and commanded by Taha Yasin Ramadan, which had a complement of 75,000 in 1979. A further indication of the leadership's concern for its own self-preservation was that in 1978 the Ministry of Interior employed over 150,000 individuals, almost a quarter of all public employees[48]. During this same period there were a number of apocryphal stories in circulation which, although by their nature not susceptible of empirical proof, gave some indication both of the length of the regime's arm and the extent of its determination to eradicate dissent.

By the middle 1970s the Ba'th Party had become an efficiently organised and powerful apparatus, increasingly penetrating every possible sphere of life. The smallest unit was the party cell, *halqa*, consisting of between three and seven members, organised at the neighbourhood or workplace level. It was in these cells that party members received their directives from the leadership; although the directives were supposedly discussed within the cells, the discussions were a matter of form and amounted largely to the acceptance of the orders of the leadership, particularly after the middle 1970s, when the personality cult of Saddam Husain was already in full swing. The next unit was the division, *firqa*, usually consisting of several cells and either covering residential areas such as urban quarters or villages, or units such as factories, government departments, schools, universities, trade unions, or hospitals. The next steps up the hierarchy were the section, *shu'bah*, consisting of five divisions; the branch, *far'*, which consisted of at least two of the former and operated on the provincial level; the regional command, *qiyada qutriyya*, which operated on the national level; and finally the national command, *qiyada qawmiyya*, supposedly functioning on a Pan–Arab level. The whole apparatus was penetrated by the various security services, which were linked directly to Saddam Husain. It was the duty of every party member to report any 'suspicious' behaviour on the part of his neighbours, friends and families.

Although this structure derived from the original organisational plan laid down by 'Aflaq in the 1940s and 1950s, it must be emphasised that it only assumed this degree of uniformity *after* the assumption of power by the Ba'th in 1968. In the course of the early 1970s the party and its affiliated bodies were transformed into effective and efficient organisations. The gradual concentration of power within a small circle at the top was accompanied by the virtual removal of all restrictions on recruitment, resulting in a significant expansion in party membership, which gradually became more or less obligatory for those with career ambitions. Thus the Ba'th claimed to have 10,000 'activists' and half a million 'sympathisers' in 1976; by the early 1980s these figures had expanded to 25,000 and 1.5 million respectively[49]. The regime now had a highly-organised machine at its disposal that it could use for the indoctrination, mobilisation and control of the population whenever required.

This transformation of the Party into an instrument of the leadership was itself a major stabilising factor for the regime. The expansion in numbers also meant that the Party came increasingly to resemble a national rally in which the adulation of itself and the leadership came to take the place of whatever ideological discourse may have existed formerly. On the other hand, as it became increasingly hazardous to engage in non-Ba'thist politics, and criticism of government policies became almost equally dangerous, many people turned away from politics altogether, confining their social activities to a close-knit circle of relatives and trusted friends, and the acquisition of consumer goods.[50].

In addition, Party members were encouraged to report on each other and on their neighbours, colleagues and workmates[51]. A series of Ba'thist organisations was founded to cater for all age groups and walks of life; indoctrination began at primary school, where children were taught poems and songs lauding the achievements and personality of Saddam Husain (and in the beginning also of Ahmad Hasan al-Bakr), and was gradually extended throughout the educational system, so that political rectitude became equivalent to academic excellence. In the same way the much vaunted adult literacy campaign was also pressed into service as a propaganda vehicle for the regime[52].

By the beginning of 1978 the break with the Communists was only a matter of time. In March *Tariq al-Sha'b* carried a series of articles criticising the regime's policies on the Kurds and the economy, implying that it was moving too close to the West for its own good. In reply, an article by Tariq 'Aziz in May in the Ba'th newspaper *al-Rasid* accused the Communists of being excessively subservient to Moscow[53]; three weeks later, it was announced that twelve Communists had been executed for allegedly carrying out political activity in the Army. This 'crime' was a contravention of the terms of the National Front, which had stipulated that no other party than the Ba'th was allowed to carry out any form of political or organisational activity in the armed forces; this had been decreed a capital offence in 1976[54]. However, the application of the ordinance in 1978 against soldiers belonging to the ICP was more out of a desire to put the ICP in its place than out of any real fear of large scale Communist infiltration.

At the end of May 1978 *al-Thawra* warned members of the other political parties that 'the revolutionary punishment of execution' would be meted out to those who tried to penetrate the armed forces; in July the RCC enacted a blanket decree making non-Ba'thist political activity (such as reading the Communist Party newspaper) illegal for all former members of the armed forces, with the death penalty prescribed for offenders[55]. In a country with universal conscription, this provision meant that any adult male discovered engaging in non-Ba'thist political activity was liable to be sentenced to death; at this stage, it should be remembered, the National Front was still officially in existence. In the summer and autumn, there were further reports of executions of Communists and of widespread arrests of Party members[56]. The regime tortured many hundreds of its victims to death in prison over the next months and years; people were dragged out of their houses and never seen again; in some cases, their bodies were thrown in front of their families' houses, dreadfully mutilated; in others, relatives were forced to collect corpses from police stations, and jeered, abused or assaulted while doing so[57]. The outbreak of the war with Iran in September 1980 provided an excuse for an intensification of these bestial practices.

It was not only the Communists who were victimised in this manner; once again the Ba'th was indiscriminate in its savage repression of real or potential opposition. Thus dissident Kurds and members of the clandestine Shi'i parties that sprang up in the 1970s were persecuted along with the Communists as the campaign of terror gathered momentum, and the personality cult — and ultimately the dictatorship — of Saddam Husain took root. Even the Ba'thists themselves were not immune from the attentions of the security services, especially those who were either bold enough or foolhardy enough to question the wisdom of the leadership. In addition individuals were increasingly obliged to demonstrate their positive support for the regime by constant declarations of their approval of the actions of the Ba'th Party and its leader, to the extent that it became more and more difficult even to profess political neutrality[58].

The Kurds, 1975–1979

Although the Algiers Agreement had dealt a fearful blow to the Kurdish movement, the brutal and repressive policies pursued by the regime in the area ensured that the spirit of resistance was not completely crushed. Nevertheless, it can be said that the cultural identity, and even on occasion the physical existence, of the 3 million Kurdish Iraqis has been seriously under threat since 1975[59]. As we have seen, the regime had implemented an ordinance for the self-governing Kurdish area in March 1974. The 'autonomous region' (*mintaqa al-hukm al-dhati*) excluded the Jabal Sinjar, the area between 'Aqra and Mosul, the environs of Kirkuk, Kifri, and the area along the Iranian border between Maidan and Badra. According to Vanly, whose evidence is clear and convincing, the 'autonomous region' accounts for less than half the total area of Iraqi Kurdistan[60]. The boundaries of the provinces of Kirkuk (renamed Ta'mim, nationalisation) and Salah al-Din (a new province based on Takrit) were redrawn to ensure that 'Kirkuk' now had an Arab majority[61]. Apart from the construction of a modern road system in the area and the inauguration of a few scattered development projects, the inhabitants gained little from the new arrangements, and those who were able to do so began to migrate to the cities of northern and central Iraq. There was very little in the way of instruction in Kurdish inside the 'autonomous region' and none at all in the areas outside it in the late 1970s[62].

However, the greatest hardship suffered by the population of the area was brought about by the forcible transfer of large numbers of Kurds either to distant parts of the country or to parts of the area itself that were more accessible to government control. Estimates of the numbers 'resettled' vary greatly, especially as the process continued for several years after the Algiers Agreement, and also because some of them were subsequently allowed to return, but as many as 250,000–300,000 people may have been involved. Generally, the deportees fell into three broad categories: first, those who had been closely involved in the fighting, and had surrendered themselves to the Iraqi authorities either immediately after March 1975 or under the terms of subsequent amnesties; second, the Kurdish inhabitants of ethnically-mixed areas, especially around Kirkuk; and finally the entire populations of villages situated close to the frontiers with Iran and Turkey, where the regime set up a *cordon sanitaire* between itself and its neighbours in order to 'prevent infiltration'[63]. Thus many families were rounded up at the end of 1975 and the beginning of 1976, put on trucks and taken to southern Iraq, where they were distributed in Arab villages in groups of up to five families. The Kurdish villages were then destroyed or re-occupied by Arabs, either Iraqis or Egyptians[64]. Apart from the fact that very few of the deportees would have spoken Arabic, they were often intimidated by the flat and desolate landscape of the Arab South, and disoriented by the destruction of their communities and the disruption of their traditional way of life. Thus, as the regime must have intended, the mere threat of deportation could be used as a powerful weapon of control in the Kurdish area. However, there were also attempts to obtain their support; huge payments were given to a number of individuals and families, some of whom found themselves in possession of considerable sums of money for the first time.[65].

In the course of the implementation of the *cordon sanitaire* policy many of the inhabitants of the border areas were 'resettled' in specially constructed villages, situated on the outskirts of towns or next to main roads in Southern Kurdistan or on the Kurdish plains, often surrounded by barbed wire[66]. Ironically, the Ba'th pointed to these new agglomerations, and its increased spending in the North, as evidence of its commitment to 'modernise' and 'develop' the 'autonomous region'; of course, whatever amenities the new structures may have had, those who were made to live in them could no longer continue with their traditional agricultural or pastoral way of life[67].

Under such circumstances, the leaders of the Kurdish resistance took some time to regroup and reorganise their forces, but, in view of the regime's evident determination to pacify the area, it was remarkable that they were able to do so and to begin to mount guerilla operations in the area by the beginning of 1977. Briefly, after the debacle of March 1975 the Kurdish movement split into two principal rival factions, the KDP-Provisional Leadership (KDP-PL) led by Mas'ud Barzani, and the Patriotic Union of Kurdistan (PUK), founded and led by Jalal Talabani, the Barzanis' long-standing political rival. The extent to which their father had miscalculated, and his personal responsibility for the defeat in 1975, meant that the claim of Mas'ud Barzani and his younger brother Idris to succeed him as leaders of the movement did not pass unchallenged. Talabani, the son-in-law and successor of Ibrahim Ahmad, a highly-sophisticated, shrewd politician and unscrupulous operator who had opposed Mulla Mustafa's 'feudal' style of leadership since the latter's return from the Soviet Union in 1958, was keen to step into his place and to establish his own hegemony over the whole of Kurdistan. Talabani claimed to be building up a party based on 'Marxist–Leninist' ideology, and to be pursuing a policy of revolutionary armed struggle to achieve autonomy for Kurdistan[68]. The two parties are still in conflict with each other for the leadership of the movement at the time of writing.

The Communists' decision to take up arms against the regime in 1979 meant that they became the third guerilla organisation in Kurdistan, concentrating their activities particularly in areas where they had traditionally enjoyed strong support. No permanent alliance was forged between them and either of the two Kurdish parties, although attempts in this direction were made from time to time. However, the presence of the Communists was an important factor in the constant balancing act between the KDP-PL and the PUK, and their actual or potential supporters in Tehran and Damascus. Subsequently, Baghdad also took advantage of the conflict to try to attach one or other of the factions to itself against the others.

Since most of the information about Kurdish politics since 1975 comes from the parties themselves, it is difficult to obtain an accurate picture either of their numerical strength or their support on the ground. Nevertheless, there were reports of sporadic guerilla activity in the area at least since the beginning of 1977, and the regime continued to maintain substantial numbers of troops there all through the 1970s[69]. In general, the Iraqi regime was able to maintain the upper hand while the border with Iran remained closed, but the situation changed dramatically with the fall of the Shah in February 1979. After the Iranian Revolution the Algiers

Agreement collapsed, and the Ba'th was suddenly faced with a
resurgence of the problem that it had managed to contain since
1975. In addition, the virtual anarchy that prevailed in Iran
encouraged some of the Iraqi Kurds to set up new bases in Iranian
Kurdistan. Clearly alarmed by these activities, the Ba'th invited
the Turkish military leader General Evren to Baghdad in April
1979 to coordinate the Kurdish policies of the two countries, and in
July it was announced that anyone attempting to penetrate into
Iraq across the Turkish border would be executed[70].

The Shi'i Opposition

It is a commonplace of much historical and political analysis of
recent and contemporary Iraq that there is a fundamental and
decisive conflict, sometimes latent and sometimes open, between
the Sunni and Shi'i sects, and furthermore that acceptance of this
'fact' is vital for a proper understanding of contemporary events.
According to this argument, the principal tensions in Iraqi society
derive from the fact that a minority Sunni regime is ruling over a
predominantly Shi'i population. Supporters of this view will no
doubt feel that they have been vindicated by events, and that the
war between Iran and Iraq that began in the autumn of 1980 must
be seen as a particularly dramatic, but otherwise entirely 'natural',
expression of this age old, almost primordial, conflict. However,
the 'real' nature of Sunni/Shi'i relations is much more complex
than this attractive but ultimately inadequate approach can
accommodate. Furthermore, it is important to stress that there is
no sense in which the Sunni rulers of Iraq in the 1970s and 1980s
have tried to promote Sunni sectarianism, or are in any way
'representing', or, indeed, regarded as representing, Sunni Islam[71].

Some years ago we tried to put this thesis in perspective, coming
to the conclusion that while sectarian affiliation has always been
important and should not be ignored, the fundamental division,
whether or not perceived as such either by those involved or by
outsiders, was not 'religious' or 'sectarian', but socio-economic,
between the haves, and the have-nots, who were distributed
between both the sects[72]. Of course, as the bulk of the population
lived in the rural South, and as the overwhelming majority of these
rural-dwellers were Shi'is, the Shi'is accounted for the majority of
the rural poor. In addition, as the Shi'i inhabitants of the southern

provinces began to migrate to Baghdad in increasing numbers, they also came to constitute the majority of the urban poor in the slums that grew up around Baghdad and other cities after the Second World War. Naturally, the Shi'i poor, both those still living in villages and those who had migrated to the cities in search of work, were poor not because they were Shi'is but because, in the comparatively recent past, the great tribal *diras* (estates) of the South on which they lived had been appropriated by powerful tribal leaders, and the tribesmen had been left either entirely without land or with insufficient land for their subsistence. Needless to say, almost all the great tribal landlords of the rural South, the principal exploiters of the rural poor, were themselves Shi'is.

The arrival of increasing numbers of migrants from the countryside had the effect of creating a new social grouping in the towns, which, although almost entirely Shi'i, had little or no contact with the established urban Shi'i population, still less with the 'high Islam' of the Holy Cities, Batatu has pointed out that many of the Shi'is of the rural South had only relatively recently converted to Shi'ism, whose:

> Anti-governmental motif, its pre-occupation with oppression, its grief-laden tales and its miracle play representing Husayn's passion accorded with the instincts and sufferings of tribesmen-turned-peasants . . .[73]

In addition, their Shi'ism was worn fairly lightly, and found its main expression not in prayers and fasting but in participation in the great festivals and processions, which were also the main occasions on which they would come into contact with their urban co-religionists.

The traditional *urban* Shi'is, who had been settled in Karbala', Najaf, Kadhimain and in other parts of Baghdad for centuries, were engaged primarily in trade and handicrafts in the bazaars, or in the various religious occupations, in very much the same way as their counterparts in Iran. In contrast to the new migrants, who eagerly sought the security of government employment, the longer established urban Shi'is had traditionally tended to distrust and distance themselves from the central government, (whether Ottoman, British or Arab), and to look to their relations or to local patrons for employment and assistance. This was perhaps in part due to a residual attachment to the belief that service in a temporal government is somehow 'unsuitable' as a career[74], although it is also true that such notions gradually became outmoded with the spread of modern education[75]. For very similar reasons, few Shi'is joined the armed forces as officers under the mandate and monarchy, and of those who did very few rose to high rank[76], although as more than half of the population were Shi'i, they formed a correspondingly high proportion of the ordinary conscript soldiers.

The traditional disinclination of the established urban Shi'i population to seek employment in government service was only in part because of religious 'scruples'. The Ottoman Empire had been a Sunni institution, and its administrators in Iraq were almost entirely either Sunni Turks or Sunni Arabs from the educated and notable families of Baghdad and Mosul. Further-more, such government educational facilities as existed in late Ottoman Iraq were Sunni institutions. Hence, when the British came, the Sunni Arab townsmen continued to supply the main cadres for the administration and the Army, both from the old notable families or from the ranks of the so-called nationalists, many of whom were ex-Ottoman officers and officials. For obvious reasons, there were very few Shi'is available for these functions, which meant that in numerical terms the Shi'is were grossly under-represented in government service and also, for similar reasons, in all the cabinets of the pre-revolutionary period, although, because of the nature of the institution, many Shi'i tribal leaders occupied parliamentary seats.

In addition, apart from a number of notorious but otherwise isolated incidents, such as the retribution exacted from the inhabitants of Najaf after the murder of a British Assistant Political Officer there in March 1918[77] and the expulsion of a number of Shi'i 'ulama' who refused to renounce their public opposition to the Anglo-Iraqi Treaty in June 1923[78], the govern-ments of the mandate and monarchy had generally been careful not to interfere with the internal affairs of the Shi'i holy cities, and this circumspection continued under the regimes of Qasim and the 'Arifs. Furthermore, since the Revolution of 1958 began as a coup d'état organised by a secret committee of fifteen military officers, only two of whom were Shi'is, the familiar pattern continued to reproduce itself, although by this time, with the spread of education among all classes and sects of the urban population, the Shi'is had begun to make a proportionally greater contribution to the ranks of the civil service, including the teaching profession.

During the period between the Second World War and the late 1960s a series of important developments had affected the urban Shi'i population as a whole. In the first place, large scale migration to the towns continued, and it was accompanied by the burgeoning of slum areas on the outskirts of Baghdad and other large cities. As has been indicated, there was very little contact between the new arrivals and the old-established urban Shi'i communities, partly for social reasons, and partly because the institutions of Shi'ism had never been widely-spread in the Iraqi countryside. Thus the new migrants had little exposure to what may be called 'orthodoxy', and, very broadly speaking, much of their Shi'ism was cultural and more superstitious than formally religious. Furthermore, especially in their new and extremely deprived urban setting, many of them were attracted to the egalitarian values and principles of the Communist Party, which was at the forefront of the national struggle between 1945 and 1958, and large numbers joined its ranks. Of course, it would be wrong to suggest that the rural migrants had any profound understanding of the theories of Marxist/Leninism: the appeal of the Communist Party lay in its uncompromising calls for the overthrow of a regime that was self-evidently controlled by foreign strategic and economic interests, and for an end to the exploitation and poverty of which this particular constituency was only too aware. In addition the Communist Party also found strong support among important sections of the traditional urban Shi'i population, as is evident from the number of prominent early Communists who originated from this background[79].

Over this same period a decline had been taking place in the social status and economic standing of all but the most prominent Shi'i *mujtahids* (experts in jurisprudence). The main reason for this was the rise of secularism in the Middle East, which made the religious professions less attractive and also resulted in a drop in the contributions of the faithful for the upkeep of the shrines and the salaries of the Shi'i clergy, who did not have the benefit of the *waqf* (pious endowment) incomes of their Sunni counterparts[80]. Furthermore, as Batatu has suggested, in Iraq, in contradistinction to Iran with its much longer *settled* rural tradition, there was little formal religious activity outside the towns, of the kind that ensured the presence of a mulla in almost every Iranian village, and required a constant supply of graduates from the theological institutes. In addition, the gradual spread of modern education to even the hardiest Shi'i centres, the expansion of career opportunities in government service and the growing attraction of such careers for many sections of the Shi'i population resulted in an inevitable reduction in the number recruited into the religious professions[81].

Furthermore, it is important to consider the attraction exercised by the various political currents of the time on the Shi'i population. As we have seen, the ideological arena before the Ba'th seized power in 1968 was divided between Arab nationalism on the one hand and communism on the other. Although both ideologies are professedly secular, Arab nationalism, particularly Nasserism, has almost inescapably Sunni connotations, and the various unity schemes bandied about in the late 1950s and early 1960s were largely unattractive to the Shi'is, most of whom felt themselves to be more Iraqi than Arab and also feared that any such arrangement with Egypt or Syria might lead to their being drowned in a 'Sunni ocean'.

Similarly, Ba'thism, although not directly identified with Sunni Islam, also has definite aspirations towards Arab unity, an ideal for which the majority of Iraqi Shi'is have never expressed much positive enthusiasm. Thus, while not wishing to suggest that all politically articulate Shi'is were attracted to communism, it is safe to say that few of them were positively attracted either to Arab nationalism or to Ba'thism. The only major exception to this was the group around Fu'ad al-Rikabi, the Shi'i founder of the Ba'th party in Iraq in 1952. As he recruited primarily among his friends and relatives, many of the first Iraqi Ba'thists were Shi'is. However, it must be emphasised that they were al-Rikabi's family and associates before anything else, so that when he left the Ba'th in 1959 almost all of them left with him. Furthermore, when control of the Ba'th passed into the hands of the Takritis after 1968, there were no Shi'is *at all* in the higher echelons of the party, a state of affairs that did not change until the appointment of four Shi'is to the RCC in September 1977[82].

Although Shi'is did join the Ba'th Party after it had established itself in power, and a number rose to important positions in the course of time, it can safely be asserted that the majority of the Shi'i population remained indifferent to Ba'thism. It was only after the

Ba'th began to concern itself with the situation of the Shi'i poor, especially the fallahin, that some of the barriers were broken and more Shi'is began to support the Party, although they were probably more attracted by its social policies than by its ideology. However, it should be emphasised that by the middle 1970s it was becoming increasingly difficult for both Sunnis and Shi'is *not* to show 'enthusiasm' for the regime, and any evidence of 'growing Shi'i support' should also be considered in this light.

So far, we have discussed the recent politicisation of the urban Shi'is in somewhat narrow terms, in the context of their recruitment to, or enthusiasm for, the political parties of the 1940s, 1950s and 1960s. Of course, many devout Shi'is, and in particular many professional men of religion, viewed these developments with great apprehension and disapproval, particularly in the context of the growing hold that atheist communism seemed to be exerting on many members of their community. This concern did not find very much practical expression under the monarchy, although a leading divine, Ayatullah Kashif al-Ghita', had expressed his concern about the rising tide of communism as early as 1953[83]. However, in the years immediately after the revolution of 1958, when the threat of communism appeared to be particularly acute, the tide of clerical alarm and opposition gathered greater momentum.

In the autumn of 1958, some of the leading *'ulama'* of Najaf took the unusual step of founding a political organisation, *Jama'at al-'Ulama' fi Najaf al-Ashraf* (the Association of Najaf *'ulama'*), whose members formed the nucleus of what became *al-Da'wa al-Islamiya* (the Islamic Call, or Mission) in 1968. The declared purpose of the Association was to raise the consciousness of the community and to combat atheism, which was then more or less synonymous with communism and Marxism, as Ba'thism was still not particularly influential, and, like Nasserism, had little or no echo among the Shi'i population. Since the Association was a secret society, it is difficult to obtain accurate information about its origins and membership, but it is clear that Muhammad Baqir al-Sadr, then aged about thirty, played an important role in its activities, and appears to have been the author of many of its publications[84].

In the late 1950s and early 1960s, the two senior *marji'-s* (supreme legal authorities) in Iraq, Muhsin al-Hakim (al-Tabataba'i) and Abu'l-Qasim al-Khu'i, were living in Najaf, where they were joined in 1964 by the exiled Ruhallah Khumaini. In 1960 Muhsin al-Hakim issued a *fatwa* (decree) forbidding membership of the Communist Party, which was then at the height of its influence[85]. At the same time his much younger colleague Muhammad Baqir al-Sadr was establishing his reputation as the leading Iraqi Shi'i intellectual of his day, with his two major works *Falsafatuna* (Our Philosophy) and *Iqtisaduna* (Our Economic System), which appeared in 1959 and 1961 respectively. In spite of its title, *Falsafatuna* is a wide-ranging critique of European philosophy rather than an exposition of Islamic thought, and testifies to its author's breadth of reading and analytical skill; while *Iqtisaduna*, a highly influential work that has gone into at least eleven editions[86], is a book of some 700 pages containing a long discussion of European economic and social thought as well as an outline of the ideological foundations of an Islamic economic order. It is significant that almost a third of the text of *Iqtisaduna* is an attempt to refute Marxism and dialectical materialism in what may be described as rational rather than religious terms, reflecting the concern of its author in the late 1950s and early 1960s to try to produce convincing counter-arguments to what was evidently the principal political current of the day. In very general terms, although al-Sadr's work apparently does not contain a single reference to any work of Khumaini's, and the two do not seem to have been in close contact with each other during the latter's exile in Najaf between 1964 and 1978, their ideas on the proper form of the Islamic polity have many similarities, as was also clear from al-Sadr's enthusiastic approval of the Iranian revolution in 1979[87].

Although opinions differ on the precise circumstances of its foundation, it seems that al-Sadr, who had himself attained the rank of *marji'* at or about the same time, was at least the moving spirit behind the formation of *al-Da'wa* in 1968. Unlike the Association of *'ulama'*, *al-Da'wa*, although a clandestine organisation, was aimed at a wider constituency. Its founders attempted to set up a secret network of members, whose task was to assist in the creation of an Islamic order along the lines proclaimed in the underground periodical *Sawt al-Da'wa*. Abstracting from al-Sadr's writings, the basic principles of the organisation have been summarised as follows:

Even in the early centuries of its foundation, the religion of Islam was not practised as it should have been, but it was nevertheless the principal and only determinant of the Islamic polity. In those days, it was sufficient to correct abuses. However, since the establishment of the dominion of the imperialist powers over the Islamic world, Islam has lost its function as the basis of the social order, and essentially alien principles, such as capitalist democracy and Marxist socialism, have taken its place. As well as having begun to determine the outward development of Muslim society, these ideologies have had an adverse effect on the development of Muslim thought, in the sense that many Muslims have lost the ability to conceive of Islam as the all-embracing spiritual foundation of their lives. In this situation, mere reform or correction is not sufficient, and the various un-Islamic social orders and their ideological principles must be replaced by the principles of Islam, and the achievement of this goal is a revolutionary task[88]. An important feature of this writing is that much of it is addressed to Muslims in general rather than to Shi'is in particular.

The possibility that such doctrines might gain widespread acceptance was unlikely to be welcome to a regime whose secularism could scarcely be doubted, and *al-Da'wa* and the other Shi'i movements began to cause the Ba'th considerable alarm by the early 1970s, when a separate branch of the security services was created to deal specifically with potential Shi'i opposition groups. Although the original impetus behind the foundation of Shi'i political organisations in the 1950s had been to act as a counterweight to the Communists, the phenomenon of *al-Da'wa* and of similar organisations, both Sunni and Shi'i, in other Muslim countries in the 1960s should be understood more in terms of a reaction against secularism, and in particular against the increasing encroachment of the state into every sphere of life.

In the context of the Iraqi Shi'i hierarchy such intrusions were the more unwelcome for having been of relatively recent origin, since, as we have seen, they had been left more or less to their own devices by the Ba'th's predecessors in government since the formation of the state in 1920. With the Ba'th however, the *'ulama'* faced two simultaneous challenges to their authority. In the first place, the regime proclaimed itself to be uncompromisingly secular, and in this respect, incidentally, as offensive to religious Sunnis as to religious Shi'is. Secondly, it was profoundly committed to asserting its right to control all areas of public life without exception, which constituted a potentially serious threat to the status quo as far as the traditional position and privileges of the *'ulama'* were concerned.

As early as 1969, Ayatullah Muhsin al-Hakim had found it necessary to protest to the Ba'th against what he termed its 'degradation of the religious leaders' in the holy cities, accusing government officials there of being 'infidels'[89]. However, the first widely-reported indirect indication of the existence of Shi'i opposition groups was the execution, for reasons that were not made public at the time, of five *'ulama'* in December 1974[90]. These exemplary sentences seem to have had the effect of dampening down opposition from that quarter for some time, since there were no further signs of specifically Shi'i unrest over the next two years.

A much more ominous incident, indicating a far wider degree of public involvement, took place in February 1977, on the occasion of the 'Ashura celebrations in the Islamic month of Muharram, when thousands of pilgrims gather at the shrines of Karbala' and Najaf. On 5 and 6 February the clergy appeared at the head of large protest demonstrations that seem to have taken the regime by surprise. Troops were dispatched to the holy cities, and a number of pilgrims were killed in the fighting which followed. Some 2000 people were arrested, including Muhammad Baqir al-Hakim, the son of the Ayatullah Muhsin al-Hakim, who had died in 1970[91]. The actual course of events is somewhat obscure, as the Ba'th used the occasion as a pretext for intensifying its campaign against its Syrian counterparts, with whom it had been locked in a long-standing dispute over the amount of water from the Euphrates that the Syrians were prepared to allow to flow into Iraq after the construction of the Tabqa dam[92]. A Syrian soldier was apparently caught planting explosives in the main mosque in Karbala', and this was seized upon as evidence of Syrian complicity in the disturbances. In this way the regime was able to gloss over or play down the extent to which the demonstrations were expressions of opposition organised by members of the religious establishment.

At the end of February a special court under Dr 'Izzat Mustafa, a member of the RCC and Minister of Municipal and Rural Affairs, Fulayyih Hasan al-Jasim, the Minister of State for Kurdish Affairs, and Hasan 'Ali al-'Amiri, the Minister of Trade, was set up to investigate the incidents in Karbala' and Najaf and to punish those responsible. al-Jasim and al-'Amiri, who were both Shi-is, had been appointed to the Ba'th Regional Command in January.

As a result of the court's activities eight *'ulama'* were executed and fifteen sentenced to life imprisonment[93]. These punishments seem to have been considered excessively lenient, and two of the 'judges' (Mustafa and al-Jasim) were dismissed from their RCC and cabinet posts and expelled from the Ba'th Party in the course of an emergency Party congress at the end of March[94].

Although the Ba'th had made great play of the Syrian bogey in the aftermath of the Muharram incidents, it can be surmised from the declarations of Saddam Husain in the following months that the regime did take the affair very seriously and was also aware of the real underlying causes. A clear change in tone was discernible from a speech in August, in which he announced that the Ba'th was 'on the side of belief always', but also warned against the use of religion as a cloak for opposition to the regime and its policies[95]. Of course, in the prevailing social climate the Ba'th had come to terms with the fact that religion and the influence of the religious hierarchy could not be stamped out simply by the adoption of draconian measures. In consequence it tried to change its image by adopting a more overtly Islamic stance, while also attempting to win over some of the *'ulama'*.

However, the majority of the Shi'i clergy were not to be convinced in this way, and Muhammad Baqir al-Sadr, although managing to avoid an open confrontation with the regime at this stage, gradually emerged as the main symbol of Shi'i opposition. At the same time *al-Da'wa* continued to constitute a threat to the regime, although it is difficult to determine how strong the movement actually became. Of course, it was not so much the numerical strength of *al-Da'wa* that was decisive, but rather that such an organisation could not easily be controlled or penetrated by the security apparatus, and also that, given the nature of the Shi'i politico-religious tradition, any Shi'i movement could always be a potential focus of spontaneous revolt[96].

An uneasy *modus vivendi* continued on both sides until the expulsion of Khumaini in October 1978 and the inauguration of the Islamic Republic in Iran a few months later. Particularly in its early stages, before it had begun to discredit itself with acts of brutality and inhumanity, the Iranian Revolution engendered a tremendous sense of optimism and enthusiasm among a wide body of Muslim opinion, and this atmosphere evidently encouraged *al-Da'wa* and its leaders to engage the Ba'th in open conflict, attacking Party offices and police posts and making open declarations of their support for the Iranian Revolution[97]. The Ba'th responded with its familiar carrot and stick tactics, first by making a series of apparently conciliatory gestures, including setting aside large grants (over ID 24 million in 1979 alone) for religious purposes, 'showing increasing deference to Islam' in public statements, and by arranging televised visits to the Shi'i South and Madinat al-Thawra during which television sets and gifts of money were distributed in public, usually by Saddam Husain in person[98].

At the same time, it launched a ferocious campaign against *al-Da'wa* and its leaders. Large numbers of those suspected of being members of the organisation were arrested, and actual membership was made punishable by death[99]. al-Sadr himself was taken to Baghdad for interrogation in the spring of 1979; when he refused to make a public recantation of his position, he was put under house arrest in Najaf, with no contacts with the outside world after water, electricity and the telephone were cut off in July[100]. Eventually, after an attempt on the life of Tariq 'Aziz at Mustansiriyah University early in April 1980, allegedly carried out by an Iranian, al-Sadr and his sister Bint Huda were once more taken to Baghdad, where they were executed by the Ba'th on 9 April. The regime's ruthlessness, which we have already seen operating against all other real or potential opposition, seems to have been effective to the extent that no major Shi'i demonstrations were reported after al-Sadr's seclusion in 1979. Furthermore, to the Ba'th's inestimable advantage, the war with Iran pre-empted the possibility of any effective re-formation of the movement in Iraq itself by creating a situation in which the idea of a 'Shi'i polity' became synonymous with treason.

Foreign Relations, 1975–1980

Although Iraq's tentative attempts to disassociate itself from its leftist stance in the middle 1970s were welcomed by most of its neighbours, their continuing distrust and the regime's own unpredictable and erratic behaviour meant that the process of Iraq's reintegration into the 'higher counsels' of Middle Eastern politics was somewhat uneven. However, the changing political circumstances in the region after 1973 produced an atmosphere that put growing pressure upon Iraq to put an end to its 'radicalism' and to its strident extremism. In this situation the gradual weakening of ties with the Soviet Union, the new oil wealth, and the agreement concluded with Iran meant that Iraq was now in a better position to improve its relations with its neighbours and also to play a more vigorous part in the politics of the region. Thus during the period between the Algiers Agreement in March 1975 and the outbreak of the war with Iran in September 1980 Iraqi foreign policy can be seen as a combination of fence-mending with potential allies and belligerency towards rivals, accompanied, almost as a logical corollary, by an equal mixture of extreme verbal militancy and profound practical caution on the Arab–Israeli conflict.

Even before the signature of the Algiers Agreement, the Iraqi regime was proclaiming its intention of pursuing better relations with Kuwait and Sa'udi Arabia[101]. Iraqi–Kuwaiti relations had never quite recovered from Qasim's ill-conceived attempt to annex Kuwait in 1961, and there had been border clashes between the two states as recently as March 1973. However, a process of reconciliation was initiated, and by June 1975 the long-standing border dispute had been settled[102]. Similarly, Prince Fahd's visit to Baghdad in June 1975 marked the beginning of improved relations between Iraq and Sa'udi Arabia, and the two countries came to an agreement on the delimitation of the neutral zone on the borders between them later in the year[103]. In the course of his speech on the seventh anniversary of the Ba'th's seizure of power, on 17 July 1975, al-Bakr declared that 'in accordance with our clear pan-Arab outlook we have sought to deepen understanding with the Arab countries of the Gulf, particularly Sa'udi Arabia, and to solve the issues pending with them'[104].

These protestations of goodwill on the Iraqi side and expressions of correct, if somewhat guarded, enthusiasm on the part of Iraq's neighbours continued over the next few years, in spite of Sa'udi Arabia's clear financial and 'moral' commitment to Syria, Iraq's principal rival in the region. In April 1976, in the course of a visit to Jidda, Saddam Husain affirmed the need for joint action between Sa'udi Arabia 'and all the states of the Gulf', and in October 1977 a series of important joint technical and trade agreements was announced[105]. Again, after the Iraqi leadership had begun to adopt a more consistent policy in response to Sadat's visit to Jerusalem, it managed to obtain a large measure of support from Sa'udi Arabia and the Gulf states[106], which continued through and beyond the brief and ultimately unavailing period of Iraqi–Syrian amity between November 1978 and July 1979. A high point of the hyperbole of the period, and particularly indicative of his eagerness to demonstrate his anti-Communist credentials, was Saddam Husain's declaration in April 1979, a few weeks after the conclusion of a Sa'udi/Iraqi security treaty in the immediate aftermath of the Iranian revolution, that Iraq would never allow Sa'udi Arabia to be occupied by the Soviet Union[107].

Although it was easy for the Iraqi regime to make the case that the claims of Arab brotherhood and solidarity made it imperative for it to pursue good relations with its Arab neighbours, it was both less inclined and less able to extend such cordiality to its Ba'th brothers in Syria. In order to maintain some degree of credibility it had to continue to phrase its policies in nationalist and unionist terms and appear to be more militant and more Arab than the Syrians, notably, of course, on Palestine. In this and other ways it tried to uphold its claim to the leadership of Arab radicalism throughout the latter part of the 1970s, while simultaneously maintaining that the achievement of Arab unity was constantly being frustrated by ill-will or intransigence on the Syrian side, a charge that the Syrians were equally ready to level at Iraq.

Apart from a brief explosion of ecstatic good neighbourliness, which lasted from the autumn of 1978 to July 1979, Iraqi–Syrian relations between 1968 and 1980 were never particularly cordial and were in fact more often downright hostile. As we have mentioned[108], the Ba'th Party was founded as a Pan-Arab organisation for which the boundaries between Arab states were essentially artificial divisions, and it was to be the Party's task to remove these boundaries and eventually to reunite the Arabs within a single political entity. Thus Ba'thist ideology always refers to the ensemble of the Arab countries as the 'Arab homeland' (*al-watan al-'arabi*), and to each Arab country as a 'region' (*qutr*) of the homeland. However, in 1966 there was a split within the Party between its founders, Michel 'Aflaq and Salah al-Din Bitar and their Iraqi supporters on the National Command on the one hand, and (mostly Syrian) members of the so-called 'Neo-Ba'th' led by Salah Jadid on the other, which resulted in the expulsion of 'Aflaq and Bitar from Syria. The Party now became divided into two wings, effectively the Syrian Ba'th and the Iraqi Ba'th, each of which claimed to be the sole legitimate representative of the party in the 'homeland'[109]. Bitar dropped out of active politics almost immediately, but 'Aflaq became secretary general of the Baghdad-based wing of the Party after the Ba'th came to power in 1968.

Although neither the Syrians nor the Iraqis would accept the truth of this assertion, there is no fundamental *ideological* disagreement between 'two Ba'ths', so that the legitimacy of the one derives naturally from the illegitimacy of the other, which explains the bitterness of the differences between them and by extension the constant need to assert these differences. In such circumstances any re-establishment of links between the two seemed, *a priori*, almost unimaginable, since the resolution of the conflict would have to take the form of a merger or the absorption of one side by the other. It also explains why the struggle between them for hegemony or influence intensified in direct proportion to Iraq's success in manoeuvring itself into a position where it could exert more leverage in the region.

However, the situation in the Middle East as a whole was greatly altered by Sadat's decision to go to Jerusalem in November 1977, since this marked such a major departure from the previous norms of inter-Arab politics as to require a fundamental change in the ground rules; even those states that had never enjoyed particularly cordial relations with each other were obliged at least to make public profession of some form of solidarity against Sadat. These circumstances also combined to bring about a situation in which Saddam Husain was increasingly tempted to assert his own and Iraq's pretensions to fill the leadership vacuum, for which, given Sa'udi Arabia's more circumscribed political style, Syria was the only other serious contender. Thus readers of *al-Thawra* were informed in the run-up to the Baghdad summit that 'The eyes of the Arabs everywhere have been turned towards your great revolution in this country and to your brave Party which has shouldered the trust and responsibility of the pan-Arab struggle for over thirty [sic] years'.

Of course, expressions of outrage, vows to resist Sadat's policies to the bitter end and other professions of unrelenting hostility were accompanied by the adoption of measures on Iraq's part that effectively impeded 'the creation of a viable anti-Sadat front'[110], notably its failure to sign the final communiqué of the 'rejectionist' conference in Tripoli in December 1977[111] and its boycott of the Algiers conference (February 1978) on the grounds that both meetings implied an indirect acceptance of UN Resolution 242.

This apparent intransigence was primarily a ploy to enable Saddam Husain to manoeuvre himself into a position where he could take a leading part in coordinating 'opposition' to Sadat, and in the process carve out a major role for himself in inter-Arab affairs[112]. In this he was aided by the more moderate Arab states, who had no desire to take any particularly strong or punitive measures against Egypt and wished to find some face-saving formula to restrain the hardliners in Algiers, Damascus and Tripoli.

Having rejected the measures proposed by the latter in Tripoli and Algiers on the grounds that they were too modest, Saddam Husain invited his Arab allies to meet in Baghdad in November 1978 to coordinate the action to be taken in the aftermath of the initialling of the Camp David Accords on 17 September[113]. However, apart from asserting the 'Arab nation's commitment to a just peace'[114], the Baghdad summit did not go beyond threatening to take various economic sanctions against Egypt if and when the treaty with Israel was formally signed. In fact, when this did happen early in 1979, there was no further mention of sanctions, and a second, lower level Baghdad summit (convened in March 1979) opted merely for the diplomatic isolation of Egypt, which amounted to her expulsion from the Arab League and the transfer of the League's headquarters from Cairo to Tunis.

A curious, but in some ways, logical, by-product of these events was a sudden and dramatic improvement in relations between Iraq and Syria. On 7 November, Baghdad and Damascus announced that the two countries were 'one state, one Party and one people', and that preparatory measures leading ultimately to complete unity between the two countries would immediately be set in motion. The sheer unreality and irrelevance of such declarations had been proved on so many occasions in the past that neither the slow progress towards 'unity'[115], nor the total rupture of relations between the two states the following July after the 'discovery' of a 'plot' against the Iraqi regime allegedly masterminded by Syria, came as the slightest surprise. Nevertheless the episode is interesting as an illustration of the kind of accommodation, however temporary and unreal, which Iraq's, or Saddam Husain's, changing role required.

The period between the Baghdad Summit and the beginning of the war with Iran in 1980 marks the culmination of Saddam Husain's attempts to launch himself as a, if not *the*, leading Arab statesman. By 1978, his fence-mending with Iraq's more moderate neighbours had evidently begun to bear fruit; as well as having good relations with pre-revolutionary Iran, Sa'udi Arabia and the Gulf States, Iraq's relations with Jordan had improved significantly, with King Husain in attendance at the Baghdad summit, and, as we have seen, largely because of Iraqi astuteness, the Arab states had admonished rather than bludgeoned Egypt.

On a wider international level, the Ba'th began to move more openly away from the Soviet Union. Thus in May 1978 Iraq threatened to break off diplomatic relations if the Soviet Union continued to support the Ethiopian regime against the 'fraternal' Eritrean secessionists[116]. On 17 July Ahmad Hasan al-Bakr's anniversary speech made no mention of the Soviet Union or the Soviet Friendship Treaty[117], and the regime began to move more vigorously and more openly against the Communist Party in the course of 1978 and 1979[118], showing that it was no longer interested in taking Soviet sensibilities into account. In the course of a long interview in an American newspaper Saddam Husain appeared to have forgotten his recent enthusiasm for the Soviet Union, declaring that it 'will not be satisfied until the whole world is Communist'[119]. By April 1979, in the wake of the confusion of the Iranian revolution, the 'slide to the right' had already reached such proportions for the *Guardian* to be able to comment:

> It is not far-fetched to suggest, as the Ba'th's critics do, that after the revolution in Iran the Ba'thists are aiming to present themselves, if not exactly as America's gendarme in the Gulf, at least as a guarantor of its stability along with the Sa'udis.[120]

As the following months and years were to show, it was in fact the Iranian Revolution, and Saddam Husain's misjudgement of its potential, that came to constitute the fatal and unforeseen obstacle to his further development as an international statesman.

The Struggle for Power within the Ba'th Party — Saddam Husain and his Rivals, 1976-1980

It will be remembered that when the Ba'th came to power in July 1968 most of the leadership was unknown in the country at large, with the exception of al-Bakr, who had been a Free Officer in 1958 and Prime Minister between February and November 1963. Saddam Husain, then aged 31, had achieved a certain notoriety because of his involvement in the attempt to assassinate Qasim in 1959, but had no other claims to distinction, at least outside the ranks of the Ba'th Party. We have already shown the development of the inter-dependence between the two men, based largely on their links with and control over the Ba'th Party hierarchy inside and outside the armed forces. After the dismissal of Hardan al-Takriti and 'Ammash and the foiling of Kazzar's plot in July 1973, there were no serious challenges to the leadership of al-Bakr and Saddam Husain; at least on the surface, apart from a few purges and dismissals, the two seemed firmly in control. At the same time, while establishing the Party's increasingly exclusive control over every sphere of life, Saddam Husain was using his newly-acquired diplomatic and political skills to make sure that every single organ in the state or Party eventually came under his control.

al-Bakr's personal influence with senior officers had un-doubtedly been important in establishing the regime in power in the first few years of its existence. However, the rapid Ba'thisation of the armed forces in the late 1960s and 1970s, involving the appointment of Party commissars at all levels, and the enforced retirement, normally on generous pensions, even of officers sympathetic to the Party if their total commitment could not be guaranteed, gradually subordinated the armed forces to the Party to such an extent that al-Bakr's function as mediator between 'the military' and 'the civilians' became increasingly redundant.

In January 1976, Saddam Husain, who had no military background, had himself 'promoted' to the rank of general, retrospectively from 1 July 1973. A few weeks later, it was announced that the complement of the People's Militia, the Ba'th Party's own military force under the command of Taha Yasin Ramadan would be doubled[121]; over the next few years, its equipment was gradually built up sufficiently for it to be able to act, if necessary, as a counterweight to the regular armed forces. In October 1977, al-Bakr handed over the portfolio of Defence to his son-in-law, Colonel 'Adnan Khairallah, who is also the brother of Saddam Husain's wife. In April 1978, Khairallah then aged thirty-eight, was also promoted to the rank of general. While regular officers had excellent pay and working conditions, and access to sophisticated weapons, the gradual build-up of the People's

Militia as an 'anti-army', accompanied by the absolute control of the armed forces by Saddam Husain's own family, had the effect of neutralising the regular Army's potential as a source of opposition to the regime and transforming it into a reliable and dependable bedrock of support[122]. In addition, the various internal security services grouped together under the General Directorate of Intelligence reported directly to Saddam Husain, generally through his cousin, Sa'dun Shakir, and surveillance and control of the Party organisation were institutionalised through 'morale officers' and Party commissars, who also reported directly to the Vice-President[123]. Although the regime is not *purely* military, as in countries where a few generals seize power and subsequently create a fake party, the army remains one of the main pillars on which it rests, and in such circumstances it is both misleading and inaccurate to characterise it as 'civilian' rather than 'military', since the two spheres are so closely inter-connected[124].

This systematic Ba'thisation of the state apparatus, of the means of coercion and of every sphere of political life, together with the marginalisation or outlawing of all other political forces, was accompanied by and intertwined with a complex struggle for power and positions within the Ba'th leadership itself. Although it is difficult to trace the actual pressures and manoeuvres that were taking place behind closed doors at the time, the most important factor for many within the leadership was the threat posed by Saddam Husain's gradual acquisition of one power position after another, since, with al-Bakr's indifferent health, the former's emergence as sole dictator could be only a matter of time. Apart from the fact that many of the leaders considered themselves to be Saddam Husain's equals, and thus entitled to at least a degree of influence within the decision-making process in both the Party and the government, they must have feared that if his power became too absolute they were likely to find themselves unable to protect their own lives.

The close connection between the process of Ba'thisation and the foundations of Saddam Husain's personal rule was reflected in the absorption of the Ba'th Regional Command into the RCC in September 1977, which signified the end of the Ba'th Party as an independent body. Typically, it was claimed that this step, which was in fact part of a long-term strategy of absorbing (or buying) anyone posing a real or potential threat as long as he could not be weakened or exterminated, was designed to 'deepen collective participation and democracy'[125].

As we have already mentioned, the Regional Command of the Ba'th Party had been increased to twenty-one members in January 1977. Two of them, Dr 'Izzat Mustafa (also a member of the RCC) and Fulayyih Hasan al-Jasim, were dismissed two months later, allegedly for failing to hand down sufficiently stiff sentences at the trials of the Shi'i demonstrators at Karbala' and Najaf, and were replaced by Burhan al-Din Mustafa and Muhi 'Abd al-Husayn al-Mashhadi. In September all the members of the Regional Command were appointed to the RCC, which, with twenty-two members (Ghaidan was in the RCC but not the RC), was now larger than it had ever been. One of the first 'decisions' of the enlarged RCC was to issue a decree transferring all aspects of oil policy and oil marketing from the Ministry of Oil to the Follow-Up Committee for Oil Affairs and Implementation of Agreements[126], now to be chaired, needless to say, by the Vice-President and Deputy Chairman of the RCC, Saddam Husain. The decree stipulated that the Chairman was 'responsible for all aspects of oil policy, coordination and operations, and that no decision on oil marketing could be taken without his approval'[127].

Thus it seemed that a degree of harmony had been established within the leadership, and in any case the necessity to close ranks against a variety of internal and external 'threats' and in the face of the rapidly-changing political circumstances in the Middle East (Camp David, the Iranian Revolution) had the effect of papering over the divisions for the time being. As well as the continuing clampdown on manifestations of Shi'i disaffection that had begun in 1977, the anti-Communist campaign began in earnest in the spring of 1978, a ruthless scorched earth policy was inaugurated in Kurdistan at the same time[128], and numerous executions and dismissals took place within the armed forces. At the same time Saddam Husain began his first major foray into inter-Arab politics with the Baghdad Summit and the ensuing 'reconciliation' with Syria. It was only with al-Bakr's resignation in 1979 that the latent rebelliousness of Saddam Husain's colleagues broke out into the open once more.

On 16 July 1979, the eve of the eleventh anniversary of the Ba'th takeover, al-Bakr appeared on television to announce his resignation, and Saddam Husain was 'sworn in' immediately as President, a transfer of power that had been as meticulously prepared as it had been long expected. In his speech al-Bakr commended Husain as the best man for the post and warmly endorsed his 'candidature'. 'Izzat al-Duri, a long-standing and loyal lieutenant of Saddam Husain, was appointed Vice-President. However, a few days before al-Bakr's resignation, there were already indications that something else was afoot, with the announcement that the RCC secretary, Muhi 'Abd al-Husain Mashhadi, was to be replaced by Tariq Hamad al-'Abdullah.

The full significance of this emerged a fortnight later, on 28 July, when it was declared that a 'plot' to overthrow the regime, masterminded by Syria, had been uncovered; a special Party court of seven RCC members was immediately set up under Na'im Haddad, and within a few days twenty-two people had been executed, including Mashhadi and four of his colleagues on the RCC, 'Adnan Hamdani, Muhammad 'Ayish, Muhammad Mahjub, and Ghanim 'Abd al-Jalil, as well as 'Abd al-Khaliq al-Samarra'i, who had been in prison since July 1973 because of his alleged involvement in Kazzar's attempted coup[129]. These 'democratic executions', as Na'im Haddad described them, were carried out by Saddam Husain and the remaining members of the leadership in person[130]; and the 'trials', and in particular the 'confession' of Mashhadi, were filmed, with video versions widely circulated among inner circles of the Party, as proof of the plotters' guilt and of Syria's involvement in the affair[131].

This episode was particularly remarkable in view of the fact that many of those executed had been among Saddam Husain's most intimate associates, particularly Hamdani, a close personal friend of long standing. The fact that even those closest to him could fall so suddenly and fatally from favour was clear for all to see, and it was evident that no opposition whatsoever, whether inside or outside the Party, would be tolerated. It was widely rumoured that some of those executed had been unwise enough to venture their misgivings at the over-centralisation of power that seemed to be taking place: Mashhadi had voiced concern over Saddam Husain's 'dynastic power base'[132]; and 'Ayish had objected to Saddam Husain's claim to have been elected unanimously, since he himself had not voted for him[133]. While the extent of Syrian involvement will never be known, Husain made full use of the allegation as a means of ridding the regime of any pressing obligations to consummate the much-vaunted union between the two countries.

After the purge, the RCC was reduced to sixteen members, only eight of whom managed to survive a further round of dismissals in June 1982. Although those who were dropped on the second 'reshuffle' did not suffer the same fate as their colleagues in 1979, the events of June 1982 pointed to the existence of a closely-knit inner circle within the RCC, and it is worth attempting to gather together the biographical information available on these individuals. Table 6.1 shows the composition of the post-purge RCC in

Table 6.1 *The RCC in August 1979 and June 1982*

RCC August 1979	*RCC June 1982*
Saddam Husain (Nov 1969)	Saddam Husain
'Izzat al-Duri (Nov 1969)	'Izzat al-Duri
Taha Yasin Ramadan (Nov 1969)	Taha Yasin Ramadan
Sa'dun Ghaidan (July 1968)	
Na'im Haddad (RC 1.74/RCC 9.77)	Na'im Haddad
Tayih 'Abd al-Karim (RC 1.74/RCC 9.77)	Hasan 'Ali al-'Amiri
Tahir Tawfiq al-'Ani (RC 1.74/RCC 9.77)	
'Abd al-Fattah Ibrahim (RC 1.74/RCC 9.77)	
Hasan al-'Amiri (RC 1.74/RCC 9.77)	
Sa'dun Shakir (RC Res 1.74/RCC 9.77)	Sa'dun Shakir
Ja'far Qasim Hammudi (RC Res 1.74/RCC 9.77)	Tariq 'Aziz
Tariq 'Aziz (RC Res 1.74/RCC 9.77)	
'Abdullah Fadil (RC 1.77/RCC 9.77)	'Adnan Khairalla
'Adnan Khairalla (RC 1.77/RCC 9.77)	
Hikmat Ibrahim al-'Azzawi (RC 1.77/RCC 9.77)	
Burhan al-Din Mustafa (RC 3.77/RCC 9.77)	
Tariq Hamad al'Abdullah (RCC 16/7/79)	
	Taha Muhi al-Din Ma'ruf (June 1982)

RC = date of promotion to Regional Command
Res = reserve member of Regional Command

1979, and the streamlined RCC in 1982; individuals have been grouped in chronological order of their first entry into the RCC.

Table 6.2 shows the biographical data available on the 'inner circle'; it will be noted that Sa'dun Ghaidan, one of those originally involved in the coup of July 1968, was dropped in June 1982. The inclusion of Taha Muhi al-Din Ma'ruf, the Kurdish Vice-President of the Republic, was intended as a gesture to Kurdish sensibilities. All the others, who were of course considerably younger than Ma'ruf, had been more or less exclusively involved with the Ba'th Party all their adult lives and had several years of close association with each other.

Table 6.2 *Biographical Data of the RCC, June 1982*

Saddam Husain, b. Takrit 1937; party worker.

'Izzat al-Duri, b. al-Dur (nr Samarra') 1942; party worker; Deputy Chairman of RCC since 1979.

Taha Yasin Ramadan (al-Jazrawi), b. Mosul 1939; ex bank-clerk; Commander of People's Militia since (at least) 1976.

Na'im Haddad, (Shi'i) b. nr Nasiriya; Baghdad University; Speaker of National Assembly since 1980.

Hasan 'Ali al-'Amiri, (Shi'i); Minister of Trade since 1976.

Sa'dun Shakir, b. Takrit 1939; a cousin of Saddam Husain, Director-General of Intelligence in 1972; Minister of Interior, 1980.

Tariq 'Aziz, b. Mosul 1936; Baghdad University; editor of *al-Thawra*, 1969; Minister of Foreign Affairs.

'Adnan Khairallah, b. Takrit 1937; cousin and brother-in-law of Saddam Husain; professional soldier; Minister of Defence since 1978.

Taha Muhi al-Din Ma'ruf; active in the Kurdish *Rizgari* Party after the Second World War; served as a representative of the Talabani faction in al-Bakr's first cabinet after the coup of July 1968; ambassador to Italy at the time of his appointment as Vice-President of the Republic in April 1974.

A number of points emerge from Table 6.2. First, Takriti origin had evidently ceased to be the sole criterion for entry to the innermost circle at the very top, although the core of the leadership in the early and middle 1980s, still came either from Takrit and the small Euphrates towns or from Mosul, two of the main centres of Arab nationalism in the 1950s and 1960s. It must remembered that the close ties between Saddam Husain and his RCC colleagues were forged in blood, in the sense that almost all of them were implicated jointly in the executions of 1979, and are thus bound by the knowledge that when Saddam Husain falls they will fall with him. Discounting Ma'ruf, there is an inner circle, consisting of al-Duri and Ramadan, who are associates of very long standing, Shakir and Khairallah, who are both relatives of Saddam Husain, and 'Aziz. al-Duri's evident lack of ambition makes him an invaluable prop for the leader; Ramadan has important contacts in Mosul and with the People's Army; 'Aziz, an experienced organiser and publicist, is the regime's main mouthpiece to the world outside the Middle East; while Shakir, as Minister of Interior, has been in charge of internal security services at least since the end of the 1970s. Since July 1982 there have been no significant changes in the composition of this group, which constitutes the country's sole decision-making body, if such a term is appropriate apart from Saddam Husain himself.

Looking back on the way in which Iraqi politics have evolved since 1958, the following observations may be of interest. When the indigenous colonial elite in a relatively undifferentiated society is removed as a result of an anti-colonial revolution or coup, the legitimacy of the 'revolutionary' government will be assured for a period, generally as long as it can be seen to be representing popular aspirations vis-à-vis the former colonial or semi-colonial power. However, in the course of time, particularly when formal political independence appears to have been secured, popular support for the new government may begin to wane for a multiplicity of reasons.

At this point those in power (or their successors) will try to find new sources of support in an attempt to bypass or to exclude both existing democratic organisations and other contenders for power. A struggle now ensues within the elite in which each of the contenders attempts to build up his own regional or family network. Those who succeed in seizing power in such circum-stances usually attempt to ensure their survival and continuation in government by relying on these personal and regional ties. In Iraq, the Qasim regime was the only post-revolutionary government that did not depend on such alliances, since it was sustained, at least at the beginning, by the immense popular support generated by the Revolution itself. Since the fall of Qasim every group that has seized power has relied to a very considerable extent on regional or family support. An important function of the 'single party' or 'leading party' in Iraq and other similar states is to prop up, and to some extent to conceal, these very personalised political systems.

Chapter Seven

Economy and Society since 1958

As we have suggested in the previous chapters, the last two decades have witnessed a series of rapid and fundamental transformations within Iraqi economy and society. These changes have set in motion processes of social differentiation that are still continuing and whose nature can still not be fully grasped. In the broadest terms, however, the social and economic policies pursued by the Ba'th since 1968 have tended to produce conditions that exhibit characteristics resembling forms of state capitalism existing elsewhere in the Third World[1], which means that the question of whether such policies are (or ever were) leading towards 'socialism' or the 'noncapitalist mode of production' has now become entirely redundant.

Regrettably, political conditions in Iraq have long prevented scholars from carrying out detailed empirical research and fieldwork, except within a highly circumscribed and heavily restricted official framework[2]. As a result, the researcher has to rely on official government statistics and on a number of doctoral theses scattered in various university libraries, many of which turn out to be based largely on these same statistics[3]. In the analysis that follows we shall begin with a brief discussion of the main social and economic trends that manifested themselves under the various governments that came to power in the decade between the Revolution of 1958 and the Ba'th takeover, and then continue with a more detailed examination of the effects of the social and economic policies pursued by the Ba'th.

Oil and the Iraqi Economy, 1958–1963

Any analysis of modern Iraqi economy and society must emphasise the paramount importance of oil. Since the end of the Second World War Iraq has been almost entirely dependent on oil revenues[4], that is, on a source of income deriving from an industry that is both capital intensive and self-contained, with few direct linkages to the rest of the economy[5], and employing only a very small proportion of the labour force. Thus in common with many other exporters of primary products[6] the Iraqi state derives its principal income from a commodity for which demand is generated abroad, that is, outside its own processes of social reproduction. Hence, at the time of the Revolution of 1958, apart from the oil sector, the economy exhibited most of the features familiar from other under-developed countries: manufacture, though expanding, accounted for less than 10% of GNP[7] and the bulk of private capital was tied up in trade, landed property, speculation and services. At the same time, a very high proportion of the economically-active population was engaged in agriculture, and largely excluded from the domestic market either because of its poverty or because of the persistence of the subsistence economy in the rural areas, especially in the South and Centre[8]. Very often ties of tribe, clan, family, region and confession were stronger than allegiance or loyalty to the nation state.

As we know, the Iraqi state was created 'from above' in the course of the peace settlement after the First World War, on political and constitutional principles that had been imported from Britain. The new institutional structures that were created were directed primarily towards ensuring the protection and furtherance of the interests of Britain, and of the landowning classes that came to constitute the principal social base of the monarchy. This political system had of course evolved in a highly differentiated capitalist society; in Iraq it had been superimposed upon a society that was still both relatively undifferentiated and highly fluid, where the bourgeoisie had not yet been able to establish its dominance and where capitalism, although evidently penetrating all spheres of economic life[9], was not predominant in the country as a whole. Thus although the middle classes had been accumulating industrial, commercial and real estate capital since the early days of the British mandate, their economic interests remained highly dispersed.

Hence, the pre-revolutionary state was not underpinned by a broad and homogeneous bourgeoisie controlling the process of capital accumulation. Instead, it was based on a constellation of social forces allied to British, that is, *external*, interests, relying ultimately for its survival on its control of the means of coercion, and on the threat — and, on some occasions the use — of military force, represented first by the Royal Air Force and subsequently by the Iraqi Army and Air Force. Lacking the social foundations and the consensus that would have formed the basis of a strong and stable political system, the Iraqi state was inherently weak. In addition, the oil revenues, which, as we have emphasised, derive from sources essentially external to the 'rest' of the economy, permitted the state a substantial degree of economic independence, and enabled it to expand its apparatus and to widen its control and influence over society as a whole. As long as these revenues remained comparatively modest (between the 1950s and the middle 1960s) this tendency was not particularly marked, but it has become abundantly clear since the late 1960s, and especially since the price explosions after 1973, that this income has played a decisive role in increasing the autonomy of the state[10]. Under these circumstances control over the state, that is, the composition of the social and political forces in charge of the state apparatus, came to be of paramount importance for the development of the country and for the determination of the direction of future capitalist penetration.

Thus the Revolution of 1958 and the fierce conflicts that took place in the years that followed must be seen primarily in terms of a struggle for control of the state apparatus. The broadly-based political movement that supported the Revolution was heterogeneous both in its social composition and in its economic and political interests. The antagonisms inherent within it remained largely concealed as long as the independence struggle was still going on, since the latter had been directed essentially against an external enemy and its internal allies, but the fragility of the coalition was rapidly revealed in the period immediately after the Revolution. As we have seen, the bourgeoisie under the monarchy was disparate and economically weak, and had not built up an effective party machinery of its own[11], and thus was unable to take over control of the state apparatus when the opportunity presented itself. Thus it was only possible to carry out effective opposition underground, a factor that favoured radical rather than reformist politics. Hence, in the immediate aftermath of the Revolution, the bourgeoisie was either unable or unwilling to provide the political underpinning that the military leadership expected of it, and in addition the expectations of those who had welcomed the Revolution with enthusiasm were often considerably more to the left than those who had actually carried it out.

Thus when the military came to power in 1958 there were no functioning and established bourgeois democratic parties to which they could hand over power, (even if they had been prepared to do so), and they therefore held on to power themselves in order to ensure the survival of the Revolution, relying on popular support to defend it. At the same time Qasim tried to build a bridge to the 'progressive' bourgeoisie, and accordingly invited a number of prominent liberal personalities[12] who had not been identified with the monarchy to serve in his first government. However, he never attempted to institutionalise the mass support that the Revolution had generated by creating a functioning democratic system, most probably because this would have involved giving formal recognition to the widespread support enjoyed by the Communists[13].

As a result the military remained the principal institutional base of Qasim's regime, and, as the public's previous experience of 'democratic government' under the monarchy had not been a happy one, it was prepared to accept military rule to the extent that 'the military' were now part of a 'revolutionary government' that would change everything. However, as we have seen, Qasim's failure to build up a functioning network of support outside the state apparatus had the effect of increasing his relative dependence on the military, which meant that he would be entirely at their mercy if — as in fact was to happen — they were to abandon him, or if a group within the military decided to oust him.

Qasim's principal achievement was to inaugurate many of the economic and social reforms that had been almost universally demanded throughout the period of the monarchy. One of his most important measures was a programme of land reform, which, for all its limitations, generally succeeded in destroying the political and economic power of the great shaikhs and landlords. Later, he gained widespread acclaim for his attempts to restrict the activities of IPC, which culminated in the promulgation of Law 80 in December 1961. Equally unexceptionable was his campaign to build houses for the *sarifa* dwellers of Baghdad in a special district,

Madinat al-Thawrah, the construction of a new canal through Baghdad and other socially desirable measures. Such actions ensured that until the very end Qasim enjoyed great personal popularity. However, it must be stressed that none of these measures was in any sense 'socialist' or 'radical', and that there was never any hint in Qasim's time of the nationalisations that were to be a prominent feature of the 'economic policies' of his successors.

Economy and Society Under the 'Arif Brothers

In 1963 a coalition of Ba'thist and nationalist officers took advantage of the extreme precariousness of Qasim's situation to oust him by a military coup, and subsequently took terrible revenge on the Communists and their sympathisers. In fact the coup was directed less against Qasim himself than against the Communist-influenced or Communist-led forces that had become too strong for the liking of many of their adversaries. However, as Qasim had derived much of his legitimacy as head of state from his position as leader of the Revolution, those who ousted him had to couch their own appeal for support in terms of the original aspirations of the Revolution; that is, national independence, social justice and economic progress.

'Arif and many of his associates were themselves of this general persuasion, and in addition, as supporters and followers of Nasser, they were in favour of a more thorough-going form of state-directed economic development, which they called socialism, provided that the Communists could be kept in check and that these policies would not seriously threaten the existing economic and social order. Having ousted his Ba'thist allies a few months after their joint coup, 'Arif built up his power base by relying primarily on his own relatives and kin, and in this way managed to consolidate his grip on the state and the military without attracting extensive popular support. Apart from an entirely unsuccessful attempt to launch an Iraqi version of the Arab Socialist Union, and vague declarations on al-Bazzaz' part of a desire to return to democratic government, neither of the 'Arifs succeeded in creating an institutional base for their rule outside the armed forces. Thus the social and political foundations of the state remained weak, and continued to be vulnerable to threats from disaffected groups within the military.

Despite their 'socialist' rhetoric and policies, 'Arif and his government had come to power on a platform of appeasement and containment rather than of change. However, while he and his followers wanted to ensure that the forces of radical revolution were kept in check, they wanted to be revolutionaries at the same time, at least in the sense of wishing to transform the old order and to bring about greater social justice and a more equitable distribution of wealth. In consequence some of their economic policies appeared to be threatening the interests of those social classes that might otherwise have rallied to their support. Although these groups had welcomed the fall of Qasim and the subsequent clampdown on the Communists and the left, they quickly became alarmed at some of the pronouncements and activities of the new regime.

'Abd al-Salam 'Arif's economic 'strategy' culminated in the nationalisation of banking, insurance, foreign trade and a number of key industries in 1964. However, these policies were only rather erratically pursued in the years that followed, partly because his own commitment to them seems to have waned fairly quickly[14], and also because his brother 'Abd al-Rahman, who succeeded him in 1966, did not have such a firm base within the armed forces and was thus far less in control. In consequence the later 'Arif governments took a much more tentative line on most economic questions and, although the state continued to play an important part within the economy, it was unable to set in motion the programmes of development and growth that had been widely expected to accompany the Revolution. In fact the general atmosphere of uncertainty that prevailed created considerable confusion among the business community, and substantial amounts of capital were spirited abroad. Hence, the Iraqi economy remained largely stagnant between 1963 and 1968 (Table 7.1), although the policies introduced in this period did contain a much more substantially *dirigiste* component than those of any previous Iraqi regime, and provided the essential foundation for the subsequent introduction of similar measures under the Ba'th.

One of the most striking features of the various efforts made to change the structure of the economy in the general direction of greater state participation was the extent to which these goals were *not* achieved, and the degree to which private capital not only succeeded in surviving this initial period of uncertainty, instability and nationalisation, but even managed to expand its activities.

Table 7.1 *Distribution of GDP by Economic Sector (in Absolute and Relative Terms) 1954–1969, at Current Prices in ID Million*

	1954*		1964		1969	
Agriculture,						
forestry, fishery	84.7	22.6%	148.1	19.5%	191.0	17.2%
Crude oil	149.5	39.9%	266.9	35.1%	335.9	30.3%
Other mining						
and quarrying	0.9	0.2%	1.9	0.2%	7.3	0.6%
Manufacturing	21.9	5.8%	63.4	8.3%	103.0	9.3%
Construction	17.2	4.6%	18.7	2.3%	38.5	3.5%
Electricity, water,						
gas	1.8	0.5%	7.7	1.0%	16.8	1.5%
Transport,						
communication,						
storage	22.1	5.9%	54.9	7.2%	69.1	6.2%
Wholesale/retail						
trade	20.7	5.5%	44.5	5.8%	90.1	8.1%
Banking, insurance,						
real-estate	3.6	1.0%	7.0	1.0%	15.5	1.4%
Public administration						
and defence	20.8	5.5%	81.1	10.7%	117.8	10.6%
Services	19.3	5.1%	51.4	6.7%	80.0	7.2%
GDP at factor cost	374.4	100.0%	761.2	100.0%	1109.7	100.0%
GNP at factor cost	306.7		637.5		955.0	
National product	284.0		595.8		885.1	

Source: Government of Iraq, *Annual Abstract of Statistics* 1974, 1976
* 1954 figures have been included to give a wider perspective.

Thus in 1970, two years after the fall of 'Abd al-Rahman 'Arif, the contribution of private capital to GDP (Table 7.2) was still more than 80% in the commodities sector, nearly 70% in distribution, and had even experienced a slight increase over the previous five years in the services sector. In manufacturing industry, where the value added contribution of the public sector increased its share from 32.3% in 1964 to 45.5% in 1970, the private sector continued to produce 65.6% of the value of output, 73% of the value of input and 44.9% of value added, and employed 65% of the industrial labour force[15] (Table 7.3).

Table 7.2 *Comparative Contributions of the Public and Private Sectors to GDP in 1964 and 1970 in ID Million*

	1964 Private		1964 Public		1970 Private		1970 Public	
Commodities (excluding oil)	202.8 –	86%	32.2	14%	312.2	82%	69.1	18%
Distribution	92.5	80%	23.1	20%	129.0	67%	58.5	33%
Services	44.8	27%	123.4	73%	74.7	28%	187.5	72%

Table 7.3 *Value of Outputs, Inputs, Value Added, Number of Workers, in Manufacturing Industries (More Than 10 Workers) in the Public and Private Sectors in ID Million at Current Prices, 1964 and 1970*

Years	Sector	Value of Output ID mn	%	Value of Input ID mn	%	Value Added ID mn	%	No. of Employees	%
1964	Public	39.702	23.3	19.139	17.4	20.563	34.3	—	—
	Private	130.383	76.7	91.208	82.6	39.355	65.7	—	—
	Total	170.085		110.167		59.918		114,840	—
1970	Public	109.013	23.4	57.414	27.0	51.599	50.1	53,536	34.8
	Private	206.912	65.6	155.428	73.0	51.484	44.9	100,089	65.2
	Total	315.925		212.842		103.083		153,625	

Source: H.K. al-Hayally, *Industrialisation and Regional Development in Iraq, with Special Reference to the Concentration of Manufacturing Industry in the Central Macro-Region.*

Similarly the number of small private manufacturing enterprises and workshops (employing less than ten people) rose by one third, from 20,999 to 27,248 between 1964 and 1969, indicating the continuing dynamism and also the proliferation of this sector, as well as the likely shortage of capital available to many of the owners of such enterprises. Private capital was also able to hold its own in what are described in the statistics as 'large' industrial establishments — employing more than ten people — which still employed at least a quarter of all workers in the manufacturing sector in 1971[16].

Like all 'post-revolutionary' regimes, the 'Arifs were committed to the improvement of housing and other social and educational services, with the result that the construction industry experienced a boom during these years. While the state was prepared to finance such projects it did not have either the intention or the facilities to carry them out itself, and invited private firms and contractors to carry out the work. In this way, whether by accident or design, the pursuit of these egalitarian or welfare state policies on the part of the government brought lucrative business for private capital[17]. Thus the number of private construction firms increased from 3,557 firms employing 27,095 workers in 1963 to 5,009 firms employing 40,046 workers in 1969, a tendency which increased even more rapidly in later years.

Similarly, the purpose of the nationalisation of foreign trade in 1964 was more to give the state greater control over the volume and type of imports and exports than to exclude private capital. Thus private business imported 55.3% of total imports and exported 59% of all non-oil exports in 1969[18]. Hence although the state was beginning to play a much more important role within the economy, and now controlled all banking and insurance and much of foreign trade, this was not achieved at the expense of private capital and indeed many of the government's policies created lucrative opportunities for the private sector.

Although substantial in absolute terms, oil income in the 1960s was relatively modest in comparison with the 1970s, so that the capacity of the state to initiate economic development and growth was still very limited. Nevertheless, revenues doubled between 1961 ($266 million) and 1970 ($521 million), and in broad balance of trade terms the country would have been in a state of constant deficit without oil (Table 7.4), a dependence which has increased dramatically since the Revolution[19].

Table 7.4 *Development of Foreign Trade at Current Prices in ID Million*

Year	Total Imports	Exports Other Than Oil	Oil Exports	Balance of Trade Without Oil	Balance of Trade With Oil	% of Oil Exports to Total Exports
1954	72.683	24.013	157.406	− 48.670	+108.736	86.7
1958	110.115	16.706	197.860	− 93.409	+ 94.451	96.7
1963	113.992	19.880	258.966	− 94.112	+164.854	92.9
1968	144.165	25.956	344.154	−118.209	+225.945	93.0

Source: A.K. Mirmis, *Industrial Location and Regional Economic Growth in Iraq.*

A similar picture emerges from a survey of some of the internal indicators (Table 7.5) over the period, such as the relationship of oil revenue to government expenditure, where the overall picture is of gradual and continuous increase. There was an equally gradual rise in ordinary and investment expenditure, reflecting the general expansion of the civil service, particularly in areas such as education and health[20].

Table 7.5 *Oil Revenues and Government Expenditure 1956/57–1968/69 (ID Million)*

Year	Oil Revenues	Ordinary Budget Expenditure	Government Investment Expenditure	Total Expenditure	Total Income
1956/57	68.84	70.28	43.041	113.321	113.84
1960/61	95.09	114.29	47.565	161.855	151.29
1964/65	129.66	180.13	75.275	255.405	222.43
1966/67	151.67	205.51	68.914	274.424	292.16
1968/69	174.72	241.94	74.406	206.346	308.94

Source: 'Isam al-Khafaji, *al-Dawla w'al-Tatawwur al-Ra'smali fi'l-'Iraq 1968–1978.*

Under these circumstances it is hardly surprising that the relative contribution of industry to GNP remained almost static and that the rate of industrial growth even dropped slightly between 1964 and 1968 despite increased state investment (Table 7.6). However, some large industrial enterprises did expand their workforce over these five years, particularly in the food processing and clothing industries, as is clear from Table 7.7. This table also gives some indication of the small size and dispersed nature of the Iraqi working class; it does not include an estimated 650,000 workers employed in small workshops or in transport, services, trade and construction[21].

Table 7.6 *Contribution of the Industrial Sector to GNP (Constant Prices) During 1964–1968*

Year	GNP in ID Million	Industrial Sector in ID Million	Contribution of Industrial Sector to GNP	Percentage Growth of Industrial Production
1964	702.7	78.1	11.1	—
1965	766.3	82.8	10.8	6.0
1966	807.1	85.3	10.6	3.0
1967	798.7	85.7	10.7	0.3
1968	877.5	90.2	10.3	5.3

Source: H.K. al-Hayally, *Industrialisation and Regional Development in Iraq, with Special Reference to the Concentration of Manufacturing Industry in the Central Macro-Region.*

With regard to agriculture, on which the majority of the population still depended, the picture changed surprisingly little over the 1960s from the point of view of the fallahin. Although the 1958 land reform had fundamentally weakened the position of the great landowners, it had not broken the dominance of private landed property, and there is in fact little indication that this had ever been part of the reformers' intentions. One of the most important results of the reform was that it created conditions that favoured the commercialisation of agriculture and led to the gradual incorporation of the countryside into the domestic market. It is primarily in this sense that the land reform was one of

Table 7.7 *Number of Workers in Large Industrial Establishments,*
1961–1975

Industry	1961	1965	1970
Food, beverages, tobacco	14,000	16,000	24,500
Textiles, clothing, leather	12,300	15,300	23,000
Paper and printing	4,100	4,500	5,000
Chemicals	2,900	3,300	7,000
Non-metallic minerals	17,600	19,000	18,700
Basic metal manufacturing	7,800	8,000	9,800
Other manufacturing	5,900	5,900	6,400
Water and electricity	8,700	10,700	13,300
Total	73,000	83,300	105,800

Source: H.K. al-Hayally, *ibid.*, p. 57

the most important achievements of the July Revolution; it was
evidently a failure in terms of agricultural production, which
declined drastically, largely because of the dislocations brought
about by the reform itself and the inadequate provision of credit,
guidance and assistance to the fallahin and to the new cooperatives
on the part of the various administrative bodies[22].

In practice, the implementation of the land reform had been
pursued rather half-heartedly under both Qasim and the 'Arifs,
and after the first months of euphoria at the abolition of large
landownership things were left very much as they were. While
expropriation was undertaken quite rapidly, distribution proceeded only slowly; much of the land that had been expropriated
was left either uncultivated or made available for rent[23]. Furthermore, many of the landless fallahin remained landless, and most
of those who had benefitted from the land reform were either left
to fend for themselves or given assistance that was generally
inadequate or hampered by complicated bureaucratic regulations.
Naturally, the former landowners kept the best and most fertile
land for themselves and made sure that they continued to control
access to irrigation channels; they also owned most of the
agricultural equipment, especially the mechanical irrigation
pumps[24]. In brief, while the pattern of land tenure had certainly
improved in the peasant's favour in comparison with the situation

before the Revolution, the landowners were often able to uphold or to re-establish their influence in many areas[25].

The most visible indictment of the land reform that had generated so much hope among the fallahin at the time was the extent of the rural to urban migration that took place in the years after its enactment, showing that the dramatic demographic transformation of Iraqi society was set in motion by default rather than design. In the thirteen years between 1957 and 1970 the urban population increased from 38.9% to 57.8% of the total population with a corresponding fall in the rural population (Table 7.8). Most of those who left the countryside of southern and central Iraq, where the landowners had always been particularly repressive, were landless fallahin with little or no links to the land.[26] They usually left their villages together with their families and settled on the outskirts of Baghdad, mostly in Madinat al-Thawra and Shura, which soon turned into overcrowded slums. Another major consequence of this dramatic demographic transformation was that the migrants flooded the city labour market and greatly increased the demand for foodstuffs and other urban goods and services. The cumulative effects of this population movement exploded with particular vigour in the middle 1970s, as we shall show.

Table 7.8 *Urban and Rural Population, 1957–1970*

Year	Total Population	Urban	Rural	% Urban	% Rural
1957	6,298,900	2,445,200	3,853,700	38.9	61.2
1965	8,047,400	4,111,800	3,935,600	51.1	48.9
1970	9,440,100	5,452,400	3,987,700	57.8	42.2

Source: Fiches du Monde Arabe, No. 924, 5 April 1978.

Economy and Society under the Ba'th

After the coup that brought it back to power in July 1968 the Ba'th Party was a somewhat disparate body, still extremely unpopular in many quarters because of the reign of murder, torture and terror for which it had been responsible in 1963. However, in contrast to its previous period in power, it was now in sole control of the state apparatus and the military. In spite of any appearances to the contrary, the Ba'th, like its predecessors, was not committed to 'building socialism' or to the radical transformation of existing relations of production, but to maintaining and sustaining the existing capitalist economic order. Again, although a relative newcomer to the Iraqi political scene, the Ba'th, in common with its nationalist and Communist competitors, had emerged as a political force during the struggle for national independence before 1958, so that the Party and many of its potential sympathisers were implicitly committed to principles of social justice and the equitable distribution of wealth that were widely shared by the population at the time.

Unlike the 'Arif brothers, however, the Ba'th leaders under-stood that they could only establish themselves permanently within the state if they were able to reach out and appeal to the more politically conscious popular forces on as wide a scale as possible. In order to do this they presented their rule as such governments usually do, as representative of the general will and as serving the interests of the nation as a whole. For this purpose, the 'doctrine' of Arab socialism, which advocated social harmony and national solidarity 'among the Arab masses', was particularly suitable[27]. In addition the regime built an institutional base for its rule by expanding and reorganising the Party in such a way that the Ba'th — and thus the state — eventually penetrated into almost every sphere of public and domestic life.

If its policies were to be acceptable and convincing to significant sections of the population, the Ba'th had to make perceptible progress in fulfilling popular political and material aspirations, especially as such aspirations were shared by many rank and file Ba'th party members and potential sympathisers, whose views would have to be taken into account if the Party was to be forged into an effective political organisation. Again, as the Communist Party was still the Ba'th's main competitor, and probably the most influential political force among the organised urban masses, it was important to obtain its support or at least its acquiescence, in order to incorporate or coopt the Party and its sympathisers. The Ba'th were probably also aware that in the long run such tactics would be the most effective way of weakening and eventually of disarming the Communists[28].

The most obvious result of this attempt to win over or recruit its competitors was the Ba'th/Communist National Front, which materialised in 1973. As we have seen, the Communist Party leadership had gradually come round to the view that the Iraqi state was not a bourgeois institution to be destroyed, but an instrument through which society could be radically transformed with the assistance and under the influence of the Communist-inspired popular forces[29]. For its part, the Ba'th leadership, still entangled in fierce and ruthless internal power struggles in the early 1970s, unable to solve the Kurdish question, and having taken a major step into the unknown by nationalising IPC, was clearly attempting to buttress itself by its Treaty of Friendship with the Soviet Union and its alliance with the Communists. At the same time it continued to build up an extensive civil and military security apparatus, using the most up-to-date surveillance techniques, thus giving the state formidable power and a degree of autonomy that gradually brought about 'the relative loosening of ties between the state and its social base'[30], a process that was further accelerated by the enormous increases in oil revenues after 1973.

Following the nationalisation of IPC, the subsequent oil price rise and the 'solution' of the Kurdish problem in March 1975, the Ba'th felt much more confident. By 1977–78 the armed forces had been almost entirely Ba'thised, and the leadership felt sufficiently secure to base itself more directly on the state apparatus, the bureaucracy and the Party organisation. As Saddam Husain's personal power grew, the regime relied increasingly on the personality cult of the 'great leader' and on the 'masses' that the Party organisation was able to mobilise and control[31]. In the process, Ba'th 'ideology' became emptied of whatever actual content it may ever have had and the Party's doctrines became couched in increasingly emotional and mystical language. Everything that was authentically popular or even remotely critical came under suspicion and was ruthlessly suppressed. By the end of the 1970s the Ba'th had begun a campaign of savage repression against the Communists, who had managed to increase their membership in the more liberal political climate of the early 1970s, and also against the underground Shi'i opposition, whose growing potential was beginning to make itself felt.

On the economic level the Ba'th transferred the state's vast oil revenues to the domestic market and used part of the new wealth to create the infrastructure needed to support its development projects. Unlike most other Third World countries, Iraq's wealth was sufficient to enable it to sustain a distributive welfare state system at the same time as supporting the capitalisation of private and public enterprises. In this way it was able to provide opportunities for social and economic advancement for many sections of the middle classes and even to offer the possibility of social and economic incorporation and advancement to social groups that had hitherto existed only on the margins of society, such as the urban poor and the rural migrants.

Given the paramount role of oil within the Iraqi economy, the extent of the impact of the nationalisation of IPC in June 1972 can hardly be over-estimated, on both political and economic levels. Politically, it was almost universally acclaimed, since the achievement of independence from IPC was widely regarded as the culmination of a process that had begun with the Revolution in 1958. Although a number of vital preparatory steps had been taken over the previous fourteen years, the Ba'th claimed that the nationalisation was entirely the result of their own efforts and their refusal to bow to the dictates of the oil companies, thereby adding to their 'revolutionary' and 'progressive' credentials.

As far as the regime itself was concerned, nationalisation meant that the Ba'th was now in total control of the country's principal economic asset, which gave it a degree of power and independence never enjoyed by any previous government. This newly-acquired strength was further compounded by the enormous increases in the price of oil that took place quite fortuitously only eighteen months later. Furthermore, since real power in Iraq now lay with a small group within the RCC, and as these individuals themselves were not answerable to any other institutions or organs of democratic accountability, the position of the Ba'th leadership, and their control over government spending, became increasingly unassailable.

In the late 1960s and early 1970s, when the Ba'th was primarily concerned with entrenching itself within the state and its institutions and was beginning to create a social base for itself, economic decisions were largely determined by considerations of social welfare and the redistribution of wealth, and of the expansion and the modernisation of the country's infrastructure. In time, and especially after the nationalisation of oil, the way in which the new-found power and wealth was used resulted in the emergence of new social groups — particularly around the leadership in the capital and in the regions of Takrit, Ramadi, and Mosul — who either found that their fortunes were increasingly linked with those of the regime, or that their interests were in one way or another served by its policies. The extent of the state's new economic might in comparison to former periods is dramatically illustrated by the oil production figures in Table 7.9. Production doubled in ten years, from 1.322 mb/d in 1965 to 2.262 mb/d in 1975, and the rapid price increases meant that the rise in revenues was very much greater. Since these revenues constitute the most important component of the country's national income and GDP it is useful to try to evaluate them against this background. As Table 7.10 shows, national income doubled from ID 1,412.1 million in 1973 (itself an enormous increase on the averages for the 1950s and 1960s) to ID 3,002.5 million in the space of a single year, and tripled within the next two years, to ID 4,478.8 million in 1976. GDP and per capita income increased at a comparable rate, implying a similarly rapid rise in demand for consumer goods of all kinds and the expansion of the home market.

Table 7.9 *Oil Production in Millions of Barrels Per Day*

1950	*1965*	*1975*	*1979**	*1980*	*1983***
0.136	1.322	2.262	3.477	2.514	0.922

Source: Exxon Background Series, 'Middle East Oil and Gas', December 1984, p. 12.

* In 1979 oil exports averaged ca. 3.3 million b/d, an increase of one third over 1978, in an attempt to offset the lower level of Iranian exports.

** Three separate pipelines were used to tranport Iraqi crude to eastern Mediterranean and Gulf terminals. In 1980 exports through Lebanon (transporting 1.1 million b/d from Kirkuk) were halted over disagreements on transit fees, and exports to the Gulf were terminated because of the war with Iran. In April 1982 crude oil movements over Syria were discontinued, leaving the single export route via the 1 million b/d line through Turkey, which terminates at Dörtyol.

Table 7.10 *GDP, National Income and Per Capita Income at Current Prices, 1967–76, 1979, 1982*

Year	Per Capita Income in ID	National Income in ID Million	GDP in ID Million
1967	89.6	754.2	937.7
1968	96.9	840.6	1,062.6
1969	98.4	897.2	1,103.3
1970	103.9	956.9	1,197.3
1971	110.9	1,081.3	1,375.0
1972	115.8	1,166.9	1,388.8
1973	135.5	1,412.1	1,587.5
1974	278.9	3,002.5	3,347.7
1975	337.2	3,750.5	3,970.5
1976	387.2	4,478.8	4,582.8
1979	825.9	10,588.5	4,714.2
1982	874.2	12,334.6	5,374.5

Source: *AAS*, 1977, p. 128; *AAS*, 1984, pp. 119–124.

Whether or not they made overall economic 'sense', the enormous expenditures on the part of the state had the effect of making it the principal customer for goods and services within the economy. In consequence, since the majority of the numerous development projects set in motion were carried out by private companies, both foreign and domestic, the state thereby acted as the 'generator' or 'motor' for the accumulation of private capital. In this way the regime provided tremendous opportunities for 'instant' enrichment and the accumulation of wealth, thus contributing to and facilitating the rapid transformation of Iraqi society[32]. This eventually created a situation in which the market became an important determinant of the regime's economic and other policies.

The close relationship between increased government expenditure and consumption on the one hand and the accumulation of private capital on the other becomes clearer from the growth of what are described as 'large industrial establishments', capital intensive industries requiring a level of expenditure and investment normally beyond the economic capacity of domestic private capital in Third World countries. It is, of course, not surprising that the state should dominate in this sector, and that it should have

expanded its economic role within it after the oil price rises of the
1970s (Table 7.11). However, even here private capital investment
rose at precisely the same rate as that of the state, a clear indication
of the close dependence, at least for the time being, of private
capital on state expenditure. In fact the rate of increase in both
input and output in large state industrial concerns was approximately the same, and the private sector was even slightly ahead:
output rose by 213% in the private sector and 203% in the public
sector; while input rose by 220% and 205% respectively.

Table 7.11 *Large Industrial Establishments, 1972–1977, 1982*

Year	Sector	Number of Establishments	Employees (in 000)	Value of Output (Mill. ID)	Value of Input (Mill. ID)
1972	Public	182	71.1	171.81	101.50
	Private	1107	44.7	63.96	54.01
	Total	1289	116.4	235.77	146.51
1973	Public	185	79.1	224.70	141.86
	Private	1090	41.6	67.41	46.07
	Total	1275	120.7	292.11	187.93
1974	Public	198	86.16	264.34	196.08
	Private	1043	37.80	87.39	63.16
	Total	1241	123.96	351.73	259.24
1975	Public	204	93.6	315.78	230.25
	Private	1145	41.0	120.65	86.46
	Total	1349	134.6	436.43	316.71
1976	Public	225	99.5	428.07	283.15
	Private	1254	43.2	161.83	115.62
	Total	1479	142.7	589.90	398.77
1977	Public	266	105.7	521.53	310.45
	Private	1282	44.4	200.25	144.15
	Total	1548	150.1	721.78	454.60
1982	Public	270	134.3	1110.75	631.26
	Private	1084	38.8	410.52	285.93
	Total	1384	173.1	1520.77	917.19

Source: *AAS*, 1976, p. 124; *AAS*, 1978, p. 91; *AAS*, 1984, p. 93.

Table 7.12 *Small Industrial Establishments, 1970–1976, 1982*

Year	Value of Input (IDmn)	Value of Output (IDmn)	Wages and Advantages	Total	Unpaid Workers*	Paid Workers	No. of Establishments
1970	29.004	52.827	4.881	62,071	40,249	21,822	28,180
1971	31.031	60.781	5,947	67,481	39,553	27,928	29,940
1972	33.179	59.797	6,491	65,832	37,289	28,543	29,583
1973	55.848	85.883	5,525	59,876	32,833	27,043	26,377
1974	60.492	93.616	5,578	58,771	32,755	26,016	26,332
1975	176.592	278.298	26,632	101,993	49,589	52,405	39,275
1976	158.874	267.944	19,316	85,460	46,808	38,652	37,669
1982	426.905	737.722	56,895	79,019	—	—	34,782

Source: AAS, 1977; *AAS*, 1984, p. 104.

* Usually the owners or family members.

Similarly, the number of small workshops, requiring relatively less capital outlay, also increased rapidly (Table 7.12). As can be deduced from official government statistics, most of these workshops (in the statistics they are described as 'small industrial establishments') seem to be family enterprises, employing only two or three people. While the value of input and output rose steadily from the early 1970s onwards, Table 7.12 shows very clearly the immediate and direct effect of increased state income and expenditures on the input, output and number of such workshops. Thus between 1974 and 1976 (the figures for 1975 seem to be unusually high and are therefore not used here) input rose from ID 60.492 million to ID 158.874 million, more than double, and output rose from ID 93.616 million to ID 267.944 million, an almost threefold increase, and the number of such workshops increased from 26,332 to 37,669. It is worth noticing that these workshops did not expand significantly in terms of numbers of employees, so that the increase denotes proliferation rather than expansion of operations. With regard to employment in 'industry' the private sector employed about 130,000 people altogether in 1977 while the public sector employed 105,700. The overall resilience of private capital in medium-sized industries (employing between ten and 250 people) is shown in Table 7.13, which shows that the private sector contributed around 80% of input and output in the early 1980s.

Table 7.13 *Public and Private Sector Shares of Inputs and Outputs of Industrial Establishments Employing 10–250 Employees, 1981–1982*

| | 1981 | | 1982 | |
	Inputs	*Outputs*	*Inputs*	*Outputs*
Public sector	18.7	23.6	18.9	20.1
Private sector	81.3	76.4	81.1	79.9

Source: R. Springborg, *Infitah, Agrarian Transformation and Elite Consolidation in Contemporary Iraq*.

Since state expenditure was concentrated largely in infrastructural projects, it was not industry which benefitted most. The

contribution of the various sectors to GDP for 1977–1979 (Table
7.14) shows clearly that the total contribution of construction, of

Table 7.14 *GDP 1977–1979 in ID Million*

	1977	1978	1979
Agriculture, forestry and fishing	412.1	473.0	—
Mining and quarrying	2,818.7	2,990.8	5,868.5
Manufacturing industries	388.8	464.5	504.3
Electricity, water, gas	34.5	45.6	49.5
Construction	277.7	317.6	344.8
Trade, restaurants, hotels	263.9	308.4	334.8
Transport, communications, storage	290.7	339.6	368.7
Finance, insurance, banking	118.8	138.9	150.8
Government services	101.1	118.2	128.7
Other services	635.2	742.3	805.9
GDP at factor costs	5,291.0	5,938.9	8,556.0
Net indirect taxes	378.8	890.1	1,007.7
GDP at market prices	5,670.0	6,829.0	9,563.7

Source: *Arab Economic Report, 1982*, General Union of Arab Chambers
of Commerce, Industry & Agriculture, Beirut, 1983.

trade, restaurants and hotels, of transport, communications and
storage, amounted to approximately double that of industry. Thus
these three sectors alone contributed ID 832.3 million to GDP in
1977, ID 965.6 million in 1978 and ID 1048.3 million in 1979. In
other words, while the contribution of the industrial sector
amounted to less than 7% of GDP, that of the three sectors
contributed to more than 14% in 1977 and 1978, and slightly more
than 10% in 1979. In absolute terms these three sectors contributed
more than double the total of manufacture or of agriculture.
Incidentally 'Mining and Quarrying' refers primarily to the
contribution of oil to GDP.

The services sector is also significant here, contributing ID 635.2
million in 1977, ID 890.1 million in 1978, and ID 805.9 million in
1979, a much higher absolute figure than industry or agriculture. It
is particularly unfortunate that there is no further explanation of

Table 7.15 *Distribution of Investments 1971–1978 in ID Million*

Year	1971	1972	1973	1974	1975	1976	1977	1978
Agriculture	60.0	23.2	65.0	190.0	207.5	268.0	386.9	495.2
Industry	50.0	28.0	60.0	225.0	448.0	709.0	966.0	1352.4
Transport and communication	28.0	16.0	40.0	120.0	166.0	242.5	351.6	439.5
Construction and services	28.0	22.0	45.0	175.0	188.0	213.2	288.2	380.4
Total allocation of production sectors	166.0	89.2	210.0	710.0	1009.5	1432.7	1992.7	2667.5
Total investments	119.8	88.1	168.2	458.4	629.2	—	—	—

Source: *Fiches du Monde Arabe*, No. 936, 19 April 1978.

the category 'other services' in this table, since it accounts for between 10 and 12% of the total. For our present purposes the relative contribution of each economic sector to GDP is more significant, since the rates of growth in each of these sectors are obscured by the lack of accurate information about the rate of inflation, which makes it impossible to measure 'real' development or growth over these years.

Table 7.15 shows the distribution of investment over the 1970s. Here the direct impact of the oil price rise in 1973 is particularly marked, since investment in all economic sectors trebled or even quadrupled between 1973 and 1974 and continued to rise steadily for the rest of the 1970s. Although such investments have, as we have seen, had a highly stimulating effect on the economy as a whole, its overall structure and the contribution of the various sectors to GDP seem to have remained constant, at least until the outbreak of the war with Iran in 1980[33].

Not surprisingly, the construction sector experienced a tremendous boom and it is here that the dominance of private capital has become particularly marked. In 1980, the private sector contributed 87.8% of GDP, rising to 93.8% by 1982[34]. According to official statistics the number of people employed in public sector construction in the 1970s increased from 29,457 in 1973 to 38,021 in 1974 to 62,595 in 1975, rising to 92,580 by 1978[35]. The numbers

Table 7.16 *Numbers and Average Monthly Wages of Employees in Construction in 1978*

Grade of Employee	Public Sector		Private Sector	
	No.	Wages	No.	Wages
Engineers	3,934	213.8	41	143.9
Labourers	92,242	88.5	66,526	97.4
Administrators	4,159	113.2	45	105.5
Guards	7,547	36.8	5,519	18.9
Others	5,519	95.4	—	—
Total	113,428		72,131	

Source: 'Isam al-Khafaji, op.cit., 1983, pp. 44–47.

employed in the private construction sector are more difficult to calculate accurately because they included large numbers of seasonal labourers, and often migrants who had newly arrived in the city, who were often not officially registered. However, al-Khafaji estimates that there were 72,131 in 1978 (Table 7.16). Table 7.17 also illustrates the increased demand in the construction sector; the number of building and repair permits trebled between 1968 and 1977 and their value rose tenfold over the same period.[36].

The increasing significance of the construction industry within the Iraqi economy is also evident from Table 7.18, which refers to the *muhafadha* of Baghdad. This shows the rise in wages in the public and particularly the private sector, both in absolute terms and relative to comparable employment in other parts of the economy. The very close relationship between the construction boom and the rise in oil revenues is directly reflected in the particularly sharp increase in wages in the years after 1974; as early as 1976 wages in the private sector began to overtake those in the public sector, an indication that the state was already having to compete with the private sector in order to keep its labour force.

Since most business was generated by government projects contracted out to private firms, both domestic and foreign, contracting became one of the most lucrative activities. In the nature of things it is extremely difficult to obtain any accurate information on actual profits in this sphere and any estimate must be very tentative. In 1970/71 there were 829 contractors officially registered with the Planning Council; three years later there were 2,788. Similarly, profits in the private building and construction sector leaped from ID 35.04 million in 1975 to ID 155.77 million in 1976, an increase of 400% in a single year[37]. As many of these contractors were newcomers to the business, the rapid rise in their numbers gives a particularly clear indication of its attractiveness. Many, though by no means all, of those who benefitted most had some sort of privileged access to the regime: out of the thirty-one wealthiest contracting and consultancy firms four came from Baghdad (Qahtan and Hisham al-Midfa'i, Khalid Tabra, Salman al-Janabi and the Sahu family); eight from Ramadi; seven from Takrit; two from Najaf; two from Basra; and eight from other places[38]. The preponderance of those from the old nationalist strongholds of the centre and north is striking.

Table 7.17 Permits for Building and Repairs and Estimated Costs, 1968–1977, 1979, 1983

Year	Building Permits Cost ID Million	No.	Repair Permits Cost ID Million	No.	Total Cost ID Million	No.
1968	29.436	23,742	.380	6,744	29.816	30,486
1969	35.278	25,664	.415	6,284	35.693	31,948
1970	36.351	26,570	.490	8,101	36.841	34,671
1971	35.769	25,514	.463	8,056	36.232	33,570
1972	41.667	27,594	.963	12,567	42.360	40,161
1973	43.182	26,818	.815	12,820	43.997	39,638
1974	54.930	27,910	1.242	15,747	56.172	43,657
1975	86.217	29,902	2.228	13,147	88.445	43,049
1976	181.253	49,891	2.871	15,304	184.124	65,195
1977	245.552	63,180	5.802	30,590	251.354	93,770
1979	509.196	100,476	8.346	26,429	517.542	126,905
1983	912.456	66,621	13.322	15,971	925.778	82,592

Source: AAS, 1978, p.11; AAS, 1984, p. 256.

Table 7.18 *Average Annual Wages Received by Construction and Other Labourers, Baghdad muhafadha, 1965–1976, in ID*

Year	Construction Industry			Other Industries		
	Private Unskilled	*Private Skilled & Unskilled*	*Public Skilled & Unskilled*	*Small Scale Industries*	*Service Industries*	*Large Scale Industrial Estates*
1965	143.760	215.965	334.002	112.700		292.660
1968	188.520	269.880	303.082	111.024		311.570
1969	195.920	286.330	309.960	98.976		331.260
1970	200.494	294.750		223.673		336.000
1971		289.710	311.870	248.750		384.170
1972	223.487	318.170	308.298	272.980		400.644
1973	172.742			204.510	173.540	423.320
1974	275.010	397.210		186.648		510.012
1975	409.040	664.680				591.350
1976	525.650	765.600	721.477	297.600	421.000	657.100

Source: I. A. al-Hashimi, *A Theoretical Analysis of the New Private Housing Market in the muhafadha (District) of Baghdad*, p. 71.

These opportunities for private capital accumulation were accelerated in the late 1970s and 1980s and further assisted by a number of governmental decrees enacted during the Iran/Iraq War, notably Law 115 of 1982 and Company Law 36 of 1983, which raised the ceiling for private sector investments from a maximum of ID 200,000 to ID 2 million for limited companies and to ID 5 million for joint stock companies and increased tax benefits at the same time. In more general terms, loans granted by the Industrial Bank increased from ID 0.61 million in 1967/68 to ID 12.5 million in 1977. With easy access to credit, little actual capital was required to start up a new business, particularly if it had anything to do with construction. In addition, the regime provided the private sector with subsidised raw materials and machinery imported free of duty. Thus contractors could either purchase or hire machinery or equipment from the state at preferential rates, which could either be used on several projects at once or leased to smaller contractors. The state normally gave the contractor 40% of the total value of the contract before work commenced, which enabled him to use it for his own purposes for a relatively long period[39]. The overall influence of private capital within the economy is illustrated in Table 7.19, which shows that it was dominant in construction and transport and highly involved in agriculture, industry and trade.

These favourable conditions encouraged entrepreneurs to try to fill some of the gaps between the supply and demand of various foodstuffs, and to engage in a variety of capital intensive industrial enterprises such as chicken batteries, dairy and livestock production and other agriculturally related activities:

> Medium and high ranking state employees and party
> officials joined private businessmen and professionals in
> buying or leasing land especially in the environs of
> Baghdad. Through the state importation company they
> were able to purchase pumps, reticulation, plastic sheets
> and other accoutrements of modern plasticulture and drip
> and sprinkler irrigation. Returns to these investors have
> been impressive, particularly when one considers that a
> large proportion of invested funds are provided by the
> government on favourable terms[40].

Among the most prominent and wealthy individuals engaged in

this field at the end of the 1970s were Khairullah Tulfa, the uncle and father-in-law of Saddam Husain; the Talib family from Mosul; Hazim Jawad, an early Ba'thist from Najaf; the Mirza brothers, also from Najaf; 'Abd al-Sattar al-Duri from Baghdad; and the Yawar and Mufti families from Mosul[41].

Table 7.19   *Private and Public Sector Percentage Shares of GDP for Selected Economic Sectors, 1980–1982*

	1980		1981		1982	
	Public	Private	Public	Private	Public	Private
Agriculture	46.9	53.1	51.3	48.7	52.7	47.2
Manufacturing	62.9	37.1	54.6	45.4	59.2	40.8
Construction	12.2	87.8	6.4	93.6	6.2	93.8
Transport/ Communication	28.8	71.2	27.5	72.5	24.0	76.0
Trade	59.3	40.7	55.4	44.6	56.2	43.8
Mining/Quarrying	99.7	0.3	98.6	1.4	98.7	1.3
All above plus Electricity and Water, Banking, Insurance, Ownership of Dwellings, Social/ Personal Services	81.4	18.6	67.4	32.6	61.2	38.8

Source: Springborg, ibid., p. 25.

At first sight, this table seems to indicate that there is a roughly equal balance between the private and public sectors in agriculture. However, since what is actually being described here is land *ownership*, it will be appreciated that the picture given is somewhat misleading, since a large proportion of state land was rented out to private individuals either directly by the state itself or by those peasant beneficiaries of the various land reforms who preferred not to work their plots themselves. As a result, although such land was not, strictly speaking, privately owned, it was used for private profit. Such arrangements were further encouraged by the fact that, in the nature of things, land distribution always lagged behind sequestration, and many former owners or *sirkals* were able to make use of their traditional authority to become 'tenants' on their old holdings[42]. In addition, the former landlords had usually been able to keep the best and most fertile land for themselves, and continued to control access to irrigation water and agricultural machinery[43]. Hence Table 7.19 shows how the reforms have weakened the power of the old semi-feudal shaikhs and landowners, and the expansion of the state into the countryside, but it does not reveal the changing character of the dominant relations of production, which were developing towards the commercialisation of agriculture, with a concomitant decline in subsistence farming.

We have seen that while the original intention of the reformers was to create greater social justice in the countryside, they did not believe that private ownership in land should be abolished. The sequestrated land was to be distributed to landless or poor fallahin, and land reform cooperatives on the Egyptian model were to be introduced. In practice, however, the fallahin usually parcelled out the land among themselves and their families, and 'cooperation' was primarily confined to marketing and to activities traditionally undertaken on a collective basis, such as the digging and maintenance of irrigation canals[44]. Nevertheless, by 1977 there were apparently 1889 such cooperatives, cultivating an area of about 7.75 million hectares as well as thirty-one agricultural state farms. Many of the cooperatives were not particularly successful and found it difficult to make efficient use of the machinery made available to them by the state because of lack of capital or technical expertise[45]. In many areas, especially the southern and central regions where agriculture had deteriorated for a variety of ecological and other reasons, most fallahin voted with their feet and continued to migrate to the cities, especially Baghdad, in even greater numbers[46].

As we have seen, in the early years of its rule, when the Ba'th was still attempting to win over the Iraqi left, it put further limits on individual landownership under Law 117 of 1970, and abolished all compensation payments by the beneficiaries. As a result more land was sequestrated, making a total of 2.575 million hectares by 1975. Out of this 1.55 million hectares were distributed by 1975 to 169,175 beneficiaries, leaving the remainder available for rent. In fact the number of individuals renting land in 1975 was at least 172,000, slightly exceeding the number of persons to whom land had been distributed[47]. A further and final reform in 1975 continued this process, and by the end of 1976, a total of 1.9 million hectares had been distributed to 235,559 individuals, while 0.9 million hectares were made available for rent to 115,972 individuals. No more sequestrations or distributions were undertaken subsequently, and the pattern of landownership does not seem to have altered substantially since that time[48]. Hence, in spite of the stated intentions of the various reforms, and in fact very largely as a result of many of the mechanisms that they have set in motion, the use of agricultural land for private profit has become or remained dominant, although, as the bureaucratic nature of the land reform organisations often had the effect of hindering rather than generating increases in production and productivity, private capital was unable to exploit the land as efficiently and extensively as it might have done.

As long as the Ba'th regime had sufficient resources to compensate both for the general decline in agriculture and for its inability to keep up with increasing consumer demand simply by importing foodstuffs, there was no pressing need for it to pay serious attention to the deficiencies in this sector. However, the war with Iran seems to have forced it to try to increase the country's agricultural self-sufficiency and to attempt to reduce the food bill, which amounted to $1.4 billion in 1980[49]. In general, the results have been far from spectacular: apart from poultry, where there has been a threefold increase, livestock and milk production has either declined or remained constant since 1979, and the only other major improvement has been in the production of fruit and vegetables[50]. Given the extent of the problem, it is unlikely that there could have been any realistic hopes that the food bill could be substantially reduced in a short space of time, particularly as the amount of food imported reflects increases in income and changes in consumption patterns as much as the stagnation in agriculture. Furthermore, it was also important in the early years of the war for the regime to keep up morale and carry the population behind it by attempting to ensure adequate supplies of fruit, vegetables and poultry, as well as to continue to satisfy the substantial numbers of 'new' entrepreneurs engaged in production in this sector.

Thus the regime began to give more systematic legal expression to a situation that had been existing for some time. Law 35 of 1983 permits Iraqi nationals to rent unlimited areas of land from the Ministry of Agrarian Reform, for periods of between five and twenty years, at rates far below those prevailing on the market[51].

Loans to the private sector by the Agricultural Cooperative Bank have apparently increased substantially[52] and the prices of 'virtually all commodities have been increased, not just as a result of irresistible market forces, but as a consequence of explicit policy decisions'[53].

Another important indicator of the degree to which the structure of society changed, and the upheavals and dislocations this must have generated in the lives of individuals, can be deduced from the population statistics. As Table 7.20 shows, rural to urban migration (which had begun to accelerate even further in the post-revolutionary period) continued unabated in the 1970s. By 1980, 69% of the population lived in cities and only 31% in the countryside, representing an almost direct reversal of the proportions in the 1947 census.

Table 7.20 *Population of Iraq 1970–1983*

	Total	Urban	Rural	Proportion (%) Urban	Rural
1970	9,440,100	5,452,400	3,987,000	57.8	42.2
1975	11,124,300	7,083,900	4,040,400	63.7	36.3
1977	12,029,760	7,640,675	4,389,085	63.5	36.5
1980	13,214,100	9,120,300	4,013,800	69	31
1983	14,586,000*				

Source: Fiches du Monde Arabe, No. 294, 5 April 1978; *AAS*, 1984, p. 48.
* Estimate

During the period 1977–1980 the anticipated annual growth rate in the urban areas was about 6.1%, while it was negative (-2.9%) in the rural areas. The principal pole of attraction was Baghdad, with a population of 3.036 million, or 26.4% of the total in 1977. The other major cities lag far behind: Basra had 400,000, Mosul 300,000 and Kirkuk 200,000 inhabitants.

As in other oil rich Middle Eastern countries, migration from the countryside took place for a combination of reasons, partly because the gap between town and countryside increased rather than decreased over these years, and also because health and educational facilities in the city improved much more than those in the countryside. From a survey of migrants to Baghdad in 1975 it emerged that few villages in Southern Iraq had piped water or electricity, and rural housing had hardly improved over the previous decade. Despite major state investments, agricultural production and productivity continued to decline in many parts of the country, partly because of long term deterioration over the previous half century, but also because of the haphazard and uncoordinated nature of these investments and, again, because of the *dirigiste* and bureaucratic fashion in which the reforms were implemented[54]. In addition, the city offered higher wages[55] and greater opportunities for work. In fact, the majority of respondents in the 1975 survey[56] felt that the availability of employment and the desire for higher incomes and better food were more important motives for migration from the countryside than the superior educational or health facilities available in the cities.

This rapid transformation also had a considerable effect both on the composition of the working class communities and on their political awareness. In comparison to the older established urban workforce, the new migrants had little or no experience of either political or trade union activity, and it is impossible to judge whether migration to the cities was accompanied by a process of proletarianisation. Such evidence as is available suggests that some migrants have experienced considerable upward social mobility, and have become engaged in a wide variety of employment, particularly in the service sectors, occasionally even becoming contractors or sub-contractors. Like their Egyptian or Syrian counterparts who migrate to work in the Gulf, these individuals move up the social ladder by making use of the new opportunities provided by the oil revenues[57].

The rapid growth in the urban population worsened the already difficult housing situation and created great overcrowding in Baghdad, especially in the districts of Madinat al-Thawra and Shura. By 1975 these two parts of the city, which had been built originally to house a few thousand inhabitants, were accommodating more than a million. While the population of Baghdad as a whole tripled between 1962 and 1975, these districts grew tenfold over the same period and developed into 'a tremendous physical and social slum'[58]. In addition, the continuous influx of migrants drove up house prices and increased opportunities for land and real estate speculation, as well as having contributed substantially to the boom in the construction sector discussed

earlier. The new migrants also supplied the urban labour market
with relatively cheap labour, but here demand gradually became
sufficiently acute to require large numbers of additional workers
from abroad, now estimated at nearly two million, mostly from
Egypt and Morocco but also from South and South East Asia.

A substantial number of the newcomers from the countryside
were employed in the state sector, which expanded rapidly in the
1970s as is shown in Table 7.21. Of an estimated 990,000 rural
migrants who entered the urban labour market between 1968 and
1977, 265,000 were employed by the state, excluding those in the
armed forces[59]. By 1978 there were 662,000 employees in government service, almost double the figure in 1972. However, as the
public industrial sector ('large industrial establishments') only
employed 105,700 people in 1977[60], the overwhelming majority of
state employees (ca. 550,000) were working in administrative or
other non-productive areas. Table 7.22 gives a detailed breakdown
of the numbers employed in each ministry: here the high figure of
151,000 employees in the Ministry of Interior, some 22.8% of the
total, gives some indication of the character of the bureaucracy,
since the primary function of this ministry is the provision of
internal surveillance and security services.

Table 7.21 *Numbers Working in the Government Sector, 1972–1978*

Year	Total Number
1972	392,954
1973	404,454
1974	438,997
1975	482,131
1976	526,578
1977	580,132
1978	662,656

Source: AAS, 1978, p. 278

Although the bureaucracy and the other parts of the public
sector expanded substantially, employing some 660,000 individuals,
with an additional 200,000 in the armed forces in 1977, the
overwhelming majority of the working population including, as

Table 7.22 *Number of Workers in the Public Sector in 1978*

Ministries	Total Number	%
Presidential Affairs	57,768	8.7
Ministry of Foreign Affairs	841	0.1
Ministry of Planning	3,187	0.4
Ministry of Industry & Minerals	94,761	14.2
Ministry of Oil	39,012	5.8
Ministry of Trade	26,592	4.3
Ministry of Agriculture & Agrarian Reform	58,182	9.3
Ministry of Irrigation	6,022	1.0
Ministry of Communications	37,453	5.6
Ministry of Transport	27,985	4.2
Ministry of Housing & Reconstruction	13,745	2.0
Ministry of Labour & Social Affairs	7,066	1.0
Ministry of Higher Education & Scientific Research	18,811	2.8
Ministry of Education	38,000	5.7
Ministry of Interior	151,301	22.8
Ministry of Youth	2,863	0.4
Ministry of Justice	5,729	0.8
Ministry of Finance	17,197	2.7
Ministry of Health	44,308	6.7
Ministry of Information	4,366	0.6
Ministry of Endowments	2,864	0.4
Ministry of Culture	4,803	0.7
Grand Total	662,656	100.0

Source: AAS, 1978, p. 270.

we have seen, some three-quarters of the rural migrants, continued to derive their income from the private sector. As the principal employer, the private sector also continued to determine wage levels, with which the state had to compete[61]. According to one source, wages in the private sector rose five times as much as those in the state sector in spite of numerous regulations to the contrary, and a number of legislative measures were passed in an attempt to retain skilled and specialist labour within the public sector[62].

As in such countries as Sa'udi Arabia, where the role of the state is even more paramount, major industrial investments and expenditure on infrastructural facilities such as roads, bridges, electricity, and public buildings has had the effect of strengthening the role of the state within the economy. However, as we have seen, domestic private capital has benefitted directly from this situation, and the new social groups or strata that are emerging are developing a vested interest in the maintenance of the system. This, as well as the all-pervading surveillance and repression employed by the regime, is an important explanation of its staying power.

On a broader level, the regime was aware that private domestic capital lacked the capacity and experience to be able to carry out the ambitious development programmes and projects that it was anxious to inaugurate, and it was also widely believed that the state could buy instant 'development' on the world market simply by spending the oil money appropriately. Thus it turned to the multinationals, who had the experience and know-how to

Table 7.23 *Total Value of Imports, Exports, Re-Exports and Transit Trade, 1958–1978, 1979, 1982 in ID Million*

Year	Transit	Re-Export	Non-Oil Exports	Imports
1958	8.057	2.458	14.248	109.956
1964	1.666	2.887	15.291	147.448
1968	20.492	4.541	23.029	144.165
1969	20.356	3.937	22.002	157.169
1970	27.942	2.164	22.566	181.651
1971	33.808	.497	22.782	247.870
1972	65.485	2.394	28.614	234.680
1973	56.095	.272	32.523	270.317
1974	89.724	.805	28.130	773.432
1975	118.141	.002	35.565	1426.858
1976	121.947	—	46.530	1150.898
1977	150.075	—	42.670	1323.153
1978	93.056	—	62.914	1473.576
1979	101.875	—	83.687	1738.906
1982	209.888	—	15.544	2942.420

Source: AAS, 1977, p. 166; *AAS*, 1984, p. 158.

undertake such major projects as the construction of an entire petro-chemical industry or a new transport system for Baghdad, and huge contracts were awarded to multinationals and other foreign companies. Between 1970 and 1975 the value of such contracts amounted to ID 682.4 million, and rose sharply in the second half of the 1970s, reaching ID 1065.5 million in 1978, ID 4077.2 million in 1980, and ID 7134.3 million in 1981[63].

Apart from making Iraq the second most important Middle Eastern market for the West and Japan after Sa'udi Arabia[64], these policies also ensured that Iraq became more deeply integrated than ever into the Western economy. This emerges from the import statistics for the period, which show, first, that imports rose very sharply after the oil price rise in 1973, and secondly that capital goods formed 50% of imports between 1974 and 1976, thus dramatically increasing the country's dependence on Western technology (Tables 7.23 and 7.24). Table 7.25 shows that the vast bulk of imports come from the West and Japan, while the combined total for the Soviet Union, China, and all the other socialist countries accounted for only 11%, 9.2%, and 6.9% of imports in 1977, 1978 and 1979, a period when Iraqi–Soviet relations were regarded as especially close[65].

Although there was an absolute and relative increase in trade with the developing countries (12.3%, 13.0%, 13.7%) between 1977 and 1979, imports from Japan and the West formed about 75% of the total in each year. Similarly, exports (Table 7.26), consisting primarily of oil, went largely to the West. The sharp increase in exports between 1978 and 1979 reflects the situation after the Iranian Revolution, when Iraq began to take up Iran's 'lost' production. What is most significant, however, is that it is still oil, and oil alone, that is the country's most important export commodity, a state of affairs that raises the question of whether (in purely developmental terms) Iraq has been able to change its economic structure in any fundamental manner; that is, whether foundations are being laid that can sustain the economy if, for example, oil was to run out, or if income from oil was to become radically reduced[66]. The very great neglect of agriculture, where intensive development would be vital for the creation of an integrated and diversified economy, seems to indicate that Iraq is in fact not moving in the direction of self-sustained or sustained growth. Unfortunately, as has already been indicated, the war with Iran and the lack of adequate information makes it impossible to

Table 7.24 *Composition of Foreign Trade 1974–76 in ID Million*

	Imports			Non-Oil Exports		
	1974	1975	1976	1974	1975	1976
Food and live animals	184.34	192.47	138.71	10.47	13.17	14.28
Beverage and tobacco	2.26	2.42	5.16	0.15	0.04	0.10
Crude materials inedible, excluding fuels	29.06	39.42	31.85	5.77	4.81	5.20
Mineral fuels, lubricants and related materials	2.01	3.44	1.85	8.38	15.48	25.58
Animal and vegetable oils and fat	12.63	22.70	6.12	0.05	—	—
Chemicals	42.33	73.24	53.44	0.89	0.69	0.64
Manufactured goods classified by materials	226.12	371.50	273.49	1.74	1.05	0.61
Machinery and transport equipment	184.53	510.51	483.22	0.16	0.15	0.06
Misc. manufactured articles	16.53	28.04	29.24	0.52	0.20	0.07
Unclassified commodities and transactions	0.28	1.02	1.84	—	—	—

Source: *AAS*, 1978.

Table 7.25 *Geographical Distribution of Imports in US $ Million, 1977–1979*

	1977	1978	1979
Industrial countries of which:	3,393	4,682	7,559
United States	218	349	486
Japan	789	1,054	1,759
United Kingdom	307	458	470
West Germany	802	882	1,258
France	252	557	877
Oil Exporting Countries	50	197	205
Developing countries (excluding oil exporting countries) of which:	553	808	1,351
African	6	14	24
Asian	224	267	421
European	173	321	483
Middle East	56	74	167
Western Hemisphere	94	132	256
Soviet Union and socialist countries and China	485	580	678
Total	4,481	6,267	9,793

Source: General Union of Arab Chambers of Commerce, Industry and Agriculture, *Arab Economic Report*, p. 193.

answer the question accurately, but, on the basis of the figures we have quoted, it seems likely that, in essence, Iraq's situation differs little from that of the other oil rich Arab states, despite all claims to the contrary.

Hence the enormous growth in oil revenues has led to the state playing a paramount and determining role within the economy. This in turn has resulted in an unparalleled growth in the might of the state and of its apparatuses of coercion and surveillance; never before have the police and security forces in Iraq (or in the rest of the Arab world) enjoyed such limitless powers as they do today. Unlike such countries as Morocco or Brazil, where multinational companies themselves have made investments, in Iraq, as has

already been pointed out, it is the state itself that has become the
main investor and thus the main customer of private capital, both
local and international. Although new social strata are emerging,
as in other Third World countries[67], the economic dominance of
the state persists, and the new capital that is being accumulated
seems to be proliferating and diversifying rather than expanding,
and will probably continue to be dependent on the state as the
main generator of investment opportunities. In general terms, it
seems most likely that this situation will persist as long as the state
continues to obtain huge revenues that are not generated
organically within society.

Table 7.26   *Geographical Distribution of Exports in US $ Million,
1977–1979*

	1977	1978	1979
Industrial countries of which:	6,223	7,178	11,230
United States	382	241	610
Japan	674	712	1,636
United Kingdom	528	867	762
West Germany	115	192	302
France	1,665	1,922	3,063
Oil exporting countries	16	18	23
Developing countries (excluding oil exporting countries) of which:	4,037	4,585	7,695
Africa	413	446	788
Asia	698	897	1,511
Europe	1,521	1,456	2,635
Middle East	165	349	636
Western Hemisphere	1,240	1,437	2,125
Soviet Union and socialist countries and China	29	32	52
Total	10,305	11,813	19,000

Source: General Union of Arab Chambers of Commerce, Industry and
Agriculture, *Arab Economic Report*, p. 193.

Chapter Eight

Epilogue

The War between Iraq and Iran

Iraq and Iran, 1975–1979

Apart from its undoubted importance, both in the context of the Kurds and more generally in initiating the process of Iraq's return from the diplomatic wilderness, the Algiers Agreement of March 1975 was also significant in that for the first time for many years the Iraqi regime no longer needed to concern itself seriously with the security of its eastern frontiers. The degree of cordiality in the relationship between Baghdad and Tehran for the next four years was a source of continual puzzlement to those who persisted in regarding Iraq as a satellite of the Soviet Union. These good relations lasted until the fall of the Shah in February 1979, when it became evident that a complete reassessment of the links between the two countries would be required.

In spite of obvious and important differences in the political cultures of the two countries, the main factors contributing to the rise of 'religious' opposition in Iran in the 1970s were similar in nature and origin to those we have described in Iraq in 1977, namely the almost total lack of more conventional 'political' alternatives for the expression of dissent. When the Shah's fall became increasingly likely, the Ba'th began to make contact with the opposition, although the closeness of its links with the former regime could scarcely be concealed. When it came, the Iranian Revolution was evidently greatly unwelcome to Iraq, but Saddam

Husain could do little more than recognise the new Iranian
government, which he did on 12 February 1979, the day after it
seized power.

Relations very rapidly became strained. The old quarrel over
the Gulf islands was resurrected, and each side accused the other
of attempting to undermine its authority, the Iraqis pointing to
Iranian appeals to Iraqi Shi'is to overthrow the regime, and the
Iranians accusing the Iraqis of fomenting rebellion in Khuzistan/
Arabistan. On the Iraqi side, *al-Da'wa* and Ayatullah Baqir al-
Sadr hastened to show their support for the new regime in Iran; in
a congratulatory telegram to Khumaini, al-Sadr expressed the
opinion that 'other tyrants have yet to see their day of reckoning'[1].

The tensions mounted throughout 1979 and the first half of
1980, especially as the Iranians made no secret of their desire to
export the Islamic revolution to Iraq as well as to Sa'udi Arabia
and the Gulf states. In June 1979 an Iraqi air raid across the
Iranian border killed six people; in spite of a formal apology a
week later, such incidents took place regularly over the next fifteen
months, occurring almost daily between February and September
1980[2]. On 12 June 1979 large crowds demonstrated outside the
Iraqi Embassy in Tehran, 'taunting the ... Ba'th government ...
with slogans usually reserved for imperialism or Zionism'[3]. In
November, a few days before the occupation of the American
Embassy in Tehran, Iraq warned Iran that it would have to
'revise' the Algiers agreement, give up the three Gulf islands, and
provide self-rule for its Arab, Kurdish and Baluch minorities[4].

Much of the literature on the conflict, which is nearing the end
of its sixth year at the time of writing, considers that its origins lie
in disagreements over territory, or the profound mutual antipathy
that is said to characterise the attitudes of Iraqis and Iranians
towards each other[5]. While any Iraqi regime must be concerned to
maintain access to the waters of the Gulf via the Shatt al-'Arab,
this particular right has never been seriously at issue, since the
Algiers agreement divided the waterway at the *khalweg* or
midpoint, and the channel is self-evidently wide enough to
accommodate the shipping of both the riparian states; the other
territorial claims, to Khuzistan/Arabistan and the Gulf islands,
are largely rhetorical.

The initial Iraqi response to the Iranian Revolution has been
discussed within the context of the overall political situation in
Chapter Six and will not be recapitulated here. Two essential

miscalculations on Saddam Husain's part have to be pointed out. First, the Ba'th leadership over-estimated the degree to which the Iraqi Shi'i population as a whole was in sympathy with, or prepared to support, the establishment of a theocratic regime in Iraq. On the other hand this over-reaction on the part of Saddam Husain can only be properly understood in the light of an important feature of his rule, his desire to ensure his total and absolute control over every sphere of political life. The Iranian Revolution was felt to be a threat to that absolute control and likely to promote the emergence of pockets of opposition that he was unwilling to tolerate.

Secondly, Saddam Husain under-estimated the force of patriotic and Islamic fervour that the Iranian Revolution had engendered in Iran itself and assumed that the apparent chaos in the Iranian armed forces presented him with an unique opportunity to oust the highly inconvenient Khumaini regime by a surprise attack. Such a victory would have ensured the continuation of his absolute control over the country as a whole, including the holy cities of Karbala' and Najaf, and a weakened and defeated Iran might also be more prepared to cooperate with Iraq on similar lines as the Shah had been with regard to the Kurds. A victory over Iran would also have made Saddam Husain almost undisputed master of the Gulf and would thus have catapulted him — at a single stroke — into the position of one of the most, if not *the* most, important leaders in the Arab world, a position to which he had long aspired. In addition, the fall of the Shah had been a severe blow to the United States and the conservative states of the Gulf, and the overthrow of Khumaini and the restoration of 'normality' to the region would be in their interests as well, especially if this could be achieved with no direct intervention on their part. Given his high self-esteem and his belief in the insurmountable economic might of his country, the temptation to launch the war seems to have become irresistible.

The Course of the War

The appeal of the advantages likely to result from a quick and spectacular victory over Iran was evidently so dazzling as to have prevented Saddam Husain and his circle from taking a more realistic view of the strategic situation, since even the apparently

parlous state of battle preparedness of the Iranian armed forces
could not alter certain basic facts of demography and geography.
In the first place, the population of Iran (about 42 million) is
roughly three times that of Iraq (about 13.5 million); secondly,
Tehran is some 850 kilometres from Baghdad, 650 of which are
inside Iran; and thirdly, the two countries share a common
frontier 1300 kilometres in length. Given the further constraints
that Syria was highly unlikely to support him and that Jordan
would be able to offer only limited support, it was surely the
greatest folly on Saddam Husain's part to imagine that he would
ever have been able to *defeat* Iran.

However, despite all the logistical and other difficulties, the
Iraqi regime managed to hold its own fairly successfully until the
spring of 1982. In this it was aided by the strength of its
accumulated foreign exchange reserves and the weaknesses and
divisions within the main opposition groups in Iraq. In addition,
the bulk of the Shi'i population acquiesced and stood at the side of
their country rather than the side of Islam. However much the
Islamic Republic of Iran may attempt to represent the war as a
struggle between the forces of Islamic righteousness in Iran and
those of the Great Satan in Baghdad, only a very few Iraqi Shi'is,
mostly from the traditional religious families of the Holy Cities,
have actually gone over to the Iranian side. While this must in part
be a reflection of the highly repressive nature of the Iraqi regime,
which did not permit any popular expression of Shi'i sympathies,
the fact remains that the Iranians have not been able to make
much propaganda capital about mass desertions, (or attempted
mass desertions), from the Iraqi Army, where the vast majority of
conscripts and ordinary soldiers are Shi'is. Thus while the Iraqi
regime is widely feared, even hated, at home, the prospect of its
replacement by something akin to the Islamic Republic of Iran is
apparently at least equally, if not more, unpalatable to most Iraqis,
and it is in these terms that they view the conflict.

The course of the war has been documented in detail elsewhere[6],
but a brief summary may be useful. As we have seen, violations of
the frontier by both sides took place with increasing frequency
during the first half of 1980, and in April the Iraqis deported some
40,000 Shi'is 'of Iranian origin' to Iran, a process that has
continued ever since, with the result that there are now more than
100,000 Iraqi Shi'i refugees in Iran and Syria[7]. Diplomatic
relations between the two countries were severed in June; on 17

September Saddam Husain announced that he intended to abrogate the Algiers Agreement immediately, and fighting broke out in earnest a few days later.

For the first few months, until about March 1981, it seemed that the Iraqis had the upper hand. By the end of 1980 they had established a vital bridgehead at Khorramshahr, across the Karun, and had forced the evacuation of the civilian population of most of the towns of the south-western Iranian province of Khuzistan/Arabistan, although the Arab population of the area showed little enthusiasm at the arrival of their Iraqi brethren from the other side of the Shatt al-Arab. However, in spite of these gains, the Iranian air force managed to inflict serious damage on Iraqi oil and industrial installations in the Basra region, to the extent that Iraq has been unable to export oil from the southern fields since December 1980 and has thus been fundamentally weakened since the very beginning of the conflict.

By the end of March 1981 the Iranians had begun to rally. Iraqi forces failed to capture Susangerd, and were gradually pushed back towards the international frontier in the course of the next few months. Of the other Middle Eastern states, only Syria and Libya declared themselves for Iran, but apart from Syria's closure of her pipeline to Iraqi oil in April 1982, neither has involved itself very directly in the conflict. Jordan came out clearly on Iraq's side, and Kuwait effectively replaced Basra as Iraq's major port. In addition, the Gulf states and Sa'udi Arabia, which, while anxious to prevent the spread of Khumaini's message among their own populations, were initially not entirely averse to Iraq's being considerably weakend by the conflict, are estimated to have lent Iraq about $1 billion a month since the beginning of the war[8].

In September 1981, the Iranians drove the Iraqis back from Abadan, and Saddam Husain called for a one month ceasefire to coincide with Ramadan, which the Iranians rejected. In March 1982, the Iranians launched a major offensive, which culminated in their regaining Khorramshahr in May. The recapture of this strategic city was a major turning-point, and at this juncture Saddam Husain attempted to find some face-saving formula to end the fighting. By this time, however, Khumaini had managed to turn the war into an Iranian national crusade, with Saddam Husain the Satan who had to be cast out; the demand for his removal was always to loom large in subsequent negotiations. After May 1982, Iraq only held on to a very few enclaves immediately west of

Dizful and around Qasr-i Shirin, and by the autumn most of the fighting had shifted to the Iraqi side of the frontier, where it has been concentrated ever since. In July 1982 Iranian forces penetrated to the outskirts of Basra, but the Iraqis managed to prevent them advancing further, with enormous loss of life on both sides.

While the Iraqi regime has never been able to make the kind of domestic spiritual, national and moral capital out of the conflict that its enemy was able to utilise so effectively (especially as the Iranian regime's anti-Western stance could scarcely be doubted), the shift of the war to Iraqi territory had two major consequences. In the first place, although the Iraqi regime had itself initiated the conflict, it could now present itself as being on the defensive, and call for a closing of ranks against the threat of external invasion. Secondly, the Soviet Union, Iraq's main arms supplier, which had apparently taken umbrage at Iraq's decision to launch the war without consulting it (in breach of the Iraqi/Soviet Friendship Treaty of 1972), was no longer able to remain aloof and resumed supplies in the course of 1982. Hiro considers that this change in the Soviet attitude was further strengthened by the Iranians' subsequent crackdown on the Tudeh Party in the autumn, but it seems equally likely that by this time the Soviet Union had come to the conclusion that it could cope more easily with a chastened Iraq than with a victorious Iran, with all the implications this might have for other parts of the region. For obvious reasons, the United States has also tended to support Iraq against Iran, with the bizarre consequence that both powers are essentially on the same side in the conflict.

Nevertheless, even with the Exocets and Super-Étendards that it obtained from France in the summer and autumn of 1983, Iraq was either unable or unwilling to strike a decisive blow against the Iranian oil installations at Kharg[9], and by the beginning of 1984 the Iranians were still firmly entrenched in the marshlands on the west side of the Shatt al-'Arab. On 27 October 1984 Iraq resumed full diplomatic relations with the United States, (which had been broken off in October 1967) although this was largely a formality because links between the two countries had been close for a number of years, and the 'United States interests section' of the Belgian Embassy in Baghdad was one of the largest missions in the capital[10].

Since the beginning of 1981, the Iraqis had been on the

defensive, and were unable to launch any serious assaults on Iran apart from a brief and unsuccessful attempt to capture Shahrani in March 1983. However, although casualties continued to mount on both sides, neither of the combatants was able to achieve any decisive advantages on the battlefield, and both remained dug in to their respective positions in Iraqi territory for the next two and a half years, until early 1986. The conflict became 'internationalised' early in 1984, when both sides, particularly Iraq, started attacking oil tankers in the Gulf, and the 'tanker war' continued intermittently during 1984 and 1985. At the same time, in an attempt to avoid being forced to a humiliating defeat at whatever cost, the Iraqis resorted to the use of poison gas against the Iranian forces. Although the Iraqis routinely denied the charge, a United Nations report published in March 1986 confirmed that 'in the areas around Abadan inspected by the (sc. United Nations) mission chemical weapons have been extensively used against Iranian positions by Iraqi forces'[11]. In February 1986, the Iranians, clearly determined not to end the war until Iraq was defeated and Saddam Husain overthrown, massed their forces for a daring surprise attack on Fao, across the Shatt al-'Arab. However, although Fao was occupied, there was no further advance into Iraq.

In terms of foreign relations, as the brief account given above indicates, the war has had the effect of increasing Iraq's dependence on the West and the West's conservative Arab allies, including Egypt and Jordan, the former providing useful spare parts for Soviet weapons in the early part of the war when the Soviet Union was disinclined to become closely involved, and the latter providing a vital transit route for imports from the port of 'Aqaba. For the benefit of some of his Arab audiences Saddam Husain has linked Iran and Zionism, against which the forces of the 'noble Iraqi Army' are pitted; hence the war 'is an international Zionist conspiracy aimed not only at Iraq but at the entire region'[12]. Arab imagery has constantly been employed to generalise the conflict and to make Iraq's neighbours feel responsible for its survival; constant reference has been made to the Iranian threat to 'the Arab nation, the Arab East, the Arabian Peninsula and the Arab Gulf'[13], a tactic which, given the fears aroused by Khumaini in the Gulf and Sa'udi Arabia, has been fairly successful.

Part of the 'price' that Iraq was prepared to pay for United States' support was a considerable modification of its famously hard line on the Arab–Israeli conflict. A few days after the resumption of

relations with the United States, Tariq 'Aziz declared on American
television that his country would support 'any just, honourable
and lasting settlement between the Arab states and Israel', and
went on to say that 'Iraq does not consider itself to be a direct party
to the conflict, because Israel is not occupying any part of Iraqi
soil'[14]. Given Iraq's previous record of vigorously denunciatory
inaction in this sphere, such pronouncements are perhaps less
remarkable than they may seem.

The Political and Economic Impact of the War on Iraq

The failure of Iraq to win an immediate victory over Iran, and the
long war which has followed, has greatly weakened the political
and economic capacity of the Iraqi regime. Politically, the
devastation caused by the war, with which the regime and its
leader have identified themselves so closely, the defeats sustained
by the Army, and the high casualty rate at the front — at least
200,000 killed and wounded, over 1% of the entire population —
have together amounted to a great loss of face for the Ba'th Party
and for Saddam Husain, and it is only his skilful use of
propaganda and the fears on the part of the Iraqi population of the
possible installation of an Islamic Republic in Iraq, together with
the utter ruthlessness of the security forces, that has maintained it
in power. Economically, Iraq will be in debt to its neighbours for
the foreseeable future, and the combination of the damage to the
physical infrastructure and the sharp fall in oil prices that began
in 1984 means that the regime will have far less resources at its
disposal to attract domestic support than it did in the 1970s.

Throughout the period of the war the cult of Saddam Husain
has continued unabated; the report of the 9th Regional Congress
of the Ba'th Party in June 1982 states that:

> Saddam Husain is a symbol of freedom, independence,
> pride, integrity and a hope for a better future for Iraq and
> the Arab nation, and this fact ... urges us to continue to
> march behind the banner which he is raising with all
> possible devotion, self-denial and courage.

A year later a journalist reported:

It is scarcely possible to walk the streets here without
encountering a photograph or larger than life poster of
Saddam Husain, in military uniform, Savile Row suit or
in traditional Arab dress. Children's balloons bear his
image.[15]

At the beginning, the war was known as 'Saddam's Qadisiya'
after the legendary victory of the Muslims over the Persians in AD
636, (although this appellation tended to fall by the wayside as
the prospect of 'victory' receded). Similarly, Madinat al-Thawra,
the Baghdad suburb built for the poor by 'Abd al-Karim Qasim in
the early 1960s, was renamed Madinat Saddam in October 1982.
Saddam Husain can be heard daily on Baghdad radio and
television, and his speeches fill the pages of *al-Thawra* and *al-
Jumhuriya*. It must be remembered that anyone born since, say,
1964, has been subjected to an incessant barrage of propaganda
about the Ba'th Party and its leader since he or she could first read
a newspaper, or listen to radio or television.

Thus the regime retains much of its self-confidence and
bravado. It has been able to maintain some semblance of a
'normal' way of life for most of the inhabitants of Baghdad, whom
visitors reported as remarkably unaffected by the conflict as late as
the autumn of 1985. Of course it is impossible to gauge the depth of
feeling against the war, because the regime has so cowed the
population with its enormous internal security forces, surveillance
operations, and the atrocious punishments meted out against all
manifestations of opposition either to the war or to its own
continuation in power, that the virtual absence of any *expression* of
opposition is not particularly significant. In July 1982, for
example, it was decreed that 'those who [commit] the crimes of
desertion or absence and who have failed to rejoin their units shall
be punished by execution', which was also to be the fate of those
'who committed the crime of absence for more than five days'[16]. In
the first years of the war the regime gave lavish financial
compensation to the families of those killed at the front, in the
form of cars, plots of land, and interest-free loans to build houses,
but after six years of fighting, during which about 1.5% of the entire
population has either been killed, wounded or captured such
'generosity' is no longer possible.

As we have seen, there has been little in the way of effective Shi'i
opposition to the Iraqi regime, though there have been rather

more dangerous expressions of opposition on the part of the Kurds and the Communists. All these groups have been hit extremely hard. Many Shi'is, Kurds and Communists have been imprisoned and executed; in March 1985 there was a report that 8000 Kurds who had been taken prisoner in 1983 had 'disappeared', and in March 1986 an apparently authentic eye-witness report appeared of a mass execution of about 4000 political prisoners at Abu Ghuraib prison in 1984[17]. However, it is also the case that the Shi'i, Communist and Kurdish opposition is gravely weakened by the fact that the three groups are often antagonist towards one another, which is almost inevitable given their very different objectives. For the most part the Shi'is are unwilling to co-operate with the Communists, and one of the principal Kurdish groups, Jalal Talabani's Patriotic Union of Kurdistan, has been in frequent contact with the Ba'th in Baghdad, and was evidently behind a joint attack in collaboration with Turkish forces against a Kurdish and Communist stronghold in Julamerk in May 1983.

As far as it is possible to ascertain, the internal dynamics of the regime continue to function much as before, in the sense that Saddam Husain remains in increasingly absolute personal control. As we have seen, a slimmed down RCC of nine members emerged after the Ninth Regional Congress in June 1982; in November 1982, it was reported that the Minister of Health, Dr Riyadh Ibrahim Husain, had been executed, allegedly for profiteering in medicines but apparently for suggesting that Saddam Husain should step down in favour of Ahmad Hasan al-Bakr, whose own death passed almost unnoticed at the end of 1982. In October 1983, two of Saddam Husain's half-brothers, Barzan, head of the security services, and Watban, the governor of Salah al-Din (Takrit) province, were dismissed from their positions[18], apparently for acting too independently of their brother. In addition, the regime continued to execute its opponents; thus executions of members of the Communist Party, members of *al-Da' wa* and of various other Shi'i and Kurdish organisations were reported throughout 1983, 1984 and 1985[19]. Again, in an obvious attempt to prevent the growth of both individual hero figures and the emergence of opposition groups within the armed forces, the generals commanding the various fronts are rotated regularly, and rarely mentioned by name in the official press. In such circumstances it would appear that, apart from some major

Iranian breakthrough, a serious threat to the regime is only likely to emerge from within its own ranks.

The Economic Effects of the War

For the first two years of the war the regime still had sufficient funds at its disposal to be able to insulate Iraqi society from most of the shortages and rationing that normally accompany military mobilisation. In the beginning, the slogan was very much 'business as usual'[20], and a wide variety of foodstuffs and consumer goods was available; similarly, it was not until 1983 and 1984 that work on major development projects (apart, of course, from those located in the vicinity of Basra, which had been damaged by Iranian action) began to slow down or cease. This was possible partly because, at least as far as the international financial community was concerned, the economy was in a reasonably healthy state before the war started, and partly because some of Iraq's principal clients, particularly in France and Japan, came to be owed so much money that the extension of further credit seemed the only guarantee that their debts would eventually be repaid.

By 1983, however, the pinch was beginning to be felt, and state and other organisations began to fall increasingly behind in payments to foreign contractors. The cost of living rose sharply, the dinar was devalued, and ceilings set upon the remittances that the two million foreign workers in the country[21] were allowed to send home. Individuals were 'asked' to 'donate' money and jewelry, particularly gold, to the war effort, and lists of 'donors' — about $400 million was apparently raised in this way — were read out regularly on the radio[22]. By August 1983 Iraq's foreign reserves had fallen from $30 billion at the end of 1980 to $3 billion, and the country was almost entirely dependent on handouts from Sa'udi Arabia and the Gulf; however, as Sa'udi oil revenues declined from $113 billion in 1981 to $40 billion in 1984, largesse on this scale may not be possible for ever. In addition, the size of the loans contracted in the course of the war ensures that Iraq will be in debt to its neighbours and the international banks for the foreseeable future[23].

The war has accelerated the expansion of the private sector of the economy, which, as we have described, had been booming long before it started. After the military reverses of the summer of 1982, Law 113 of 1982 provided substantial investment incentives in the form of tax concessions and low interest loans to private and mixed industrial firms, with particular favour being shown to joint stock companies. The encouragement of larger firms means that private capital is now able to move into relatively 'big business', formerly the sole preserve of the state sector, thus indicating a partial reversal of the nationalisations of 1964. At the beginning of 1984, the regime announced that budget allocations for the private industrial and trade sector would be increased by 171%.

Developments in agriculture have shown a similar pattern; here again the war has generally had the effect of intensifying trends that have been inherent in government policies at least since the middle 1970s. In spite of considerable investment in agriculture on the state's part, production levels have not greatly improved, and shortages of labour and other constraints connected with the war have combined to necessitate fairly large-scale imports of foodstuffs, including a purchase of 820,000 tons of grains from the United States in December 1982. At the same time, 80% of all loans to the agricultural sector in 1981 were to private firms or individuals, and a form of agricultural 'reprivatisation' has taken place, under an arrangement in force since January 1983 by which the Ministry of Agriculture offered leases of between five and twenty years to individuals or to local and Arab companies prepared to grow commercial crops[24]. Farmers were no longer required to belong to or sell through agricultural cooperatives or state farms, and could now sell direct to public sector or private wholesale markets. The war conditions evidently proved extremely beneficial to individuals with the know-how and facilities to exploit the regime's desperate need for both industrial and agricultural products.

An Endless Conflict?

It is difficult and unwise to predict the future course of events, although it is worth pointing out the unfortunate fact that apart from the human tragedy involved, there are few immediately compelling pressures to end the war. Apart from the inevitable economic shortages, and the fact that the casualties are sufficiently high to involve almost all classes of the population on both sides, neither the Iranian nor the Iraqi regimes show signs of buckling under the strain. Iran has managed to export substantial quantities of oil throughout the war, and Iraqi exports have also picked up since the opening of the pipeline from the Kirkuk fields across northern Sa'udi Arabia to Yanbu' on the Red Sea in 1985.

In the ideological sphere, all those who fall in battle on the Iraqi side are awarded the doubtful distinction of honorary membership of the Ba'th Party. The ethos promoted by the regime was illustrated in an edition of *al-Thawra* in February 1986, showing a picture of Saddam Husain decorating a man who had shot his own son dead for refusing to go to the front. Needless to say, the cult of martyrdom is even more assiduously fostered by the Iranian authorities, and young boys and old men are apparently equally eager to die for the faith in the battle against the Great Satan. There is no doubt that the Iraqi regime has been fairly successful in using the conflict to justify its continuation in power, and the bogey of what may happen to Iraq if it is overrun by Iran is a particularly powerful propaganda weapon for the regime.

The prospect of external forces ending the conflict is also remote. The early 1980s was a period of constant crisis for the oil-producing states, with the price of oil dropping with alarming regularity. In 1978 and 1979 Iraq produced about 3 million barrels per day; in 1981–83 the figure was well below 1 million. Comparable figures for Iran are 3.1 million b/d in 1979 and 2.49 million b/d in 1983; the fall of production in the Gulf area as a whole was even more remarkable, from 21.3 million b/d in 1979 to 11.3 million b/d in 1983[25]. As two associates of the Brookings Institute confirmed in 1984, 'the ... scenario of prolonged stalemate probably helps ensure relatively soft oil markets for the next few years'[26]. In this light, it is neither in the interests of the producers nor the consumers of oil that the war should end.

On a different level, given their present budget difficulties, the Gulf states and Sa'udi Arabia now find themselves in a serious dilemma. While the continuation of the war has come to act as a serious drain on their economies, it is difficult for them to stop financing Iraq, since although Iraq may not be able, will probably never be able, to defeat Iran, she is in an important sense protecting her 'allies' by preventing the export of the Iranian Revolution. In addition, the human and economic toll that the war has brought to Iraq means that the country presents increasingly less of a threat to its neighbours than it did at the end of the 1970s. That the falling price of oil may eventually prevent Iraq's allies from continuing to bail her out on the scale they have done in the past is a possibility that must be considered, but it seems unlikely that they would ever be able to contemplate the prospect of a victorious Iran, with all its implications for their own domestic security. Hence, short of an outright Iranian victory or a successful thrust by an opposition that would need to be far more united than it has ever been in the past, the prospects either of a speedy end to the conflict or of a change of regime in Baghdad appear equally dismally remote.

Notes

Chapter 1 Iraq before the Revolution of 1958

1 S.H. Longrigg's *Four Centuries of Modern Iraq*, London, 1925, is still the standard work on Ottoman Iraq. See also P.M. Holt, *Egypt and the Fertile Crescent 1516–1922, a Political History*, London, 1966, especially pp. 134–48, 247–54. The latter part of the Mamluk period is the subject of a valuable study by Tom Nieuwenhuis, *Politics and Society in Early Modern Iraq: Mamluk Pashas, Tribal Shayks and Local Rule between 1802 and 1931*, The Hague, 1982, which makes excellent use of contemporary French archives.

2 Mosul was formally incorporated as a *vilayet* (under the administrative system set out under the *Law of Vilayets* of 1864) in 1879 and Basra in 1884.

3 British commercial supremacy in the region had been virtually unchallenged since the beginning of the eighteenth century. Beginning with the capitulations agreement of 1675, continuing with Britain's political and military pre-eminence in the East following the Seven Years' War (1756–63) and culminating with the Anglo–Ottoman Commercial Treaty of 1838, British goods, and British traders and their protégés, enjoyed a wide range of privileges and advantages. See Hanna Batatu, *The Old Social Classes and the Revolutionary Movements of Iraq: a Study of Iraq's Old Landed and Commercial Classes and of its Communists, Ba'thists and Free Officers*, Princeton, 1978, p. 236. For the econmomic history of Iraq in the nineteenth century, see Roger Owen, *The Middle East in the World Economy 1800–1914*, London, 1981, pp. 180–188, 273–286.

4 M.S. Hasan, 'The Role of Foreign Trade in the Economic Development of Iraq 1864–1964: a Study in the Growth of a Dependent
   Economy', in M.A. Cook (Ed.) *Studies in the Economic History of the
   Middle East from the rise of Islam to the Present Day*, London, 1970, pp.
   346–372.
5 Owen, op.cit., p. 273.
6 The Code, in which the definitions of 'owner', 'occupier' and
   'cultivator' are rather vague, states that usufructuary rights to land
   (*haqq al-tasarruf*) 'will henceforth be acquired by leave of and grant by
   the agent of the Government appointed for the purpose' and that this
   grant will be confirmed by the issue of title deeds, *tapu sanads*. See
   Marion Farouk-Sluglett and Peter Sluglett, 'The Transformation of
   Land Tenure and Rural Social Structure in Central and Southern Iraq,
   c. 1870–1958', *International Journal of Middle East Studies, 15* (1983), pp.
   491–505; and Peter Sluglett and Marion Farouk-Sluglett, 'The
   Application of the 1858 Land Code in Greater Syria: some Preliminary
   Observations', in Tarif Khalidi (Ed.), *Land Tenure and Social
   Transformation in the Middle East*, Beirut, 1984, pp. 409–21. The text of
   the Code is reproduced in Stanley Fisher, *Ottoman Land Laws*,
   London, 1919.
7 See Gabriel Baer, 'The Evolution of Private Landownership in Egypt
   and the Fertile Crescent' in Charles Issawi (Ed.), *The Economic History
   of the Middle East 1800–1914*, Chicago and London, 1966, pp. 79–90;
   Kemal Karpat, 'The Land Regime, Social Structure and Modernisation
   in the Ottoman Empire' in William R. Polk and Richard L. Chambers
   (Eds.), *Beginnings of Modernization in the Middle East: the Nineteenth
   Century*, Chicago and London, 1968, pp. 69–90.
8 Small-scale landownership had never developed to any significant
   extent in Ottoman Iraq, and was found only on the Middle Euphrates
   between Hit and Haditha, in the Khalis and Lower Diyala valleys,
   around Basra and on the Hindiyya and Shamiyya *shatts*. See Batatu,
   op. cit., p. 55.
9 Holt, op. cit., p. 251.
10 Albertine Jwaideh, 'Midhat Pasha and the Land System of Lower
   Iraq', in Albert Hourani (Ed.), *St. Antony's Papers, III*, London, 1963,
   pp. 105–136.
11 Owen, op. cit., p. 186.
12 For a more detailed discussion see Marion Omar Farouk, *Der Wandel
   der Produktions — und Machtverhältnisse auf dem Lande im Irak unter
   der britischen Kolonialherrschaft 1914–1932*. Dr. Phil. thesis, Humboldt
   University, Berlin, 1974.
13 Robert A. Fernea, *Shaykh and Effendi: Changing Patterns of Authority
   among the El Shabana of Southern Iraq*, Cambridge, Mass., 1970, p.
   121.

14 Albertine Jwaideh, 'Aspects of Land Tenure and Social Change in Lower Iraq during Late Ottoman Times', in Tarif Khalidi (Ed.), op.cit; pp. 333-356.

15 Batatu, op. cit., p 77.

16 M.S. Hasan, 'The Growth and Structure of Iraq's Population 1867-1947', *Bulletin of the Oxford University Institute of Economics and Statistics*, 1958, pp. 339-352. The balance (24% in 1867, 24% in 1905 and 25% in 1930) consisted of townsmen.

17 It has been suggested that Hasan's aggregate population figures, which are based largely on estimates by Western observers and visitors, are too low. See Justin McCarthy, 'The Population of Ottoman Syria and Iraq 1878-1914'. *Asian and African Studies, 15*, 1, (1981), pp. 3-44.

18 For example, in Mosul between 1895 and 1911, one man, Mustafa Chalabi Sabunji, was virtual dictator of Mosul town, far more powerful than any of the numerous *walis* sent from Istanbul. See Batatu, op. cit. For an interesting description of Mosul between the Young Turk revolution of 1908 and the attempted counter-revolution of 1909, see Vice-Consul H.E. Wilkie Young, Mosul, to Sir Gerard Lowther, Constantinople, 28 January 1909, reproduced with an introductory note by Elie Kedourie in *Middle Eastern Studies*, 7, (1971), pp. 229-235.

19 See Roderic Davison, *Reform in the Ottoman Empire, 1856-1876*, Princeton, 1963.

20 These ideas are discussed in detail in Albert Hourani, *Arabic Thought in the Liberal Age 1798-1939*, London, 1962, pp. 67-102, 260-91; and in Bassam Tibi, *Arab Nationalism, a Critical Enquiry*, London, 1981, pp. 69-80.

21 See S.J. and E.K. Shaw, *History of the Ottoman Empire and Modern Turkey: Volume II, Reform, Revolution and Republic: the Rise of Modern Turkey 1808-1975*, London, 1977, pp. 255-82.

22 See Bernard Lewis, *The Emergence of Modern Turkey*, 2nd edition, London 1968, pp. 175-238.

23 Whom some thought should be chosen from the family of the Sharifs of Mecca; see Hourani, op.cit; pp. 260-91.

24 For further details see Ghassan R. Atiyyah, *Iraq 1908-1921; a Political Study*, Beirut, 1973; and Wamidh 'Umar Nadhmi, *The Political, Social and Intellectual Roots of the Iraqi Independence Movement of 1920*, Durham University Ph.D., 1974.

25 The import statistics are from Batatu, op. cit., pp. 239-40; overall figures for British trade are from the report of the Holland Wilson Commission, published in 1919 as *Prospects for British Trade in Mesopotamia and the Persian Gulf*, India Office, London, Letters, Political and Secret 10, 1283/1913/19/5/8193.

26 Arthur Marder, *From Dreadnought to Scapa Flow. Volume I, The Road to War 1904-1914*, London, 1961, p. 45.

27 See Stephen Longrigg, *Oil in the Middle East: Its Discovery and Development*, London, 1954, pp. 16-32.

28 For a vivid description of the events leading up to the Ottoman-German alliance see Barbara Tuchman, *August 1914*, 2nd edition, London, 1980, pp. 139-162.

29 Philip Ireland, *Iraq: a Study in Political Development*, London, 1937, p. 21. This book provides the most detailed available account of the operation and function of the British Occupation administration between 1914 and 1920; the section on the Mandate (pp. 338-456) has generally been superseded by later works that incorporate information from British archival sources not available to Ireland in 1937.

30 See A.J. Barker, *The Neglected War*, London, 1967.

31 For further details see Peter Sluglett, *Britain in Iraq 1914-1932*, London, 1976, pp. 9-14.

32 cf. '. . . the Turkish menace has apparently been removed. But another has taken its place, of a different kind, and one which, I think, makes it imperative for us to get to work. What I mean is that we must at least consider the possibility of a peace which will not give us the absolute political control of Mesopotamia that we should like to have . . .' Sir Arthur Hirtzel, India Office, to W.H. Clark, Department of Overseas Trade, Private, 31 December 1917. FO 368/1999/1071.

33 For an interesting interpretation of the significance of the Fourteen Points, see William Stivers, *Supremacy and Oil: Iraq, Turkey and the Anglo-American World Order, 1918-1939*, Ithaca and London, 1983, Chapter 2.

34 The full text is in *Accounts and Papers*, 1938-39, xiv, (Cmd. 5974), pp. 50-51.

35 J.S. Mann (Ed.), *An Administrator in the Making: J.S. Mann, 1893-1920*, London, 1921, p. 182. Mann was subsequently killed during the rising of 1920.

36 'The principal cause of the rising in Mesopotamia is that after the Arabs had been firmly promised that they should control their own affairs under advisory guidance, the British authorities proceeded to act as though we meant to take over the whole country, lock, stock and barrel'. Leader in *The Times*, 6 September 1920.

37 A.S. Klieman, *Foundations of British Policy in the Arab World: the Cairo Conference of 1921*, Baltimore and London, 1970.

38 For further details see Sluglett, op. cit., pp. 42-73.

39 Sluglett, op. cit., Chapter VII, pp. 259-272.

40 See H. al-Nakib, *A Critical Study of Saiyid Talib Pasha al-Nakib of Basra in the Setting of his Time and Environment*, Leeds University M.Phil., 1972-73.

41 cf. '. . . most of the 100 representatives who had been elected [to the Constituent Assembly in 1924] were believed to favour ratification . . . Only about fifteen were known to be definitely opposed . . .'. Ireland, op. cit., p. 394.

42 Batatu, op. cit., pp. 53-61.

43 Particularly in southern Iraq; see Farouk-Sluglett and Sluglett, op. cit., p. 498; and Sluglett, op. cit., Appendix II; Tenurial and Taxational Arrangements in 'Amara Liwa under the Mandate, pp. 317-331.

44 These attacks were effective at least to the extent that Bonar Law was clearly prepared to give up Mosul and the mandate for Iraq rather than risk another confrontation with Turkey.

45 This took place on 10 June, the day after the Mosul dispute was formally referred to the League of Nations for arbitration, and the last sentence of the ratification resolution finally agreed upon (by 37 votes to 24, with 8 abstentions, out of a Chamber of 100) declared that 'This Treaty and its subsidiary Agreements shall become null and void if the British Government fails to preserve the rights of Iraq in the Mosul Wilayet'. Quoted in Ireland, op. cit., pp. 403-04.

46 cf. 'You need not be alarmed about our 25 years' mandate. If we go on as fast as we've done over the last two years, Iraq will be a member of the League before five or six years have passed, and our direct responsibility will have ceased'. Gertrude Bell to Sir Hugh Bell, 13 January 1926. Lady Bell (Ed.), *The Letters of Gertrude Bell*, London, 1927, Volume II, p. 747.

47 A despatch from the American Legation in Baghdad in 1932 illustrates this point: 'Although Iraq became a member of the League of Nations as an Independent and free state, the fact cannot be hidden that perhaps the Iraqian without exception feels that his country is still tied to Great Britain both by written and by implied terms of the Anglo-Iraqi treaty, to an extent which still leaves it under a sufficiently powerful influence of Great Britain which make it impossible for Iraq to be considered or to act as a fully independent state. I believe that I am correct in saying that these views are held by every Iraqian without exception'. Sloan, Baghdad, to State Department, 17 November 1932, United States National Archives 890 g.00/223; quoted in Mudhaffar Amin, *Jama'at al-Ahali: its Origin, Ideology and Role in Iraqi Politics 1932-1946*, Durham University Ph.D. thesis, 1980, p. 16.

48 For further details of this period see Mohammad Tarbush, *The Role of the Military in Politics: a Case Study of Iraq to 1941*, London 1982.

49 Although it is true that resentment against the Assyrian Levies had always run high, since they were used by the British in combined operations with the RAF and were generally more highly thought of in British military circles than the Iraqi Army, most of those actually

killed in the operations carried out against them by the army in 1933 were the dependents of the Levies rather than Levies themselves. See R.S. Stafford, *The Tragedy of the Assyrians*, London, 1935. Khaldun S. Husry's article 'The Assyrian Affair of 1933', Parts I and II, *International Journal of Middle East Studies*, (1974), Nos 2 and 3, pp. 161–176, 344–360, which, although critical of Stafford on points of detail and interesting on the way in which the incident appealed to contemporary nationalist sentiment, rather glosses over the fact that the Army's greatest 'success' was essentially a massacre of 'unarmed villagers, clustered at the [Sumayyil] police station for protection'. (Phebe Marr, *The Modern History of Iraq*, Boulder and London, 1985, pp. 57–59.)

50 See Tarbush, op. cit. p. 123. The contemporary rumour that Britain was somehow behind the coup seems without foundation, as the following exchange between the British Ambassador, Sir Archibald Clerk Kerr and George Rendel of the Foreign Office illustrates: 'My dear George, I am sorry to have to sling that *coup d'état* at you without a word of warning. But Hikmat Sulaiman and Bakr Sidqi were unreasonable enough not to warn anyone at all.' FO 371/20014, E 7184/1419/93, 5 November 1936.

51 See the detailed study by Amin, op. cit., and Tarbush, op. cit., pp. 129–133.

52 Colonels Salah al-Din al-Sabbagh, Muhammad Fahmi Sa'id, Mahmud Salman and Kamil Shabib. For al-Sab'awi', see Khaldun S. al-Husry, 'The Political ideas of Yunis al-Sab'awi', in Marwan Buheiry (Ed.), *Intellectual Life in the Arab East, 1890–1939*, Beirut, 1981, pp. 165–175.

53 See Marion Farouk-Sluglett and Peter Sluglett, 'Labor and National Liberation; the Trade Union Movement in Iraq, 1920–1958', *Arab Studies Quarterly*, Vol 5, No 2 (1983), pp. 139–154.

54 See Anica, op. cit., pp. 68–95.

55 al-Husri's career and influence have been studied in detail in B. Tibi, op. cit., especially pp. 90–172.

56 See Tarbush, op. cit., pp. 80–82, which provides a sample of 61 senior officers in the Iraqi Army and Air Force in 1936; there are 58 Sunnis, 2 Christians and one Shi'i.

57 For details see Batatu, op. cit., pp. 297–300.

58 cf. Sir John Simon's comment in the *New York Times*, 7 February 1935, that neither the present Iraqi regime nor its predecessors had 'taken any action to prejudice the position of the British government in Palestine.' Quoted in Barry Rubin, *The Arab States and the Palestine Conflict*, Syracuse, 1981, p. 56.

59 For a complete list see Majid Khadduri, *Independent Iraq 1932–1958: a Study in Iraq Politics*, 2nd revised edition, London, 1960, p. 371.

60 For details see Lukasz Hirszowicz, *The Third Reich and the Arab East*,
    London, 1966, pp. 67–68; Tarbush, op. cit., p. 170. Hirszowicz'
    treatment of German–Iraqi relations immediately before and during
    the War is still the most detailed account available.

61 The text of the treaty is reproduced in full in Tarbush, op. cit., pp. 198–
    208. Diplomatic relations with Germany had been broken off on 5
    September 1939.

62 Batatu, op. cit., p. 453. The Communists, as Batatu remarks a few
    pages later 'could not in June 1941 radically alter their appraisal of the
    nationalist movement without giving affront to popular sentiment, or
    even risking ostracism. But it was not purely a matter of sensitivity to
    local realities. Many of the Communists were themselves not
    unaffected by the wave of bitterness that swept through the nation'. (p.
    462). However, with hindsight, perhaps in view of the anti-Communist
    sentiments of Rashid 'Ali and most of his circle, and presumably even
    more because of the subsequent invasion of the Soviet Union by Nazi
    Germany, the Party came to reject this analysis and to regard its
    support for the movement as a 'political mistake' (p. 461).

63 See the detailed account by Walid Hamdi, *Iraq, Britain and the Axis
    Powers, a Political and Military Study of the 1941 Crisis*, Ph.D. thesis,
    University of Birmingham, 1985.

64 For a trenchant appraisal of Nuri's career and influence, see Elie
    Kedourie, 'The Kingdom of Iraq, a Retrospect', in Elie Kedourie, *The
    Chatham House Version and other Middle Eastern Studies*, London, 1970,
    pp. 280–82.

65 Wm. Roger Louis, *The British Empire in the Middle East 1945-1951:
    Arab Nationalism, The United States and Postwar Imperialism*, Oxford,
    1984, p. 313.

66 The central section of Batatu's monumental work on the political and
    social history of Iraq is devoted to the Communist movement from its
    origins until the Revolution of 1958. Chapter 17, entitled 'Of the
    General Causes That Made for the Increase of Communism in the
    Two Decades Before the July Revolution' (op. cit., pp. 465–484) is the
    source of much of the material in the following paragraphs.

67 For the labour movement before 1958, see Farouk-Sluglett and
    Sluglett, op. cit., 1983b.

68 Tarbush, op. cit., pp. 131–32.

69 Batatu, op. cit., pp. 442–443.

70 See William Eagleton Jr, *The Kurdish Republic of Mahabad*, London,
    1963, pp. 14–24; and Sir Arnold Wilson, *Mesopotamia 1917-1920: a
    Clash of Loyalties*, London, 1931, pp. 29–38.

71 Sluglett, op. cit., p. 117; see also C.J. Edmonds, *Kurds, Turks and Arabs:
    Politics, Travel and Research in North-Eastern Iraq, 1919-1925*, London,
    1957, pp. 28–78.

72 The speech is quoted in Sluglett, op. cit., pp. 182–183.
73 See C. Kutschéra, *Le Mouvement Nationale Kurde*, Paris, 1979, pp. 113–121. Kutschéra's book, which is concerned with the Kurdish movement as a whole, is generally the most comprehensive and reliable guide to the subject.
74 Sa'ad Jawad, *Iraq and the Kurdish Question 1958–1970*, London, 1981, pp. 13–14; Kutschéra, op. cit., pp. 136–137; Ferhad Ibrahim, *Die Kurdische Nationalbewegung im Irak: eine Fallstudie zur Problematik Ethnischer Konflikt in der Dritten Welt*, Berlin, 1983, pp. 387–390.
75 For further details of Kurdish Communist politics under the monarchy and the ICP's activities in Kurdistan, see Majid 'Abd al-Ridha, *al-Qadhiya al-Kurdiya fi'l-'Iraq* (The Kurdish Question in Iraq), Baghdad, 1975; and Su'ad Khairi, *Min Ta'rikh al-Haraka al-Thawriya fi'l-'Iraq: Thawra 14 Tammuz* (The History of the Revolutionary Movement in Iraq: the Revolution of 14 July [1958]), Beirut, 1980. There were disagreements on policy between the Communists and the KDP (see below) largely over whether the Kurds were a minority within Iraq (the Communist view) or whether the Iraqi Kurds formed a part of the Kurdish nation (the KDP view). This point is discussed by Ibrahim, op. cit., pp. 417–426.
76 S.H. Longrigg, *Iraq 1900 to 1950*, London, 1953, pp. 277–302.
77 Barzani to Cornwallis, 25 December 1943, FO 371/40038, quoted in Kutschéra, op. cit., pp. 139–140.
78 See W. Eagleton Jr., *The Kurdish Republic of Mahabad*, London 1963; and Archie Roosevelt Jr., 'The Kurdish Republic of Mahabad', *Middle East Journal*, Vol 1, no 3, 1947. (Reprinted in Gerard Chaliand (Ed.), *People Without a Country: the Kurds and Kurdistan*, (trs. Michael Pallis), London, 1980, pp. 135–152.)
79 This period in Iranian history is best followed in Ervand Abrahamian, *Iran Between Two Revolutions*, Princeton, 1982; and Nikki R. Keddie, *Roots of Revolution; an Interpretative History of Modern Iran*, New Haven and London, 1981, pp. 113–141.
80 The British authorities certainly knew what they were doing. A report of 1917 states: 'Settled agriculture and extended civilisation have tended to disintegrate the tribe and to weaken the influence of the shaikhs. To restore and continue the power of the tribal shaikhs is not the least interesting of the problems in land administration which the Baghdad *wilayet* presents'. Administrative Report, Revenue Board, Baghdad, for the period 22 March to 31 Decemeber 1918, FO 371/3406/139231. Again, the Revenue Commissioner noted in 1919: 'We must recognise that it is primarily our business not to give rights to those who have them not, but to secure their rights to those who have them'. Lt.Col. E.B. Howell, *Note on Land Policy*, Baghdad, 1919, FO 371/4150/127807.

81 Major Pulley, Hilla, to Civil Commissioner, Baghdad, 6 August 1920. India Office, LP & S 10/4722/18/1920/8/6305; Sir A. Wilson, *Mesopotamia 1917–1920: A Clash of Loyalties*, London, 1931, p. 96.

82 Doreen Warriner, *Land and Poverty in the Middle East*, London, 1949, p. 99.

83 In 1921, there were 143 pumps in Iraq; in 1929 there were 2,066; and in 1944, 3,000. Warriner, op. cit., p. 106; Marion Omar Farouk, op. cit., pp. 107–127.

84 Muhammad al-Suri, *al-Iqta' fi Liwa' al-Kut*, Baghdad, 1958, pp. 80–81.

85 See Batatu, op. cit., p. 129 and note 45 above.

86 See Sluglett, op. cit., p. 92; and David Pool, 'From Elite to Class; The Transformation of Iraqi Leadership 1920–1939', *IJMES*, *12*, 3 (November 1980), pp. 331–350.

87 Y. Sayigh, *The Economies of the Arab World: Development Since 1945*, London, 1978, p. 28.

88 H.M. Government, *Special Report . . . on the Progress of Iraq 1920–1931 for the Permanent Mandate Commission of the League of Nations*, London, 1931.

89 M.S. Hasan, op. cit., p. 352.

90 Ahmad Fahmi, *Taqrir hawl al-'Iraq*, Baghdad, 1926, p. 103.

91 Thus: 'Had the British understood the local situation more clearly . . . they might have been able to introduce a system for settling land titles which gave the great tribal shaikhs . . . smaller opportunities to acquire tribal lands for themselves and form a large class of absentee landlords'. E. & E.F. Penrose, *Iraq: International Relations and National Development*, London and Boulder, 1978, p. 15.

92 Some of these contrary opinions are quoted in Sluglett, op. cit., pp. 231–238.

93 Professor M. Critchley, quoted in Rony Gabbay, *Communism and Agrarian Reform in Iraq*, London, 1978, p. 29.

94 See Sluglett, op. cit., pp. 251–253, 317, 321.

95 Doris G. Phillips, 'Rural Migration in Iraq', *Economic Development and Cultural Change*, 7, (1959), p. 409; Batatu, op. cit., pp. 133–34. For demographic developments during this and later periods, see F. Baali, *The Relation of the People to the Land in Southern Iraq*, Gainesville, Fla., 1966; the important short study by Richard Lawless, 'Iraq: Changing Population Patterns' in J.I. Clarke and W.B. Fisher (Eds.), *Population in the Middle East and North Africa*, London 1972, pp. 97–127; and M.M. Azeez, 'Geographical Aspects of Rural Migration from Amara Province, Iraq, 1955–1964' Durham University Ph.D. thesis, 1968.

96 In a recent and otherwise rather disappointing study of the area that became Madinat al-Thawra, the major low-cost development initiated by 'Abd al-Karim Qasim's government in 1961,

Ansari notes that about 80% of the population present there in 1963 had migrated from what is now Maisan province, formerly 'Amara, which, although relatively rich in agricultural terms, was an area of particularly acute landlord exploitation. Bassim al-Ansari, *al-Thawra, Quartier de Bagdad*, thèse du 3e cycle, EHESS Paris, 1979.

97   Real wages declined between the late 1930s and the mid 1950s. Batatu, op. cit., pp. 473–75.

98   Sluglett, op. cit., pp. 198–99.

99   Khair al-Din Haseeb, *The National Income of Iraq 1953-1961*, London, 1964, p. 20.

100 Khair al-Din Haseeb, op. cit, p. 25.

101 Hasan, op. cit., p. 364.

102 Batatu, op. cit., p. 274; Hasan, op. cit., p. 364.

103 See Elisabeth Longuenesse, *La Classe Ouvrière en Syrie; une Classe en Formation*, thèse du 3e cycle, EHESS, Paris, 1977.

104 Batatu, op. cit., pp. 348–50.

105 In the words of one of the leading Iraqi Communist historians of the period, this episode showed the population at large that the government was perfectly prepared to kill Iraqi workers in defence of British interests. Su-ad Khairi, *Min Ta'rikh al-Thawriyya al-Mu'asira fil-'Iraq* (The History of the Contemporary Revolutionary Movement in Iraq), Baghdad, 1975, pp. 150–152.

106 Batatu, op. cit., p. 546 cf. 'This treaty was certainly an improvement on the Treaty of 1930. It sought to establish the alliance on the basis of respect for Iraqi independence and mutuality of interest. . . . And yet [it] was repudiated by a popular coup d'état as soon as the news of its signature reached Baghdad'. M. Khadduri, *Independent Iraq 1932-1958: a Study in Iraq Politics*, London, 1960 p. 267.

107 Chancery, Baghdad, to Eastern Department, Foreign Office, 16 July 1946, FO 371/52315/E 7045; quoted in Louis, op. cit., p. 309.

108 cf. Pelham, Baghdad, to Attlee, 25 January 1948: 'Iraqi opinion, in common with other Arab opinion, has grown steadily more and more concerned with what seems to them the manifest injustice of the National Home policy in Palestine . . . The man in the street and in the coffee house has been excited by the successive outrages in Palestine since the partition decision, and Palestine has formed one of the subjects of slogans shouted in all the recent demonstrations in Baghdad'. FO 371/68446/E 2217, quoted in Louis, op. cit., pp. 339; see also p. 340–344 which contain some useful *post hoc* explanations of the crisis by British officials in the Foreign Office.

109 Batatu, op. cit., p. 548.

110 These incidents are movingly described in Batatu, op. cit., pp. 545–566.

111 P. Marr, *The Modern History of Iraq*, Boulder and London, 1985, p. 104.
112 Batatu, op. cit., pp. 563, 611-14, 626-27.
113 Batatu, op. cit., pp. 568-69.
114 Including Zaki Khairi, 'Aziz al-Hajj, 'Abd al-Salam al-Nasiri and Mahdi Hamid.
115 Louis, op. cit., p. 593.
116 Batatu, op. cit., pp. 666-670; Marr, op. cit., pp. 112-13.
117 Batatu, op. cit., p. 669; Khadduri, op. cit., p. 284.
118 Batatu, op. cit., p. 687.
119 See P.J. Vatikiotis, *Nasser and his Generation*, London, 1978, pp. 225-248.
120 See, e.g. E. & E.F. Penrose, op. cit., pp. 199-201; Marr, op. cit., p. 120; 'Caractacus', (pseud.), *Revolution in Iraq*, London, 1959.
121 Batatu, op. cit., p. 743. The figure (actually 289) is based on a membership list seized by the police in June 1955.

Chapter 2 1958-1963

1 See H. Batatu, *The Old Social Classes and the Revolutionary Movements of Iraq: a Study of Iraq's Old Landed and Commercial Classes and of its Communists, Ba'thists and Free Officers*, Chapter 41, 'The Free Officers, the Communists and the July 1958 Revolution', pp. 764-807.
2 Batatu, op. cit., p. 783.
3 Uriel Dann, *Iraq under Qassem: a Political History*, London, 1969, p. 27.
4 Batatu, op. cit., pp. 803-04.
5 E.g., in Batatu, op. cit., pp. 800-07; E. & E.F. Penrose, *Iraq: International Relations and National Development*, pp. 199-210; U. Dann, *Iraq under Qassem; a Political History*, pp. 28-32.
6 Batatu, op. cit., p. 802, where the full text of the proclamation is given.
7 Personal recollections in Baghdad, July–September 1958.
8 See Maxime Rodinson, 'The Political System' in P.J. Vatikiotis (Ed.) *Egypt since the Revolution*, London, 1968, pp. 87-113.
9 For a comprehensive discussion of the events of this period, see M. Tarbush, *The Role of the Military in Politics: a Case Study of Iraq to 1941*, London, 1982.
10 On the Euphrates, Hit seems to have been exceptional in being relatively unaffected by Arab nationalism and being more influenced by the ICP. On the question of ICP membership, the figure of 500 for 1954 given by Batatu op. cit., p. 704) and repeated by P. Marr (*The*

Modern History of Iraq, p. 166), seems extremely small. It is most unlikely that such a small number of individuals could have organised the huge demonstrations that took place in Baghdad in 1958 and 1959, and it is also unlikely that the Party was able to recruit substantial numbers in the years between 1954 and the Revolution, when repression was particularly severe.

11 See particularly Majid Khadduri, *Republican Iraq: a Study in Iraqi Politics Since the Revolution of 1958*, London, 1969, pp. 86, 88, 230, etc. and Marion Farouk-Sluglett, 'Contemporary Iraq: some Recent Writing Reconsidered', *Review of Middle Eastern Studies, 3*, 1978, pp. 82–104.

12 See Batatu, op. cit., p. 750; and Henri Grimal, *Decolonisation: the British, French, Dutch and Belgian Empires, 1919–1963*, trs. S. de Vos, London and Boulder, 1978.

13 K.S. Abu Jaber, *The Arab Baath Socialist Party*, Syracuse, 1966, pp. 43–44; Batatu, op. cit., pp. 822–23.

14 'The quickened tempo and successful conclusion of the desultory talks between Egypt and Syria caught everyone by surprise ... Without doubt, the Communists have been taken aback. Khaled al-Azem was the only member of the Government to oppose the plan; the sole Communist deputy has left the country and known Communists are reported to be noticeably more reticent than in the recent past. A reliable source reports that the Russian Embassy in Damascus was very angry at the sudden move ...' K. Bradford, British Bank of the Middle East, Beirut, to H. Musker, British Bank of the Middle East, London, 3 March 1958.

15 For details see Dann, op. cit., pp. 79–81; Penrose & Penrose, op. cit., p. 215; Batatu, op. cit., p. 828.

16 Or were told daily on Cairo Radio, *Sawt al-'Arab*.

17 See Khadduri, op. cit., 1969, p. 87; Dann, op. cit., pp. 79, 89.

18 Batatu, op. cit., p. 808.

19 Dann, op. cit., p. 128; Penrose & Penrose, op. cit., p. 221; Khadduri, op. cit., 1969, p. 101.

20 American troops had landed in Lebanon on the same day as the Iraqi Revolution, 14 July.

21 Taha al-Shaikh Ahmad stayed with Qasim to the end and died with him. He also retained his position throughout Qasim's purges of Communist officers in the early 1960s, and indeed led some of them. On the basis of conversations with an officer who worked for him in 1958–1959, it seems most likely that al-Shaikh Ahmad had been using his former Communist connections (see Batatu, Table 45-1) for his work as Qasim's security chief, but that his loyalties lay with Qasim rather than with the Party. On the other hand, the fact that he was widely believed to be a member of the ICP or at least sympathetic to it,

increased the false impression that party members were occupying important positions of power and that Qasim was particularly reliant upon them.

22 Batatu, op. cit., p. 849.
23 Dann, op. cit., p. 114.
24 See, for example, the 'Statement of the ICP to the Iraqi People on 14 July 1958' (quoted in Batatu, op. cit., pp. 829–30) and 'Statement of the ICP concerning Union with the UAR and Yemen' (p. 830).
25 Dann, op. cit., pp. 134–35.
26 Personal experience in Baghdad, 1958–60.
27 See Batatu, op. cit., pp. 953–54.
28 Batatu, op. cit., pp. 858, 892–93; Dann, op. cit., p. 103. Of those named here, only Fakhri was definitely a full member of the ICP; al-Awqati and Tahir were sympathisers, but not members.
29 Batatu, op. cit., pp. 861–62.
30 This is stressed by Penrose & Penrose, op. cit., p. 223.
31 Vice-Consul H.E. Wilkie Young, Mosul, to Sir Gerard Lowther, Constantinople, 28 January 1909; see Chapter 1, note 21.
32 They were replaced either by Free Officers loyal to Qasim or by civilians associated with the NDP. See Batatu, op. cit., pp. 844–45.
33 Khadduri, op. cit., 1969, p. 107.
34 Batatu, op. cit., p. 879.
35 Khadduri, op. cit., 1969, p. 111.
36 Batatu, op. cit., pp. 866–89.
37 For a contemporary description of these demonstrations, see the account in Penrose & Penrose, op. cit., pp. 228–29.
38 Batatu, op. cit., p. 898.
39. Personal recollections.
40 Batatu shows that pressure was also brought to bear on the ICP by the Soviet Union, as was also to be the case in 1973; Batatu, op. cit., p. 903.
41 Dann, op. cit., pp. 219–20.
42 It is instructive to compare Khadduri's and Batatu's accounts of the same incident (Khadduri, op cit., 1969, pp. 124–125; Batatu, op. cit., pp. 912–21).
43 Personal recollections.
44 There is a French translation of this document in *Orient* 11, no 3, (1959), pp. 175–221.
45 Including 'Abdullah al-Rikabi, 'Ayad Sa'id Thabit, and Khalid 'Ali al-Dulaimi; see Dann, op. cit., p. 253.
46 For the trial, see Dann, op. cit., pp. 247–49; Khadduri, op. cit., pp. 111–12.
47 Dann, op. cit., p. 249; Batatu, op. cit., pp. 931–32.
48 Saddam Husain managed to escape to Egypt, where he spent much of

the next five or six years. See Batatu, op. cit., p. 1084; and Khadduri, op. cit., 1969, pp. 128n., 130, where he appears as 'Sudam Tikriti'.

49 al-Sayigh had been given a licence to publish a newspaper, *al-Mabda'*, in November 1959.

50 Kamil Chadirchi, one of the founder members of the NDP and a respected member of the moderate opposition under the monarchy, dissociated himself from the NDP at this stage because of his dislike of military rule and his fears that Qasim was degenerating into a military dictator. See Khadduri, op. cit., 1969, p. 143.

51 For the elections to the Teachers' Union, see Dann, op. cit., p. 286; and Batatu, op. cit., pp. 950, 952–53. The ICP gained 91% of the votes in the elections in February 1961.

52 Batatu, op. cit., p. 947. For the background to ICP involvement in the unions in the port of Basra and on the railways see Farouk-Sluglett & Sluglett, 'Labour and National Liberation; the Trade Union Movement in Iraq, 1920–1958', *Arab Studies Quarterly* Vol 5, No 2 (1983), pp. 139–154.

53 In April and June anti-Communism *fatwas* were issued by two prominent Najaf *ulama*; see below, pp. 195.

54 See Dann, op. cit., p. 289; Batatu, op. cit., p. 951.

55 For further details, see Penrose & Penrose, op. cit., pp. 240–252. Land reform is discussed in Ronay Gabbay, *Communism and Agrarian Reform in Iraq*, London, 1978; industrialisation in Ferhang Jalal, *The Role of Government in the Industrialisation of Iraq*, London, 1971. See also Khair al-Din Haseeb, *The National Income of Iraq 1953–1961*, London, 1964.

56 For a particularly interesting discussion of middle class house-building and house-purchasing after 1958 see L.N. Rauf, *Development and Housing in Iraq*, Sussex University D.Phil., 1981, especially pp. 330–78.

57 The sympathy for Qasim among the poorer elements of the urban Shi'i population was probably more to do with his concern for their welfare than his own Shi'i background. In any case Qasim was often accused either of atheism or of indifference to religion — one of the Revolutionary Command Council's proclamations referred to him as ''adu al-Karim', the enemy of God — while 'Abd al-Salam 'Arif and Ahmad Hasan al-Bakr both came from fairly conservative Sunni backgrounds, and thus attracted some support both from religious Sunnis and religious Shi'is.

58 These developments are analysed in greater detail in Chapter 7.

59 Batatu, op. cit., p. 836.

60 Khadduri, op. cit., 1969, p. 161; Penrose & Penrose, op. cit., pp. 275f.

61 The negotiations, and the earlier history of the concession, are

described in detail in Penrose & Penrose, op. cit., pp. 137–62, 257–73.

62 Penrose & Penrose, op. cit., p. 269.

63 Dann, op. cit., p. 36.

64 The Iraqi Kurds could not have been encouraged by the experiences of the Kurds in the Syrian part of the UAR. See Mustafa Nazdar, 'The Kurds in Syria', in G. Chaliand (Ed.), *People Without a Country: the Kurds and Kurdistan*, London, 1980, pp. 211–19.

65 For details of these contacts see Sa'ad Jawad, *Iraq and the Kurdish Question 1958–1970*, London, 1981, pp. 108–112.

66 Dann, op. cit., p. 269.

67 For further details see Dann, op. cit., pp. 349–53; Khadduri, op. cit., 1969, pp. 166–73.

68 The formal organisational structure of the Ba'th Party is described on pp. 108-11, 119-20, 135-37, 184-85.

69 See Batatu, op. cit., p. 1010; and Christine Moss Helms, *Iraq, Eastern Flank of the Arab World*, Washington, 1984, p. 75.

Chapter 3 1963–1968

1 H. Batatu, *The Old Social Classes and the Revolutionary Movements of Iraq: a Study of Iraq's Old Landed and Commercial Classes and of its Communists, Ba'thists and Free Officers*, Princeton, 1978, pp. 1011–12.

2 Batatu, op. cit., p. 982.

3 Batatu, op. cit., pp. 985–86. Batatu quotes King Husain as saying that 'what happened in Iraq on 8 February had the support of American intelligence', and a high-ranking former official of the State Department has confirmed to us that Saddam Husain and other Ba'thists had made contact with the American authorities in the late 1950s and early 1960s; at this stage, the Ba'th were thought to be the 'political force of the future', and deserving of American support against 'Qasim and the Communists'.

4 There is considerable disagreement about the relative primacy of the early leadership. Thus in Abu Jaber's *The Arab Baath Socialist Party*, Syracuse, 1966, al-Arsuzi is not mentioned at all, and J.F. Devlin's *The Ba'th Party; a History from its Origins to 1966*, Stanford, 1976, contains only a few references. Presumably because of their Iraqi rivals' close association with 'Aflaq, the Asad regime in Syria has always claimed al-Arsuzi as the source of its ideology. For 'Aflaq, see N.S. Babikian, 'Michel Aflaq; a biographic Outline', *Arab Studies Quarterly*, 2, ii, (1980), pp. 162–79.

5 These events are discussed in greater detail by Patrick Seale, *The*

Struggle for Syria; a study of Post-War Arab Politics, 1945-1958, London, 1965.

6 'L'Islam est cette pulsion vitale qui a mis en branle les forces latentes de la nation arabe . . . . Muhammad fut l'incarnation de tous les Arabes; que chaque Arabe soît donc aujourd'hui Muhammad! . . . Les Chrétiens arabes . . . lorsqu'ils retrouveront leur caractère originel, reconnaîtront que l'Islam est pour eux une culture nationale au sein de laquelle ils doivent s'immerger et de laquelle ils se rassasieront, afin de la comprendre et de l'aimer au point d'être attachés a l'Islam comme a l'évènement le plus précieux de leur arabisme'. Michel 'Aflaq, 'Fi dhikr al-rasul al-'arabi' (1943), trs. J. Viennot, *Orient*, 9, xxxv, (1965), pp. 147-58.

7 'The relation between Arabism and the moment of overthrow' (1950), in Michel Aflaq, *Choice of Texts From the Ba'th Party Founder's Thought*, Florence, 1977, p. 59.

8 See 'The Party of the Arab Ba'th: Constitution' in Sylvia Haim, (ed. and trs.) *Arab Nationalism; an Anthology*, London and Berkeley, 1962, 1976, pp. 23-41.

9 Devlin, op. cit., p. 31.

10 For further details see Seale, op. cit., Itamar Rabinovich, *Syria under the Ba'th, 1963-1966: the Army-Party Symbiosis*, Jerusalem, 1972; Nikolaos Van Dam, *The Struggle for Power in Syria*, London, 1979, 1981; Elisabeth Picard, 'La Syrie de 1946 à 1979', and Olivier Carré, 'Le mouvement idéologique ba'thiste', both in André Raymond (Ed.), *La Syrie d'Aujourd'hui*, Paris, 1980, pp. 143-84, 185-224; Robert W. Olsen, *The Ba'th and Syria 1947-82*, Princeton, 1982.

11 Batatu, op. cit., p. 808.

12 *al-Jarida*, 8 April 1967. Immediately after this 'Abd al-Rahman 'Arif announced that he was committed to the principle of holding a general election, but that he wished to avoid a repetition of the Communist victory in the student elections, an indication of the regime's perception of the continuing strength of Communist support in the country as a whole. *ARR*, 15-30 April 1967.

13 Devlin, op. cit., p. 259.

14 cf. p. 65; see Batatu, op. cit., p. 1028.

15 Batatu, op. cit., p. 1028.

16 E. Penrose & E.F. Penrose, *Iraq: International Relations and National Development*, London and Boulder, 1978, p. 318-21.

17 Penrose & Penrose, op. cit., pp. 322-24; Batatu, op. cit., pp. 1031-32; A. et A. Guerreau, *L'Irak: Devéloppement et Contradictions*, Paris, 1978, p. 43.

18 Penrose & Penrose, op. cit., p. 382.

19 Penrose & Penrose, op. cit., pp. 387-90.

20 Batatu, op. cit., p. 1034.

21 Penrose & Penrose, op. cit., pp. 333-52.
22 Penrose & Penrose, op. cit., pp. 333-52.
23 Penrose & Penrose, op. cit., p. 341.
24 For details of the succession process, see M. Khadduri, *Republican Iraq: a Study in Iraqi Politics since the Revolution of 1958*, London, 1969, pp. 263-66.
25 Khadduri, op. cit., 1969, pp. 284-85.
26 These negotiations are summarised in Penrose & Penrose, op. cit., pp. 390-94.
27 Penrose & Penrose, op. cit., p. 467. The official mainly responsible for the nationalisations, Khair al-Din Hasib, was removed from his post after only a year in office.
28 *al-Waqa'iya' al-'Iraqiya*, (Iraq Government Gazette), No. 975, 14 July 1964, quoted in Nabil al-Nawwab, *State Intervention in the development of Social Welfare in Iraq during the period 1958-1968*, Keele University Ph.D., 1979, p.171.
29 Five years is of course too short a time to assess economic performance and our aim here has been to list the various projects undertaken during these years in addition to the 1964 nationalisations and the developments in the oil sector. A more wide-ranging assessment of economic development over the whole period since 1958 will be found in Chapter 7.
30 See pp. 97-8.
31 For further details, see Sa'ad Jawad, *Iraq and the Kurdish Question 1958-1970*, London, 1981, pp. 218-19. The various factions in Iraqi Kurdish politics are well described in the relevant sections of C. Kutschéra, *Le Mouvement Nationale Kurde*, Paris, 1979.
32 Khadduri, op. cit., 1969, p. 259; Jawad, op. cit., pp. 192-93.
33 Khadduri, op. cit., 1969, p. 179.
34 Khadduri, op. cit., 1969, pp. 198-200.
35 This section is based on the highly detailed information given in Batatu, op. cit., pp. 1027-73.
36 Batatu, op. cit., p. 1036.
37 Batatu, op. cit., p. 1040.

Chapter 4 1968-1972

1 H. Batatu, *The Old Social Classes and the Revolutionary Movement of Iraq: a Study of Iraq's Old Landed and Commercial Classes and of its Communists, Ba'thists and Free Officers*, Princeton, 1978, p. 1063.
2 At a meeting in September 1967, the Baghdad Chamber of Commerce asked 'Abd al-Rahman 'Arif for clarification of his government's policies towards land reform, the nationalisation of

industry, the scope of the public, private and mixed sectors of the economy, and foreign trade, claiming that the absence of a clear line was detrimental for business. *Middle East Record*, 1967, Vol III, pp. 360–361.

3 cf. *L'Orient* (Beirut), 6 May 1967; *Le Monde*, 10 October 1968.

4 E.g. J.F. Devlin, *The Ba'th Party; a History from its Origins to 1966*, Stanford 1976, *passim*; Majid Khadduri, *Socialist Iraq; a Study in Iraqi Politics since 1968*, Washington, 1978, pp. 36–41; C. Helms, *Iraq, Eastern Flank of the Arab World*, New York, 1984, pp. 83–131.

5 See Marion Farouk-Sluglett and Peter Sluglett, 'Iraqi Ba'thism: Nationalism, Socialism and National Socialism', in Campaign Against Repression and For Democratic Rights in Iraq (CARDRI), *Saddam's Iraq: Revolution or Reaction?*, London, 1986, pp. 89–107.

6 However, it is important not to overstate the case, since it was essential for any splinter group to be seen to be attached to one main faction or another. Thus al-Sa'di's reign of murder and terror earned him the disapproval of 'Aflaq and the less ruthless elements in the Iraqi Party, so that his 'derecognition' meant that he could be more easily disowned as an embarrassment by the Ba'thist officers around Ahmad Hasan al-Bakr in November 1963. In the same way the al-Bakr/Husain group sought 'Aflaq's approbation in the late 1960s after the Syrian and Iraqi factions had split, showing their concern to have some form of institutional links to the National or Regional Commands. cf. P, Marr, *The Modern History of Iraq*, Boulder and London, 1985, p. 188, which refers to al-Sa'di's 'radicalism' and his 'military wing' as 'doctrinaire to the core'.

7 Amazia Baram, 'Saddam Husain: a Political Profile', *Jerusalem Quarterly*, 17, Fall 1980, pp. 115–144.

8 M. Khadduri, *Socialist Iraq; a Study in Iraqi Politics since 1968*, Washington, 1978, p. 17.

9 See p. 90 above.

10 *ARR*, 16–31 May 1966.

11 E.g., May 1966; *ARR* 16–31 May 1966; August 1966, in the context of al-Bazzaz' resignation on 6 August; *ARR* 1–15 August 1966: May 1967; *Egyptian Gazette*, 7 May 1967: April 1968, when thirteen senior retired army officers including Ahmad Hasan al-Bakr, Hardan al-Takriti and Salih Mahdi 'Ammash visited 'Abd al-Rahman 'Arif to try to persuade him to establish a coalition government; *New York Times*, 22 April 1968.

12 *L'Orient* (Beirut), 6 May 1967; *Egyptian Gazette*, 7 May 1968; *Le Monde*, 10 October 1968.

13 *New York Times*, 22 April 1968; cf. *Middle East Record*, 1968, pp. 514–15.

14 *ARR*, 1–15 July 1968.

15 Khadduri op. cit., 1978, p. 22.
16 *Middle East Record*, 1968, pp. 515-17. Cf. Marr, op. cit., p. 205.
17 Batatu, op. cit., pp. 1011, 1025, 1062-63, 1073-74.
18 *Le Monde*, 9 October 1968.
19 Batatu, op. cit., pp. 1075-76.
20 For al-Shihab's connections with al-Bakr, see E. Penrose & E.F. Penrose, *Iraq: International Relations and National Development*, London and Boulder, 1978, p. 354; for Ghaidan's political background, see Batatu, op. cit., p. 1074.
21 Cf. *Le Monde*, 11 October 1968.
22 For details see above, pp. 100-01.
23 *Daily Telegraph*, 18 July 1968; *Le Monde*, 18 July 1968; *Le Monde*, 23 July 1968.
24 Khadduri, op. cit., 1978, pp. 28-29.
25 *Middle East Record*, 1968, p. 523.
26 *Middle East Record*, 1968, p. 521; the Arabic *wahdawi* has been mistranslated as 'united'.
27 Batatu, op. cit., p. 1092.
28 *Le Monde*, 1 August 1968, 12 August 1968.
29 *Le Monde*, 11 October 1968.
30 See *Le Monde*, 24 September 1968. A second provisional constitution was promulgated in 1969, and a number of important revisions were made in 1973 and 1974. Khadduri op. cit., 1978, pp. 183-198) gives a composite version of the document, which has survived in this form of suspended animation (in the sense that it has never been subjected either to a referendum or to the national assembly or formed the basis for the day to day activities of the government) at the time of writing (1986).
31 According to a source generally well-disposed towards the Ba'th regime, 'there is reason to believe that in peace time (the national assembly) would provide a stable and predictable support group for the civilian Ba'thists'. Helms, op. cit., p. 102.
32 See Batatu, op. cit., pp. 1099-1100; Penrose & Penrose, op. cit., pp. 344-45.
33 See *Le Monde*, 15 November 1968. In a demonstration on 7 November in which at least three participants were killed by the National Guard, more than thirty demonstrators were arrested and themselves accused of murder. *L'Humanité*, 14 December 1968.
34 For biographical details, see Batatu, op. cit., pp. 1221-22. The only professional in the group was 'Izzat Mustafa, a physician. The useful phrase 'Sunni triangle' seems to have originated with Abbas Kelidar; see his pamphlet *Iraq: the Search for Stability*, London: Institute for the Study of Conflict, 1975.
35 Batatu, op. cit., p. 1093.

36 *Middle East Record*, 1969-70, p. 703.
37 In the course of an interview on Baghdad Radio on 6 February 1969, the president of the Revolutionary Court, Lt.Col. 'Ali Wudwud, said that 'one of the first provisions of [words indistinct] court procedure stipulates that no lawyers shall be appointed members of the court. However, the court has a legal adviser who does the legal work of the court. The adviser is consulted when legal decisions are made'. BBC, *SWB*, 8 February 1969.
38 *Guardian* 30 June 1969.
39 This episode, Majid Khadduri remarks in somewhat pained tones, 'stirred a storm of protests, mainly by Jewish organizations in Western countries, on the grounds of ethnic and religious discrimination. . . . The Grand Rabbi of Baghdad', Khadduri continues with no apparent irony (the man was eighty-nine years old), '*disturbed by Jewish overreaction in the West* (our italics) made public statements in which he declared that the trial was fair and that the Jewish community in the country enjoyed freedom and security under the Iraqi regime'. Khadduri op. cit., 1978, p. 51.
40 While these allegations will always remain a matter for conjecture, it is neither impossible nor particularly unlikely that Britain, the United States, Israel and Iran should have had agents working in Iraq in the 1960s.
41 "C'était eux ou nous" a declaré le Général Hardan al-Takriti' (*Le Monde*, 26 January 1970). See also *Guardian*, 31 January 1970; *Christian Science Monitor*, 3 March 1970.
42 Batatu, op. cit., pp. 1069-71, 1098-1101. See also Abbas Kelidar, 'Aziz al-Haj: a Communist Radical' in Abbas Kelidar (Ed.), *The Integration of Modern Iraq*, London, 1979, pp. 183-92. al-Hajj also wrote a detailed recantation of his 'errors'; see his *Ma' al-'Awam: Sahafat min Ta'rikh al-Shiu'yya fi'l-'Iraq 1958-1969*, (With the Years: Pages from the History of the Communist Movement in Iraq, 1958-1969), Beirut, 1981.
43 Penrose & Penrose, op. cit., p. 426.
44 *Times*, 5 February 1968. See also Chapter 2 p. 19 above.
45 Significantly, those most closely involved in the ERAP negotiations were among the first to be arrested after 30 July. However, the ratification of the agreement by the 17 July regime was never reversed, and the Ba'th has always maintained cordial relations with France and with French oil interests, a policy that has stood it in good stead at certain crucial moments, notably in the immediate aftermath of the oil nationalisation in 1972 and in the course of the war with Iran.
46 *Financial Times*, 7 July 1969; *Times*, 9 July 1969.
47 See Sluglett, *Britain in Iraq 1914-1932*, London, 1976, pp. 103-140 and Helmut Mejcher, *The Imperial Quest for Oil, Iraq 1910-1928*, London, 1976.

48 See Michael E. Brown, 'The Nationalisation of the Iraq Petroleum Company', *IJMES*, 10, 1979, pp. 107–24, and in particular the reference to the activities of the Basra Petroleum Company on p. 116. Compare the testimony of an executive of Continental Oil Company before the Senate Foreign Relations Sub-Committee on Multinational Corporations on 27 March 1974 to the effect that 'IPC actually drilled wells to the wrong depth and covered others with bulldozers in order to reduce productive capacity'. Quoted Joe Stork, *Middle East Oil and the Energy Crisis*, London and New York, 1975, p. 140.

49 Brown, op. cit., p. 114.

50 *L'Humanité*, 14 December 1968.

51 Cf. *Neue Züricher Zeitung*, 12 May 1970.

52 *Financial Times*, 2 May 1969.

53 See Batatu, op. cit., p. 1208.

54 Sa'ad Jawad, *Iraq and the Kurdish Question 1958–1970*, London, 1981, pp. 108–12.

55 Jawad, op. cit., pp. 238 and 271n.

56 *Times*, 19 December 1968.

57 C. Kutschéra, *Le Mouvement National Kurde*, Paris 1979, pp. 267–68; *Financial Times*, 4 March, 15 March 1969; *Sunday Times*, 11 May 1969.

58 I.e. Iran declared that it would treat the Shatt al-'Arab as an international waterway rather than as part of Iraqi territory.

59 *International Herald Tribune*, 24–25 May 1969; BBC, *SWB*, 29 June 1969.

60 *Observer Foreign News Service*, 30 October 1969; I.S. Vanly, 'Kurdistan in Iraq' in Gerard Chaliand (Ed.), *People Without a Country: the Kurds and Kurdistan*, London, 1980, pp. 153–210, especially p. 174.

61 Principally relating to the use of Kurdish as a language of instruction in the area, the publication of Kurdish newspapers and the creation of a Kurdish Literary Academy.

62 For 'Aziz Sharif, see Batatu, op. cit., pp. 854–55. See also Jawad, op. cit., p. 255.

63 According to Mahmud 'Uthman, Sami 'Aziz al-Najm, a member of the Ba'th Regional Command was the first official Ba'th emissary; when more detailed talks got under way in January and February 1970, the Ba'th team included Hamad Shihab, Sa'dun Ghaidan, 'Abd al-Khaliq al-Samarra'i and Murtada al-Hadithi (all from the RCC), and 'Aziz Sharif and Fu'ad 'Arif, with Saddam Husain participating from time to time. The Kurdish delegation included Salih al-Yusufi, who had been prominent in earlier contacts with the Ba'th in 1963, Dara Tawfiq, a member of the KDP Politburo, formerly of the ICP, Muhsin Dizahi, who had served in al-Nayif's cabinet between 17 and 30 July 1968 and then briefly in al-Bakr's before resigning in protest at the inclusion of Taha Muhi al-Din Ma'ruf, and two of Barzani's sons, Mas'ud and Idris. See Jawad, op. cit., pp. 259–60, 275n.; and Ferhad Ibrahim,

Die kurdische Nationalbewegung im Irak: eine Fallstudie zur Problematik Ethnischer Konflikt in der der Dritten Welt, Berlin, 1983, pp. 562-64.

64 See p. 122 above.

65 'Il semble que ce sont les négotiations entreprises depuis quelque temps a Baghdad entre représentants irakiens et représentants de ... Barzani qui ont améné les opposants au règlement de cette affaire à un tel règlement risquant, à leurs yeux, de renforcer considerablement l'autorité du Parti Baas sur l'ensemble du territoire irakien.' (*Le Figaro*, 26 January 1970)

66 See Uriel Dann, 'The Kurdish National Movement in Iraq', *Jerusalem Quarterly*, 9 (1978), p. 141.

67 The full text is given in Khadduri, op. cit., 1978, pp. 231-40, from which this quotation is taken.

68 See Vanly, op. cit., pp. 171 f.

69 One minor consequence of the Manifesto was that the Ahmad/ Talabani faction now became redundant, and dissolved itself in the course of 1970. See Ibrahim, op. cit., p. 578.

70 For the text of a speech by Rogers outlining the plan on 9 December 1969, see T.G. Fraser, *The Middle East 1914-1979 (Documents of Modern History)*, London, 1980, pp. 123-26.

71 BBC, *SWB*, 2 August, 4 August 1970.

72 *New York Times*, 11 October 1970. How far the Palestinian guerillas really constituted a threat to Husain (in terms of their actual capacity to unseat him) must be a matter of conjecture; Helena Cobban's account of Black September suggests that Husain considered he had no alternative to taking them on. See *The Palestinian Liberation Organisation: People, Power and Politics*, Cambridge, 1984, pp. 49-52.

73 BBC, *SWB*, 11 September 1970.

74 BBC, *SWB*, 7 October 1970.

75 *'ando kull miftah bi-jaybo*, (he has all the keys in his pocket), as the saying goes in Iraqi colloquial.

76 E.g. while recognising the importance of personal animosities, Khadduri tends to discuss the events of this period in terms of military/civilian rivalry, as if the Ba'th had a coherent set of ideological principles. See Khadduri, op. cit., 1978, pp. 57-63. Helms' more general discussion of Ba'th ideology shows similar tendencies; op. cit., pp. 103-125.

77 For examples of the rumours circulating at the time about events in RCC meetings, see *Neue Züricher Zeitung*, 22 November 1970.

78 According to one correspondent in Baghdad in October 1970, the 'Ba'thists still do not control the army completely'. *Egyptian Mail*, 17 October 1970.

79 'Hardan al-Takriti als Sündenbock'; *Neue Züricher Zeitung*, 22 November 1970.

80 *New York Times*, 16 October 1970; *Guardian*, 16 October 1970; the *New York Times* had Hardan al-Takriti cast in the more heroic role.

81 Two other senior officers, Taha al-Shakarji and Hasan al-Naqib, were removed from command positions at the same time.

82 Adapted from Table 58-2 in Batatu, op. cit., pp. 1086-89.

83 Batatu, op. cit., p. 1078, and personal information.

84 Just over 59% of the 3.8 million acres affected by the Law had been confiscated by 1963, and this figure had risen to about 91% by June 1968. See R. Gabbay, *Communism and Agrarian Reform in Iraq*, London, 1978, pp. 114, 121-22. As Gabbay himself points out, the figure of 3.5 million (see his Table 10, p. 203) is contradicted by other Iraqi statistics, such as the Annual Abstract of Statistics for 1974, which gives a figure of 2.1 million. [The original figures, in *donums*, have been converted to acres; 1 acre = 2 *donums*].

85 By 1963 only about 40% of the sequestrated area had been redistributed, and although confiscation continued until 1968, only 1.25 million out of the total of 3.5 million acres had been reallocated. See Marion Farouk-Sluglett, ' "Socialist" Iraq 1963-1978 — Towards a Reappraisal', *Orient*, 23, ii, (1982), pp. 206-19.

86 Robin Theobald and Sa'ad Jawad, 'Problems of Rural Development in an Oil-Rich Economy', in Tim Niblock (Ed.), *Iraq: the Contemporary State*, London, 1982, p. 203.

87 Jawad Hashim, *Development Planning in Iraq: Historical Perspective and new Directions*, quoted by Rodney Wilson, 'Western, Soviet and Egyptian Influences on Iraq's Development Planning', in T. Niblock (Ed.), *Iraq: the Contemporary State*, London, 1982, pp. 224-225.

88 *Annual Abstract of Statistics*, 1973, p. 71.

89 Workers' Pension and Social Security Law No. 112 of 19 July 1969. See Batatu, op. cit., p. 1127-28.

90 Khadduri, op. cit., 1978, p. 138.

91 The only exception appears to be K. al-Jader's Sussex University D.Phil thesis (1972-73) entitled *Labour Organisation in Iraq: an Analysis of the effects of Social, Political and Economic Forces on the Structure and Organisation of Labour Unions in Iraq*, which is unfortunately not available for consultation.

92 Khadduri, op. cit., 1978 p. 138.

93 See Farouk-Sluglett & Sluglett, 'Labour and National Liberation; the Trade Union Movement in Iraq, 1920-1958'.

94 Cf. 'the policies of the Iraqi state towards the working class are not noticeably different from those of regimes [more] . . . openly in the service of capitalist development'. Joe Stork, 'Oil and the Penetration of Capital in Iraq', in P. Nore & T. Turner (Eds.) *Oil and Class Struggle*, London, 1980, pp. 172-198.

95 Batatu, op. cit., p. 1102. Cf. *Le Monde*, 8 April 1970, 9 May 1970, quoting

Beirut Communist newspapers. 'Au profit de qui est menée la campagne contre le PCI? . . . les milieux réactionnaires est impérialistes ont accueilli avec satisfaction cette campagne anti-communiste'. *L'Humanité*, 1 June 1970. The attacks continued throughout the summer of 1970; on 15 June *L'Humanité* reported further persecutions, with the bodies of Communists being thrown into the Tigris; cases of torture were reported in the *Morning Star* on 21 June and 28 June, and on 27 August *Le Monde* noted that the Communists were the principal victims of 'les milices baasistes qui ont depuis reçu un statut légal sous l'appellation d'Appareil du Sûreté Nationale'.

96   BBC, *SWB*, 2 June 1970.
97   BBC, *SWB*, 13 July 1970.
98   In addition, 'creating loyalties inside the armed forces other than loyalty to the Revolution (= the Ba'th)' was not to be permitted. See Batatu, op. cit., p. 1103.
99   See, for example, R.A. Uljanovskij, 'Besonderheiten und Schwierigkeiten der national-demokratischen Revolution auf dem nicht-kapitalistischen Entwicklungsweg', in *Asien und Afrika im Revolutionären Weltprozess*, Berlin-GDR, 1972, pp. 23–54; the discussion in *Problems of Peace and Socialism*, January/February 1972, and G. Brehme (Ed.), *Die national-demokratische Staat in Asien und Afrika*, Berlin-GDR, 1976. The development of these theories specifically in the context of Soviet/Middle Eastern relations has been discussed by Hélène Carrère D'Encausse in *La Politique Soviétique au Moyen Orient, 1955–1975*, Paris, 1975. In January 1972, the GDR newspaper *Neues Deutschland* reported that the Ba'th's National Action Charter showed the regime's intention 'den kapitalistischen Entwicklungsweg grundsätzlich abzulehnen'.
100   BBC, *SWB*, 15 November 1970.
101   *New York Times*, 5 January 1971. However, a more realistic trend was noted in the *Neue Züricher Zeitung* on 29 April: 'Interessant ist . . . das langsame — aber doch stetige — Ansteigen der Importe aus den Ostblockstaaten, die keine so spectakularen Zuwachsraten zeigen wie die Lieferungen die westliche Länder'.
102   See *ARR*, 10 February 1971, 10 May 1971; Batatu, op. cit., p. 1105.
103   Conversations with some of those arrested and tortured, 1975-76.
104   BBC, *SWB*, 25 March 1970, 8 July 1970.
105   BBC, *SWB*, 25 April, 8 May, 8 June, 9 August 1970.
106   BBC, *SWB*, 29 May 1970.
107   See Articles 5 (b), 7, 8 (c); the text is in Khadduri, op. cit., 1978, pp. 183-198. The other 'minorities' referred to include the Assyrians and Turcomans.
108   For Barzani's complaint that local Christian leaders were assisting the Ba'th to 'Arabise' Kirkuk, see *Le Monde*, 25 May 1971.

109 Ghareeb does not mention that the Ba'th's refusal to consider Karim
     came only six months after the proclamation of the March
     Manifesto. Edmond Ghareeb, *The Kurdish Question in Iraq*, Syracuse,
     1981, p. 105. Cf. *Le Monde*, 12 September 1970.
110 Ghareeb, op. cit., p. 109.
111 See Barry Rubin, *Paved with Good Intentions; the American Experience
     and Iran*, London, 1981, pp. 125–35.
112 The text is quoted in full in Khadduri, op. cit., 1978, pp. 199–229. It is
     of some interest that the word 'Islam' does not appear in the
     document.
113 See note 111 above.
114 Brown, op. cit., p. 113.
115 See *Fiches du Monde Arabe*, Iraq 1–i24a, 26 April 1978.
116 Penrose & Penrose, op. cit., p. 406.
117 *Times*, 14 December 1971.
118 *Le Monde*, 21/22 November 1971.
119 See below, pp. 151-54.
120 BBC, *SWB*, 13 January 1972; *ARR*, 10 February 1972.
121 BBC, *SWB*, 25 February 1972.
122 *ARR*, 1 April 1972.
123 Saddam Husain had spent a week in Damascus in March.
124 *Financial Times*, 9 June 1972.

Chapter 5 1972–1975

1 E.g. see BBC, *SWB*, 27 May 1973.
2 See 'Isam al-Khafaji, 'The Parasitic Base of the Ba'thist Regime', in
   CARDRI, *Saddam's Iraq; Revolution or Reaction?* London, 1986, pp.
   73–88.
3 C. Helms has the Ministers appointed *after* the formation of the
   National Front, which is incorrect. *Iraq, Eastern Flank of the Arab
   World*, New York, 1984, p. 77.
4 In the context of the Front, therefore, it is difficult to maintain 'that the
   [Communist] leaders were concerned above all with the problem of
   gaining or maintaining power'. (E. Penrose & E.F. Penrose, *Iraq:
   International Relations and National Development*, London and Boulder,
   1978, p. 370). In the first place, the Front's composition (8 Ba'thists, 3
   Communists, 2 Independents, 3 members of the KDP) meant that
   although the Communists could use it as a forum and give the CP
   leaders direct access to their Ba'th counterparts, they could not use the
   Front to 'gain', still less to 'maintain', power.
5 See note 7 below.
6 See Chapter 2.

7 This is one of the themes that emerges from the collection of essays edited by Michael Confino and Shimon Shamir, *The USSR and the Middle East*, Jerusalem, 1973.

8 See Helms, op. cit., pp. 75, where the Ba'thist version of these events is reproduced quite uncritically, as if it was an objective account. Cf. H. Batatu, *The Old Social Classes and the Revolutionary Movements of Iraq: a Study of Iraq's Old Landed and Commercial Classes and of its Communists, Ba'thists and Free Officers*, Princeton, 1978, pp. 866–889, 912–921.

9 Penrose & Penrose, op. cit., pp. 430–31.

10 Iraq was France's third supplier after Sa'udi Arabia and Libya; see *Le Commerce du Levant*, 8 November 1972.

11 *Times*, 7 June 1972.

12 Penrose & Penrose, op. cit., p. 414.

13 *International Herald Tribune*, 9 December 1975; *ARR*, 8 December 1975. It has been suggested that the oil policies pursued by successive Iraqi regimes since the promulgation of Law 80 in 1961 were detrimental to the country's economic development, in the sense that the tensions that arose between IPC and the various regimes had the effect of reducing the amount of oil that the former might have been prepared to produce in more cordial circumstances. However, in the first place, it would have been politically impossible for any regime to have gone back significantly on Law 80, and secondly, at least during the early years of the decade before nationalisation, market and price conditions were sufficiently adverse as far as sellers (that is, governments), were concerned to cast some doubt on how confidently it could have been predicted that better relations would necessarily have produced better financial returns. See J. Stork, 'Oil and the Penetration of Capital in Iraq', in P. Nore and T. Turner (Eds.), *Oil and Class Struggle*, London, 1980, p. 191; P. Stevens, 'Iraqi Oil Policy: 1961–1976', in Niblock (Ed.), *Iraq, the Contemporary State*, London, 1982, pp. 182–3.

14 Stork, *Middle East Oil and the Energy Crisis*, London and New York, 1975, p. 55.

15 *Times*, 9, 14 June 1972.

16 *Times*, 17 July 1972; *Guardian*, 7 August 1972.

17 BBC, *SWB*, 28 June 1972.

18 BBC, *SWB*, 2 March 1973.

19 It seems the policy of cutbacks and embargo had greater propaganda value than political or economic effect; at the height of the 'embargo', in December 1973, deliveries of oil from the Arab states to the United States were only 7.4% below pre-October levels. Stork, 1975, op. cit., p. 230.

20 BBC, *SWB*, 8 November 1973.

21 *Le Monde*, 17 May 1972.
22 *al-Ahram*, 16 December 1971; *al-Dustur*, 9 January 1972.
23 *Times*, 1 March 1973.
24 Cf. *Le Monde*, 27 August 1971: 'Ce sont, à definitive, les Communistes, seul force reéllement organisée en Iraq au dehors des nationalistes Kurdes et les baasistes, qui semblent avoir été les principales victimes des milices baasistes'.
25 *L'Humanité*, 15 June 1971.
26 See BBC, *SWB*, 2 October 1971.
27 M. Khadduri, *Socialist Iraq; a Study in Iraqi Politics since 1968*, Washington, 1978, p. 204.
28 *ARR*, 17 November 1971.
29 BBC, *SWB*, 4 December 1971; 25 February 1972.
30 *Le Monde*, 25 May 1971.
31 *Guardian* 18 January 1971.
32 E. Ghareeb, *The Kurdish Question in Iraq*, Syracuse, 1981, p. 89.
33 F. Ibrahim, *Die Kurdische Nationalbewegung im Irak: eine Fallstudie zur Problematik Ethnischer Konflikt in der Dritten Welt*, Berlin, 1983, p. 717.
34 It emerges from the leaked Pike report that Barzani was little more than a pawn in the hands of both the Iranians and the American security service from the time that he obtained the 'undertakings' from the CIA in May 1972; see C. Kutschéra, *Le Mouvement National Kurde*, Paris, 1979, pp. 282–84. Furthermore, the Kurds did not obtain adequate supplies of 'offensive' weapons until February 1975; see Ibrahim, op. cit., p. 723.
35 *al-Nahar* (Beirut), 12 July 1972; *al-Hayat* (Beirut), 13 August 1972.
36 *SWB*, 20, 31 October; 15, 17, 18 November 1972.
37 *Times*, 4 November 1972.
38 Eric Rouleau in *Le Monde*, 19, 21 July 1973.
39 Khadduri, op. cit., 1978, pp. 63–64.
40 This appointment did not, apparently, interfere with his studies; Khadduri remarks, without apparent irony, that although he had not yet completed his course at the Technological Institute before being promoted, 'he passed the final examination and received the diploma in 1970'. Khadduri, op. cit., 1978, p. 63, note 24.
41 See BBC, *SWB*, 6 July 1973, quoting *al-Anwar* (Beirut). This impression is partly confirmed by a RCC report of 10 July that mentions that Kazzar was personally in charge of the 'second investigation committee', an organisation whose apparent independence of the 'public security body' would have given him a degree of autonomy that he did not want to lose. For further details, see the articles in *Le Monde* by Jean Gueyras (3 and 4 July) and Eric Rouleau (19, 20 and 21 July).

42 BBC, *SWB*, 3 July 1973.
43 Khadduri, op. cit., 1978, p. 65.
44 Khadduri, op. cit., 1978, p. 65.
45 'A left winger, a party theoretician, and the most popular member of the Ba'th command . . .' Batatu, op. cit., p. 1094; cf. also p. 1097.
46 Batatu, op. cit., p. 1094. He was described on the radio as a member of the Regional Command (BBC, *SWB*, 7 July), but there is no supporting evidence for this.
47 *al-Thawra*, 10 July 1973.
48 *Le Monde*, 20 July 1973.
49 BBC, *SWB*, 6 July 1973.
50 A. Kelidar, *Iraq: the Search for Stability*, London: Institute for the Study of Conflict, 1975, p. 9; Penrose & Penrose, op. cit., p. 365.
51 The text is in Khadduri, op. cit., 1978, pp. 195–96.
52 Murtada al-Hadithi was dropped in 1974, and made ambassador to Moscow. He was replaced at the Ministry of Foreign Affairs by Shadhil Taqla, and 'Ammash, his predecessor in Moscow, was transferred to Paris; see *Egyptian Gazette*, 24 June 1974. 'Izzat Mustafa was dropped in March 1977; see p. 239 below.
53 BBC, *SWB*, 19 July 1973.
54 *Saddam Hussein on Current Events in Iraq*, London, 1977, p. 18.
55 BBC, *SWB*, 4 September 1973.
56 BBC, *SWB*, 6 July 1973.
57 BBC, *SWB*, 18 July 1973.
58 Kutschéra, op. cit., pp. 290–98.
59 Apparently trained by Savak in Iran; see Fred Halliday, *Iran; Dictatorship and Development*, London, 1979, p. 272.
60 For further details, see Mirella Galletti, 'L'ultima rivolta curda in Iraq', *Oriente Moderno*, 55, 1975, pp. 462–72.
61 BBC, *SWB*, 27 September 1973.
62 Kutschéra, op. cit., p. 286; Galletti, op. cit.
63 *Saddam Hussein on Current Events in Iraq*, London, 1972, p. 29. It is worth pointing out that Ghareeb's account (op. cit, pp. 151–52) is apparently based solely on this source!
64 Saddam Hussein, op. cit., p. 21.
65 Cf. 'Le PDK [=KDP] estime que seule une '*démocratie reélle*' qui mettrait fin au role dirigeant du Party Baas au sein du Conseil de la Revolution, de l'armée et du gouvernement peut restaurer le climat du confiance entre les deux principales ethnies du pays.' Jean Gueyras in *Le Monde*, 13 March 1974.
66 Saddam Hussein, op. cit., p. 31.
67 BBC, *SWB*, 18 July 1973.
68 BBC, *SWB*, 3 April 1974.
69 I.S. Vanly, 'Kurdistan in Iraq', in G. Chaliand (Ed.), *People Without a*

Country: the Kurds and Kurdistan, London, 1980, pp. 171-76.

70 In the past the ICP and the KDP had often cooperated, and had been drawn together more recently by their joint antipathy to the Ba'th (in spite of the Kurds' equivocation in 1963). However, as we have seen, the ICP had moved round to a position where it felt that it should support what it regarded as the 'progressive wing' of the Ba'th in the situation in which the regime now found itself. See *Le Monde*, 13 March 1974.

71 *Tariq al-Sha'b*, 21 November 1973, quoted in BBC, *SWB*, 21 November 1973. Similar comments in the following months indicate that the situation continued to deteriorate; cf. BBC, *SWB*, 15 December 1973, and 26 April 1974, which quotes *Tariq al-Sha'b*'s deep regret at the KDP line.

72 *Guardian*, 11 February, 7 March 1974; *Times*, 12 February 1974; *Le Monde*, 22 February 1974.

73 *Times*, 14 August 1974; *International Herald Tribune*, 29 August 1974; *Financial Times*, 7 September 1974; *Times*, 17 December 1974; *Le Monde*, 1 January 1975; *Times*, 10 February 1975.

74 Saddam Hussein, op. cit., p. 33.

75 Summarised in Ghareeb, op. cit., pp. 156-58.

76 Galletti, op. cit., p. 464, quoting several Beirut newspapers.

77 Kutschéra, op. cit., p. 298. One of the doubters was Dara Tawfiq; see *Christian Science Monitor*, 25 March 1974.

78 Galletti, op. cit.

79 BBC, *SWB*, 8, 16 April 1974; *Times*, 22 March 1974.

80 Kutschéra, op. cit., p. 305. Vanly gives the figure of 145,000; op. cit., p. 181.

81 According to contemporary reports, some by journalists who visited the area during or immediately after the bombing, 130 people were killed in a bombing raid on Qala' Diza on 24 April, 43 in a raid on Halabja on 27 April, and 29 in a raid on Galala on 29 April. David Hirst, *Guardian*, 7 May 1975. See also *Fiches du Monde Arabe*, 1401/5, 23 July 1980, which notes that the Iraqi Army had built a 700-mile road network in the mountains between 1970 and 1974.

82 Kutschéra, op. cit., pp. 307, 312.

83 *Financial Times*, 25 October 1974; *Daily Telegraph*, 18 November 1974. The casualty figures are from *Le Monde*, 6 May 1975.

84 *Fiches du Monde Arabe*, 1401/9, 27 August 1980.

85 Albeit, in Galletti's words, under 'un controllo draconiano'; Galletti, op. cit., p. 465.

86 *Le Monde*, 1 January 1975; BBC, *SWB*, 3 January 1975.

87 Ibrahim, op. cit.

88 See the Pike Report (quoted at length in Kutschéra, op cit.) and Galletti, op. cit. The Iranian Kurds' situation as an ethnic minority

was even less favourable than their fellows in Iraq. cf. *Le Monde*, 8 March 1975, where the ferment caused among the Iranian Kurds is given as an important reason for the convergence of Iranian and Iraqi interests.

89 See *ARR*, 1 June 1973, quoting *al-Nahar* (Beirut). The matter was also apparently discussed during Marshal Grechko's visit in March 1974; see *Christian Science Monitor*, 25 March 1974; *Daily Telegraph*, 30 March 1974.

90 Kutschéra, op. cit., pp. 322–23; Ibrahim, op. cit., p. 728.

91 *Financial Times*, 24 March 1975.

Chapter 6 1975–1980

1 Reproduced by M. Khadduri, *Socialist Iraq; a Study in Iraqi Politics Since 1968*, Washington, 1978, pp. 245–60.

2 *Fiches du Monde Arabe*, Iraq 1301/3, 2 May 1979, No. 1258.

3 Thus the Foreign Minister of the United Arab Emirates acclaimed the Agreement as 'a major step in ensuring the security and stability of the Gulf'; see *Fiches Monde Arabe*, Iraq 1301/2, 18 April 1979, no. 1247.

4 Cf *Daily Telegraph*, 25 August 1973; 18 November 1974.

5 *Fiches du Monde Arabe*, Iraq III-i8, 12 September 1979, no. 1376.

6 For the United States, see *New York Times*, 2 April 1975; for Japan and West Germany, see *ARR*, 27 July 1973, 3 September 1973, 5 October 1973, 14 July 1974 and BBC, *SWB*, 15 January 1974. However, Iraq was never in any sense 'economically dependent' on the Soviet Union as P. Marr claims; *The Modern History of Iraq*, Boulder and London, 1985, p. 238.

7 See Chapter 7.

8 See H. Batatu, *The Old Social Classes and the Revolutionary Movements of Iraq: a Study of Iraq's Old Landed and Commercial Classes and of its Communists, Ba'thists and Free Officers*, Princeton, 1978, pp. 1096–97.

9 R. Theobald & S. Jawad, 'Problems of Rural Development in an Oil-Rich Economy', in T. Niblock (Ed.), *Iraq: the Contemporary State*, London, 1982; Keith McLachlan, 'Iraq: Problems of Regional Development', in A. Kelidar, (Ed.), *The Integration of Modern Iraq*, London, 1979, pp. 135–149.

10 John Townsend, 'Industrial Development and the Decision-Making Process', in Niblock (Ed.), op. cit., pp. 256–277.

11 See Hamid al-Shawi, 'Le contenu de le contestation communiste en Irak et en Syrie', *Maghreb/Machrek*, 63, 1974; and cf. 'repoussant ces adversaires à la périphérie du système sut asseoir solidement son autorité en dépolitisant la population et l'armée'. Y. Schémeil, 'Le

système politique iraqien enfin stabilisé?' *Maghreb/Machrek*, 74, 1976, p. 44.

12 For the Communist Party, this was the time when it was still attempting to get something out of the Ba'th and also to defend its positions, a struggle that it was bound to lose, given the existing constellation of forces.

13 Cf. *Le Monde*, 21 July 1973. Marr does not make it sufficiently clear (P. Marr, *The Modern History of Iraq*, Boulder and London, 1985, pp. 27–28) that these organisations had always been dominated by the Communists.

14 Ara Khajadur, *Min Tajarib Shakhsiya fi'l-'Amal al-Niqabi al-'Ummali fi'l-'Iraq*, (Personal Experience of Work in the Trade Union Movement in Iraq), n.p., 1984.

15 Khajadur, op. cit.

16 Khajadur, op. cit., p. 52.

17 Khajadur, op. cit.

18 Apart from large-scale attempts to buy off some opposition either by the creation of numerous low-level civil service posts (such as caretakers for schools that did not yet exist) or payments to compensate for relocation. Personal information, Paris 1985.

19 See *Report of an Amnesty International Mission to the Government of the Republic of Iraq, 22–28 January 1983*, London, 1983; and Chapter 4, Note 81.

20 See BBC, *SWB*, 7 March 1974, 12 March 1974. The report was also published in English; Arab Ba'th Socialist Party, *Revolutionary Iraq 1968–1973: The Political Report Adopted by the Eighth Regional Congress of the Arab Ba'th Socialist Party — Iraq*, Baghdad, 1974.

21 See M. Farouk-Sluglett and P. Sluglett, 'Iraqi Ba'thism: Nationalism, Socialism and National Socialism', in CARDRI, *Saddam's Iraq: Revolution or Reaction?*, London, 1986, pp. 102–5.

22 P. Seale, *The Struggle for Syria; a Study of Post-War Arab Politics, 1945–1958*, London, 1965.

23 For an earlier example: 'In the five days from 6 to 11 November [1973] Kissinger succeeded in concluding the first bilateral disengagement agreement between Egyptian and Israeli forces'. H. Cobban, *The Palestinian Liberation Organisation: People, Power and Politics*, Cambridge, 1984, p. 59.

24 See F. Halliday, *The Threat from the East?*, London, 1982, pp. 63–80.

25 Peter Gubser, *Jordan: Crossroads of Middle Eastern Events*, Boulder and London, 1983, p. 106.

26 Syria purchases its arms from the Soviet Union with funds donated to it by Sa'udi Arabia and the Gulf states. Although the donors have a certain amount of leverage, Syria's position as a front line state makes this rather less effective than it might be.

27 BBC, *SWB*, 31 October 1973. See also Hamid al-Shawi, 'Iraq et le dernier conflit israélo-Arabe', *Maghreb/Machrek*, 64, 1974, pp. 19–23.

28 The new members were Sa'dun Shakir (a cousin of Saddam Husain); Ja'far Qasim Hammudi (a Sunni); Tariq 'Aziz (a Christian from Mosul); 'Abdullah Fadhil (a Sunni from Samarra'); 'Adnan Khairallah (Saddam Husain's brother-in-law); Hikmat Ibrahim al-'Azzawi (a Sunni); Muhammad 'Ayish (a Sunni, secretary general of the Iraqi Trade Union Federation); Burhan al-Din Mustafa (a Sunni from Takrit); and Muhi 'Abd al-Husain Mashhadi (a Shi'i).

29 Cf. M. Farouk-Sluglett, '"Socialist" Iraq 1963–1978 — Towards a Reappraisal', *Orient* 23, ii, (1982), pp. 206–19; and Chapter 7 below.

30 *Sunday Times*, 4 February 1974; Batatu, op. cit., pp. 1095–96.

31 *Financial Times*, 21 January 1977.

32 See Alya Sousa, 'The Eradication of Illiteracy in Iraq', in Niblock, op. cit., pp. 100–108.

33 For Brown and Root, see *ARR*, 23 September 1973; the contract was worth $117 million; for Mannesmann, see *Le Commerce du Levant*, 14 July 1974, *Le Monde*, 5 January 1977; for the Tharthar canal, see BBC, *SWB*, 26 October 1976.

34 *New York Times*, 19 March 1975.

35 *Financial Times*, 27 July 1973.

36 *Guardian*, 2 April 1974.

37 See *Financial Times*, 22 October 1974; *Daily Telegraph*, 18 November 1974; *New York Times*, 2 April 1975; *International Herald Tribune*, 11 April 1975.

38 For 1974–75, see *Neue Züricher Zeitung*, 12 June 1976; 1981, see K. Dawisha, 'The USSR in the Middle East; Superpower in Eclipse?', *Foreign Affairs*, Winter 1982–83, pp. 438–52. Incidentally, it is not correct that the Ba'th's relations with the Soviet Union deteriorated in the early 1970s, or that the Soviet Union was 'particularly displeased' about the Algiers Agreement of 1975, as Marr suggests (op. cit, p. 238), especially as the Soviet Union had been attempting to mediate between the two sides since 1973. See above, Chapter 4, note 90.

39 C. Kutschéra, *Le Mouvement National Kurde*, Paris, 1979, p. 324.

40 A consignment of helicopters had already been purchased in 1974; France remains Iraq's principal Western supplier, and the volume of this trade has increased significantly since 1980.

41 *Fiches du Monde Arabe*, Iraq-1401/8.

42 According to official figures, *al-Thawra* sold about 18 million copies over this period; Batatu, op. cit., p. 1110.

43 Personal observation in Baghdad in March 1976.

44 *ARR*, 1–15 April 1976; *Neue Züricher Zeitung*, 12 June 1976.

45 See *Watha'iq al-Mu'tamar al Watani al-Thalith al-Hizb al-Shiu'i al-*

'*Iraqi*, (Documents of the Third National Congress of the Iraqi Communist Party), Baghdad, 1976, pp. 46-50.

46 *Guardian*, 11 February, 1976; *International Herald Tribune*, 12 April 1976; *Neue Züricher Zeitung*, 12 June 1976; *Guardian*, 7, 8, 16 December 1976.
47 Khadduri, op. cit., 1978, pp. 43-44.
48 See below, Chapter 7, Table 22.
49 Batatu, op. cit., p. 1078; C. Helms, *Iraq: Eastern Flank of the Arab World*, New York, 1984, p. 87.
50 No empirical research has been undertaken in this field, but imports of consumer durables have increased tremendously over these years.
51 Colin Legum and Haim Shaked (Eds.), *Middle East Contemporary Survey* Volume 1, 1976-77, London and New York, 1978, p. 403. [Subsequently *MECS* and appropriate year/s].
52 Helms, op. cit., p. 97.
53 This was first reported in the international Communist press (see *ARR*, 26 May 1976) and subsequently confirmed by the regime (*ARR*, 7 June 1976).
54 The point had already been made some years earlier by the President and Vice President. See BBC, *SWB*, 20 November 1971, containing an interview with al-Bakr; cf. Saddam Husain in *SWB*, 3 March 1972. See also Amnesty International, *Report of an Amnesty International Mission to the Government of the Republic of Iraq, 22-28 January, 1983*, London, 1983, p. 20.
55 See RCC Resolution 884 of 17 July 1978, quoted in Amnesty International, op. cit., pp. 19-21.
56 *Morning Star*, 18 July 1978; *ARR*, 5 August 1978; *Morning Star*, 9 November 1978; *Tariq al-Sha'b*, 21 November 1978; *L'Humanité*, 6 December 1979; *Morning Star*, 27 December 1978; *International Herald Tribune*, 3 January 1979.
57 See, for example, CARDRI, op. cit., pp. 108-119.
58 Personal contacts.
59 Mirella Galletti, 'Sviluppi del problema curda negli anni 1976-1978', *Oriente Moderno*, 58, 1978, pp. 463-74.
60 I.S. Vanly, 'Kurdistan in Iraq', in G. Chaliand (Ed.), *People Without a Country: the Kurds and Kurdistan*, London, 1980, pp. 153-210.
61 Thus Kifri, Chamchamal and Klar were taken from Ta'mim and assigned to Sulaimaniya, and Tuz Khurmatu assigned to Salah al-Din. See Galletti, op. cit., p. 465.
62 Galletti, op. cit.; Vanly, op. cit
63 See Saddam Husain, *Khandaq am Khandagani?* (One Trench or Two Trenches?), Baghdad, 1977, pp. 34-35.
64 Galletti, op. cit., p. 464; Vanly, op. cit., pp. 192-99.

65 Personal information, Paris, August 1985.

66 Eyewitness report by James Litherland MP.

67 E. Ghareeb, *The Kurdish Question in Iraq*; Syracuse, 1981, p. 178; *MECS*, 1976-77, pp. 410-11.

68 Galletti, op. cit., p. 467.

69 According to Galletti (op. cit.), 90% of the Iraqi Army was stationed in the North in 1978. *Die Zeit* (20 October 1978) claimed that 33% out of a total of 160,000 troops were in the area; 'Das autonome Kurdistan ist ein militärisch besetzes Land'.

70 *Daily Telegraph*, 26 April 1979; *Guardian*, 16 July 1979.

71 This point is made by Michael Hudson in 'The Islamic factor in Syrian and Iraqi Politics', in James Piscatori (Ed.), *Islam and the Political Process*, Cambridge, 1983, pp. 73-97.

72 Marion Farouk-Sluglett and Peter Sluglett, 'Some Reflections on the Present State of Sunni/Shi'i Relations in Iraq', *Bulletin of the British Society for Middle Eastern Studies*, 5, (1978), pp. 79-87.

73 Hanna Batatu, 'Iraq's Underground Shi'a Movements: Characteristics, Causes and Prospects', *Middle East Journal*, 35, (1981), pp. 578-94.

74 Ibid., p. 587.

75 Also, by extension, those who were in a position to do so sent their children to Shi'i private schools; conversation with 'Isam al-Khafaji.

76 Tarbush, *The Role of the Military in Politics: a Case Study of Iraq to 1941*, London, 1982, pp. 80-82.

77 Sir A. Wilson, *Mesopotamia 1917-1920: A Clash of Loyalties*, London, 1931, pp. 72-76.

78 P. Sluglett, *Britain in Iraq 1914-1932*, London, 1976, pp. 82-85.

79 Batatu, 1978, op. cit., pp. 752, 1000.

80 See Shahrough Akhavi, *Religion and Politics in Contemporary Iran; Clergy State Relations in the Pahlavi Period*, Albany, 1980, pp. 1-22.

81 See F. Jamali, 'The Theological Colleges of Najaf', *Muslim World*, 50, i, (1960); quoted in Batatu, 1981, op. cit., p. 586, where the exact numbers are given.

82 Na'im Haddad and Hasan 'Ali al-'Amiri joined the Regional Command in 1974. Muhi 'Abd al-Husain al-Mashhadi and 'Adnan Hamdani became members of the RCC in September 1977; Haddad and al-'Amiri became RCC members at the same time.

83 Batatu, 1981, op. cit., p. 588.

84 The society is supposed to have published a secret journal, *al-Adwa'*, for six years. See Andreas Rieck, (ed. and trs.), *"Unsere Wirtschaft'; Eine gekurzte kommentierte Übersetzung des Buches "Iqtisaduna" von Muhammad Baqir as-Sadr'*, Berlin, 1984, p. 45.

85 S. Akhavi, *Religion and Politics in Contemporary Iran; Clergy State Relations in the Pahlavi Period*, Albany, 1980, p. 98.

86 Rieck, op. cit., p. 68. A less favourable view is expressed by Michael M.J. Fischer, *Iran: From Religious Dispute to Revolution*, Cambridge Mass. and London, 1980, p. 157.

87 Rieck, op. cit., p. 59.

88 Freely adapted from Rieck, op. cit., p. 53 ff.

89 Akhavi, op. cit., p. 131.

90 *Guardian* 16 December 1974; *Times*, 8 January 1975.

91 *Le Monde*, 12 February 1977; *Guardian* 12 February, 1 March 1977. Muhammad Baqir al-Hakim is currently the leader of the Iraqi Shi'i opposition in exile in Iran.

92 See below; there have also been suggestions that the drought caused by the construction of the Tabqa Dam (and the acceleration of migration which followed) was an important factor behind the growth of Shi'i protest generally and the February 1977 incidents in particular.

93 *Le Monde*, 26 March 1977.

94 This reduced the RCC to 5 members: Ahmad Hasan al-Bakr, Saddam Husain, Sa'dun Ghaidan, Taha Jazrawi, 'Izzat al-Duri. See Ofra Bengio, 'Shi'is and Politics in Ba'thi Iraq', *Middle Eastern Studies*, 21, (1985), pp. 1-14.

95 On 11 August 1977; see his speech entitled 'Nazra fi'l-Din wa'l-Turath' (Considerations on Religion and Heritage), quoted in Batatu, 1981, op. cit., p. 591. Cf. Bengio, op. cit.

96 See e.g., Fischer, op. cit.; Akhavi, op. cit.

97 Batatu, 1981, op. cit., p. 590.

98 *MECS*, 1978-79, pp. 570-71; and personal conversations with Iraqis.

99 Amnesty International, op. cit.

100 Rieck, op. cit., pp. 62-63.

101 BBC, *SWB*, 6 January, 27 February 1975.

102 BBC, *SWB*, 26 June 1975.

103 Cf. BBC, *SWB*, 7 June 1975, and Zehra Onder, *Saudi-Arabien: Zwischen islamischer Ideologie und westlicher Ökonomie*, Stuttgart, 1980, pp. 246-247.

104 BBC, *SWB*, 19 July 1975; visits were also exchanged with Qatar; *SWB*, 4 July, 15 July 1975.

105 BBC, *SWB*, 20 April 1976; *ARR*, 3 October 1977.

106 See *ARR*, 17 April, 12 August, 2 October 1978.

107 *Guardian*, 11 April 1979. Iraq and Sa'udi Arabia had signed a mutual security agreement only one month after the fall of the Shah, at the end of February 1979.

108 See Chapter 3 above.

109 See Olivier Carré, 'Le mouvement idéologique ba'thiste', in André Raymond (Ed.) *La Syrie d'Aujourd'hui*, Paris, 1980.

110 *MECS*, 1977–78, p. 523.
111 According to David Hirst, the disruptions caused by Taha Yasin Ramadan's constant departures from the conference chamber to telephone Baghdad and the general recalcitrance shown by the Iraqi delegation indicated a desire on Iraq's part to prevent the conference reaching an agreed position.
112 *ARR*, 17 April, 12 August, 9 September, 1 October 1978.
113 H. Cobban, *The Palestine Liberation Organisation: People, Power and Politics*, Cambridge, 1984, pp. 100–102.
114 *MECS*, 1978–79, p. 216.
115 Cf. Saddam Husain's statement that 'unity is not to be achieved at the expense of precision', *Financial Times*, 31 January 1979.
116 *Financial Times*, 27 May 1978.
117 *Le Monde*, 18 July 1978.
118 *Guardian*, 2 June 1978; *Morning Star*, 9 November, 27 December 1978; *International Herald Tribune*, 3 January 1979; *Guardian* 27 February 1979.
119 *International Herald Tribune*, 10 July 1978.
120 *Guardian*, 11 April 1979.
121 BBC, *SWB*, 9 February 1976.
122 Even in the course of the present war, it is rare for the names of individual officers to be mentioned publicly, in order to avoid anyone making a reputation for themselves.
123 *MECS*, 1976–77, p. 403.
124 This is not, of course, to imply that 'the military' or 'the generals' were actually in power.
125 *al-Thawra*, 5 September 1977.
126 See P. Stevens, 'Iraqi Oil Policy: 1961–1976', in Niblock, op. cit., pp. 173–74.
127 *Middle East Economic Survey*, 19 September 1977.
128 *MECS*, 1977–78, pp. 521–2.
129 *New York Times*, 28 July 1979; *International Herald Tribune*, 30 July 1979.
130 *Die Zeit*, 7 August 1979.
131 We have seen a copy of this film.
132 *Observer Foreign News Service*, 3 August 1979.
133 It is sometimes claimed that the contest was in some way ideological, but we have not found any evidence of disagreements of this kind.

Chapter 7 Economy and society since 1958

1 Notably in Latin America; see F.H. Cardoso and E. Faletti,

Dependency and Development in Latin America, London and Los Angeles, 1979; E.V.K. Fitzgerald, *The Political Economy of Peru, 1956-1978: Economic Development and the Restructuring of Capital*, London, 1979; Bryan Roberts, *Cities of Peasants*, London, 1978.

2 Very little anthropological and sociological fieldwork has been carried out over the last few years; compare the research carried out before the revolution. See here R.A. Fernea, *Shaikh and Effendi: Changing Patterns of Authority Among the El Shabana of Southern Iraq*, Cambridge, Mass. and London, 1980; S.M. Salim *Marsh Dwellers of the Euphrates Delta*, London, 1962; and of course H. Batatu's immense work which has been cited so frequently over the previous chapters, *The Old Social Classes and the Revolutionary Movements of Iraq: a Study of Iraq's Old Landed and Commercial Classes and of its Communists, Ba'thists and Free Officers*, Princeton, 1978. Iraqis receiving state postgraduate studentships are required to submit copies of their dissertations to the Iraqi Embassy, with the result that the version given to the Embassy may be very different from the one deposited in the University Library, which is all too often — but for perfectly understandable reasons — not available for public consultation (personal experience). Furthermore, very few of the theses cited later in this chapter have been published, either in their entirety or as articles.

3 This situation has been made more difficult in recent years by the government's failure to publish complete national statistical series since 1978. We have now obtained the *Annual Abstract of Statistics* for 1984, which is extremely patchy in comparison with earlier volumes, with the result that many of our tables do not go beyond 1977. The later figures used in the original draft were made available by Professor Robert Springborg, who kindly allowed us to use the tables in his 'Infitah, Agrarian Transformation and Elite Consolidation in Contemporary Iraq', unpublished paper presented to the International Political Science Association conference, Paris, July 1985.

4 Oil formed 81% of Iraqi exports as early as 1954; see F.A. Mahdi, *An Appraisal of an Alternative for Iraqi Planning and Development with Emphasis on Foreign trade and the 1961/62-1969/70 Experience*, Birmingham University, Ph.D., 1974, p. 30.

5 C. Issawi, *An Economic History of the Middle East and North Africa*, New York, 1982, p. 205.

6 Cardoso & Faletti, op. cit., p. 74.

7 M. Farouk-Sluglett, 'Contemporary Iraq: Some Recent Writing Reconsidered', *Review of Middle Eastern Studies*, 5, (1978), p. 89.

8 See M. Farouk-Sluglett & P. Sluglett, 'The Transformation of Land Tenure and Rural Social Structure in Central and Southern Iraq. c. 1870-1958', *International Journal of Middle East Studies*, 15, (1983), pp. 491-505.

9 'The city was throbbing with vigour'; cf. the long passage in Batatu, op. cit., p. 78.

10 This was and is also true for states receiving aid rather than oil; compare the situation in Egypt and Syria.

11 See above, Chapter 2.

12 Such as Kamil Chadirchi and Muhammad Hadid; Chadirchi refused to accept a ministerial position.

13 This was also seen as a major obstacle by 'Abd al-Rahman al-Bazzaz; see above, Chapter 3.

14 Given his pronouncedly conservative views, 'Arif's nomination of al-Bazzaz as Prime Minister suggests that his own enthusiasm for 'socialism' may already have begun to wane.

15 See M. Farouk-Sluglett, '"Socialist" Iraq 1963–1978 — Towards a Reappraisal', *Orient*, 23, ii, (1982), p. 211.

16 Ibid., p. 212.

17 In fact the projects initiated after the foundation of the Development Board in 1952 had already begun to affect the economy in the same way, but as the scale was so much smaller the effects were less immediately perceptible.

18 Naturally, this was soon followed by the emergence of a brisk black market in import licences, and a whole host of new administrative bottlenecks.

19 The main non-oil exports were and continue to be dates, barley, raw cotton, raw wool, raw leather, and cement.

20 The number of civil servants increased from 207,966 in 1960 to an estimated 346,000 in 1969, and their average income rose by 63.9% over the same period compared with an average rise of 42.3% in the country as a whole. F.A. Mahdi, op. cit., p. 22

21 Government of Iraq, *Statistical Pocket Book 1960–1970*, Baghdad 1971, p. 27.

22 Officially, there were 608 cooperatives with 76,272 members working 903,000 hectares of land in 1973; *AAS*, 1973, p. 73.

23 Farouk-Sluglett, op. cit., 1982, p. 213.

24 In 1973, 95.2% of irrigation pumps were privately owned. See A.L. Khammo, *The Role of Mechanization in the Development of Agriculture in Iraq*, Leeds University Ph.D., 1977, p. 430.

25 See R. Theobald & S. Jawad, 'Problems of Rural Development in an Oil-Rich Economy', in T. Niblock (Ed.), *Iraq: the Contemporary State*, London, 1982, p. 202; for the continuing role of local credit, see M.S. Fattah, *Bargaining, Trust and Credit Between Crop Traders in an Iraqi Market*, Manchester University Ph.D., 1974.

26 See Fattah, op. cit., p. 33–34; see also A.K. Hirmis, *Industrial Location and Regional Economic Growth in Iraq*, Manchester University Ph.D., 1979, pp. 11–12. In 1969, average per capita income was below ID 40

in 1969 in the rural areas and between ID 120 and ID 150 in the cities. Nationally, per capita income averaged ID 117 in 1971. In general, the situation was somewhat better from the peasants' point of view in the 'Sunni triangle', where relations between shaikh and tribesmen were better, or more accurately, the shaikh's role was more paternalistic. For an interesting discussion of this see 'Isam al-Khafaji, *al-Dawla wa'l-Tatawwur al-Ra'smali fi'l-'Iraq, 1968-1978*, (The State and Capitalist Development in Iraq), Cairo, 1983, p. 174-5.

27 See Farouk-Sluglett, 1982, op. cit., p. 210; M. Farouk-Sluglett & P. Sluglett, 'Iraqi Ba'thism: Nationalism, Socialism and National Socialism', in CARDRI, *Saddam's Iraq: Revolution or Reaction?*, London, 1986.

28 Even Iraqis not sympathetic to the Communist Party were questioning the wisdom of this move. See Hamid al-Shawi, 'Le contenu de la contestation communiste en Iraq et en Syrie', *Maghreb/Machrek*, 63, 1974.

29 See Chapter 4 above.

30 Cardoso & Faletti, op. cit., p. 212.

31 See Richard Kühnl, (Ed.), *Texte zur Faschismusdiskussion 1: Positionen und Kontroversen*, Hamburg, 1974; and *Faschismustheorien: Texte zur Faschimusdiskussion 2, Ein Leitfaden*, Hamburg, 1979.

32 Mahmud Bunya is one of the wealthiest entrepreneurs in Iraq, with numerous interrelated enterprises; other include the family of Muhammad Hadid (Qasim's first Minister of Finance), the Kubaisi family from Ramadi, 'Ali Hajj Yunis from Mosul and others, many of whom have contacts with foreign companies. al-Khafaji, 1983, op. cit., pp. 102–03.

33 Springborg, op. cit., p. 23.

34 Springborg, op. cit., p. 25.

35 *AAS*, 1978, p. 116.

36 al-Khafaji, 1983, op. cit., pp. 44–47.

37 'Isam al-Khafaji, 'The Parasitic Base of the Ba'thist Regime', in CARDRI, 1986, op. cit., pp. 77.

38 al-Khafaji, op. cit., 1983, p. 84.

39 'Isam al-Khafaji, op. cit., 1986, pp. 76–77.

40 Springborg, op. cit., p. 17. Springborg attributes these developments to the new policies pursued since 1979/80, but all the evidence suggests that the process had started long before that time and was only intensified by the war. See here for instance al-Khafaji, 1983, op. cit., passim.

41 al-Khafaji, op. cit., 1983, pp. 115–16.

42 See Farouk-Sluglett, op. cit., 1982, p. 213; Fattah, op. cit.

43 Salim I. Ibrahim, 'Socio-Economic Status and the Utilisation of Agricultural Machinery in Iraq', Arab Planning Institute, Kuwait,

1979–80, pp. 25–37; Khammo, op. cit., p. 430.

44 Private information.

45 There were four different kinds of cooperative; see Ibrahim, op cit., pp. 34–37.

46 W.A. Hilmi, *Internal Migration and Regional Policy in Iraq*, Sheffield University Ph.D., 1978, pp. 53, 361, 413.

47 Later statistics do not indicate any changes; see *AAS* 1978, pp. 108–09.

48 According to Ibrahim, ca. 30% of the total cultivated area (25 million out of 82.5 million donums) has remained in private hands, with the proportion differing from area to area. Thus in the districts of Anbar, Ninawi and Ta'min (Kirkuk) the proportion was nearer 50%. Salim Ibrahim, op. cit., pp. 37, 44.

49 Springborg, op. cit., p. 3.

50 Springborg, op. cit., Tables 4 and 5, pp. 14–15.

51 In order to establish a direct chain of command between himself and the appropriate bureaucracy Saddam Husain abolished the Higher Agricultural Council (a 14-man Party body) in 1980. See Springborg, op. cit., pp. 7–8; and R. Springborg, 'Ba'thism in Practice: Agriculture, Politics and Political Culture in Syria and Iraq', *Middle Eastern Studies* 17, 2, (1981), pp. 191–209.

52 See M. Farouk-Sluglett, P. Sluglett, & J. Stork, 'Not Quite Armageddon: the Impact of the [Gulf] War on Iraq', *MERIP Reports*, 125–26, July–September 1984, p. 30.

53 Springborg, op. cit., p. 11.

54 Hilmi sees the deterioration of agriculture as the main reason for migration. He also states that migration is undertaken in one step; migrants (who are mostly landless peasants) normally doubt the government's sincerity or its capacity to change conditions in the countryside. Also migration is generally total, in the sense that no family members are left behind. Hilmi, op. cit., pp. 52–53, 561, 891.

55 al-Khafaji, 1986, op. cit., pp. 14–16.

56 Hilmi, op. cit., pp. 301–02.

57 Khajadur describes how old working class ICP members have become totally outnumbered by a completely different sort of worker, with little experience of political activity, largely apolitical and primarily concerned with making money; A. Khajadur, *Shakhsiya fi'l-'Amal al-Niqabi al-'Ummali fi'l-'Iraq* (Personal Experience of Work in the Trade Union Movement in Iraq), n.p., 1984, p. 54. A similar situation has been described in Syria; see E. Longuenesse, *La Classe Ouvrière en Syrie; Une Classe en Formation*, 3e cycle, EHESS, Paris, 1977.

58 Hilmi, op. cit., p. 294.

59 al-Khafaji, 1983, op. cit., p. 46.

60 See above, p. 15.

61 al-Khafaji, 1983, op. cit., p. 53.

62 Khajadur, op. cit., p. 54; there are also a number of regulations designed to keep state employees from moving to the private sector. Personal contacts, 1980–84.

63 Figures for 1978 and 1979 from Economist Intelligence Unit, *Iraq: a New Market in a Region of Turmoil*, London, 1980, p. 87; for 1980 and 1981 from John Townsend, 'Economic and Political Implications of the War; the Economic Consequences for the Participants', in M.S. El Azhary (Ed.), *The Iran–Iraq War*, London, 1984, pp. 60–62. ID = $3.39.

64 Farouk-Sluglett, Sluglett & Stork, op. cit., p. 30.

65 K. Dawisha, 'The USSR in the Middle East; Superpower in Eclipse?', *Foreign Affairs*, Winter 1982–83, pp. 438–52.

66 It is of course not clear to what extent the recent fall in oil prices has affected Iraqi oil revenues. However, although the fall in oil prices has been quite drastic and will certainly leave its mark on the economies of the oil-producing countries, their long term effect will not be as radical as may be assumed at first sight. In Iraq and elsewhere oil revenues will continue to be the main source of income for the foreseeable future, although somewhat diminished by the recent changes in prices.

67 Cf. the situation in Peru. E.V.K. Fitzgerald, *The Political Economy of Peru, 1956–1978: Economic Development and the Restructuring of Capital*, London, 1979, passim.

Chapter 8 Epilogue: the war between Iraq and Iran

1 *Guardian*, 28 February 1979.

2 See the list over 80 border incidents in *MECS*, 1979–80, pp. 518–21.

3 *Guardian*, 12 June 1979.

4 *Financial Times*, 1 November 1979. There were also persistent rumours of an imminent Iraqi attack on Iran: *Guardian*, 18 June 1979; *International Herald Tribune*, 19 June 1979; *New York Times*, 15 December 1979.

5 See Tareq Y. Ismael, *Iraq and Iran: Roots of Conflict*, New York, 1982; Shirin Tahir-Kheli & Shaheen Ayubi (Eds.), *The Iran-Iraq War: New Weapons, Old Conflicts*, New York, 1983; M.S. El-Azhary (Ed.), *The Iran-Iraq War*, London 1984. See also the discussion in Chapter 6 above.

6 See Dilip Hiro, 'Chronicle of the Gulf War', *Merip Reports*, No 125/

126, July/September 1984, pp. 3-14, from which most of the factual account in the next paragraphs has been taken.

7 Dilip Hiro, *Iran under the Ayatollahs*, London, 1985, p. 167. Thus in June 1980 the Revolutionary Command Council announced that 'Any Iranian family which is proved to be disloyal to the [Iraqi] revolution and the homeland is subject to deportation even if it holds the Iraqi nationality certificate'. Another aspect of the campaign against 'Iranians' has been the encouragement of Iraqis to divorce their 'Iranian' wives; in 1981 the RCC passed a resolution to the effect that 'Any Iraqi national who is married to a woman of Iranian origin is eligible to ID 4000 if he is a member of the armed forces or ID 2500 for civilians if he divorces his wife or if she is deported'. Amnesty International, *Report of an Amnesty International Mission to the Government of Iraq, 22-28 January 1983*, London, 1983.

8 See Hiro, 1984, op. cit., p. 6; *Financial Times*, 9 February 1983, 24 August 1983. Most of the aid appears to come directly from Sa'udi Arabia; see *Frankfurter Allgemeine Zeitung*, 2 April 1985.

9 It is also possible that Iraq's allies took seriously Khumaini's threat that if Iranian oil exports were interfered with 'not a drop of oil [would flow] through the Hormuz Straits' and pressed Iraq not to attack Kharg. See Hiro, 1984, op. cit., p. 11.

10 Thus 'For the first nine months of the current fiscal year beginning October 1 1979 US food imports to Iraq totaled $251 million . . . Although Iraq has not maintained diplomatic relations with the United States since 1967 . . . the expansion of trade has advanced strongly since about 1974'. *New York Times*, 30 September 1980. The same article has a graph showing that US exports to Iraq rose from under $50 million in 1973 to about $420 million in 1979. After an interview with the US Secretary of State George Schultz in Washington in the summer of 1982, the Iraqi Foreign Minister Sa'dun Hammadi claimed that the United States was 'serious about its intentions for a peace initiative in the Middle East'. *Frankfurter Allgemeine Zeitung*, 23 October 1982.

11 There have been two United Nations missions to the area, the first between 13 and 19 March 1984 and the second between 26 February and 3 March 1986. The second mission published its report on 14 March 1986.

12 BBC, *SWB*, 8 January 1983.

13 BBC, *SWB*, 29 July 1983.

14 *al-Nahar* (Beirut), 2 December 1984.

15 The report of the Ninth Regional Congress is quoted in *MECS*, 1981-82, pp. 588-90. *International Herald Tribune*, 3 August 1983; cf. *Frankfurter Allgemeine Zeitung*, 24 July 1984, 24 July 1985.

16 BBC, *SWB*, 10 July 1982.

17 For the 'missing' Kurds see *Times*, 1 March 1985; the Abu Ghuraib massacre was described in a press release issued by Ann Clwyd M.P. on 14 March 1986.

18 See *Guardian*, 7 November 1983.

19 E.g. see *Times*, 23 June 1983 reporting the execution of six members of the al-Hakim family; *Le Monde*, 6 February 1983 reporting that Tayih 'Abd al-Karim, a former oil minister, had been executed at the same time as Riyadh Ibrahim Hasan; *Times*, 19 March 1984, reporting the execution of about forty Kurds; *Guardian*, 24 June 1984, reporting the execution of a further three Kurds; *Le Monde*, 6 April 1984 reporting at least 300 executions in 1983.

20 See 'No compelling reason to end the war', *Arab Economist*, 136, January 1981, p. 18; Economist Intelligence Unit, *Quarterly Economic Report, Iraq*, Nos 1–4, 1981.

21 See *Le Monde*, 5 April 1984.

22 *Financial Times*, 9 December 1983.

23 Some indication of the extent of Iraq's indebtedness is given in *Financial Times*, 9 May 1984, where it is mentioned *inter alia* that $7.5 billion had been borrowed over the previous year.

24 *Middle East Economic Digest* reported on 13 January 1984 that the government had signed 300 contracts with local and Arab agricultural companies in the course of 1983. Law 35 of 1983 permits leases of up to 400 hectares to private individuals.

25 Exxon Background series, 'Middle East Oil and Gas', 1984, p. 5.

26 'Oil and the Outcome of the Iran–Iraq War', quoted in *Merip Reports*, No 125/126, July/September 1984, pp. 40–42.

Bibliography

Theses

Amin, Mudhaffar, *Jama'at al-Ahali: its Origin, Ideology and Role in Iraqi Politics 1932–1946*, Durham University Ph.D., 1980.

al-Ansari, Bassim, *al-Thawra, Quartier de Bagdad*, 3e cycle, EHESS, Paris, 1979.

Azeez, M.M., *Geographical Aspects of Rural Migration from 'Amara Province, Iraq, 1955–1964*, Durham University Ph.D., 1968.

Fattah, M.S., *Bargaining, Trust and Credit Between Crop Traders in an Iraqi Market*, Manchester University Ph.D., 1974.

Hamdi, Walid, *Iraq, Britain and the Axis Powers, a Political and Military Study of the 1941 Crisis*, Birmingham University Ph.D., 1985.

al-Hashimi, I.A., *A Theoretical Analysis of the New Private Housing Market in the muhafadha (District) of Baghdad*, Manchester University Ph.D., 1979.

al-Hayally, H.K., *Industrialisation and Regional Development in Iraq, with Special Reference to the Concentration of Manufacturing Industry in the Central Macro-Region*, University College of Swansea, University of Wales, M.Sc., 1978.

Hilmi, W.A., *Internal Migration and Regional Policy in Iraq*, Sheffield University Ph.D., 1978.

Hirmis, A.K., *Industrial Location and Regional Industrial Growth in Iraq*, Manchester University Ph.D., 1979.

al-Jader, K., *Labour Organisation in Iraq: an Analysis of the effects of Social, Political and Economic Forces on the Structure and Organisation of Labour Unions in Iraq*, Sussex University D.Phil., 1972–73.

Khammo, A.L., *The Role of Mechanization in the Development of Agriculture in Iraq*, Leeds University Ph.D., 1977.

Longuenesse, Elisabeth, *La Classe Ouvrière en Syrie; une Classe en Formation*, 3e cycle, EHESS, Paris, 1977.

Mahdi, F.A. *An Appraisal of an Alternative for Iraqi Planning and Development with Emphasis on Foreign Trade and the 1961/62–1969/70 Experience*, Birmingham University, Ph.D., 1974.

al-Nakib, H., *A Critical Study of Saiyid Talib Pasha al-Nakib in the Setting of his Time and Environment*, Leeds University M.Phil., 1972–73.

al-Nawwab, Nabil, *State Intervention in the Development of Social Welfare in Iraq during the period 1958–1968*, Keele University Ph.D., 1979.

Omar Farouk, Marion, *Der Wandel der Produktions- und Machtverhältnisse auf dem Lande im Irak unter der britischen Kolonialherrschaft 1914–1932*, Humboldt University, Dr.Phil., Berlin, 1974.

Rauf, L.N., *Development and Housing in Iraq*, Sussex University D.Phil., 1981.

'Umar Nadhmi, Wamidh, *The Political, Social and Intellectual Roots of the Iraqi Independence Movement of 1920*, Durham University Ph.D, 1974.

Newspapers

Christian Science Monitor
Le Commerce du Levant
Daily Telegraph
Egyptian Gazette
Egyptian Mail
Le Figaro
Financial Times
Guardian
L'Humanité
International Herald Tribune
Le Monde
Morning Star
Neue Züricher Zeitung
Neues Deutschland
New York Times
Observer Foreign News Service
L'Orient (Beirut)
Sunday Times
The Times

News Reports, Yearbooks etc

Arab Report and Record
Fiches du Monde Arabe
Middle East Contemporary Survey
Middle East Record

Books and articles

'Abd al-Ridha, Majid, *al-Qadhiya al-Kurdiya fi'l-'Iraq*, (The Kurdish Question in Iraq), Baghdad, al-Tariq al-Jadid, 1975.

Abrahamian, Ervand, *Iran Between Two Revolutions*, Princeton, Princeton University Press, 1982.

Abu Jaber, K., *The Arab Baath Socialist Party*, Syracuse, Syracuse University Press, 1966.

'Aflaq, Michel, 'The relation between Arabism and the moment of overthrow' (1950), in Michel 'Aflaq, *Choice of Texts from the Ba'th Party Founder's Thought*, Florence, Cooperativa Lavoratori Officine Grafiche, 1977, p. 59.

'Aflaq, Michel, 'Fi dhikri al-rasul al-'arabi' (1943), trs. J. Viennot, *Orient*, 9, xxxv, (1965), pp. 147–58.

Akhavi, Shahrough, *Religion and Politics in Contemporary Iran; Clergy State Relations in the Pahlavi Period*, Albany, State University of New York Press, 1980, pp. 1–22.

Amnesty International, *Report of an Amnesty International Mission to the Government of the Republic of Iraq, 22–28 January 1983*, London, 1983.

Arab Ba'th Socialist Party, *Revolutionary Iraq 1968–1973: The Political Report Adopted by the Eighth Regional Congress of the Arab Ba'th Socialist Party — Iraq*, Baghdad, n.p., 1974.

Atiyyah, Ghassan, *Iraq 1908–1921; a Political Study*, Beirut, Arab Institute for Research and Publishing, 1973.

el-Azhary, M.S., (Ed.), *The Iran–Iraq War*, London, Croom Helm, 1984.

Baali, Fu'ad, *The Relation of the People to the Land in Southern Iraq*, Gainesville, Fla., Florida University Press, 1966.

Babikian, N.S., 'Michel 'Aflaq; a biographic Outline', *Arab Studies Quarterly*, 2, ii, (1980), pp. 162–79.

Baer, Gabriel, 'The Evolution of Private Landownership in Egypt and the Fertile Crescent', in Charles Issawi (Ed.), *The Economic History of the Middle East 1800–1914*, Chicago and London, University of Chicago Press, 1966, pp. 79–90.

Baram, Amazia, 'Saddam Husain: a Political Profile', *Jerusalem Quarterly*, 17, Fall 1980, pp. 115–144.

Barker, A.J., *The Neglected War*, London, Faber, 1967.

Batatu, Hanna, *The Old Social Classes and the Revolutionary Movements of Iraq: a Study of Iraq's Old Landed and Commercial Classes and of its Communists, Ba'thists and Free Officers*, Princeton, Princeton University Press, 1978.

Batatu, Hanna, 'Iraq's Underground Shi'a Movements: Characteristics, Causes and Prospects', *Middle East Journal*, 35, (1981), pp. 578–94.

Bell, (Lady Bell), (Ed.). *The Letters of Gertrude Bell*, London, Benn, 1927.

Bengio, Ofra, 'Saddam Husayn's Quest for Power and Survival', *Asian and African Studies*, 15 (1981), pp. 323–341.

Brehme, G., (Ed.), *Der national-demokratische Staat in Asien und Afrika*, Berlin-GDR, Staatsverlag der DDR, 1976.

Brown, Michael E., 'The Nationalisation of the Iraq Petroleum Company', *International Journal of Middle East Studies*, 10, (1979), pp. 107-24.

Caractacus, (pseud.), *Revolution in Iraq*, London, Gollancz, 1959.

Cardoso, F.H. & Faletti, E., *Dependency and Development in Latin America*, London and Los Angeles, University of California Press, 1979.

CARDRI, (Campaign Against Repression and For Democratic Rights In Iraq), *Saddam's Iraq: Revolution or Reaction?*, London, Zed Press, 1986.

Carré, Olivier, 'Le mouvement idéologique ba'thiste', in André Raymond (Ed.), *La Syrie d'Aujourd'hui*, Paris, 1980, pp. 185-224.

Carrère d'Encausse, Hélène, *La Politique Soviétique au Moyen Orient 1955-1975*, Paris, Cahiers de la Fondation Nationale des Sciences Politiques, 1975.

Chaliand, Gérard (Ed.), *People without a Country: the Kurds and Kurdistan*, trs. Michael Pallis, London, Zed Press, 1980.

Cobban, Helena, *The Palestinian Liberation Organisation: People, Power and Politics*, Cambridge, Cambridge University Press, 1984.

Confino, Michael, & Shamir, Shimon, *The USSR and the Middle East*, Jerusalem, Israel Universities Press, 1973.

Dann, Uriel, *Iraq under Qassem; a Political History*, London, Pall Mall, 1969.

Dann, Uriel, 'The Kurdish National Movement in Iraq', *Jerusalem Quarterly*, 9 (1978), pp. 131-44.

Davison, Roderic, *Reform in the Ottoman Empire 1856-1876*, Princeton, Princeton University Press, 1963.

Dawisha, Adeed, 'Invoking the Spirit of Arabism; Islam in the Foreign Policy of Saddam's Iraq', in Adeed Dawisha (Ed.), *Islam in Foreign Policy*, Cambridge, Cambridge University Press, 1983, pp. 112-128.

Dawisha, Karen, 'The USSR in the Middle East; Superpower in Eclipse?', *Foreign Affairs*, Winter 1982-83, pp. 438-52.

Devlin, J.F., *The Ba'th Party; a History from its Origins to 1966*, Stanford, Hoover Institution Press, 1976.

Eagleton, William Jr., *The Kurdish Republic of Mahabad*, London, Oxford University Press, 1963.

Economist Intelligence Unit, *Iraq: a New Market in a Region of Turmoil*, London, Economist Publications, 1980.

Edmonds, C.J., *Kurds, Turks and Arabs; Politics, Travel and Research in North-Eastern Iraq, 1919-1925*, London, Oxford University Press, 1957.

Exxon Background Series, 'Middle East Oil and Gas', December 1984.

Fahmi, Ahmad, *Taqrir hawl al-'Iraq*, Baghdad, 1926.

Farouk-Sluglett, Marion, 'Contemporary Iraq: Some Recent Writing Reconsidered', *Review of Middle Eastern Studies*, 3, (1978), pp. 82-104.

Farouk-Sluglett, Marion, '"Socialist" Iraq 1963-1978 — Towards a Reappraisal', *Orient*, 23, ii (1982), pp. 206-19.

Farouk-Sluglett, Marion, & Sluglett, Peter, 'Some Reflections on the Present State of Sunni/Shi'i Relations in Iraq', *Bulletin of the British Society for Middle Eastern Studies*, 5, (1978), pp. 79-87.

Farouk-Sluglett, Marion, & Sluglett, Peter, 'The Transformation of Land

Tenure and Rural Social Structure in Central and Southern Iraq, c. 1870–1958', *International Journal of Middle East Studies*, 15 (1983a), pp. 491–505.

Farouk-Sluglett, Marion, & Sluglett, Peter, 'Labor and National Liberation; the Trade Union Movement in Iraq, 1920–1958', *Arab Studies Quarterly*, Vol. 5, No 2 (1983b), pp. 139–154.

Farouk-Sluglett, Marion & Sluglett, Peter, 'Iraqi Ba'thism: Nationalism, Socialism and National Socialism', in CARDRI, (Campaign Against Repression and For Democratic Rights in Iraq), *Saddam's Iraq: Revolution or Reaction?*, London, 1986, pp. 89–107.

Farouk-Sluglett, Marion, Sluglett, Peter and Stork, Joe, 'Not Quite Armageddon: the Impact of the [Gulf] War on Iraq', *MERIP Reports*, 125–26, July–September 1984.

Fernea, Robert A., *Shaykh and Effendi: Changing Patterns of Authority among the El Shabana of Southern Iraq*, Cambridge, Mass., Harvard University Press, 1970.

Fischer, Michael M.J., *Iran: From Religious Dispute to Revolution*, Cambridge Mass. and London, Harvard University Press, 1980.

Fisher, Stanley, *Ottoman Land Laws*, London, Oxford University Press, 1919.

Fitzgerald, E.V.K., *The Political Economy of Peru, 1956–1978: Economic Development and the Restructuring of Capital*, Cambridge, Cambridge University Press, 1979.

Fraser, T.G., *The Middle East 1914–1979 (Documents of Modern History)*, London, Arnold, 1980.

Gabbay, Ronay, *Communism and Agrarian Reform in Iraq*, London, Croom Helm, 1978.

Galletti, Mirella, 'L'ultima rivolta curda in Iraq', *Oriente Moderno*, 55 (1975), pp. 462–72.

Galletti, Mirella, 'Sviluppi del problema curda negli anni 1976–1978', *Oriente Moderno*, 58, (1978), pp. 463–74.

Ghareeb, Edmond, *The Kurdish Question in Iraq*, Syracuse, Syracuse University Press, 1981.

Grimal, Henri, *Decolonisation: the British, French, Dutch and Belgian Empires, 1919–1963*, trs. S. de Vos, Boulder, Col., Westview, 1978.

Gubser, Peter, *Jordan: Crossroads of Middle Eastern Events*, London, Croom Helm, 1983.

Guerreau, A. & Guerreau, A., *L'Irak: développement et contradictions*, Paris, Sycomore, 1978.

al-Hajj, 'Aziz, *Ma' al-'Awam: Sahafat min Ta'rikh al-Haraka al-Shiu'iyya fi'l-'Iraq, 1958–1969*, (With the Years: Pages from the History of the Communist Movement in Iraq, 1958–1969), Beirut, al-Mu'assasa al-'Arabiyya l-'il Dirasat w'al-Nashr, 1981.

Halliday, Fred, *Iran: Dictatorship and Development*, Harmondsworth, Penguin, 1979.

Halliday, Fred, *The Threat from the East?*, Harmondsworth, Penguin, 1982.

Haim, Sylvia, (Ed. and Trs.) *Arab Nationalism; an Anthology*, London and Berkeley, University of California Press, 1962, 1976, pp. 23–41.

Hasan, M.S., 'The Growth and Structure of Iraq's Population 1867–1947', *Bulletin of the Oxford University Institute of Economics and Statistics*, (1958), pp. 339–352.

Hasan, M.S., 'The Role of Foreign Trade in the Economic Development of Iraq 1864–1964: a Study in the Growth of a Dependent Economy', in M.A. Cook (Ed.), *Studies in the Economic History of the Middle East from the rise of Islam to the Present Day*, London, Oxford University Press, 1970, pp. 346–372.

Haseeb, Khair al-Din, *The National Income of Iraq 1953–1961*, London, Oxford University Press, 1964.

Helms, Christine Moss, *Iraq, Eastern Flank of the Arab World*, Washington, The Brookings Institution, 1984.

Hiro, Dilip, 'Chronicle of the Gulf War', *MERIP Reports*, 125/126, (July/September 1984), pp. 3–14.

Hiro, Dilip, *Iran Under the Ayatollahs*, London, Routledge & Kegan Paul, 1985.

Hirszowicz, Lukasz, *The Third Reich and the Arab East*, London, Routledge & Kegan Paul, 1966.

H.M. Government, *Special Report . . . on the Progress of Iraq 1920–1931 for the Permanent Mandate Commission of the League of Nations*, London, HMSO, 1931.

Holt, P.M., *Egypt and the Fertile Crescent 1516–1922, a Political History*, London, Longmans, 1966.

Hourani, Albert, *Arabic Thought in the Liberal Age 1798–1939*, London, Oxford University Press, 1962.

Hudson, Michael, *Arab Politics: the Search for Legitimacy*, New Haven, Yale University Press, 1977.

Hudson, Michael, 'The Islamic Factor in Iraqi and Syrian Politics', in James Piscatori, (Ed.), *Islam in the Political Process*, Cambridge, Cambridge University Press, 1983, pp. 73–97.

Husain, Saddam, *Khandaq am Khandaqani?* (One Trench or Two Trenches?), Baghdad, n.p., 1977.

Husain, Saddam, *Saddam Hussein on Current Events in Iraq*, London, Longmans, 1977.

Husry, K.S., 'The Assyrian Affair of 1933', Parts I and II, *International Journal of Middle East Studies*, 5, (1974), Nos 2 and 3, pp. 161–176, 344–360.

Husry, K.S., 'The Political ideas of Yunis al-Sab'awi', in Marwan Buheiry (Ed.), *Intellectual Life in the Arab East, 1890–1939*, Beirut, American University of Beirut, 1981, pp. 165–175.

Ibrahim, Ferhad, *Die Kurdische Nationalbewegung im Irak: eine Fallstudie zur Problematik Ethnischer Konflikt in der Dritten Welt*, Berlin, Klaus Schwarz, 1983.

Ibrahim, Salim, I., 'Socio-Economic Status and the Utilisation of Agricultural Machinery in Iraq', Arab Planning Institute, Kuwait, 1979–80.

Iraqi Communist Party, *Watha'iq al-Mu'tamar al-Watani al-Thalith l'il-Hizb al-Shiu'i al-Iraqi*, (Documents of the Third National Congress of the Iraqi Communist Party), Baghdad, Tariq al-Sha'b, 1976.

Ireland, Philip, *Iraq: a Study in Political Development*, London, Cape, 1937.

Ismael, T.Y., *Iraq and Iran: Roots of Conflict*, Syracuse, Syracuse University Press, 1982.

Issawi, Charles, *An Economic History of the Middle East and North Africa*, New York, Columbia University Press, 1982.

Jalal, Ferhang, *The Role of Government in the Industrialisation of Iraq*, London, Cass, 1971.

Jamali, F., 'The Theological Colleges of Najaf', *Muslim World*, 50, i, (1960).

Jawad, Sa'ad, *Iraq and the Kurdish Question 1958–1970*, London, Ithaca Press, 1981.

Jwaideh, Albertine, 'Midhat Pasha and the Land System of Lower Iraq', in Albert Hourani (Ed.), *St. Antony's Papers: Middle Eastern Affairs No. 3*, London, Chatto & Windus, 1963, pp. 105–136.

Jwaideh, Albertine, 'Aspects of Land Tenure and Social Change in Lower Iraq during Late Ottoman Times', in Tarif Khalidi, (Ed.), *Land Tenure and Social Transformation in the Middle East*, Beirut, 1984, pp. 333–356.

Karpat, Kemal, 'The Land Regime, Social Structure and Modernisation in the Ottoman Empire' in William R. Polk & Richard L. Chambers (Eds.), *Beginnings of Modernization in the Middle East: the Nineteenth Century*, Chicago and London, University of Chicago Press, 1968, pp. 69–90.

Keddie, Nikki R., *Roots of Revolution; an Interpretative History of Modern Iran*, New Haven and London, Yale University Press, 1981.

Kedourie, Elie, 'The Kingdom of Iraq, a Retrospect', in Elie Kedourie, *The Chatham House Version and other Middle Eastern Studies*, London, Weidenfeld & Nicolson, 1970, pp. 280–82.

Kedourie, Elie, (Ed.), 'Vice Consul H. Wilkie Young, Mosul, Mosul, to Sir Gerard Lowther, Constantinople, 28 January 1909', *Middle Eastern Studies*, 7, (1971), pp. 229–235.

Kelidar, Abbas, *Iraq: the Search for Stability*, London, Institute for the Study of Conflict, 1975.

Kelidar, Abbas, (Ed.), *The Integration of Modern Iraq*, London, Croom Helm, 1979.

Kelidar, Abbas, 'Aziz al-Haj: a Communist Radical' in Abbas Kelidar (Ed.), *The Integration of Modern Iraq* London, 1979, pp. 183–92.

Khadduri, Majid, *Independent Iraq 1932–1958: a Study in Iraq Politics*, 2nd revised edition, London, Oxford University Press, 1960.

Khadduri, Majid, *Republican Iraq: a Study in Iraqi Politics since the Revolution of 1958*, London, Oxford University Press, 1969.

Khadduri, Majid, *Socialist Iraq; a Study in Iraqi Politics since 1968*, Washington, Middle East Institute, 1978.

al-Khafaji, 'Isam, *al-Dawla wa'l-Tatawwur al-Ra-smali fi'l-'Iraq, 1968–1978*, (The State and Capitalist Development in Iraq), Cairo, Dar al-Mustaqbal al-'Arabi, 1983.

al-Khafaji, 'Isam, 'The Parasitic Base of the Ba'thist Regime, in CARDRI, *Saddam's Iraq . . .*, pp. 73–88.

Khairi, Su'ad, *Min Ta'rikh al-Thawriyya al-Mu'asira fil-'Iraq*,   (The History of the Contemporary Revolutionary Movement in Iraq), Baghdad, Matba'a al-Adib al-'Arabi, 1975.

Khairi, Su'ad, *Min Ta'rikh al-Haraka al-Thawriya fi'l-'Iraq: Thawra 14 Tammuz* (The History of the Revolutionary Movement in Iraq: the Revolution of 14 July [1958]), Beirut, Dar Ibn Khaldun, 1980.

Khajadur, Ara, *Min Tajarib Shakhsiya fi'l-'Amal al-Niqabi al-'Ummali fi'l-'Iraq*, (Personal Experience of Work in the Trade Union Movement in Iraq), n.p., 1984.

Khalidi, Tarif, (Ed.), *Land Tenure and Social Transformation in the Middle East*, Beirut, American University of Beirut, 1984.

Klieman, A.S., *Foundations of British Policy in the Arab World: the Cairo Conference of 1921*, Baltimore and London, Johns Hopkins University Press, 1970.

Kühnl, Reinhard (Ed.), *Texte zur Faschismusdiskussion 1: Positionen und Kontroversen*, Hamburg, Rowohlt, 1974.

Kühnl, Reinhard (Ed.), *Faschismustheorien; Texte zur Faschismus-Diskussion 2: ein Leitfaden*, Hamburg, Rowohlt, 1979.

Kutschéra, Chris, *Le Mouvement Nationale Kurde*, Paris, Flammarion, 1979.

Lawless, R.I., 'Iraq; Changing Population Patterns', in J.I. Clarke & W.B. Fisher (Eds.), *Population in the Middle East and North Africa*, London, London University Press, 1972, pp. 97–127.

Longrigg, S.H., *Four Centuries of Modern Iraq*, London, Oxford University Press, 1925.

Longrigg, Stephen, *Oil in the Middle East: Its Discovery and Development*, London, Oxford University Press, 1954.

Louis, Wm. Roger, *The British Empire in the Middle East 1945–1951: Arab Nationalism, The United States and Postwar Imperialism*, London, Oxford University Press, 1984.

McCarthy, Justin, 'The Population of Ottoman Syria and Iraq 1878–1914', *Asian and African Studies*, 15, 1, (1981), pp. 3–44.

McLachlan, Keith, 'Iraq: Problems of Regional Development', in A. Kelidar, (Ed.), *The Integration of Modern Iraq*, London, 1979, pp. 135–149.

Mann, J.S., (Ed.), *An Administrator in the Making: J.S. Mann, 1893–1920*, London, Longmans, 1921.

Marder, Arthur, *From Dreadnought to Scapa Flow. Volume I, The Road to War 1904–1914*, London, Oxford University Press, 1961.

Marr, Phebe, *The Modern History of Iraq*, Boulder, Col., Westview, 1985.

Mejcher, Helmut, *The Imperial Quest for Oil, Iraq 1910–1928*, London, Ithaca Press, 1976.

Nazdar, Mustafa, 'The Kurds in Syria', in G. Chaliand (Ed.), *People Without a Country: the Kurds and Kurdistan*, London, 1980, pp. 211–19.

Niblock, Tim, (Ed.), *Iraq: the Contemporary State*, London, Croom Helm, 1982.

Nieuwenhuis, Tom, *Politics and Society in Early Modern Iraq: Mamluk*

Pashas, Tribal Shayks and Local Rule between 1802 and 1831, The Hague, Nijhoff, 1892.

Olson, Robert W., *The Ba'th and Syria 1947–82*, Princeton, Kingston Press, 1982.

Onder, Zehra, *Saudi-Arabien: Zwischen islamischer Ideologie und westlicher Ökonomie*, Stuttgart, Klett-Cotta, 1980.

Owen, Roger, *The Middle East in the World Economy 1800–1914*, London, Methuen, 1981.

Penrose, E., & Penrose, E.F., *Iraq: International Relations and National Development*, London, Benn, 1978.

Phillips, Doris G., 'Rural Migration in Iraq', *Economic Development and Cultural Change*, 7, (1959), pp. 405–21.

Picard, Elisabeth, 'La Syrie de 1946 à 1979', in André Raymond (Ed.), *La Syrie d'Aujourd'hui*, Paris, 1980, pp. 143–84.

Pool, David., 'From Elite to Class; The Transformation of Iraqi Leadership 1920–1939', *International Journal for Middle East Studies*, 12, 3 (November 1980), pp. 331–350.

Rabinovich, Itamar, *Syria under the Ba'th, 1963–1966: the Army–Party Symbiosis*, Jerusalem, Israel Universities Press, 1972.

Raymond, André, (Ed.), *La Syrie d'Aujourd'hui*, Paris, Editions du CNRS, 1980.

Rieck, Andreas, (Ed. and Trs.), *"Unsere Wirtschaft": Eine gekurzte kommentierte Übersetzung des Buches "Iqtisaduna" von Muhammad Baqir as-Sadr*, Berlin, Klaus Schwarz, 1984.

Roberts, Bryan, *Cities of Peasants*, London, Arnold, 1978.

Rodinson, Maxime, 'The Political System', in P.J. Vatikiotis (Ed.), *Egypt Since the Revolution*, London, Allen & Unwin, 1968, pp. 87–113.

Roosevelt, Archie Jr., 'The Kurdish Republic of Mahabad', *Middle East Journal*, Vol 1, no 3, (1947) [reprinted in Gerard Chaliand (Ed.), *People Without a Country: the Kurds and Kurdistan*, London, 1980, pp. 135–152.]

Rubin, Barry, *Paved with Good Intentions; the American Experience and Iran*, Harmondsworth, Penguin, 1981.

Rubin, Barry, *The Arab States and the Palestine Conflict*, Syracuse, Syracuse University Press, 1981.

Salim, Shakir M., *Marsh Dwellers of the Euphrates Delta*, London, Athlone Press, 1962.

Sayigh, Yusuf, *The Economies of the Arab World: Development since 1945*, London, Croom Helm, 1978.

Schemeil, Yves, 'Le système politique iraqien enfin stabilisé?' *Maghreb/Machrek*, 74, 1976.

Seale, Patrick, *The Struggle for Syria; a Study of Post-War Arab Politics, 1945–1958*, London, Oxford University Press, 1965.

Shaban, M.A., *Islamic History, a new Interpretation. Vol I, A.D. 600–750*, Cambridge, Cambridge University Press, 1971.

Shaw, S.J., & Shaw, E.K., *History of the Ottoman Empire and Modern Turkey: Volume II, Reform, Revolution and Republic: the Rise of Modern Turkey 1808–1975*, Cambridge, Cambridge University Press, 1977.

al-Shawi, Hamid, 'Le contenu de la contestation communiste en Irak et en Syrie', *Maghreb/Machrek*, 63, 1974.

al-Shawi, Hamid, 'Iraq et le dernier conflit israélo–Arabe', *Maghreb/ Machreq*, 64, 1974.

Sluglett, Peter, *Britain in Iraq 1914–1932*, London, Ithaca Press, 1976.

Sluglett, Peter, & Farouk-Sluglett, Marion, 'The Application of the 1858 Land Code in Greater Syria: some Preliminary Observations', in Tarif Khalidi (Ed.), *Land Tenure and Social Transformation in the Middle East*, Beirut, 1984, pp. 409–21.

Sousa, Alya, 'The Eradication of Illiteracy in Iraq', in T. Niblock (Ed.), *Iraq: the Contemporary State*, London, 1982, pp. 100–108.

Springborg, Robert, 'Baathism in Practice: Agriculture, Politics and Political Culture in Syria and Iraq', *Middle Eastern Studies* 17, 2, (1981), pp. 191–209.

Springborg, Robert, 'Infitah, Agrarian Transformation and Elite Consolidation in Contemporary Iraq', unpublished paper presented to the International Political Science Association conference, Paris, July 1985.

Springborg, Robert, 'Iraqi Infitah: Agrarian Transformation and the Growth of the Private Sector', *Middle East Journal*, 40, 1, (1986), pp. 33–52.

Stafford, R.S., *The Tragedy of the Assyrians*, London, Allen & Unwin, 1935.

Stevens, Paul, 'Iraqi Oil Policy: 1961–1976', in T. Niblock (Ed.), *Iraq: the Contemporary State*, London, 1982, pp. 168–190.

Stivers, William, *Supremacy and Oil: Iraq, Turkey and the Anglo-American World Order, 1918–1939*, Ithaca and London, Cornell University Press, 1983.

Stork, Joe, *Middle East Oil and the Energy Crisis*, New York, Monthly Review Press, 1975.

Stork, Joe, 'Oil and the Penetration of Capital in Iraq', in P. Nore and T. Turner (Eds.), *Oil and Class Struggle*, London, Zed Press, 1980.

al-Suri, Muhammad, *al-Iqta' fi Liwa al-Kut*, Baghdad, 1958.

Tahir-Kheli, Shirin, & Ayubi, Shaheen, (Eds.), *The Iran–Iraq War: New Weapons, Old Conflicts*, New York, Praeger, 1983.

Tarbush, Mohammad, *The Role of the Military in Politics: a Case Study of Iraq to 1941*, London, Kegan Paul International, 1982.

Theobald, Robin, & Jawad, Sa'ad, 'Problems of Rural Development in an Oil-Rich Economy', in T. Niblock (Ed.), *Iraq: the Contemporary State*, London, 1982, pp. 191–218.

Tibi, Bassam, *Arab Nationalism, a Critical Enquiry*, trs. Marion Farouk-Sluglett & Peter Sluglett, London, Macmillan, 1981.

Townsend, John, 'Industrial Development and the Decision-Making Process', in T. Niblock (Ed.), *Iraq: the Contemporary State*, London, 1982, pp. 256–277.

Townsend, John, 'Economic and Political Implications of the War; the Economic Consequences for the Participants', in M.S. El Azhary (Ed.), *The Iran–Iraq War*, London, 1984, pp. 51–65.

Tuchman, Barbara, *August 1914*, 2nd edition, London, Macmillan, 1980.

Uljanovskij, R.A., 'Besonderheiten und Schwierigkeiten der national-demokratischen Revolution auf dem nichtkapitalistischen Entwicklungsweg', in *Asien und Afrika im Revolutionären Weltprozess*, Berlin-GDR, Akademie Verlag, 1972, pp. 23–54.

Van Dam, Nikolaos, *The Struggle for Power in Syria*, London, Croom Helm, 1979, 1981.

Vanly, I.S., 'Kurdistan in Iraq' in Gérard Chaliand (Ed.), *People Without a Country: the Kurds and Kurdistan*, London, 1980, pp. 153–210.

Vatikiotis, P.J., *Nasser and his Generation*, London, Croom Helm, 1978.

Warriner, Doreen, *Land and Poverty in the Middle East*, London, Oxford University Press, 1940.

Wellhausen, Julius, *The Arab Kingdom and its Fall*, trs. Margaret Weir, Calcutta, Calcutta University Press, 1927.

Weulersse, Jacques, *Paysans de Syrie et du Proche Orient*, Paris, Gallimard, 1946.

Wilson, Sir Arnold, *Mesopotamia 1917–1920: a Clash of Loyalties*, London, Oxford University Press, 1931.

Index